The Georgia Peach

Imprinted on license plates, plastered on billboards, stamped on the tail side of the state quarter, and inscribed on the state map, the peach is easily Georgia's most visible symbol. Yet *Prunus persica* itself is surprisingly rare in Georgia, and it has never been central to the southern agricultural economy. Why, then, have southerners – and Georgians in particular – clung to the fruit? *The Georgia Peach: Culture, Agriculture, and Environment in the American South* shows that the peach emerged as a viable commodity at a moment when the South was desperate for a reputation makeover. This agricultural success made the fruit an enduring cultural icon despite the increasing difficulties of growing it. A delectable contribution to the renaissance in food writing, *The Georgia Peach* will be of great interest to connoisseurs of food, southern, environmental, rural, and agricultural history.

William Thomas Okie is Assistant Professor at Kennesaw State University, where he teaches American history, food history, and history education. Trained in environmental and agricultural history at the University of Georgia, he has produced work that has won prizes from the Society of American Historians, the Southern Historical Association, and the Agricultural History Society. He has written for the journal *Agricultural History* and the Southern Foodways Alliance's quarterly, *Gravy*.

T0381788

Cambridge Studies on the American South

Series Editors

Mark M. Smith, *University of South Carolina, Columbia*
David Moltke-Hansen, *Center for the Study of the American South, University of North Carolina at Chapel Hill*

Interdisciplinary in its scope and intent, this series builds upon and extends Cambridge University Press's longstanding commitment to studies on the American South. The series not only will offer the best new work on the South's distinctive institutional, social, economic, and cultural history but will also feature works in a national, comparative, and transnational perspective.

Titles in the Series

The Georgia Peach

*Culture, Agriculture, and Environment
in the American South*

WILLIAM THOMAS OKIE
Kennesaw State University

CAMBRIDGE
UNIVERSITY PRESS

CAMBRIDGE
UNIVERSITY PRESS

University Printing House, Cambridge CB2 8BS, United Kingdom

One Liberty Plaza, 20th Floor, New York, NY 10006, USA

477 Williamstown Road, Port Melbourne, VIC 3207, Australia

314-321, 3rd Floor, Plot 3, Splendor Forum, Jasola District Centre, New Delhi - 110025, India

79 Anson Road, #06-04/06, Singapore 079906

Cambridge University Press is part of the University of Cambridge.

It furthers the University's mission by disseminating knowledge in the pursuit of education, learning and research at the highest international levels of excellence.

www.cambridge.org
Information on this title: www.cambridge.org/9781107417717

First published 2016
First paperback edition 2018

A catalogue record for this publication is available from the British Library

Library of Congress Cataloging in Publication data
Names: Okie, William Thomas.
Title: The Georgia peach: culture, agriculture, and environment in the American South / William Thomas Okie, Kennesaw State University.
Description: New York, NY: Cambridge University Press, 2016. |
Series: Cambridge studies on the American South |
Includes bibliographical references and index.
Identifiers: LCCN 2016023873 | ISBN 9781107071728 (hard back : alk. paper) |
ISBN 9781107417717 (paper back : alk. paper)
Subjects: LCSH: Peach – Southern States.
Classification: LCC SB371.O45 2016 | DDC 634/.250975–dc23
LC record available at https://lccn.loc.gov/2016023873

ISBN 978-1-107-07172-8 Hardback
ISBN 978-1-107-41771-7 Paperback

For Mom and Dad
And, as always, for Kelly

Take from me apples of cider flesh,
Rob me of plum and pear,
Lose every orange of juicy gold,
Let not a vineyard bear:
Apricots' rose from its cheek may fade,
Melons may dry and bleach.
If thick in the low green orchard hangs
That beautiful Georgia peach!

Mabel Swartz Withoft,
"The Georgia Peach," 1903

Contents

Figures

Tables

Acknowledgments

This book's many failings are, of course, my own responsibility, but it would not exist at all without the help of many, many people and institutions. Here is my inadequate attempt to offer thanks for some of that help. I began this project as a Ph.D. student at the University of Georgia, where the History Department provided a warm, collegial home for my graduate studies. Thanks to Robert Pratt, John Morrow, Benjamin Ehlers, Laurie Kane, and Vici Payne for providing assistantships, travel funds, and friendly and patient assistance with a range of tasks. As a prospective graduate student, I had little sense of what to look for in an adviser, but I count myself very fortunate to have fallen into Paul Sutter's hands. He welcomed me into graduate school, commented on almost everything I wrote in those years, and kept me on as his advisee even when his own career took him to the University of Colorado. He has been a model of high expectations, rigorous critique, and down-to-earth generosity. Thanks also to the rest of the committee: Pamela Voekel, Shane Hamilton, Jim Cobb, and Steve Berry, who all left their marks on the project. In addition to the faculty, graduate student colleagues made the department an exciting place to be, and I am especially grateful to the members of the Workshop on the History of Agriculture and the Environment and the Georgia's Writers Bloc.

I have benefited from the encouragement and feedback from a number of scholars beyond UGA. The members of the Critical Agrarian Studies Group for the Social Science Research Council's Dissertation Proposal Development Fellowship – especially Jenn Baka, Sara Safransky, Greta Marchesi, Aaron Jakes, Tom Fleischman, and Pablo Lepegna – gave my early proposals a broad and interdisciplinary reading and included me in a workshop in Berkeley that was a true intellectual feast. Daegan Miller reminded me that historians are, indeed, writers, and gave the dissertation a thorough and critical reading as I began manuscript revisions. The year I spent at Bowdoin College was rewarding in many ways, not least for the friendship and intellectual encouragement of Matt Klingle, Connie Chiang, and the rest of the History Department. Sheryl Vogt and the Richard B. Russell Library Scholars and Policymakers Symposium provided an unusual opportunity to share my project with policymakers. John T. Edge and the good folks at the Southern Foodways Alliance provided what was certainly the liveliest forum I have yet experienced, and one of the most supportive. At the final stage of revisions, Andrew Baker gave the manuscript a rigorous but sympathetic reading that improved it significantly.

Like any historical study, this book would not exist without archives large and small. I am especially indebted to the following: Jim Bennett and Phyllis Reed at the Glastonbury Historical Society provided invaluable assistance, and Dick and Joan Mihm hosted us in Glastonbury, Connecticut. Wayne Olson and the staff of the National Agricultural Library went above and beyond the call of duty, as did Russell McClanahan at the Rome History Museum Archives, Sue Verhoef at the Atlanta History Center, Jill Severn at the Richard B. Russell Jr. Library, and the staff of the Hargrett Rare Books and Manuscripts library at the University of Georgia. I'm also grateful to the archivists and historians at the National Archives and Records Administration in College Park, Maryland and Morrow, Georgia; the Georgia State Archives in Morrow, Georgia; the Georgia Historical Society in Savannah, Georgia; the Atlanta University Center Archives in Atlanta, Georgia; the Special Collections at the Fort Valley State University Hunt Memorial Library; and Thomas Public Library in Fort Valley, Georgia.

I also owe much to the "living archives" – the residents primarily of middle Georgia who consented to talk with me over tea or chili, in orchards and offices. The late Oliver Bateman, Robert Carrazco, Mr. Bob and Robert Dickey, Ed Dunbar, George Hancock, the Watson family, David Rumph, Hal Lowman, Al and Lawton Pearson, Nick Strickland, and Billy Dick, all sat for recorded interviews. Davine Campbell gave me a thorough tour of historic Marshallville. Deanna Grice shared with me her cache of Rumph family memorabilia and arranged for a tour of the original Samuel Rumph home at Willow Lake. At the Peach County Historical Society, Cyriline Cantrell, Constance Rainey, and Perry Swanson shared their resources and knowledge. Jim Farmer, Dawn Herd-Clark, and Berlethia J. Pitts helped me navigate the local histories of Edgefield and Fort Valley. Lamar and Jean Wilbanks not only invited me to give my first public talk to the Habersham County Historical Society, but also shared their own archives, arranged interviews with other Habersham residents, gave me my first piece of peach-related artwork, and hosted me and my entire family at their house overnight.

A variety of institutions helped to fund the research and dissemination of this project. The Social Science Research Council, with funding from the Andrew Mellon Foundation, funded a summer of research as part of its Dissertation Proposal Development Program. The UGA Graduate School, UGA History Department, and Bowdoin College likewise provided funding at crucial moments for travel to archives. Kennesaw State University has been a generous supporter of this early part of my career, and I am grateful to the Office of the Vice President of Research, the Center for Excellence in Teaching and Learning, the College of Humanities and Social Sciences, and the Department of History and Philosophy for funding, course reassignments, mentoring, and guidance. My chair, Alice Pate, and assistant chair, David Parker, and my colleagues in History Education – Jane McKinzey, Chuck Wynn, Kay Traille, Kay Reeve, Angie DeAngelo, and Bryan McGovern – have been particularly supportive. Out of the goodness of his heart, Geert Voogt translated Prosper Berckmans's journal into English. Working across the hall from Bert Way, my new partner-in-crime at the Agricultural History journal, has made my intellectual life at KSU especially rewarding.

Portions of this book appeared first as articles: "Under the Trees: The Georgia Peach and the Quest for Labor in the Twentieth Century," *Agricultural History* 85.1 (January 2011) and "The Georgia Peach in Black and White," *Gravy* (Winter 2015), 38–47. I am grateful to *Agricultural History*'s editor-in-chief, Claire Strom, and managing editor, Annabel Tudor, and *Gravy*'s editor, Sara Camp Arnold, for permission to reproduce revised versions of that work here.

At Cambridge University Press, Deborah Gershenowitz has been a model editor, displaying more confidence in the project than I had myself and reading the entire manuscript with a critical eye. Jim Giesen, David Shields, and one anonymous reader improved the manuscript immensely, and the series editor, David Moltke-Hansen, provided timely advice and feedback as well. Kristina Deusch, Marielle Poss, Siva Prakash Chandrasekaran, and Susan Thornton have likewise worked hard to make this process surprisingly smooth. Bob Ellis of Palmetto Editorial produced an excellent index. Jennifer Bell created beautiful maps out of my rudimentary ArcGIS data.

I suppose I could have done this without family and friends, but it is difficult to imagine how. Grandparents and siblings on all four sides supported and encouraged this work, especially John Thomas West, who has always believed in the open-minded pursuit of truth. My mother- and father-in-law, Janet and R. J. Clarkson, have provided countless hours of child care and other support. Thanks to my own parents, I am literally made of fruit: they kept me satisfied with peaches, as well as plums, apricots, blueberries, apples, and more, throughout my childhood near the heart of Georgia's peach belt. Many of those fruits were my father's creations – approximately half of Georgia's present-day peaches are his cultivars – and in many ways his dogged work as a peach breeder for the USDA inspired this project. My mother introduced me to the idea of stories about nature via Thornton Burgess's *Book of Birds* and *Little Joe Otter*. Beyond these particular inspirations, I owe my parents more than I can say for rearing me with love, wisdom, patience, and presence, and now for extending that same love to my own children. My daughter Aida was just a few months old when I started graduate school; she will be in double digits by the time this book is in paperback. She has since been joined by Benjamin, Eliza, and Liam, who arrived as I finished up copyedits on this manuscript. They have all shaped my life and work in ways I could not have imagined a decade ago. I am thankful for the relational intensity, the emotional color, and the sheer insanity they bring to our days.

Finally, I thank my wife, Kelly. Like this book, our life together has been shaped by a series of places: Grimy homeless missions in Chattanooga and Manhattan. The gentle rise and fall of the running trails atop Lookout Mountain. The dusty gym at The Beth and the old cemetery between the sad, lovely worlds of St. Elmo and Alton Park. The tiny apartment overlooking the wide rocky bed of the Cangrejal River and the steep paths through slashed and burned fields of *maíz* and *frijoles*. The low ceilings and warm rooms of Grandma's Broughton Street upstairs. The cinderblock walls, many playgrounds, and idiosyncratic international community of university housing. The big box stores and wide congested parkways of north metro Atlanta – and right in the midst of the frantic suburbs, our little half-acre on the scarp of Kennesaw Mountain. For the time being, we are home.

Introduction

An Invitation

Down in Georgia there are peaches
Waiting for you, yes, and each is
Sweet as any peach
that you could reach for on a tree.
Southern beauties they are famous
Georgia's where they grow.
My folks write me, they invite me,
Don't you want to go?[1]

I

Would you care for a Georgia peach?

Plucked off the tree only hours ago, it perfumes the air with a delicate sweetness, gives slightly to your touch, sits heavily in your hand: unblemished golden skin, streaked with crimson, pulled taut over a perfect orb of luscious flesh. Your mouth waters.

On the other hand, it *is* fuzzy. Argentines say, *Si te gusta el durazno, bancate la pelusa.* "If you like the peach, put up with the fuzz." But as one visitor put it to Luther Burbank, the most famous American plant breeder, "a good many of us would about as willingly bite into a spiny cactus as a fuzzy peach."[2] There is also the pit, or stone, the enamel-shattering shell at the center of the fruit. Perhaps thinking of the teeth of his older self, T.S. Eliot's J. Alfred Prufrock fretted. "Do I dare to eat a peach?"[3]

And even if you can get past the fuzz and avoid the pit, there are other considerations. For example: What are you wearing? Do you have access to a water faucet? Are you carrying a knife? How much time do you have? Other fruits do not generate the same sort of quandary. Seedless

I

grapes can be eaten in an office, at a computer, in a car. Pink Lady™
apples can be cut in the morning and still look and taste "fresh" hours
later for your drive-thru lunch from McDonald's.[4] You can buy bananas
at gas stations, confident in the sanitary and uniform quality of the eating
experience. But a tree-ripened peach demands commitment. You have
to stop, get to a sink, walk outside, lean over. The poet Wallace Stevens
wrote: "With my whole body I taste these peaches."[5] A French gardener
insisted that the fruit must be eaten "quarter by quarter." Joy, he said,
"comes with the first nectareous sap trickling down the throat, followed
by the caress of rich texture to tongue and palate; the essence of summer
sun and almondy bitterness reaches the nostrils and eventually ascends to
the spirit."[6] For California peach grower David Mas Masumoto, proper
peach consumption is sensory ecstasy: "I caress the skin ... stroking the
suture... I close my eyes... take a deep breath, carry the bouquet deep into
my lungs... I feel my teeth sink into the succulent flesh, and juice breaks
into my mouth as I seal my lips on the skin and suck the meat... My taste
buds pucker slightly." Masumoto describes his first orchard peach as the
loss of his "peach virginity."[7]

II

Would you care to read *The Georgia Peach*?

I'm afraid this book will make a poor comparison to a ripe Georgia
peach. Nevertheless, if you accept my invitation, you will learn a great
deal about *Prunus persica* here, especially its "life" since the mid-nineteenth century. But this is not a commodity study, or a consideration of
the social life of a thing, or an exercise in "thing-following."[8] A global
study of peaches is possible: the fruit grows on nearly every continent and
has cultural resonance in many parts of the world, especially in east Asia.
But with all due respect to those who have followed organisms and things
across geographical and temporal boundaries, I am pursuing a different
quarry. I have followed the story, and the story has taken me to Georgia.
More specifically, to a few places in that irregular polygon between the
Atlantic and the Caribbean, named for a long dead British monarch and
immortalized in a hymn to a more recently deceased woman.[9] There, in
Georgia, *Prunus persica* is at the center of a myth, an imaginative pattern,
a belief-embodying, meaning-shaping story.[10]

The myth has appeared in many forms. It was in the words of the
Belgian baron Louis Berckmans, who in 1859 foresaw a time when the
South would be considered "the fruit garden of America," a time when

"thousands of acres, unfit for cultivation of cotton and corn, will be converted into remunerating orchards."[11] It was in the prose poem of newspaperman John T. Boifeuillet, who declared in 1896:

Peach is now queen in Georgia. Her velvet cheeked highness rules in the state ... She comes delighting the eye of the beholder and pouring upon the altar of the air and upon the wandering zephyr her reviving perfume. She comes garlanded with summer's sweetest flowers, and on her cheeks trembles something like the first blush of the morning. With her coming, burdens of adversity vanish like mists before the rising sun. She reanimates the world... She is the emblem of prosperity.[12]

It was in the 1918 song of a New York City songwriting trio who, when they wanted to capture the spirit of the South (one of them had sojourned there as a soldier during the Great War), wrote: "Ev'ry thing is peaches down in Georgia ... Believe me, paradise is waiting there for you!" It was a song of the seductive, alluring, and above all, *available* South, embodied in a fruit, embodied in a woman's body:

> All of Georgia's full of peaches,
> They're all gorgeous, each one reaches
> Right into your heart
> and makes you part of Georgia too.
> Clingstone peaches cling right to you
> Peaches haunt your dream,
> Think of getting, always getting
> Peaches in your cream.[13]

And the myth persists in the casual statements of industry representatives today. "I'll go to my grave swearing that Georgia peaches taste better than any other peaches," fourth-generation grower Al Pearson drawled to a CBS Early Show reporter. "I'm just fortunate to be in the right place."[14]

At the level of imagery, these myth purveyors seem to be exactly right. Imprinted on license plates, plastered on billboards, stamped on the state quarter, inscribed on the state map, dropped from a tower in downtown Atlanta on New Year's Eve, the peach is easily Georgia's most visible crop. When Ben and Jerry's made a peach ice cream in 1986, they packed it with "Fresh Georgia Peaches." In 1996, when the Summer Olympics came to Atlanta, the organizers dug up four peach trees from Al Pearson's Big Six Farms near Fort Valley and transplanted them in Centennial Olympic Park.[15] In 2011, when American Idol star and Rossville, Georgia native Lauren Alaina released her debut album, "Georgia Peaches" was the first single. Lynyrd Skynyrd sang about a "funny talkin', honky-tonkin' Georgia peach" in 1977; the Allman Brothers Band released their "Eat a

Peach for Peace" album in 1972; Jimmie Rodgers declared in 1932 that "Peach pickin' time in Georgia" was "gal pickin' time" for him; and just a few years before, black gospel singer Clara Hudman began her career in New York as "the Georgia Peach."[16] Perhaps the most famous "Georgia Peach" was Ty Cobb, raised in Royston, Georgia, and making his name playing for the Detroit Tigers from 1905–1926 – though his playing style was anything but sweet.[17] Everything *does* seem to be peaches down in Georgia.

And yet Georgia ranks only third nationally in peach production, with South Carolina second and California producing the vast majority. Nor is peach production terribly important *inside* the state, at least by the numbers. *Prunus persica* covered 11,816 Georgia acres in 2014 and produced 35,000 tons of fresh fruit – a total worth about $53.5 million. But this made up less than two-fifths of a percent of Georgia's $14 billion agricultural production in 2014, ranking well below broiler chickens ($4.5 billion), pecans ($313 million), blueberries ($335 million), and even turfgrass, silage, cucumbers, pine straw and deer hunting leases. Spatially, peaches are similarly inconsequential: *Prunus persica*'s 11,816 acres pale beside the 1.38 million acres of cotton, 607,272 acres of peanuts, and 28,643 acres of blueberries.[18] If the state was known by its most significant agricultural contributions, it would be the broiler state, the peanut state, or the quail state – it was number one in all of these commodities in 2014. Even cotton has a solid claim to the state's identity: in 2012, Georgia's cotton industry was, at 1.3 million acres, worth more than $900 million, second only to Texas.[19] Peaches have made a few people wealthy, but if growers destroyed their trees tomorrow, the state's agricultural economy as a whole would experience the loss as a small bump in the road. Why, then, is "Georgia peach" a household name? Why have southerners – and Georgians in particular – clung to the fruit?

The answer to that question is a story. Peaches were everywhere in the South from the seventeenth century on, growing along fencerows and roadsides, in haphazard seedling orchards used for foraging hogs, feeding slaves, and making brandy (Ch. 1). In the mid-nineteenth century, the fruit became part of an earnest and sophisticated rural development campaign, the leaders of which were horticulturists, an eclectic collaborative of fruit growers, plant breeders, landscape architects, truck farmers, and arborists. Prominent horticulturists such as Stephen Elliott, Prosper Berckmans, and Samuel Rumph articulated a vision of a renovated southern landscape and engaged in both environmental and economic experimentation: breeding new fruit varieties and shipping commercially to northern cities (Ch. 2–3). In the 1890s and early 1900s, northern investors such as John Howard Hale of Connecticut expanded the reputation and the commercial reach of the Georgia peach industry (Ch. 4); overproduction and misdistribution led to the contraction of the industry in the 1930s, despite the best efforts of groups such as the Georgia Fruit Exchange (Ch. 5). Meanwhile, a critical mass of white self-described "progressives" such as Mabel Swartz Withoft gathered in Fort Valley and launched a campaign to create a new political unit, a "wonder county" named in honor of the fruit. Simultaneously, African Americans such as Henry Hunt, with the support of some of those white progressives, waged their own slow campaign for education, better living conditions, and economic parity (Ch. 6). In the aftermath of World War II, as black southerners left the countryside for the city and demanded equality, growers found themselves scrambling for workers willing to accept the low pay and status of field work. Meanwhile, the landscape itself seemed to rebel against growers, especially in the form of a new affliction called "Peach Tree Short Life." Georgia's peach growers sought the support of the federal government. By the 1970s, they had a new federal research lab; by the 1990s, they had a legal supply of federally sponsored Mexican guest workers, who make up most of the labor force today (Ch. 7). The fruit's cultural presence has been more lasting and just as important as its physical presence, because it emerged as a viable commodity at a moment when the South was desperate for an improved reputation – a new face. And this cultural triumph has in turn helped to keep the physical trees in place, despite the increasing difficulties of growing the crop, as peach growers used this cultural capital to call upon local, state, and federal aid in the waning decades of the twentieth century.

III

For historians of agriculture, the environment, and the American South, many parts of this story will sound familiar. For the last four decades, environmental historians have been demonstrating the ways in which the non-human world *matters*, in all its messy detail. It matters, for instance, that the Great Plains is a place of periodic drought: when farmers and financiers ignored this characteristic in the early twentieth century, plowing up grassland and betting on continual high yields, the mass migrations of the Dust Bowl resulted.[20] It matters that the Mississippi River ebbs and flows and shifts course every so often: the levees engineered to keep it in place have instead set the stage for

less frequent but more catastrophic floods.[21] In the story at hand, the
"Georgia Peach" would not have existed without the particularities of
climate and human geography that made the fruit so prolific, its production in Georgia so early, and its reception in the big population
centers of the northeast so notable. Collectively, by chronicling not just
human relationships and activity but the *world* in which we live and
breathe and move – the "world with us," as Paul Sutter recently put it –
environmental historians have filled in the historical picture. American
history is less frequently written as if it took place on the head of a pin,
hermetically sealed in some vacuum tube while characters send mind
waves back and forth.[22]

While explorations of the human-nonhuman relationship abound,
writing about that relationship has often been a vexed enterprise. To say
that nature matters is one thing; to describe with precision what nature
is, quite another. The commonsense notion of nature as something "out
there" that needed to be protected by humans in parks and wilderness
areas had, by the late 1990s, come under withering critique. "The flight
from history that is very nearly the core of wilderness," William Cronon
wrote in a defining essay, "represents the false hope of an escape from
responsibility, the illusion that we can somehow wipe clean the slate of
our past and return to the tabula rasa that supposedly existed before we
began to leave our marks on the world."[23] For stories that complicate this
troublesome human-nature, city-wilderness binary, environmental historians have looked to agriculture, which is, by definition, a human and
environmental enterprise that takes shape in hybrid landscapes. These
cultural and environmental approaches have in the last twenty years
reinvigorated agricultural history, one of the more venerable fields in
American history.[24] At the same time, not coincidentally, environmental
history has looked South, mostly because, as Mart Stewart has succinctly
observed, "in the South, man and nature were never unhitched."[25] Unlike
the supposed wildernesses of the American West, the South was a place
with no "untouched" landscapes, a place where environmental history
was agrarian history.[26]

One of the more forceful insights emerging from this literature is, on
the face of it, a pair of truisms: culture is agriculture, and agriculture is
culture. Culture is *more* material than we sometimes make it out to be,
awash as we are in a world of symbols.[27] At the same time, agriculture is
less material than we sometimes acknowledge, comprising not just soil,
plants, and animals but visions, values and narratives as well.[28] As agricultural historians have been pointing out for quite some time now, it is

only in the last century or so that it has become possible to talk about the culture of a place or people *without* considering their agriculture. The observation that prior to the late nineteenth century, most people spent most of their waking hours outside, and that understanding those people might require some attention to their agricultural context, may be "blindingly obvious," but is nevertheless crucial.[29] And the American South, with its long agrarian history and its fierce debates over the meaning of that history – over slavery and states' rights and the "southern way of life" – has been particularly fertile soil for the examination of this agriculture-culture interplay.[30]

I owe much to those histories of environment and humans, agriculture and culture, but *The Georgia Peach* is at heart a story about the power of environmental beauty. For scholars, beauty talk is usually a cover for something worse: a smokescreen for oppression, a lie told in service of some will to power, a mere marketing campaign.[31] And indeed, in some ways, the easiest story to tell about peaches would be an exposé, calling out the Georgia peach myth as a simple lie. For although those who planted and promoted peaches made constant appeals to the beauty of the fruit and the orchard landscape, and often praised the peach as a thing apart, unbleared with greed, unstained with oppression, the fruit could not really be disentangled from the wretchedness and shame of the southern story. Much of what follows confirms this truth. I have no desire to hide the oppressions and transgressions committed on behalf of the Georgia Peach.

But this dominant mode of interpretation can have a corrosive effect, implying as it does that beauty does not really matter at all. "The whole point of seeing through something is to see something through it," C. S. Lewis once observed. "To 'see through' all things is the same as not to see."[32] Or as Eve Kosofsky Sedgwick retorted to those who scorned what she called "reparative reading" as *merely* aesthetic or ameliorative: "What makes pleasure and amelioration so 'mere'?" Life and scholarship alike, Sedgwick maintained, are not only about "exposing and problematizing hidden violences" but also about repairing the "murderous" pieces into "something like a whole."[33] Beauty matters, and not just as an elegant garment for scholars to rend away, exposing the naked ugliness of power. Beauty matters, full stop. A peach tree in full bloom is a fine sight; a fresh plucked fruit is lovely and delicious. That something so fine could emerge from the land of cotton was not just remarkable, it was also good. Americans would be poorer without it.[34] We have many stories of the South's ugliness; here is one about beauty.

In tandem with a reappraisal of beauty in the southern past, then, I am also arguing for academic modesty.[35] We make our careers out of argumentative engagement, so debunking is, in some respects, the name of the game. To cultivate academic modesty would mean to cast doubts on the virtues of exposure, to acknowledge how little we know, to admit that the scholar's perspective offers only a partial vista. Historians might know this somewhat better than other scholars, working as we do with faint traces of the past: we make "mythic constellations" out of a few stars; we pull a few droplets out of a "roaring cataract" and call it history.[36] Environmental and agricultural historians should be triply humble, for we draw from ecology and plant pathology and other disciplines, and frequently write about *know-how*, the kind of knowledge that cannot be fully described at all, but only experienced through years or generations of practice.[37]

More to the point of the story at hand, cultivating the virtue of academic modesty might also restore our ability to perceive and articulate the ends to which we dedicate our critiques. The British philosopher R. G. Collingwood once described the historian as a woodsman guiding an "ignorant traveller" through the forest. "'Nothing here but trees and grass', thinks the traveller, and marches on. 'Look', says the woodsman, 'there is a tiger in that grass'."[38] As Collingwood's tiger suggests, historians tend to be serious folk, unveiling oppression, analyzing power, chronicling the great causal forces of the human past – all good gifts that we offer to each other and to the broader public. But the scholar should also be pointing out moments, however rare, of beauty, delight, wonder. We ought also be able to say, "Look, there is an orchid in that grass." Or, "Hang on! That there is a lazuli bunting!"

IV

What follows, then, is the story of the Georgia Peach and the mythology that has grown up around it. In telling this story, I am attempting to chart a course between the radical cynicism of the exposé and the credulous hunky-doryism of the human interest story. I critique the mythology of the Georgia peach, but not merely to debunk it. I am not just exposing the dirty underbelly of a Southern industry, nor just "looking away" in order to focus on its nobler features.[39] I can do neither in part because I grew up here, in the buckle of the peach belt. From the time of my birth, my father was the resident peach breeder at the USDA Research Laboratory in Byron, Georgia, and I went with him often to the orchards. I learned to emasculate flowers, removing the petals and the male pollen-bearing stamens of a blossom still in bud and leaving only the naked female pistil (this was a fun bit of knowledge to share with school-age friends); I walked through orchards with a whiffle bat, thinning green peaches and practicing my home run cut at the same time; I made peach leaf puree in search of the dreaded plum pox virus; and of course I ate pounds and pounds of peaches, plums, and apricots, fresh, frozen, and dried. My favorite birthday dish was something called "peach quiche," which, being indescribable, you will just have to imagine.

The irony here is that, proud as I was to be from the place that produced the world's best peaches – beware the soul who sought to defend the honor of *California* drupes in my presence – I was also aware that I grew up in a place not much regarded for its beauty or for its contribution to the national narrative. I looked out on my native landscape, and saw housing developments, self-storage units, big box stores, scraggly loblolly pine, sassafras, sumac, and broomsedge. Beauty was elsewhere. State parks in the Appalachian foothills or along the Gulf Coast had a small loveliness, their beauty in turn dwarfed by places even further afield: western North Carolina's ancient mountains, New England's rocky shoreline, the West's dramatic canyons. I grew up at the epicenter, as it were, of American plainness, the environmental equivalent of a yawn, perhaps even a disgusted sneer. The world was less homely the further from home I went.

In the course of this project, I discovered that beauty was right at the heart of peach culture in this ugly region. It was in the making of the Georgia peach myth, and it was also a real experience of the landscape for many of this place's inhabitants over the last two centuries. I also discovered that the ugliness of my native landscape was even deeper and more tragic than I understood. The peach has been a locus for visions of prosperity and of the good life; it has also been a way of denying the good life to whole classes, ornamenting the maintenance of poverty with paeans to agrarian harmony.

As a child, I took the omnipresence of the peach for granted; as an adult, I have returned to try and understand the place and the people who lived here, generation upon generation. Wallace Stevens's peaches that he tasted with his "whole body" conjured much more than tangy sweetness: they spoke to him the way an "Angevine" (a native of Anjou)

"absorbs Anjou"; the way "a young lover sees the first buds of spring";
the way "the black Spaniard plays his guitar;" the way

> The bells of the chapel pullulate sounds at
> Heart. The peaches are large and round,
> Ah! and red; and they have peach fuzz, ah!
> They are full of juice and the skin is soft.
> They are full of the colors of my village
> And of fair weather, summer, dew, peace.[40]

Telling a story, anthropologist Tim Ingold writes, is not always "like weaving a tapestry to cover up the world," and thus obscuring things as they really are. A story can also lead us "into the world, deeper and deeper, as one proceeds from outward appearances to an ever more intense poetic involvement."[41] Rather than exposing the lies laid across the landscape in the myth of the Georgia peach, this will book guide you anew into the landscape, whether or not you already know it firsthand.

And so I issue my third invitation. Would you care to see the good, the beautiful, the whimsical, the wicked, the wretched, and the ugly – the "colors of my village?" As you take in this story of the South, look for Collingwood's tigers, but also the orchids and buntings, the first buds of spring, the bells of the chapel, the Spaniard at his guitar. I hope these stories open up a landscape previously hidden to you, that the next time you eat a Georgia peach, you will do so, as Stevens says, having absorbed something of the place. A century and a half ago, the Georgia peach symbolized modern, progressive agriculture, a New South on the wind; today it harkens back to a lost South of rural loveliness. Let's follow the peaches – and those who grew, bred, picked, financed, marketed, regulated, ate, and praised them – into the landscape and into the southern past.

Would you care for a Georgia peach?

I

A Wilderness of Peach Trees

I

Somewhere in rural Georgia, probably en route to a state park in the mountains or by the sea, the Okie family car is on the side of the road. It is not a flat tire, or an emergency bathroom break for one of the four children. No, my father has spotted an unusual wild plum in the ragged roadside hedgerow, and even at 55 miles per hour he has noticed something curious enough to warrant investigation. An unusual blossom, an unfamiliar leaf, a striking growth habit – this *Prunus* is something more than a standard wild stone fruit.

Along with sleeping bags and tents and dry skim milk, fortunately, standard Okie camping equipment includes several rolls of bright flagging tape, a pair of red-handled Felco pruners, and clear plastic bags. My father tags the tree, cuts a few branches, and stows them with moist paper towels in plastic bags for grafting or rooting back at the station. If we pass that way again, he will notice the tag and stop to inspect the tree; if the branches take root, he will have a new piece in his expanding collection of *Prunus* accessions; if it fruits, perhaps this one will be the key genetic ingredient for a reliable, delicious, hardy southern plum.

Once you have eyes to see them, wild plums and feral peaches are remarkably common in the Southeast: thickets in ditches on the edges of ball parks; scraggly seedlings growing in fencerows. Upon our arrival in Kennesaw in 2013, we discovered that the house we had rented, sight unseen, had a pair of overgrown peach trees, which annually produce buckets of tiny, hairy, bitter drupes. The peach is everywhere in southern culture and iconography, and its uncultivated cousins also seem to be everywhere in the landscape. It is only the commercial orchard that is surprisingly rare.

But of course it was the commercial orchard that made the Georgia peach. To understand the story of the Georgia peach – to grasp the magnitude of that transformation from wilderness to orchard – we must first trace the North American career of *Prunus persica* itself, which hitched a ride to the New World with Spanish monks in the sixteenth century, spread throughout the continent via Native Americans, and became by the early nineteenth century an unremarkable part of everyday life in a region increasingly devoted to staple crop production. My father's "*Prunus* eyes" had historical counterparts among Native Americans, African slaves, and European settlers alike. All had claims on *Prunus persica*, but it was a subset of this last group – the horticulturists – who were the chief agents of the transformation of the Georgia peach.

II

Peaches are stone fruits, so-called because of the hard, kernel-encasing shell common to all members of the *Prunus* family, including plums, apricots, cherries, and almonds. The stone is what remains after eating or rotting. Indeed, in the case of the peach, the stone is the only thing solid about the fruit: cut into the skin and the flesh falls away; walk through an unkempt orchard in early autumn and the floor is a valley of dry, brown bones, waiting for the warm breath of spring to resurrect. The wrinkled husk does its job well; peach seedlings are extraordinarily prolific. Autumn's valley of brown bones is spring's lush nursery of earnest little trees.

With peaches otherwise so ephemeral, we may as well follow the pits. The durability of these husks has, in fact, been a boon for archaeologists tracing human settlement. Because of their investigations, we can surmise that the fruit was originally from East Asia, probably the Chengdu region near Tibet, where researchers have discovered peach pits in the ruins of Neolithic villages (6000–7000 BCE), and a thousand-year-old tree, six stories high and thirty feet around at the trunk.[1] Not surprisingly, the fruit has held a place in Chinese mythology at least since the second century BCE, when the peaches in the garden of the Queen Mother of the West were said to bestow immortality.[2] In the sixteenth century, Shanghai staked its reputation on the succulent "honey nectar peaches" grown in walled gardens by local elites who had made their fortunes in the region's fifteenth-century cotton boom.[3]

Peaches were widespread in Europe, too, having traveled there via the Silk Road trade sometime in the first or second century BCE. Virgil (71–19 BCE) wrote of them in his second Georgic: "And I will search our planted grounds at home / For downy peaches, and the glossy plum."[4] By then, the legend of the fruit's origination in Persia was firmly fixed, presumably because, from the Greek perspective, Persia was where they originated most immediately. The great Roman naturalist Pliny the Elder (79–23 BCE) called them "Persian Apples," or *Persica malum*; eventually the *malum* fell away, leaving only *persica*, then *persca, pesca, peske, pesche, peach*.[5] From the Mediterranean, the fruit migrated rapidly all over Europe – even Pliny believed that there was a "Gallic" peach, native to what we now call France. By the seventeenth century, peasants of the Paris suburb of Montreuil had earned a reputation among kings and nobles for growing delectable peaches, the trees strapped to south-facing stone walls to ripen them unseasonably early.[6]

Meanwhile, starting in the sixteenth century, the Montreilleux' southern neighbors, the Spanish, were fanning out across the Atlantic Ocean to seek gold, glory, and Christian converts. *Prunus persica* accompanied them as a little-mentioned piece of what the historian Alfred Crosby famously called the Columbian Exchange – when Europeans introduced epidemic diseases and large livestock in exchange for maize, potatoes, and more.[7] The pits traveled easily and germinated readily, and Jesuit friars scattered them wherever they went as part of their overall civilizing agenda for the New World. Tend orchards; attend mass. *Prunus persica* has been on the continent since the settlement of St. Augustine, Florida, in 1565, at the latest.[8]

The Seminole, Creek, and Cherokee tribes who met the Spanish were, of course, never entirely in accord with this civilizing project – they despised pigs, for instance – but peaches rapidly won their approval. The stones entered the intracontinental trade and spread all along the eastern seaboard. In 1607, according to one report, British settlers found them naturalized at Jamestown.[9]

Prunus persica was, if anything, more highly regarded by Native Americans than by the Europeans who introduced it. Aside from eating the fruit fresh, cooked, and dried, they apparently used the bark, leaves, and pits to treat nausea, parasites, fever, and skin diseases.[10] John Lawson, during his journey through the Carolinas in 1700, found that Santee and Congaree Indians grew a variety he judged to be a "Spontaneous Fruit of America" – the Indians, at any rate, claimed it as their own, since it had been "growing amongst them, before any Europeans came to America."

It was an exceptionally large, hardy tree, "thriving in all sorts of land, and bearing its Fruit to Admiration." The fruit was a freestone, which was rare at that time, downier than most, and "large and soft, being very full of juice."[11] Indians ate the fruit "barbacu'd," dried, and stewed. They also made a "quiddony," or fruit paste, which was then formed into little loaves "like Barley-Cakes" to be sliced and dissolved in water and given to the feverish as a "grateful Acid."[12] In addition to using the fruit, Native Americans actively cultivated the trees. William Bartram found numerous plum and peach orchards around the ruins of Indian towns in the 1770s, and large peach orchards pocked the Cherokee countryside in the early 1800s: Joseph Vann's estate near Dalton, Georgia, had more than a thousand trees and a distillery for making brandy.[13] What many called "the Indian peach" was not exactly native, but it may well have been a cultivar selected and propagated by Indians. Horticulturists understood "Indian peaches" as one of the principal strains of the fruit into the late nineteenth century.[14]

Like their native counterparts, English colonists and their descendants found the fruit irresistible. According to John Lawson, hogs fattened on peaches and maize produced "some of the sweetest Meat that the World affords, as is acknowledged by all Strangers that have been there."[15] Lawson boasted that peach trees came to "Perfection (with us) as easily as the weeds," as a result of their rapid and ready growth from seed. The trees bore so heavily, in fact, that the limbs sagged and broke under the weight. Sometimes the English did not even bother to take them into the towns to prepare them, instead opting to eat them right out in the orchards. But this practice created its own sort of problem, since the seedlings sprang up so thickly that the colonists had to weed them out. Otherwise, Lawson wrote, "they make our Land a Wilderness of Peach-Trees."[16]

A century after Lawson, the American South was emerging as one of the most prosperous agricultural regions in the world. Cotton production skyrocketed as short staple or upland cotton took hold; the crop thrived in the expansive southern piedmont (see Figure 1.1). By the 1850s, cotton had spread farther west and farther into the Georgia hills than ever before; by 1860, the South produced 70 percent of the world's cotton.[17]

Charles Ball had a firsthand look at this emergent cotton economy. Born into slavery around 1780 in Calvert County, Maryland, Ball was sold in 1805 to a trader who took him, along with about fifty other slaves, to be sold in Augusta, Georgia. Collared, bolted, stapled, and chained, Ball nevertheless kept a constant eye on the changing landscape.

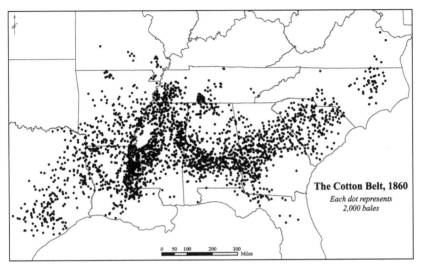

FIGURE 1.1. The cotton belt in 1860.
Source: Map prepared by Jennifer Bell, University of Georgia. Data courtesy of Minnesota Population Center, National Historical Geographic Information System: Version 2.0. (Minneapolis, MN: University of Minnesota 2011).

Traveling southward through Virginia, he saw that the agricultural landscape grew "progressively worse," marked by "weather-beaten and neglected" mansions, surrounded by decaying outbuildings and gardens and fences rotted away, in the midst of vast fields grown up in cedars and chinquapin bushes.[18] As they passed over the Yadkin River into the Carolina up-country, where cotton was "almost the sole possessor of the fields," Ball observed that the South Carolina countryside had neither barns nor hay and few crops save cotton, corn, sweet potatoes, and watermelon. The livestock consisted only of poor hogs and "thin and meagre" cattle.[19] Slaves were "deplorably abundant," usually half-naked, ashy, malnourished, and wan-faced.[20] He was not impressed with the emerging cotton belt.

Indeed, for Ball, South Carolina seemed a "bottomless pit." Its reputation was such that some Maryland owners controlled their slaves with the mere threat of selling them to South Carolina, a place where (so he had heard) slaves sometimes had to subsist on cottonseed.[21] And Ball was to be sold in Georgia, which, given the southerly direction of misery, seemed likely to be even worse. Perhaps noticing his discontent, the slave trader told him that Georgia was a "far better country than any we had seen," a land where they would live "in the greatest abundance."[22] Ball, seeing only "evil and misfortune" in his future, was not convinced.[23] "I do not marvel," he said, "that the slaves who are driven to the south often destroy themselves."[24]

In the end, Ball was sold in Columbia, South Carolina, to Wade Hampton I, master of 260 slaves, owner of vast cotton, rice, indigo, corn, and potato fields, and on his way to being one of the wealthiest men in the United States.[25] About ten days after Ball's arrival, when the cotton was all "laid by" – weeded and hilled and now only awaiting ripening – Hampton gave all the slaves a holiday: a Saturday free of work (in addition to the usual Sunday) and a supper of beef stew, bacon, puddings – and peaches. "To add to our happiness," Ball recalled, "the early peaches were now ripe," and the overseer allowed the slaves to gather some ten bushels of "very fine fruit." In South Carolina and Georgia, Ball contended, "the peach arrives at its utmost perfection." The slaves enjoyed a brief interlude of "uninterrupted happiness," a moment when Ball's new community was, for once, "immersed in pleasure," in "universal hilarity and contentment."[26] To some extent, this "felicity" continued throughout the period between cotton's laying-by and the harvest, which ended in January.

Peaches became a kind of touchstone for this fleeting felicity. During the harvest, in addition to giving the slaves a barrel of apple cider, Hampton's overseer allowed them to gather three bushels of peaches per day – though Ball estimated that they ate three times that much, "for we stole at night that which was not given us by day."[27] At Christmastime, the overseer distributed a dram of peach brandy to each slave, to be consumed along with two hogs, which had probably been fattened on fallen fruit. In August 1807, when Ball made his escape from a plantation in Morgan County, Georgia, he availed himself of this fruited landscape, filling his pockets with "fine ripe fruit" from a peach orchard near Augusta, drinking a dram of peach brandy at a friendly house farther down the road (which "did me more harm than good"), and later coming upon an orchard of Indian peaches, which Ball remembered as "the largest and finest" of any fruit, sometimes as "large as a common quince."[28] Peaches and roasted corn composed the bulk of Ball's runaway diet.

What Ball observed and experienced was the southern world of plantation and thicket, order and disorder, landscape and counterlandscape, political and vernacular landscape, that the historians Mart Stewart and Jack Temple Kirby have chronicled so well.[29] From the slaves' perspective, as Ball's narrative makes clear, the South's orchards were part of the landscape of freedom, limited though it was. The orchards, along with fish, game, nuts, and wild fruits such as plum and persimmon, prevented them from starving and meted out brief moments of pleasure. That the slaves' notion of public orchards contradicted the planters' notions of private property was precisely the point. The slaves made the landscape their own by their movement within it, notwithstanding the demarcations of those who owned them and ruled the land. "I do not feel that I committed any wrong, against either God or man," Charles Ball insisted.[30] In the antebellum South, peaches and other fruits glinted in the foliage, little vessels of comfort and joy in the midst of an otherwise bleak landscape.

Planters saw peach trees and other fruits as a kind of feral resource, a low-effort supplement to the slaves' diet. They required little care, fruiting within three years of sowing, and made excellent fodder for hogs. Unlike apples, which first had to be made into cider, peaches could be directly distilled into brandy. Peach brandy was nearly as ubiquitous as apple cider throughout the young republic, especially in the deep South.[31] From the planters' perspective, in other words, this entire landscape was an auxiliary to staple production. The peaches fed the hogs that became the salt pork that fed the slaves who picked the cotton that made the planters wealthy.

And this was the orcharded South prior to the 1850s: made by the pits, sown by Spaniards, scattered by Indians, and growing up promiscuously along fencerows and roadsides. For planters, these orchards were self-effacing servants of King Cotton. For slaves, the orchards were a part of the liminal landscape they increasingly called their own; the fruit became also a source of celebration, offering the barest moments of hilarity amid lives stolen for their masters' profit.

III

If conditions had remained as they were, there would not be much of a story to tell here. Plants grow; animals eat; seeds spread; plants grow. There would no more be a Georgia peach than there is a Georgia persimmon or a Georgia chokecherry. But conditions did not remain as they were. The cotton boom of the early nineteenth century produced unprecedented wealth for the South; it also created an insatiable demand for slave labor and left a damaged landscape in its wake. Meanwhile, the seedling peaches that grew everywhere may have been good enough for pigs and brandy, but not for an increasingly influential group of reformers, who longed to see horticulture established as a settled, scientific, beautiful enterprise in the South. These educated middle- to upper-class businessmen and landowners articulated a vision of renovated southern landscapes, corresponded with counterparts in Europe and the northern United States, and worked with imported and native plant material in a decades-long search for locally adapted, commercially viable cultivars. That vision and practice collided with the South's warm, humid climate and its cotton- and-slave-centered economy. Out of that collision grew the horticultural movement that produced the Georgia peach.

Horticulture had long been a thread in the fabric of agricultural reform. As the writer Andrea Wulf has shown, George Washington, Thomas Jefferson, John Adams, and James Madison spoke of gardening and nation building in the same breath; if the new nation was to survive, they believed, it would need gardens – which, for them, comprised scientific agriculture, new and acclimatized plant material, and elevated environmental taste.[32] Washington discovered grafting in 1760, at age twenty-eight, and continued the practice "ardently" for years. His farm diary, which he kept religiously from 1748 until 1799, is full of detailed notes about his experiments. Even at what would seem to be the most intense moments of his military and political career – at Valley Forge, for example – he never stopped tending his gardens at Mount Vernon, sending periodic instructions to his cousin and estate manager Lund Washington.[33] And as he looked toward retirement, Washington saw fruit. "At length my Dear Marquis," he wrote in a 1784 letter to his old comrade in arms the marquis de Lafayette, "I am become a private citizen on the banks of the Potomac, & under the shadow of my own Vine & my own Fig-tree."[34] Thomas Jefferson, for his part, was in public service almost constantly from 1774 on. But like Washington, he also thought almost constantly about his orchards and gardens at Monticello, which he laid out originally in 1766. While president from 1801 to 1809, Jefferson kept in touch with life at Monticello via his overseer Edmund Bacon in a correspondence that included, for instance, instructions to replant some purple beeches he was sending in place of earlier saplings, which had died.[35]

At stake with Jefferson's purple beeches and Washington's grafts was not just the appearance or provisioning of their estates, but the question of civilization in the New World. "Colonization," the historian Philip Pauly wrote, was "a high-stakes race between culture and degeneracy: would colonists improve their environments enough to make family life viable and continued immigration attractive before they became too stupid or slovenly to care?" If civilized plants such as wine grapes, French pears, flax, and wheat could be made to grow, then perhaps the United States could develop some of the glories of Western Europe – without, of course the trappings and oppressions of a European-style aristocracy. On the other hand, if only maize, tobacco, and rice could grow here, then perhaps the United States was condemned to a future of "biotic mediocrity."[36] Jefferson himself was not always optimistic on this point. "Five acres of peach trees at twenty-one feet apart," he wrote bitterly, "will furnish dead wood enough to supply a fireplace all winter."[37]

Increasingly, horticulturists were not just gentleman farmers like Jefferson and Washington, but professional floriculturists, market gardeners, fruit growers, and landscape architects. They called their collective pursuits the "science of horticulture" and formalized their aspirations by founding societies – the Horticultural Society of London in 1804, similar groups in France and the Netherlands, the New York Horticultural Society in 1818, the Pennsylvania Horticultural in 1826, and the Massachusetts Horticultural Society in 1829.[38] The Philadelphia nurseryman William Coxe's *A View of the Cultivation of Fruit Trees* (1817) set off a cascade of horticultural literature, with Charles Hovey, William Robert Prince, Thomas Green Fessenden, Robert Manning, and others all contributing books and journals.[39]

But it was Andrew Jackson Downing who emerged as the spokesman for American horticulture in the 1840s, with the publication of *A Treatise on the Theory and Practice of Landscape Gardening* (1841), *Fruits and Fruit Trees of America* (1845), and the launching of the *Horticulturist: A Journal of Rural Art and Taste* (1845). His career was remarkable and meteoric. Just twenty-six years old when he published the *Treatise*, he was by 1850 the nation's foremost expert on landscape architecture and pomology.[40] "Few men in the United States are so universally known, or so generally influential as he," the writer Catherine Sedgewick said in 1850. "Nobody, whether he be rich or poor, builds a house or lays out a garden without consulting Downing's works."[41]

Chief among Downing's tasks was to praise the aesthetic and agricultural potential of the new nation. "America is a *young orchard*," he wrote in 1845; two years later, as evidence that the work of culturing North America was well on its way, Downing cited English praise for American apples, the productivity of American orchards, and certain gardens of the Northeast, which for sheer variety were exceeded only by London's Royal Horticultural Society. It seemed to him that "Nature" herself was on America's side. "She gives us, occasionally, and almost without a direct petition," he marveled, "a new variety, in the midst of a meadow, or by the side of the garden fence." Perhaps there was something in the American soil or climate, Downing mused, "which imparts new vital powers, and gives a new type to the offspring of an old stock in the vegetable races of the other continent."[42]

The two key concepts for the horticultural movement were *culture* and *taste*. Culture, for horticulturists of the nineteenth century, was primarily a way of thinking and talking about one's biological relationships. As the historian Philip Pauly noted, prior to the twentieth century "culture" meant "tillage" and the raising and improving of plants. Culture as intellectual refinement was a "metaphorical derivative" of this basic definition. Culture as the way in which particular people or groups order their world – the definition commonly accepted today – was barely on the conceptual map.[43]

In this sense, culture *was* horticulture: the reciprocal relationship between person and place. A. J. Downing believed that horticulture intensified the practitioner's "attachment to a certain spot." This observation was not just figuratively compelling, as in "you're proud of what you work for," but also biologically precise: horticulturists actually *attached* themselves to the environment in a conscious, intentional way. There was a constant, conscious interplay between the ideal of beauty and the actual patch of earth to which one was attached.[44] Horticulture was, to borrow the anthropologist Tim Ingold's term, a "taskscape," a set of labors, ordinary and otherwise, that one performed in time. A landscape of fruit and flowers was simply the horticultural "taskscape in its embodied form."[45] A tree was not just a physical form in the landscape but an embodiment of planting, watering, pruning, and climbing. And by Downing's account, horticultural taste and culture could be contagious. "The love of country is inseparably connected with the love of home," he wrote in the first edition of the *Treatise*.

Whatever, therefore, leads man to assemble the comforts and elegancies of life around his habitation, tends to increase local attachments, and render domestic life more delightful; thus not only augmenting his own enjoyment, but strengthening his patriotism, and making him a better citizen.... In rendering his home more beautiful, he not only contributes to the happiness of his own family, but improves the taste, and adds loveliness to the country at large.[46]

Collecting paintings and sculptures was a private activity, Downing argued, beneficial only to one's family, close friends, and perhaps to posterity. The "sylvan and floral collections," however, could spread beyond the boundaries of the estate and reappear in the "luxuriant, blossoming vines which clamber over the porch of the humblest cottage by the way side."[47]

The horticultural concept of taste, no less than culture, requires a suspension of our twenty-first-century associations. Aside from the gustatory use, when we say "tasteful" or "bad taste" we mean one's likes or dislikes, perhaps according to what is generally acceptable or judged of good quality. Taste can also be, as the sociologist Pierre Bourdieu has shown, a path to distinction: for wealthy Americans laboring to measure up to European aristocracy, or for the middle class striving to set themselves apart from the "lower sorts."[48] The nature writer and historian Jenny Price has argued that taste for Downing and his ilk was "a style of consumerism" and a "statement of identity" that, in the nineteenth century "defended middle-class borders in both directions."[49]

Clearly some of this horticultural beauty talk was instrumental. Downing and others presented their work as in the public interest, but many of them were nurserymen or landscape designers whose business picked up as their stature grew. As the historian Aaron Sachs has pointed out, Downing is sometimes compared to Martha Stewart, a professional tastemaker with lines of household goods – or in his case, cottage blueprints and potted plants – that expressed his own judgments of taste; he is sometimes credited with founding the American suburb, environmentally unsustainable, racially exclusive, and architecturally questionable at best.[50] Kenneth Jackson, the great scholar of American suburbanization, called Downing a "snob and an aloof aesthete."[51] And, yes, Downing wrote without apology for the gentleman at his country seat; almost angrily he dismissed the "rural bedlams" where residents tried to do too much.[52] It was no accident, according to Price, that "tastemakers appealed en masse to Nature ... to legitimate their aesthetic."[53] For the horticulturists, taste was not arbitrary. It was the apprehension of "the Beautiful."

Before we dismiss these old fashioned notions, however, we should also note the more democratic corollary to this belief in an absolute aesthetic: the Beautiful could be discovered by careful study. To develop or "elevate" one's taste meant to refine one's perception: to see, hear, touch, smell, and, yes, taste more truly. It meant to live with heightened sensitivity to one's surroundings, with one's "internal powers, / Active and strong, and feelingly alive / To each fine impulse."[54] It meant, to borrow from William Wordsworth, to "see into the life of things."[55] Understood in this way, horticultural taste was a way of thinking about and perceiving more precisely the biological relationships we all have.

Taste and culture may seem rather far afield from the Georgia peach, but they are important to bear in mind for two reasons. First, and most obviously, people rarely exchange botanical material without also exchanging ideas about that material. This is a first principle of environmental history with abundant examples.[56] Second, the horticultural dream of embellished landscapes, refined tastes, and steady culture, represented by A. J. Downing, faced its greatest American challenge in the South.

IV

While the first movement of *Prunus persica* into North America consisted of unnumbered hundreds of peach pits multiplying rapidly into millions of trees across the landscape, the second movement – scientists refer to it as the "second wave of peach introduction" – comprised just two little trees, carefully potted, packed, and shipped across the Pacific Ocean, and ending up in South Carolina. In 1844, Robert Fortune was swashbuckling his way through China for the Royal Horticultural Society, observing and collecting plant material for the organization and the progress of civilization. Near Shanghai he discovered the delectable and already famous Shanghai peach, ripening in August and frequently "eleven inches in circumference and twelve ounces in weight."[57] In 1850, the British consul at Shanghai sent a couple of these trees to Charles Downing at Newburgh, New York. Downing did not keep them but passed them on to correspondents he thought might be able to put them to better use, including one Henry Lyons of Columbia, South Carolina, who gets credit for being the first to fruit Chinese Cling – the eventual name of the accession – on American soil, sometime in the 1850s. Lyons raised the Chinese Cling successfully, and commercial peach production was transformed.

Dreams accompanied those trees. In the South, the civilizational stakes of horticulture, the battles between "culture and degeneracy," were more pronounced than in the North. Even as nurseries, floral houses, orchards, and landscape firms flourished in the North, horticulture's future in the South was very much in doubt. Would it wilt beneath the hot sun? Succumb to the social sickness of slavery? Be neglected on the margins of the staple crop estate? The Georgia peach was the product of this collision between horticulture and cotton culture.

The costs of the short-staple cotton boom were starting to show by the mid-nineteenth century. As western lands opened up, farmers left the eastern piedmont gullied and bare. "We are awfully bad off up here," John

Trott of Troup County testified to the readers of *The Soil of the South* in 1851, "having nearly worn out one of the prettiest and most pleasant counties in the world." Trott looked out and saw not noble plantations but "waving broomsedge ... barren hillsides ... terrible big gullies."[58] Or, as the northern reformer Solon Robinson wrote of middle Georgia, "Probably no soil in the world has ever produced more wealth in so short a time, nor has been more rapidly wasted of its native fertility."[59]

In the midst of this wastage, like-minded Georgians organized the Southern Central Agricultural Society (SCAS), a group dedicated to "inquiring into the resources and facilities of agricultural pursuits and the advancement of the arts and sciences, connected therewith, and into the best method of developing the one and illustrating the other."[60] Founded in 1846 in Stone Mountain, Georgia, the SCAS was, with the Agricultural Society of South Carolina, one of the only agricultural societies in the lower South with a truly statewide reach.[61] Beginning with $61, sixty-one members, and an exhibit consisting entirely of two mules, at its height the society boasted one thousand members and annual revenues of nearly $10,000.[62] In 1851, the meeting moved to Macon, in middle Georgia, a relocation that reflected the shifting center of gravity for agricultural reform in the South. Some two-thirds of local agricultural societies in Georgia – and there were dozens of these – were formed in the counties of the old cotton belt, and more than 90 percent were organized between 1840 and 1845.[63] The SCAS gathered up the momentum of these smaller organizations and directed it toward the reformation of southern agriculture.

The members of the SCAS looked to amateur science and to old-fashioned "social and friendly intercourse between planters" to establish better husbandry in the South.[64] Their annual fairs were ceremonies of multitudinous praise, honoring the finest bushel of wheat, the tastiest lemon, the most ingenious straw cutter, the woolliest sheep, the prettiest embroidery. Cotton was the economic elephant in the room at these events, allotted a tiny space compared to its immense importance in the South at large. In 1850, members of this society founded the suggestively titled *Soil of the South*, based in Columbus, Georgia. "Why ... should we, like a set of dastards, desert the graves of our fathers, in pursuit of virgin soil?" wrote one western Georgia planter in 1853. "I, for one, am determined to hide my red hillsides and fill up my gullies."[65]

An "enlightened system of agriculture," with the power to hide red hillsides, fill gullies, and keep the South's soil and people alike in place: this was the goal of southern agricultural reform. Leaders included early soil chemists (such as Edmund Ruffin of Virginia), botanists (such as Henry

Ravenel of South Carolina), practitioners of convertible husbandry (such as John Taylor of Virginia). They were concerned with the economic vulnerability of the cotton boom, and the political vulnerability of the eastern states as out-migration shifted representation westward. But some of these improvers were also aestheticians; to them, out-migration was not only an economic and political crisis but also an aesthetic one. They deplored the ramshackle southern landscape with its scraggly fields full of broomsedge and scrub pine. Under the influence of the cotton boom, settlers had destroyed the native forests, plundered the soil of its nutrients, and, worst of all, abandoned their farms. Without soil fertility, there was no basis for continued wealth in the Southeast. The cotton boom, while it had made many of them rich, had sacrificed beauty on the altar of profit.[66]

At the 1851 meeting of the SCAS, Garnett Andrews laid out the high stakes for the work of the society and the broader reform movement: the hungry "destroying millions" of Asia and Europe would soon be swarming across the United States, said Andrews, a judge from Wilkes County. Like "flocks of locusts" they would come, from both the Atlantic and the Pacific. All "virgin soil" would be "swept off the face of the earth," and then every piece of arable land would "require patient and tedious care."[67] After thus painting a Malthusian picture of population and food supply, Andrews admonished his listeners simply to look at their landscape. "Your bleak hills, with their gullied mouths," he said, "speak more eloquently, and convincingly, on this subject than I can."[68]

And then the Rt. Rev. Stephen Elliott took the podium. Like Garnett Andrews, Bishop Elliott pointed to the southern landscape. Unlike Andrews, before discussing the landscape's wounds, Elliott underscored its original beauty: the "tangled luxuriance of our Eastern shores," the "rugged steeps of our northern mountains," and the "gently rounded hills of our midland counties," the "overarching masses of foliage and flowers," the "broad sheets of water … in pellucid brightness"; the "line of beauty" and "ever changing hues" of the mountains and gorges; the "sighing waterfalls and grassy knolls."[69] And yet this natural bounty, Elliott claimed, had yielded almost nothing in the way of horticultural refinement.

Elliott enumerated four "reasons for [Georgia's] backwardness."[70] First, Georgia's climate and soil were so amenable to the production of fruit and flowers that residents had become "mere dependent idlers on her bounty."[71] Echoing A. J. Downing, who claimed that the "patient and skilful [*sic*] cultivator" could only be found in harsher northern climates,

Elliott lamented southerners' indolent willingness to enjoy their fruits in their "wild and untrained excellence."[72]

Second, since horticulture was the art of domesticating and training natural excellence, it was the "science of a settled and permanent population, not the pursuit of a people struggling for bread."[73] Georgia was only a generation removed from being "Indian country," Elliott reminded his listeners, intoning dramatically that "within the recollection of our children, the war whoop was heard upon our Western limits." He exaggerated, of course, for most Cherokees and Creeks were by the time of removal very much a "settled population," some of whom owned extensive orchards. Much of what Elliott understood to be natural abundance, especially in peaches and apples, was the result of Cherokee cultivation and selection.[74]

Third, southern horticulturists had no books, or at least none adapted to their climate. Southerners were imitating the horticulture of London in a climate more like Tuscany's. And the dissonance between the South's soil and climate and the "book knowledge" of English horticulture was "absolutely pernicious" in its discouraging effect on experimentation.[75]

Fourth, the southern economy was not diverse enough to support nurserymen, florists, market gardeners, and orchardists. Unlike in England and the North, where prominent horticulturists all owned nurseries, the South had few nurseries and not enough urban population to create sufficient demand for flowers or fruits or vegetables. Southern horticulturists, including Elliott himself, earned their living in other trades. Profitable agriculture in the South was staple crop agriculture, and horticulture suffered from the "absorbing pursuit" of cotton.[76] Southern planters, meanwhile – the men responsible for enshrining staple crop agriculture – were, according to Elliott, their own worst enemies. Isolated lords of their demesnes, individualistic and tradition-bound, planters were notoriously difficult to "collect into societies." Societies, for Elliott, were much more than social organizations. They were "the instrumentality of the present day for the advancement of every science and art."[77] If the Southern Central Agricultural Society barely survived, how could the more specialized horticultural societies be expected to thrive? For horticulture seemed "much more connected with mere ornament and luxury."[78]

Elliott thus hinted at a critique of planters more fully developed by other reformers in this period. They were, as the historian Gavin Wright memorably put it, not landlords but "laborlords."[79] Land was relatively abundant, particularly after the removal of Native American tribes opened up the old Southwest to Anglo settlement. Their wealth tied up in slaves, planters sought to maximize the productivity of their labor rather than their land. Often this meant a modified form of swidden farming – girdling trees, burning, and planting in the ashes. A quick three or four harvests and the field would be abandoned for more fertile terrain. The political economy of slavery seemed to dictate that horticulture would always be what it was: an afterthought, a seedling orchard for slave provisioning and hog foraging and maybe a little brandy distilling. Only those who fancied plants would claim the mantle of pomology.

Stephen Elliott's perspective bore the imprint of his Beaufort–Charleston upbringing. As the historian Max Edelson has shown, the planters who fancied plants were often the very same who exhausted the soils of the southern frontier. By the time of Elliott's birth, most Charleston planters moved their slaves and the focus of rice production to newer lands in the interior, using the money they accumulated from these "labor camps" to transform the older in-town homesites into "genteel retreats," horticultural Edens.[80] When Elliott peered into Georgia's future, he saw Charleston's past: an increasingly permanent population, more interested planters, larger towns, more nurseries, and a wider circulation of journals. "Patience and perseverance," Elliott counseled. "Let us, in horticulture, as in everything else, learn a nobler ambition, and make our land what God and nature intended it should be, a land of surpassing beauty and exceeding joys."[81]

Elliott then turned his attention to pomology. "A delicious peach is handed us," he said, "whose skin peels off like that of a well boiled potato, the rich juice the while streaming down our fingers, and while the flesh melts in our mouth and the combined qualities of smell and taste and sight are gratified to the utmost." And yet this seductive drupe remained unnamed, and therefore, unknown: "'Tis still only a peach, and great astonishment is expressed at a desire to know any thing more about it."[82] Without correct nomenclature, southerners knew "neither our riches nor our poverty."[83]

Yet even the right name was no good without that indispensable quality, "taste." And the southern landscape, for Elliott, revealed southern deficiency more than anything else. "It is sickening," he wrote of middle Georgia, "to behold its deformed appearance." For although nature had made it lovely ("nothing is more picturesque than the alternation of hill and dale, the undulating sweep of a rolling country, the variety of foliage that arises from the mixture of so many species of forest trees"), the settlers had not improved its "curve line of beauty" but allowed it to decay into "the rugged wrinkles of an early decrepitude."[84] Elliott especially deplored the typical southern homestead. The houses were "the most wretched specimens of architecture" with outbuildings "arranged just in the most conspicuously awkward positions"; orchards "where our ornamental grounds should be"; vegetable gardens "thrust[ing] up their tall collards and peasticks." Southern estates were "bare red hills, crowned with great white houses glaring at you," with "negro quarters of the most ungainly aspect, with cotton and corn growing up to the very doors" along a "straight up and down clay road, flanked by straggling Virginia fences on either hand." In the estate's bare dooryard, "consumptive hogs" wallowed in "dirty puddles." There was not a proper lawn in sight.

But Elliott also saw the southern landscape as it could be: pretty country seats surrounded by tastefully arranged ornamental grounds, approached by winding roads through native forests that were cultivated into parks and groves. Slave cabins would be kept at a distance, and homes would display education, refinement, and culture. Approaching the house, visitors would see not dirty pigs but members of the family reading or debating in the cool air of the wide verandahs. All this would be possible with the progress of horticulture. Elliott concluded with a personal testimony to the refining influence of horticulture on a southern man, for it had "opened before me higher views of the beneficence of my Creator, and has taught me the important lesson – a lesson which cannot be too impressed upon an utilitarian age – that over and above the useful, the profitable, the necessary, God has deemed it wise to surround his creatures with the beautiful, the picturesque, the sublime."[85] Elliott had read his Downing, and Charleston's gardens seemed to permeate his environmental imagination.

The 1850s would see increasing correspondence with horticulturists around the Atlantic world, and an ever-increasing nursery business, but horticultural progress as Elliott would have understood it was slow. There was a market for garden ornamentals, to be sure, as planters sought to add to their profits something approximating "taste," but horticulturists and other agricultural reformers increasingly found themselves butting up against what the historian Philip Herrington calls the "environmental critique of slavery."[86] In one of the better-known passages of this critique, Alexis de Tocqueville famously contrasted Ohio and Kentucky from the vantage point of the river dividing them. In Ohio, Tocqueville wrote, the harvests were abundant, the dwellings elegant, industry humming, and everywhere the evidence of "taste and activity ... wealth and contentment." In Kentucky, on the other hand, "population is rare" except for "loitering" groups of slaves; "society seems to be asleep, man to be idle, and nature alone offers a scene of activity and of life."[87] Slave labor, the argument went, invariably led to white laziness (and sometimes to white brutality); the lack of proper cultivation led to soil exhaustion; soil exhaustion led to impermanence as white families migrated to more fertile western lands.

Horticulturists echoed this critique when they called for more careful attention to the land and the plants that grew there. Few of the leading southern horticulturists owned many slaves: of the ten members of the SCAS executive committee, only two self-identified as planters, the rest being doctors, attorneys, and entrepreneurs.[88] Their movement was essentially a campaign to replace plantations with gardens and orchards. For the horticultural revolution to take shape in the South, though, the economic system would need to change. For the economic system to change, agricultural reformers would need to confront slavery. And for such a confrontation, southern reformers had no taste.

Instead, they contented themselves with quiet, ambiguous critiques. In Augusta, Georgia – which hosted the slave market Charles Ball had so feared – the agricultural reformer and sometime-pomologist Dennis Redmond purchased a 315-acre indigo plantation, revitalized the orchards, started a nursery, and christened the place "Fruitland." In 1854, he began building what architectural historians would describe as a "Louisiana plantation house ... reminiscent of the West Indies."[89] It was the perfect home for an improving southern farmer. It was not built of the usual brick or wood, but of concrete, which was, according to Redmond, less susceptible to fire, moisture, and vermin; more suited to the southern climate (cool in summer and warm in winter); and easier to build, requiring only one "mechanic" and a crew of "common field hands." The ten-foot wrap-around verandahs, ten-foot-wide hallways running the length of both floors, and transom lights on the second floor allowed "the freest possible circulation of pure air."[90] The bottom floor housed workaday rooms – a pantry, storeroom, office, dairy room, and fruit ripening room – suggesting, as Herrington observes, "Redmond's desire to incorporate agricultural labor into the house itself." The second floor comprised bedrooms, parlors, and libraries to "provide elevated space for personal cultivation." A cupola atop the second floor gave Redmond a commanding view of his plantation and workers as well as a "beautiful prospect of the city of Augusta, the opposite hills of South Carolina, and the surrounding country, for many miles."[91] From his cupola, Redmond could survey a region brimming with reform. Across the Savannah River, in Graniteville, South

Carolina, William Gregg built one of the first large southern cotton mills and along with the botanist Henry Ravenel experimented with shipping peaches north; at Redcliffe, just five miles from Augusta, James Henry Hammond experimented with marl and expostulated on the fragile future of the South's agrarian civilization.[92]

Fruitland was, in short, the architectural embodiment of the horticultural ethos: practical, businesslike, progressive, and worthy of, as Redmond's associate Daniel Lee put it, "the Beautiful in Agriculture."[93] Redmond's new home suggested, Herrington writes, "an alternative southern agricultural landscape: a big house without slaves, without cotton, and perhaps without a plantation." But Redmond never said that slavery was incompatible with the aims of agricultural reform. Fruitland remained a "purposefully ambiguous landscape," at once a model for slave owners *and* an implicit critique of slave society.[94]

This ambivalence was common among agricultural reformers. Stephen Elliott, in his public lament for the southern landscape, seemed to wish merely that slave quarters be orderly and removed from plain view, set tastefully at a distance where perhaps they could lend an air of southern distinctiveness without offending the delicate sensibilities of visitors. Privately, Elliott confided to Swedish reformer Fredrika Bremer his belief that slavery must be eradicated. He believed Christianity would sound the death knell. "Already is Christianity laboring to elevate the being of the negro population," he told Bremer, "and from year to year their condition improves, both spiritually and physically; they will soon be our equals as regards morals, and when they become our equals, they can no longer be our slaves."[95] Elliott seemed sincere in this belief: he founded the all-black St. Stephen's Church in Savannah and put it under a black vestry. Given that masters generally compelled slaves to accompany them to white churches, this effort to give them some autonomy within the church was significant. Perhaps in gratitude, St. Stephen's vestry bore the bishop's coffin to the tomb.[96]

The reluctance of horticulturists to challenge slavery publicly was on one level rather straightforward: it was bad business to alienate the wealthiest and most powerful customers of their nurseries and periodicals. On a deeper level, though, the relationship of horticulture to capitalism, slavery, and emancipation was more complicated. As several prominent scholars have recently shown, nineteenth-century slave-powered cotton cultivation was not some sort of pre- or anticapitalist formation but was intimately entangled in the development of global capitalism and ultimately in the prosperity of the nation, North and South alike.[97] And as we will see in Chapter 2, horticulturists ultimately welcomed emancipation as a necessary precondition for commercial fruit cultivation.

V

In 1849, from his "forty acres of solid earth" at Roslyn on Long Island, William Cullen Bryant wrote a poem inviting his fellow northerners to the civilizational duties and delights of horticulture. "What plant we in this apple-tree?" he asked. Bryant's own answer took shape in the succeeding stanzas: in planting apple trees we plant shade from the sun, shelter from rain, habitat for thrushes, fragrance for all, blossoms for bees and sick children, fruit for the autumn harvest and for the long winter nights, fruit sold and shipped far away. And then, in typical Bryant fashion, the poem turns toward death: "The years shall come and pass, but we / Shall hear no longer, where we lie." What would the world look like in those distant years? Thinking, no doubt, of the fate of southern slavery in that future generation, Bryant asked:

> Shall fraud and force and iron will
> Oppress the weak and helpless still?
> What shall the tasks of mercy be,
> Amid the toils, the strifes, the tears
> Of those who live when length of years
> Is wasting this little apple-tree?[98]

Bryant's poem crystalized the horticultural vision: in planting apple trees, Americans could plant human joy, environmental diversity, civilization itself. But when Charles Ball sojourned in South Carolina in the early 1800s, he found that while peaches "ripened to perfection," apples did not do well in the Carolina climate. "This fruit of so much value in the north, is in the cotton region, only of a few weeks continuance."[99] Could culture succeed in a place where horticulture failed?

His own antislavery sentiments notwithstanding, Stephen Elliott spent his war years defending the institution of slavery. His sermons show all the marks of that twisted logic, and perhaps he recognized as much, given how quickly he turned to reconciliation within the Episcopal Church after the war. On December 21, 1866, having just returned from a trip to some of the churches under his charge, he shared a meal with his family and abruptly "fell lifeless," apparently as a result of aneurysm or heart attack.[100] Given Elliott's own belief in the immorality of slavery, the strain of holding his church together – and of preaching, again and again, that the sacrifice of the white southern youth was not in vain – all of this may have taken its toll.

Charles Ball, for his part, never made it to Augusta. If he had, he would have found it a kind of way station for the wealth of the vast upland cotton lands, which supplanted sea island cotton in the mid-nineteenth century.[101] Augusta was, as the journalist Thomas Stokes characterized it, "the pulsing, vivid capital of this new cotton empire, one that radiated from it on all sides into Georgia and South Carolina."[102] Bales streamed from the uplands of South Carolina and Georgia into Augusta, thence to Savannah, and thence to sea.

In 1856, a pair of Belgian nurserymen of noble birth purchased Dennis Redmond's experiment in horticultural renovation and extended it, training Fruitland into one of the largest and most influential nurseries in the region. From Augusta, the town cotton had made, they intended to remake the South by disseminating the knowledge and the plant material of fruits and ornamental plants. They would reverse the paths of cotton, trudging upstream while cotton floated downstream, to make a new world in the South with diligence, skill, culture, and taste. They would use the wealth generated by cotton to reshape the landscape ruined by cotton. And over time, their means for doing so would be reduced to one species: *Prunus persica.*

2

A Baron of Pears

I

One might read A.J. Downing's books, envision beautiful landscapes, sketch out brilliant plans on paper, but the essence of horticulture was feet on the ground, hand on the pruning hook, eye on the leaf. Downing died in 1852; even if Rev. Stephen Elliott had lived, his church work would have prevented him from devoting himself to horticulture. Who would take horticulture from vision to practice in the South? As it turns out, Prosper Jules Alphonse Berckmans, an aristocratic Belgian immigrant, had both the vision and the practical skill to be the South's foremost "apostle of taste." He sought to make the South's landscapes more lovely, its farms more diverse, its people more prosperous, its society more settled. Initially, Berckmans hoped that the South would become, like his native Belgium, a paradise of pears, or wine grapes, or at least apples. Peaches were at best third or fourth on his list of region-transforming fruits. As his hopes for other fruits dimmed, however, Berckmans and his colleagues in the club he founded, the Georgia State Horticultural Society, turned increasingly to *Prunus persica*. They took the feral fecundity of the South's many peach trees, combined them with the civilized virtues of imported cultivars, and, with careful attention and work, nurtured the development of the genetic material that would become the Georgia peach.

Of course, humans as well as plants populated the South. The horticulturists pursued their own labors in the social context of an economy based on slave labor; the South's horticultural taskscapes belonged as much to the people who worked for Berckmans and his ilk – potting plants, laying out orchards, picking and packing fruit – as they did to those who called themselves horticulturists.[1] The change in status of that labor force, from slave to "free" in the midst of the Civil War, was, as Berckmans himself understood, a pivotal transition in the development of commercial fruit growing in the South. Just as we saw in Elliott's life the collision of horticultural "taste" with the southern landscape, so in Berckmans's life we see the mediating work that all horticulturists did: culturing, cultivating, moving with and within the landscapes they shaped.[2] But before we can appreciate what Berckmans *did*, we have to see what he *saw* as he chose the South as his own particular mission field.

II

In 1850, as A. J. Downing sent fruit and Swedish women to the South, and as Stephen Elliott gathered his thoughts on the problems with southern taste, eighteen-year-old Prosper Jules Alphonse Berckmans boarded the *Peter Hattrick* and sailed out of Antwerp's harbor. He spent more than a month aboard with a motley crew of Belgians, Prussians, and seventeen *vauriens*, or "good-for-nothings." Then, he visited the big cities of New York, Philadelphia, and Charleston; camped in the north Georgia mountains; took a steamship up the Mississippi River; felt the spray of Niagara Falls; floated down the Erie Canal.[3] For this son of an artistic Belgian baron, raised in a castle and trained in European boarding schools, the tour of busy, topsy-turvy American society was tremendously exciting. As if to keep pace, Berckmans kept an almost-daily record of his experiences in a volume he titled, in large and elegant lettering, *Voyage en Amerique*.

Everything he witnessed needed to have a name, a place in the natural history of the world. On September 10 he saw his first sea tortoise; on September 16 he identified large stretches of marine algae as *golffoide*, or "Gulf Weed"; on September 21, a large fish called "Black fishes." One day he saw several whales he thought were called *Souffleurs*, or spouters; another he witnessed the harpooning of a porpoise and the extraction of its liver. Nearly every day of the voyage, he described the weather, wind direction and speed, animals and plants, and health of the passengers.

Occasionally, even in the terse language of the diary, beauty overwhelmed him. A "bad storm" on August 28 made the sea a "new sight," "magnificent to behold." Storm petrels skipped lightly across the "lovely" sea, "light green with great patches of grey. The birds flew partly underwater, allowing waves to "sweep over them" before they continued their flights; they reminded him of European swallows.[4] One Saturday evening, Berckmans stood on the deck of the *Peter Hattrick*, probably exhausted.

The whole ship had been ill for three straight days; the aroma of vomit must have permeated the air. But beauty broke in, and Berckmans was watching. "I see the sun set," he wrote. "It is the most beautiful sight one can see."[5] Berckmans could have been holed up in his cabin, nursing his tender stomach. Instead he had his eyes open to the world about him. He was, to borrow a phrase from Bruno Latour, "learning to be affected."[6]

As the ship approached the harbor, Berckmans's descriptions could not keep pace with his excitement. The New Jersey shoreline, dotted with country houses and resort hotels, was *"tres beau"*; the New York harbor with its "forest of masts" was *"fort beau."*[7] Once ashore, he traveled from New York to New Jersey, where he described the woods near Elizabethtown as "very picturesque," reminding him of an English garden. In the absence of a vocabulary adequate to his experience, Berckmans made lists. Near Elizabethtown he went hunting. He saw little game, though he killed a milk snake and caught a yellow tortoise. But other quarry abounded, and these he captured with his eyes and pen: oaks (*Quercus coccinea, macrocorpa, dentata, sempervirens,* and *lacinata*), maples (*Acer campestris* and three other species), cedars (*Cedrus niger*), tulip trees (*Liriodendron virgineana*), hickories (*Fagus silvestris* and *castanea*), "butternuts" (*Juglans ulmus*), lindens (*Tilia microphilla* and *platyphylla*), along with more unfamiliar herbaceous plants such as blue gentians and white orchids. He also strolled through "many orchards," though Berckmans noted summarily that the agriculture was "not advanced" and that the farmers grew only the lowly cider apple, and no pears.[8]

After some days in the mid-Atlantic region, Berckmans went south, where he spent much of his time on the 320-acre estate of a fellow Belgian, General Louis Joseph Barthold LeHardy. In 1848, LeHardy and about twenty-five others left Brussels for the United States and ended up in Rome, Georgia, a town of three thousand that was then the emerging capital of Cherokee Georgia.[9] Berckmans was impressed with the richness of the soil on LeHardy's land, as well as the "limpid and delicious" water from the many springs. New members of the little Belgian colony were still arriving during Berckmans's stay: the Gosfuins had also purchased a plantation not far from LeHardy's, and Berckmans visited and enjoyed the "excellent Bordeaux wine."[10] He took a trip across the northern part of the state to Habersham County. Near Clarksville, a haphazard little town Berckmans judged to be "in very bad taste," he noted the price and condition of several properties. One five-hundred-acre plantation contained "the best soil I that I have seen here," and listed for three thousand dollars; another pair of plantations, both with plenty of rich bottomland soil, was available for seven thousand dollars.[11] While in the neighborhood, Berckmans spent a number of days exploring foundries and other ironworks in Habersham and pronounced the region "rich in minerals and in mines of gold, silver, iron, and zinc."[12] The specificity of his observations suggests that the young Belgian was in the market for either a plantation or a mine, or both.

When it came to taste and culture, though, Berckmans was less sanguine. "There is a big contrast between the customs of ordinary life between the South, North, and West," he began, in a meandering essay that concluded the journal. "I will try to describe them faithfully if not elegantly." He was at turns charmed and repulsed by the scenes he recorded. The "call to dinner" at a northern farm was pleasantly rustic: the shining brass candelabras and flowering sprigs decorating the room; the polished floor; the "sturdy farmer's wife" blowing the dinner horn; the unbuttoned shirts and sweat, the combed hair and washed hands of the farmer, his sons, and the "peasants"; the tea and milk, water and bread, "enormous bowls" of stew, potatoes, carrots, chicken, bacon; the farmer serving all generously and merrily finishing with a "big glass of cider" while his blue-eyed daughter gave him his fruit cobbler and chunk of cheese. The food was "copious and abundant," and if lacking in "artful refinement" at least it was "simple" and "quite adequate."[13]

Not so in on the western frontier, said Berckmans, where the farmer found at dinner hour "the same food he had for breakfast and that he will have for supper, day in day out": coffee, bacon, and corn bread. This despite the fact that the prairie grass was "literally red" with "big and tasty strawberries," despite the river full of fish and its banks covered with lush watercress and heavy-laden wild plum bushes. Berckmans seemed willing to accept these shortcomings, given that the homestead was just one "stage" on the path toward civilization. But he had no kind words for the city boardinghouse, where dinner began with a "deafening gong" that "bursts your eardrums and paralyzes you as some fifty men stampede past the waiter" and begin immediately snatching up the celery, oranges, figs that have been scattered across the table, inhaling the soup, and proceeding to the main course:

You take a spoonful of potatoes, but they are very watery and filled with brown pieces that refuse to let themselves be chewed with the rest – you hesitate and try the beef: it is tasteless, so you try the macaroni: rivulets of water stream from each piece. The bread is dry.

Berckmans also found northern homes wanting, in part because of the hurry, in part because of the "uncouth" Irish peasants serving as "master chefs," and in part because of the horrifying mixing of food. "I have seen," Berckmans gravely attested, "pretty young ladies mix oysters with cabbage and fowl and cream – but *de gustibus non est disputandum*."[14]

The South, according to Berckmans, was not so afflicted by hurry, and since the food was generally served by "servants who belong to the household" – his euphemism for slaves – he found the food and the atmosphere more tolerable. But this was only true of the well-to-do, for "the common people are of the coarsest and least-civilized kind." Like the frontier family, they ate bacon, coffee, and corn bread three times a day, with the occasional "pan-fried fowl, fried eggs, simply boiled cabbage leaves," and of course whiskey and tobacco, which were "the chief pleasures" of all classes. Berckmans reserved special disgust for this last item. He attributed the American "physiognomy" to the "constant spitting and coughing up" of the golden weed: the hardened, compressed, wrinkled lips; the "pale and colorless" skin tone; the "frightening and universal scrawniness." Together with excessive whiskey drinking and the "gobbling up of one's food without chewing," tobacco was to blame for the national epidemic of "dyspepsia." "You will constantly hear people throwing up," Berckmans testified, in society and even at the table, without embarrassment.[15]

Berckmans appeared truly to believe in the transformational power of food. He quoted the French gastronome Jean Anthelme Brillat-Savarin as a proselytizer might quote scripture: "The discovery of a new dish does more for the happiness of the human race than the discovery of a star." And he insisted that the dinner table was the best evidence of a family's "refinement": "nowhere are man's sensual and selfish instincts as evident. This is the center of the family after a day of separation, this is where they are reunited after a night of oblivion, this is where we provide hospitality to stranger or friend, this is where the tongues are loosened and the soul is warmed by a generous wine." Indeed, he concluded:

The kind of food one eats is equally important to man's physical wellbeing as it is to his moral health. Food may be badly prepared, raw and indigestible; it may be over-cooked and heavy, it may be dried until the nutritious juices have all evaporated, or it may be fried in an oily mass that requires the strongest stomach to try it. Furthermore, food that originally was wholesome and good may be so drained of nutritious value by cooking methods that it has lost most of its wholesomeness. Almost any food that is put on American table suffers from one or another of the above mentioned flaws. To avoid these bad effects, and to cook food without spoiling it, and to serve economical portions is an art of civilized life: one of the most simple, but most often neglected arts.[16]

Despite these rather visceral observations of American society, Berckmans saw its shortcomings as an opportunity for his own talents. He envisioned the United States, and in particular the South, as a place to develop and cultivate. The plant lists in Berckmans's diary, then, divined his future more accurately than his mineral investigations. For just as the minerals were the raw materials for those who would extract fortunes from mines, these native plants were the raw materials for Berckmans, who would cultivate a horticultural fortune. The enormous genetic variation to which Berckmans bore witness in his diary was the foundation for a profitable culture in plants and fruits. In the hands of one who knew how to select and breed new varieties, this genetic diversity was a botanical gold mine.

III

Prosper Berckmans saw the South as a place to cultivate in part because of his background in Belgian horticulture, which, in the early nineteenth century, was avidly devoted not to the peach but to the pear. He was born into it. His father, Dr. Louis Mathieu Edouard Berckmans, was a founding member of the Belgian pear cult. Born in 1800, Louis Berckmans trained as a physician but apparently preferred playing violin and painting. Sometime in the 1820s, while traveling in the Belgian lowlands, he met and married Marie Gaudens, who was either a lowlands peasant or a direct descendent of Spanish nobility, depending on which genealogist tells the story. Marie gave birth to Prosper in 1830, while Louis was away fighting for Belgian independence from the Netherlands. She died of complications.[17] Though Louis later married again, he was haunted by the death of his first wife to the end of his days. Perhaps to console himself, Louis Berckmans threw himself into pomology.

Though Europeans had cultivated pears since the days of Homer, the fruit earned its aristocratic reputation in France in the seventeenth century, when there were some 254 distinct varieties in cultivation. Two hundred years later, there were only 238 varieties.[18] And then in the early nineteenth century, Belgian pomologists turned the French fascination with pears into an obsession, and nearly quadrupled the number of varieties in cultivation: from 238 in 1833 to 900 in 1867.[19] More significant than the number of varieties they produced, though, was the way they changed the fruit. In the eighteenth century, pears were crisp, applelike fruit, as they had been for millennia. By the mid-nineteenth century, pears were soft, melting, buttery – hence the prevalence of the term *beurre* (butter) in pear nomenclature. After centuries of cultivation, the Belgians created the modern pear in just a few decades.[20]

The Belgians also played a significant role in a pan-European effort to revitalize fruit culture. In the late 1700s, fruit growers feared that the existing varieties, most of which dated to the Renaissance, were "running out." Each year, it seemed, they produced fewer and less appetizing fruits and succumbed more readily to disease. Thomas Knight, president of the Royal Horticultural Society in London, offered one explanation: a single tree had a life span of two or three hundred years, which included all tissues of the tree, even grafts, and grafts of grafts. An apple variety found in 1550, in other words, would start to wane around the turn of the nineteenth century. Knight's solution was cross-pollination: manually taking the pollen from the stamens of a wilder tree and fertilizing the pistil of the cultivated variety. In this way, Knight hoped to produce hybrids that joined the vigor of the wild trees with the desirable eating characteristics of the old varieties.[21] His approach had unpredictable results, though. Most fruit varieties at this time were "found," chance productions of nature, and cross-pollination improved on chance only marginally. Knight's method was a kind of horticultural alchemy, relying on studied mixing to create new varieties rather than serendipitous discovery.

The Belgian Jean Baptiste Van Mons, on the other hand, explained the problem of varietal decline by arguing that older fruits had become too refined and cultivated for their own good. The horticulturist's task, then, was to develop new strains from seed, with aggressive and observant care, managing his nursery like a reform school. If Knight's garden was a laboratory, Van Mons's was a sluice box.[22] Rather than look for secret ingredients in individual varieties, he ran millions of seedlings through a grueling selection process and propagated the best still standing. Van Mons discarded the old varieties and started with trees most gardeners would consider useless, usually just one generation removed from wild seedlings. In the first generation, he cared little for the quality of the tree and instead required only that they be young and in "state of variation": thorny, perhaps, or stunted, and bearing nearly inedible fruit.[23] He selected the most promising seedlings of these, cut off their taproots and pruned them vigorously, harvested the unripe first fruits of these seedlings, allowed the fruit to rot, and then planted again. After five generations of this uninterrupted reproduction, Van Mons claimed, his pear seedlings were nearly all superior selections.

This more physical -- or, as the historian Emily Pawley puts it, "republican" -- approach posited variety development as a continual struggle between horticulturist and plant.[24] As varieties aged, Van Mons thought, they became harder to manipulate. The old varieties that he and other pomologists had inherited at the end of the eighteenth century had reached their senescence and should be allowed to die a peaceful death.

But the creation of new varieties required superhuman perseverance. As Van Mons wrote in 1835: "To sow, re-sow, to sow again, to sow perpetually, in short to do nothing but sow, is the practice to be pursued, and which cannot be departed from; and in short this is the whole secret of the art I have employed."[25]

Van Mons's monomaniacal obsession with proving his theory made his estate an astonishingly productive place. At one time, he had eighty thousand unique seedlings in his gardens; he named and propagated some four hundred new pears, forty of which were still in cultivation a century later.[26] His experiments demonstrated the value of selection as a breeding technique, and after his death in 1842, his countrymen carried on his work. Belgian's Royal Commission on Pomology, which produced the beautiful four-volume *Album du Pomologie* in 1851, was, as a model of government support for horticulture, the envy of horticultural societies around the world.[27]

The sexual behavior of fruit trees, as explored by Van Mons and Thomas Knight, was part of the larger mystery of evolutionary biology. In 1855, for example, Charles Darwin wrote to the *Gardener's Chronicle and Agricultural Gazette* and begged for correspondents who had "carefully sown named seeds and have noted the result." Van Mons, Darwin noted, had "sometimes raised from the seed of one variety of Pear a quite distinct kind," but his results were uncertain at best: "It now appears Van Mons was careless in marking the varieties sown." Do some varieties produce "truer offspring" than others? Darwin wanted to know.[28]

Evolutionary biology could apply not just to the nonhuman world, but to human civilization as well. Van Mons's theory may have been a way to work through his own "conflicted feelings about aristocracy."[29] Like the available fruits, the European aristocracies had risen to power in the late Middle Ages; by the late eighteenth century, both seemed to be "running out," sapped of their former vigor and vitality. What pieces of the old regimes that political revolutions had left in place, the Industrial Revolution was rapidly dismantling. Something new was in order.

And what better place for the new botanical order than the New World? America fascinated observers on both sides of the Atlantic not just because of the political experiment afoot but also because of the emerging horticultural possibilities. For horticulturists, using the language of nativity, vitality, and stock to talk about fruit trees was not just a metaphorical way of working out their racial fears or nationalistic ambitions; it was not just political or rhetorical work, but biological. The new republic had been planted; it would now have to be tended. And so the work of horticulture – the sowing, pruning, pollinating, cultivating, ripening, observing, selecting, grafting, protecting – was essential, in the minds of the horticulturists, for the maintenance of the nation.[30]

Prosper Berckmans was well equipped for this work. His father, Louis, had raised him in the heyday of the Belgian pear craze and sent him to botanical gardens in Paris and Tours for formal training. In 1848, Prosper Berckmans returned to Iteghem to assist in managing the estate and to collaborate with his father and Bivort on the *Album*.[31] At age eighteen, then, Prosper was already very much a part of Belgium's horticultural world. We can see something of his skill and sensibility in the *Indicateur General*, an 1846 volume from his time as manager of the family estate at Iteghem. The book divided the estate into sections, each of which someone, presumably the painter Louis, had rendered in exquisite water-color: blue ponds and streams, golden paths, green orchards, and red buildings. Each tree or shrub had a number, and the following pages listed, in a flawless hand, the variety name and relevant details: its origi-nator (Van Mons, Esperen, etc.), or, if it was a seedling, which generation. The book is a remarkable representation of the fastidious attention to detail and the aesthetic sensibilities that characterized nineteenth-century Belgian horticulture (Figures 2.1 and 2.2).

By all appearances, the Berckmans family in Belgium was well off: they had a thousand-year history of nobility and owned several "castles" near Lier, in the province of Antwerp. Louis Berckmans had chosen the right side during the Belgian independence movement, which achieved sepa-ration from the Netherlands in 1831. Economically, Belgium was on a solid footing, second only to England in iron production; a potato famine and economic crisis in the 1840s mainly affected the working class. The revolutions that shook nearly all of Europe in 1848 were mere trem-ors in Belgium.[32] There is no self-evident reason for the Berckmanses' emigration. Though some later biographers have suggested religious and political persecution as the reason, Prosper Berckmans himself mentions nothing of the kind.

But Prosper's devotion to the theory of Van Mons may offer a clue. Well into the 1870s, though he also practiced Knight's cross-pollination techniques, Berckmans instructed his American followers in what he called "the law of reversion," the idea that cultivated varieties could become too refined for their own good and would, in order to save the species, "revert" to wild. In 1876 he praised Van Mons's notion of genetic overrefinement as the "one of those provisions of Providence" that pre-vented species from becoming so refined that "to go further must end in a

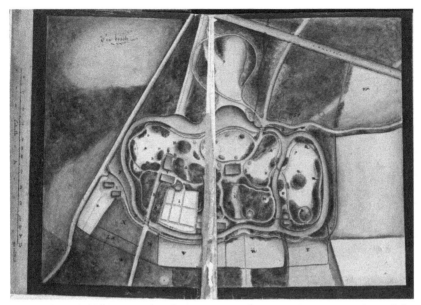

FIGURE 2.1. Frontispiece of *Indicateur Generale*, presenting an overview of the Berckmans family estate near Iteghem, Belgium.
Source: Indicateur Generale (1846). Courtesy of Hargrett Rare Book and Manuscript Library and the University of Georgia Libraries, Berckmans Family Papers, MS 122, Box 1, Folder 7.

diseased tree or imperfect seed, and consequent extinction of the race."[33] Perhaps the Berckmans family feared the decline of their ancestral bloodlines and hoped to infuse their lineage with New World wildness and vigor. Prosper did marry an American, Mary Craig, not long after settling in Plainfield, New Jersey.

As it turns out, Prosper Berckmans's youthful jaunt through the United States was a kind of house-hunting trip. Instead of returning to Belgium and carrying on the family estate at Iteghem, he returned to New York, where he welcomed his father and stepmother in 1851. Plainfield, New Jersey was a strategic choice. New Jersey had been the most advanced fruit-growing region in the country since the early 1800s, mostly because of its close proximity to the great urban markets of New York. It was the home of William Coxe, author of *A View of the Cultivation of Fruit Trees* and along with Downing one of America's best pomological writers of that time, and it was close to the New York horticultural scene as well.[34]

American horticulturists, for their part, were thrilled with the Berckmanses' transplantation. Louis Berckmans was Belgian pomology

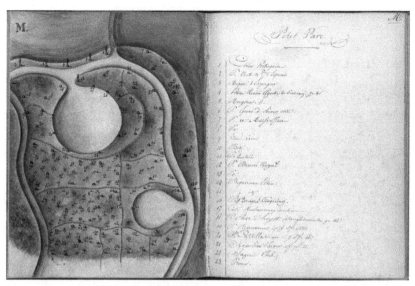

FIGURE 2.2. "Le Petit Parc" (The Little Park), a representative page from the *Indicateur Generale*. Each two page spread focused on a particular part of the estate, with the map on the left keyed to a list of plants on the right.
Source: *Indicateur Generale* (1846). Courtesy of Hargrett Rare Book and Manuscript Library and the University of Georgia Libraries, Berckmans Family Papers, MS 122, Box 1, Folder 7.

incarnate. The work of Van Mons and company, which had drifted inter-mittently across the Atlantic since the 1820s, was now present for closer examination. As Robert Manning of the Massachusetts Horticultural Society later recalled, Louis Berckmans's arrival "threw a great deal of light on what had before been obscure and uncertain, and seemed to give reality to what had previously appeared dim and unreal."[35] A. J. Downing showed up soon after their arrival "to consult with [Louis] on some pears."[36] Not to be outdone, Downing's chief rival, Charles Hovey of Massachusetts, paid a visit to Berckmans's Plainfield property the following year. Hovey marveled that Berckmans had left "his beautiful villa at Heyst-op-ten-berg, with all the attractions which taste, aided by wealth, had lavished upon it" for the "wild and uncultivated scenery" of America. Berckmans had already set out pear seedlings, Hovey found, though many had died crossing the Atlantic. They were "planted in rows, thickly, in different parts of his grounds, which are mapped off in a book, and the trees catalogued in such a way that reference may be had to any lot with the greatest facility" – an *Indicateur General* for the new continent. It was an organized, ambitious estate, and Hovey expected great things from this "co-worker in the great cause."[37]

Despite New Jersey's horticultural reputation, the Berckmans men soon found the climate too harsh for their delicate pear trees. They stayed long enough for Prosper to earn his American citizenship and to wed Mary Craig.[38] Then, in 1856, Louis and his second wife, Elizabeth, divorced. Heartbroken again, he left Elizabeth with their two sons, Auguste and Emile, and moved to Augusta, Georgia.[39]

Augusta was in many ways an obvious choice. Several nurseries already operated there. The Swedish traveler Carl Arfwedson averred that, with the exception of New Orleans, no other southern town had "a more agreeable exterior" or a "a stronger idea of comfort and wealth." Its situation was "in every respect advantageous: on the borders of two cotton-growing States, and lying close to a navigable river" that fed easily into Savannah and Charleston, the two greatest south Atlantic seaports.[40] Augusta, as its imposing cotton warehouse indicated, grew out of the upland cotton boom: a large proportion of upland cotton from both South Carolina and Georgia passed through Augusta on its way to the sea. And it was an early shipping point for southern peaches.

The town would have been familiar to the Berckmans via the southern horticultural network that emerged, in fits and starts, in the 1850s. By 1856 the little network had a name in the Georgia Pomological Society (GPS), a president in Stephen Elliott, officers in Mark Cooper, William White (author of *Gardening for the South*), and James Camak, and – suggesting that they understood themselves to be part of the national horticultural scene – corresponding members in Louis Berckmans and Patrick Barry.[41] By 1857, when the society held its first meeting, its report appeared not only in the *Southern Cultivator* but also Downing's journal the *Horticulturist*.[42] Less than a year later, Louis Berckmans was president of the GPS – for, as William White suggested, "No other man could fill the chair so well" – and in his annual report on fruits, Berckmans proclaimed progress: "In respect to correctness, great improvement is manifest the last two years, and we no longer see the same Pear, Apple, &c, exhibited under three or four different names."[43] Southern pomology, like northern pomology a decade earlier, was finally giving some order to the haphazard horticultural landscape. Though later Prosper Berckmans remembered the GPS as little more than "a social reunion of a few kindred spirits," he nevertheless boasted of the two hundred distinct fruit varieties displayed at the final meeting in 1860.[44]

One of those kindred spirits was the enterprising Dennis Redmond, who, as editor of the *Southern Cultivator*, touted the South's climatic advantages and the need for regional self-reliance. It was Redmond's home at Fruitland that, by degrees, became the Berckmans operations center in the South. In April 1857, Redmond announced an "Important New Arrangement!" with Louis Berckmans, which gave him "full access to all the grafts and buds" of "the well known" pomologist's pear collection – hundreds of named varieties plus more than twenty thousand seedlings – as well as "all the best and rarest varieties of other fruit known in Europe and America."[45] By October, only Prosper Berckmans's name was on the advertisements, under which Redmond offered a "hearty thanks" to his readers for their encouragements and endorsed the new proprietors of Fruitland. Redmond, meanwhile, had "purchased a beautiful hill-side," converted it into a vineyard, and was now devoting his attention mostly to grapes with a new business he called "Vineland."[46] In 1860 the correspondent for the R. G. Dun and Company, an early credit-rating agency, reported that Redmond had "not much means" and lived "pretty well up to his income," so that he was "slow and hard up for money generally."[47]

Prosper Berckmans, meanwhile, was on the way up. The R. G. Dun correspondent recommended "no hesitation in selling him all he wants to a reasonable extent."[48] Berckmans had the further advantage of marrying well: his wife, Mary Craig Berckmans, owned real estate worth ten thousand dollars.[49] In 1858, the *Horticulturist* editor Peter Mead described Fruitland Nurseries as "a firm commencing under uncommonly favorable auspices." Prosper Berckmans, the son of the "well-known pomologist of New Jersey," would help to build up a "first class Southern nursery" specializing in fruit. "Pomology," Mead concluded, "is advancing rapidly in that region."[50] Redmond agreed in 1861, noting with pleasure the "very hopeful and encouraging aspect of Southern Pomology" and anticipating "a degree of activity and success which must greatly redound to the prosperity and happiness of our country."[51] By 1861, Berckmans boasted that Fruitland had, along with nine hundred apple varieties, three hundred grapes, three hundred peaches, more than thirteen hundred named varieties of pears, plus ten thousand "unproduced seedlings" of pomological luminaries such as Van Mons, Pierre Joseph Esperen, William D. Brincklé, and Berckmans himself.[52]

Under Berckmans's management, Fruitland was an astonishingly productive place. To take just one year as an example, at the Georgia State Horticultural Society's third annual meeting in 1878 Berckmans exhibited thirty-nine varieties of apple, forty-five of pear, twenty-two of peaches – the Committee on Peaches and Miscellaneous Fruits made "special mention" of Pullen's Seedling and White Pine Apple Cling – fourteen of grape, two of plums, and one of cobnuts (hazelnuts).[53] Berckmans claimed to be "in constant correspondence with the principle European growers" and imported any new variety "at once." But like Berckmans himself, the nursery also translated that horticultural eminence into practical agriculture for the South. His grounds at Fruitland were extensive enough to "compare and study the influence of soil and aspect upon the same varieties," he explained. Observing the new fascination with fruit growing in the South, and convinced of the "great importance of depending mostly upon southern seedling fruits" to succeed in this pursuit, Berckmans had taken "great pains" to sift through all the cultivated varieties and offered only those "well tried as to all their merits." One could order a Fruitland fruit tree with confidence. Like Thomas Affleck and William Summers, who operated Southern Nurseries in Mississippi and Pomaria Nurseries in South Carolina, respectively, Berckmans was trading both plant material and expert authority.[54] Fruitland was an outpost of European horticulture.

IV

This auspicious beginning for Fruitland, and for southern horticulture more broadly, took place in the midst of growing sectional hostilities: Bleeding Kansas in 1855, the Dred Scott case in 1857, John Brown's raid on Harpers Ferry in 1859. And yet despite some rhetoric to the contrary, horticulture remained a partnership between North and South.[55]

The outbreak of the Civil War violently interrupted that partnership. There was little public talk of orchards or gardens during the Civil War or immediately afterward. A writer for the short-lived periodical the *Land We Love* summarized: "Unavoidable neglect, and want of a market during the war; and, since its close, the inability of many to cultivate their orchards properly, tended to check [horticulture's] progress."[56] Orchards became battlefields or, as they had some decades earlier for slaves such as Charles Ball, provisioning grounds for soldiers. To cite one representative example: in August 1862, Joshua Callaway, a volunteer in the Army of Tennessee from Coffee County, Alabama, stumbled upon a fine orchard near Chattanooga, Tennessee; purchased some fresh milk from the owners; and indulged. "Now you may *imagine* how much milk and peaches I ate and how I enjoyed it but I'm sure I can't *tell* you," he wrote to his wife.[57] Hostilities persisted in the wake of war, especially during the period of radical congressional Reconstruction in 1867–1877. Even if horticulturists felt some fellowship with northerners in this decade, they could not publicly join the "carpetbaggers" and retain their nursery customers and high standing. So it was not until 1876, as radical Reconstruction waned and the war itself seemed distant, that horticultural reformers made their first pronouncements about what had just happened.

And it was not just the cessation of hostilities and the opening of markets that made commercial horticulture possible. It was the sudden availability of *labor*. As Berckmans explained it, the Civil War, by destroying slavery, laid a new foundation for horticulture in the South. "Farming upon a smaller scale followed as a natural consequence of this change [emancipation] in our labor," he argued in 1876. "Fruit growing, which to the cotton planter was a secondary matter, [became] one of great solicitude to the farmer" only after the war.[58]

Berckmans's counterintuitive logic requires some unpacking, for the more dominant note about labor in the immediate postbellum period was uncertainty, if not outright despair. An exchange on "The Labor Question" in the Augusta-based *Farmer and Gardener* – for which Prosper Berckmans was the horticultural editor – illustrates this point. A letter writer known only as "Agricola" argued that "negro labor is better adapted to our cotton growing States, and must succeed better" than any "introduced" groups.[59] Agricola made familiar arguments about the physical superiority of former slaves for working in the "almost tropical" climate of the cotton belt – though he offered some additional specious evidence about the "thick and woolly covering of his cranium" which "fit him for the midsummer rays." The only question for this writer, then, was whether freedmen could be as efficient as slaves. He thought all that was needed was for planters to "organize into societies and pass suitable resolutions" to require recommendations from former employers. In reply, the editor of *Farmer and Gardener* accepted Agricola's premises – physical adaptation of black labor – but scoffed at the idea of societies and resolutions giving planters sufficient control over labor. The *Farmer and Gardener* was a consistent defender of immigrant labor. The freedmen were reliable enough, he said, but the "young negro" promised to become a "worthless, idle vagabond." Without white immigrant workers, the South's "fruitful fields" would become "barren wildernesses."[60]

Southern horticulturists turned this despair on its head: labor instability, they said, was an *opportunity* for commercial horticulture. Freedmen moved frequently – "lookin' for better all the time" – and they sought their own land on which to order their own time and labor.[61] These two actions of former slaves, albeit severely circumscribed by the eventual failure of Reconstruction to secure political or economic power, spelled destruction for some agriculture industries, such as low country rice, which required large-scale, intensively-managed production.[62] Southern cotton production could be scaled down, and so it expanded in the late nineteenth century. Cotton depended on a mutually unsatisfactory compromise between former masters and former slaves known as sharecropping, a system that saw no less use for all the condemnation heaped upon it. This footloose but unfree population was available to power the gospel of agricultural diversification – in particular, to harvest fruit and vegetables.

The story of Berckmans's colleague Armenius Oemler underscores this point. Armenius was the son of Augustus Gottlieb Oemler, a German immigrant who had been a correspondent of elite botanists and horticulturists around the country: A. J. Downing considered his garden "inferior to no private collection in the Union."[63] After some successful real estate deals, Armenius Oemler began buying up land and, like his father, went into gardening. While Augustus had been concerned with taste and beauty and display, though, Armenius was aggressively commercial in his approach. He purchased seventeen slaves for $13,832 in 1862 and began raising vegetables or "truck": beans, peas, cabbages, cucumbers, eggplant, potatoes, tomatoes, and watermelon.[64] By 1883, with two decades of experience and profit under his belt, he published *Truck Farming at the South: A Guide to the Raising of Vegetables for Northern Markets* with Orange Judd Company, one of the preeminent agricultural presses of the day.

Oemler gave pride of place in *Truck Farming* to the question of labor, and his considered and frankly racist conclusion was that "the negro must be accepted as the only practical solution of the labor question." The immigration of whites such as Italians or eastern Europeans was simply impractical, for they possessed the "praiseworthy desire for self-elevation." But "the negro" was the "God-given instrument for the development of the agricultural resources of the South." Landowners could use "his general wastefulness and improvidence" and instability, which Oemler understood to be fixed traits, to their advantage. By "strict justice, fairness and even kindness," the employer could make his black workers content with their lot and useful to the building up of southern society instead of leaving them to become "irritating elements of the body politic."[65]

Oemler agreed with Berckmans that there would be no truck farming without the end of slavery. He had tried growing vegetables with slaves, but he could not employ more than forty-five at one time, and only twenty-six of these could be used in the field. Savannah truck farmers routinely employed one to two hundred laborers each during the picking season. Simply put, slave labor limited the acreage one could devote to perishable crops. After emancipation, then, the prospective truck farmer needed to live close to a city. "Ex-Governor Hammond" of South Carolina, he wrote, was entirely correct when he predicted that the emancipated slave would "seek the towns."[66]

Oemler quoted here from one of James Henry Hammond's lengthy letters on slavery, addressed to the British abolitionist Thomas Clarkson in 1845 and widely disseminated across the South; it sought to defend the practice of American slavery and to make emancipation seem impossible. "The negro loves change, novelty and sensual excitements of all kinds, when awake," Hammond declared:

Released from his present obligations his first impulse would be to go somewhere. And here [unlike in the "little sea-girt West India Islands"] no natural boundaries would restrain him. At first they would all seek the towns, and rapidly accumulate in squalid groups upon their outskirts. Driven thence by the "armed police" which would immediately spring into existence, they would scatter in all directions.

Some would go north and west, "making their tracks by their depredations and their corpses." Others would "roam wild" in the southern woods and swamps, preying on southern crops and livestock until exhausted, and finally plundering "our scattered dwellings" and murdering those who dwelt there.[67] Emancipation was tantamount not just to economic suicide but to physical suicide and to homicide as well. For a southern white man to propose emancipating southern slaves was little different from proposing the murder of his southern neighbors.

It is important not to dismiss Hammond's alarmism, overwrought as it seems. Emancipation *did* represent a wrenching prospect, and to think that the transition to freedom could be peaceful and friendly discredits the ambitions of the slaves themselves. Beyond the possibility of violence, the basic demands of emancipated slaves would upend the structure of southern economic and social life. For freedmen demanded land of their own, a desire W. E. B. DuBois believed arose in part from their experience of tending their own independent gardens as slaves.[68] And where was that land to come from, if not from the plantations of their former owners?

A group of freedmen from Edisto Island, in South Carolina, expressed this desire in particularly compelling terms. They petitioned President Andrew Johnson in 1865 for the continued ownership of lands given to them by General Sherman during the war:

Here is [where] we have toiled nearly all Our lives as slaves and were treated like dumb Driven cattle, This is our home, we have made These lands what they are. we were the only true and Loyal people that were found in possession of these Lands… We wish to have A home if It be but A few acres… A Homestead right here in the heart of South Carolina.[69]

The freedmen appealed to the same ideals that motivated agricultural reformers: permanence, self-sufficiency, agrarian civilization. This was the work of culture to which the horticulturists called their fellow southerners, to make their lands their own via careful tending. Could horticulturists see black southerners as fellow workers in the great cause?

As Oemler's story suggests, the answer to that question is depressingly predictable: *no*.[70] In some ways, the horticultural landscape was paradoxically *more* closed to freed people than it had been to slaves.[71] White landowners looking to diversify their crops saw black freedom as an opportunity for reinvestment. They could be extraordinarily harsh in maintaining that "opportunity." Whereas Charles Ball had helped himself to peaches throughout the harvest season in the early 1800s, by the late 1800s landowners were policing that boundary much more carefully. In 1888, somewhere in rural Georgia, three black boys stole into a peach orchard and picked some peaches, three of which they gave to eight-year-old William Robinson. The landowner caught the boys, and, contending that "the receiver was just as bad as the rogue," charged Robinson's father twenty-one dollars for the three peaches. As Robinson remembered it ninety-five years later, the owner looked Robinson's father in the eye and said, as if to emphasize his magnanimity, " 'if he was … just a little bigger, I'd put him in jail. Put 'em on chain gang,' " he said. Robinson did not take this as an idle threat: "I was scared of it," he affirmed. "I heard them workin', heard them singin' on there and workin' the roads." The lesson Robinson drew from the experience was "Don't take that ain't yours."[72] But the threat and the harsh fine – when Robinson could just as well have been an employee of the owner, and could easily have eaten three peaches while on the job, at no real cost – suggest the kind of fearful urgency with which landowners demarcated boundaries.

Berckmans himself never owned slaves, and his early employees appear to have been mostly European immigrants. In 1860, he had in his household a twenty-nine-year old Belgian laborer named Joseph Tice, a thirty-one-year-old French nurseryman named Peter Benne, a twenty-three-year-old servant from Ireland named Rose Kelly, and a clerk and a child, both from New Jersey. Next door to Berckmans lived a thirty-five-year-old Dutch farmer named Herman Schneider and his family; a few houses down was the Danish nurseryman William K. Nelson, who later founded an important nursery near Macon, Georgia.[73] A decade later, Berckmans had in his household another Frenchman, Prosper Murat, who worked as a foreman, and (perhaps his brother) Symphorien Murat, who worked as a gardener; a German gardener, Henry Zapper, and his southern wife, Mary, lived nearby. But he also had the black farmhand John Golphin and his black wife, Maria Golphin, a domestic servant, and their four children; William Robinson and Louisa Smith, a butler and a laundress, respectively, both black; and Tobey Johnson, a twenty-nine-year old black gardener and his farmhand wife, Fannie, and their family. Many more of his immediate neighbors were black farm-hands by 1870.[74] By 1910, the next available census schedule, Berckmans employed mostly black workers: nursery laborers Freeman Payne, Elijah Stead, Hampton Key, Shed Talksley, Henry Williams; wagon drivers Dick Stolen, Charles Williams, and Booker Yarrboro; and Eugene Smith, care-taker of the nursery greenhouse.[75]

These people, for the most part, are mute in the historical record, although images surviving from the early twentieth century show black workers performing agricultural tasks in much the same way as other photographs from the period do. But the greenhouse caretaker Eugene Wesley Smith did speak. In the 1930s, he sat down with a Works Progress Administration (WPA) interviewer, who described him with the observant condescension typical of white oral historians of the WPA:

He has thin features, trembling lips and a sparse beard. His skin is a deep brown, lined and veined. His legs showing over white socks are scaly. His hands are palsied, but his mind is intelligent. He shows evidences of association with white people in his manner of speech, which at times is in the manner of white persons, again reverting to dialect.

Smith's memories of growing up in Augusta were vivid, if scattered. He was born in 1852 to an enslaved father, a porter who belonged to an Augusta jeweler, and a free mother, so he saw both sides of bondage as a boy. His mother Louisa, a laundress, had moved to Augusta from Pennsylvania with white owners, who freed her when she came of age.[76] Some slave children went to school, though it was technically against regulation. Smith saw fellow blacks on the auction block at the Augusta slave market, and he recalled the threat of speculators stealing children, taking them to plantations until they were old enough to sell, and taking them back to market. Smith remembered great "frolics" for black Augustans, but their freedom was circumscribed by curfew and pass laws. Similarly, although Smith was technically free, he had to have a white guardian. Smith fell in love at age sixteen and married five years later. He quit his butler job and took up work on the Augusta Canal, which city leaders were in the process of widening. He made $1.25 a day. "They got in some Chinese when it was near finished," Smith recalled, "but they wasn't any good. The Irishmen wouldn't work with niggers, because they said they could make the job last eight years – the niggers worked too fast. They accomplished it in about four years." Once the canal was complete, Smith continued in construction work, helping to dig the foundations of Augusta's iconic Sibley Mill and the raceway that leads from canal to river. And then he got a job at Fruitland Nurseries.

I went to Mr. Berckmans and worked for him for fifty years. All my children were raised on his place. That's how come my boy do garden work now. I worked for 50 c a day, but he give me a house on the place. He 'lowed me to have chickens, a little fence, and a garden. He was very good to us. That was Mr. P. J. Berckmans. I potted plants all day long. I used to work at night. I wouldn't draw no money, just let them keep it for me. After they found out I could read and write and was an honest fellow, they let me take my work home, and my children helped me make the apple grass and plum grass, and mulberry grass. A man come and told me he would give me $60 a month if I would go with him, but I didn't.[77]

Sixty dollars a month would have been a fine salary, quadrupling Smith's cash wages at Fruitlands. From a certain perspective, Smith's choice to stay with Berckmans might seem to be an expression of "loyalty," a trope that showed up again and again in white memories of the postemancipation South.[78] And while the stories of former slave loyalty might speak to authentic feelings of white southerners, they were on the whole not very accurate. Emancipation, for a few years at least, wrenched those fine tales of slave affection from their former owners, just as it took away the slaves themselves.

Looking closely at Smith's description, though, loyalty was not necessarily the issue. He did not choose to stay with Berckmans out of affection for the man, even if he clearly had some lingering respect for the Belgian. It was just as much, if not more, the house, the "little fence," the chickens, the garden. It was a space that he cultivated himself, in addition to the "grass" – fruit tree starts – he tended for Berckmans. This space may have been a far cry from the forty acres and a mule of the Edisto Island freedmen, but it was, for Smith, yet worth remembering.

V

By the 1870s, Berckmans's Fruitland Nursery was one of the largest in the South, and, according to the correspondent for R. G. Dun and Company, was "apparently making money" in 1875. The correspondent estimated Berckmans's worth at twenty-five thousand dollars and pronounced him worthy of large amounts of credit.[79] His public persona expanded along with his wealth: he had served the state agricultural society for several years as chairman of the horticultural committee, and he edited the horticulture department of the Augusta-based *Farm and Garden*.[80]

The time was ripe, from Berckmans's point of view, for a club: a separate horticultural organization that would collect the expertise and experience of all the planter hobbyists, commercial orchardists, truck farmers, and nurserymen of the state – and by extension, the South. The South could be made beautiful and cultured, and Berckmans's nursery business stood to make a tidy profit from it.[81] And so, in 1876, he gathered a group of men in Macon's Central City Park and chartered the Georgia State Horticultural Society to "promote and encourage the science of Horticulture in all its branches, by the most feasible means," to establish horticultural schools, to hold regular exhibitions of the state's products.[82] Berckmans was elected president of the society, an office he would hold until his death in 1910. It was one of the most enduring societies of its kind in the South.

Having organized the society that he believed would produce horticultural prosperity for the state and the region, Berckmans took the podium to deliver the inaugural presidential address, touching on themes that would occupy him for the next thirty years. He waxed eloquent on the capacity of fruit growing to deliver not only increased income but also a "refining influence" to Georgia's farmers. The establishment of the GSHS, he assured his audience, heralded a "progressive era" for the state's agriculture.[83] True to form, Berckmans's talk was much more than lofty rhetoric. He also took time in his opening salvo to address more practical questions, delineating, for example, the two methods by which his horticultural disciples could *culture* the South. In Van Mons–style "progressive improvement" one simply planted the seeds of the best fruits on the best trees; in Knight-style "cross impregnation or hybridizing" one actively intervened in sexual reproduction, taking pollen from one tree to fertilize another.[84] His annual addresses followed a similar pattern for years: philosophical meditations, practical advice, and policy recommendations. Berckmans thus assumed the role of the aristocratic educator, taking the fecund but undeveloped Southland and turning it to more civilized pursuits by instructing southerners in the finer points of horticultural practice.

Prosper and Louis Berckmans did not have in view anything like today's "Peach State." Prosper would be a good peach breeder and grower, and the Berckmanses' arrival in the South and founding of the GSHS heralded the region's promise as a fruit producer. If they had had their wish, though, Augusta would have been the next *pear* capital of the world, or the vineyard of the nation. As Dennis Redmond proclaimed to the American Pomological Society in 1859, "We have much reason to believe that in the South only is the Pear destined to arrive at its highest development and perfection." In July 1859, Louis Berckmans predicted: "I shall not see the time when the South, from Virginia to Alabama, shall be considered the fruit garden of America, but I am fully convinced that such a time must and shall come, and that thousands of acres, unfit for cultivation of cotton and corn, will be converted into remunerating orchards. All we want," he concluded, "is a little patience – a rare thing with a fast people."[85] As if to demonstrate his faith, Louis named his first home near Augusta "Pearmont."[86]

Pears never saw much success in the South. Fire blight decimated even the one notable "southern" pear, the LeConte variety, and no lasting market developed for southern pears in the North. Aside from the Berckmans themselves, few southern horticulturists had the resources or the patience to pursue the exacting Van Mons method of successive selection. The same applied to Redmond's efforts at Vineland: the promise of southern wine would remain mostly unfulfilled until the twenty-first century.[87]

Instead, southern horticulturists paid more and more attention to the more obliging *Prunus persica*. As early as 1859, Dennis Redmond recognized the peach's potential. "The South is the true home of the Peach," Redmond told the American Pomological Society.

It has long been, and is yet, the favorite fruit of the people, no less for its intrinsic excellence, than for the ease with which it may be propagated from seed, and the early period at which it comes into bearing. Thousands of the very finest seedling peaches, unnamed and comparatively unknown, are scattered thro'out the South, along the road-sides, in the open fields, and in the remote corners of fences and hedges.[88]

While the pear demanded fastidious care, peaches thrived without any care at all. If "worked" – if cultured with all the tools the horticulturist had at his disposal – the fruit could be exceedingly fine. The Berckmans may have gone south for the pear. But young Prosper would stay there for the peach.

This transition from diversified horticulture to peach monoculture was gradual. In part the peach's triumph stemmed from the difficulty of the southern environment. Despite the turgid praise heaped on the lavish beneficence of Georgia's climate, its natural advantages were actually quite limited. The Southeast's high humidity and warm winters rolled out the welcome mat to insect pests. At the same time, irregular rainfall stressed trees, making them more vulnerable to those pests as well as fungi, bacteria, and viruses. In view of these challenges as well as unpredictable springtime temperatures – with late, killing frosts every few years – fruit growers could not rely upon a profitable harvest. Citrus was confined to tropical Florida, and watermelons and tomatoes and other annual truck crops lacked the cultural sophistication of orchards and vineyards. Other orchard crops succeeded momentarily – apples in northern Georgia in the early twentieth century, wild goose plums in the cotton belt in the late nineteenth – but only peaches remained commercially viable for long.

VI

The postbellum years marked not just a change in crops but also a change in horticultural knowledge and labor. Gradually, the work of *culture* for the sake of *taste* gave way to *cultivation* for the sake of *profit*. It also produced a parting of Louis and Prosper Berckmans. The separation of the Berckmans men augured a broader shift in ways of knowing and working with plants.

In 1870, Louis completed his about-face from his days as a dashing military officer by settling, alone, in a one-room cottage atop Mount Alto, near Rome. There he lived as part of the small Belgian colony pioneered by his friend L. J. B. LeHardy some twenty years earlier, and kept his neighbors puzzled by his "interesting" habits. In his "little vine-clad cottage" he kept a "classic library" and paintings of generals from his military days in Belgium, while his grounds blossomed with fruit trees and flowers.[89] "I wish you could come up and enjoy the fine peaches and pears," he wrote to his grandsons in 1880. "I wish you could come here to see the beautiful landscape all around, and walk over the trails of our rugged mountains."[90] His favorite dish was a mixture of rice, lemons, and apples, and he never drank, even when offering "delicious wines" to visitors. He smoked a mixture of tobacco and homegrown rose leaves in a pipe. He walked everywhere he went, even into old age, and one Rome resident remembered him as unmatched in "physical ability and vigor." But deep sadness hung over his days. In one letter to his grandsons Robert and Allie he wrote, "My retired life is at least comparatively secure and I mix not with men and society, in order to escape scores of annoyances and perils." He concluded, bleakly, "This world is a battlefield filled with unknown perils."[91]

Residents of Rome, Georgia, called Louis Berckmans "The Hermit of Mt. Alto," a description he acknowledged in letters to his three grandsons when they were in school. "I live most retired," he wrote to Robert and Allie Berckmans in 1882, "pay scarcely any visits to neighbors, and keep busy with my plants and trees." He visited Fruitland rarely, in part because there he did not have a "real private room" with a fireplace. (At Fruitland "they do not believe in fireplaces!" he complained.)[92] He declined to meet the headmaster of their school. "I do not go to public gatherings any more as I had too much of that during my long life," he explained, "and I hate crowds, and public celebrations of all kinds."[93]

As these comments suggest, Louis Berckmans lived his last years in solitude. This retirement did not guarantee protection from suffering, Berckmans acknowledged, but "if misfortune befalls me, I will at least have the proven consolation that I did not seek them."[94] Twenty months after Louis Berckmans sent those words to his grandsons, on December 5, 1883, he returned to Fruitland. The next day, he walked to Augusta and back, a total distance of about three miles. The day after, December 7, he died, at age eighty-two.[95]

Prosper Berckmans would lead the GSHS to an increasingly commercial emphasis, shepherding the rise of a number of long-lived marketable peach cultivars and starting his own commercial peach orchard, even as he continued to experiment with wine grapes and pears. He died in November of 1910, and the following year's GSHS proceedings were full of mournful tributes to the old man. "I looked upon him as a friend and a counselor and a father," the University of Georgia horticulturist Thomas H. McHatton said, "and I appreciated above all things the interest that he seemed to take in me as a young horticulturist."[96] Berckmans, McHatton observed, had introduced commercial peach growing, the Japanese persimmon, the Peento (also called saturn or donut) peach, the Japanese plum, and amur privet. He had been president not just of the GSHS but of the American Pomological Society, and corresponding or honorary member of the horticultural societies of Massachussetts, Nebraska, Florida, Alabama, and Bourdeaux, France.[97]

If there has been a man in the state of Georgia that has done more toward the advancement, the welfare and the happiness of its people, I do not now recall it. We have had great politicians; we have had great orators; we have had men who probably stood in the public eye to a greater extent than the President of the Georgia Horticultural Society, but I doubt materially if we have ever had a man whose work will live after him as long as that of Prosper Julius Alphonso Berckmans. In the years to come ourselves, and our children, and our grand-children, will look upon the plants that beautify the State, and, if we just glance back into our history for a generation or so we will get back to Dr. Berckmans, the President of our Society... The Horticultural Society of the State of Georgia has lost its founder and its friend, and this country has lost a constructor, whose work will live on into time.[98]

Berckmans's cultural work would outlast the achievements of Georgia's more famous citizens. *This country has lost a constructor* – because one cannot have a country without plants to make it beautiful and fruitful. Other GSHS members concurred. "I know of no one who has died of whom it can be said that his life had accomplished so much good," one said. "His life was devoted to fruits and flowers."[99] Another remarked that "every mile-post of his pathway was wreathed in flowers as he passed along."[100] A third claimed him as a farmer, "cultured to the high-est degree." Still another compared him to Moses, leading horticulturists into the promised land.

But it was Col. B. W. Hunt of Eatonton who carried the rhetoric of the occasion to its sentimental apogee. He took the podium, perhaps shakily, and read prepared remarks out of fear that his emotion would get the best of him. Berckmans knew, Hunt declared, "that he could not leave the world without a witness to speak of him." And that is exactly what the southern landscape did:

Grandeur and glory of verdure, whose vibrant leaves would forever whisper his name from the mountains to the sea; rainbow hued flowers smiling from the sod, emanations of his life and love, would embalm his memory in their perfume. Every cup a pulpit, every leaf a book, and all living creatures telling of him. Not Solomon in all his glory was arrayed like this beauteous throng, who through unnumbered years, should swing their chalices of incense, and chant his praises through earth's green aisles.

Hunt continued, indefatigable. Berckmans was like Christ himself, dead and buried yet rising from the dead every spring with "the innumerable tenements of beauty, among the rainbow galaxies of flowers he loved, now up-springing in the light... The work of his hands still lives."[101] When, at long last, John C. Greer took up the scheduled paper for the morning, he hesitated to break the mood. "I feel like it is almost irreverent to disturb the spirit that has fallen upon this meeting with any thing I shall have to say," he began his paper, which bore the forthright if unimaginative title, "Figs."[102]

But the work had to go on, and the 1911 meeting saw the leadership of the GSHS fall, fittingly, to Prosper's sons. The meeting's opening had a dramatic moment when Vice President B. W. Hunt of Eatonton was nominated to serve as chairman of the proceedings that year. Standing, Colonel Hunt blurted, "And I would like to nominate a gentleman." *Sit down!* the members cried. "You can't put me down," Hunt replied, and went on to nominate Robert Craig Berckmans instead. "The name of Berckmans stands as no other name in Georgia," he said, "and we want one of P. J. Berckmans' hard-working sons, who has inherited his intelligence, his culture, his love for plants, and his love for the Society." The crisis was averted when R. C. Berckmans refused to serve, and was later elected to succeed his father as the president of the GSHS. But the notion that Robert and Allie (as P. J. A. Jr. was known) had inherited not just the Berckmans name, not just his "love for the plants," but his *culture* was crucial. Passing on "culture," with all that the concept entailed to one trained in horticulture, was, after all, central to Berckmans's vision for the GSHS.[103]

The work of culture, though articulated and envisioned by horticultural leaders like Berckmans, was often accomplished by the hands of others, people like Wesley Smith. A year after their father's death, the Berckmanses wrote to David Robinson of the New York News Service about the possibility of "securing good foreign labor" – about thirty men, perhaps some "thrifty Hungarians" – for their nursery. Although census records indicate that they did not follow through on this plan, Robinson's assurance that he knew "the class you want" indicates that they thought the local help to be insufficient.[104] The inquiry also suggested that the Berckmans' sons may have been somewhat less hopeful about the *culturing* of the South, eager as they were to import not just plant but human immigrants to Fruitland.

VII

In 1884, a few months after *his* father's death, Prosper had returned to Europe to collect specimens for the horticultural exhibit at the 1885 New Orleans Exposition, taking along his wife, Mary, and his son Allie for a three-month jaunt through England, Belgium, France, Switzerland, and Germany.[105] Allie was just a year younger than Prosper when he had gone to America in 1850; like his father, he kept a trip diary. But the two journals were worlds apart. Whereas the father's diary was earnest, almost obsessive in its careful records and plant lists, looking always for financial opportunity, the son's was casual, irreverent, careless, expressing the easy confidence of a successful businessman's son. They did their part as tourists, visiting cathedrals, churches, art museums, parks, and castles. He witnessed the still-unfinished Palais du Justice, "one of the finest buildings in Europe" and a late harvest of Belgian King Leopold II's brutal occupation of the Congo.[106] But Allie seemed just as interested in going out dancing with women: the "peasant girls" at a village feast, a Louise Morehead, a party of "seven young ladies," a "real pretty girl" whose husband was "so stiff" Allie wanted to choke him.[107]

Rather than looking forward into the family's future, as Prosper had during his 1850 voyage, Prosper Jr. peered into the family's past. When they were not visiting tourist sites or carrying on business with other nurserymen, they stayed with family and friends in Belgium, at Heyst-op-den-Berg, Iteghem, and Lier. "I thought we would never get done meeting old acquaintants," Allie complained.[108] Still he praised their liberal hospitality, even from the half-dozen or so old family servants, who offered the Berckmans so many quarts of beer they barely made it back to their quarters.[109] He saw his father's birthplace, the paternal estate of his recently departed grandfather, and the uniform of one of the men who died fighting beside Louis in 1832.[110]

It was probably during these visits to the old castles that Allie copied down information on the family's history of nobility. The coat of arms featured a birch tree in between two human figures; *berck* was Flemish for "birch" and *mans* Flemish for "men."[111] Thus the Berckmans were "birch men" – men of trees. When Louis named his son Prosper he prophesied. Prosper Jules Alphonse Berckmans was the man who prospered trees.

The question remained as to whether those trees would also prosper the South.

3

Elberta, You're a Peach

I

If trees were to prosper the South, the cause of horticulture could not continue to be an import from Belgium or anywhere else. Fruit growers knew that often the most productive tree was actually *two* trees: a tree with marketable fruit grafted onto a hardy, vigorous set of roots. In the same way, European and northern horticulture needed a sturdy southern rootstock for the cause to take shape in the way that Berckmans and company envisioned. Nowhere is this need more clear than in the life and mythology of the Georgia native Samuel Henry Rumph.

Travel to Marshallville, Georgia, and you can still see Rumph's story in his two houses. About two miles outside "downtown" Marshallville, you take the unpaved (and curiously named) "Juice Plant Road." A sod farm stretches out on both sides, with no plants taller than six inches for acres, pocked only by center-pivot sprinklers and corrugated metal buildings. Every now and then a trailer or modest ranch home comes into view, but the land appears only partially inhabited – raked clean by humans, but perhaps not home to them.

And then, a single story farmhouse, modest but comfortable, sheltered by a copse of tall trees that, like the house, seem incongruous out here so far from the historic homes and spreading trees of central Marshallville. A crumbling stone arch looms over a wrought iron gate and a large granite block that once bore the shoes of visiting ladies alighting from their carriages. The arch perfectly frames the entryway of the house; stepping through the gate, you notice more details: the two chimneys with decorative brickwork, the spindled porch railing and ornamental woodwork

on the eaves, the sweeping porch and floor-to-ceiling windows. The landscape, too, is thoughtfully arranged. Stately magnolias – that ubiquitous
symbol of white southern wealth – flank the walkway. Aging boxwoods
line the porch, and a large hemlock shades the northern side of the house.
This is Willow Lake, where Samuel Rumph lived in the nineteenth century. In its day it was a paragon of rural sophistication. In those days
Rumph embodied the ideals of southern horticulture, both in his gentle-
manly manner of living and in his horticultural work as the breeder of the
South's most famous peach, perhaps the most famous peach of all time,
the variety he christened "Elberta" after the wife of his youth.

Back to Marshallville, you continue west through the single inter-
section and enter the "historic district," an oak-lined avenue of white-
columned mansions. The first and largest of these is a startling two-story
structure with eight Doric columns, symmetrical porches, four chimneys, and a parapet, all in red brick and gleaming white masonry.
Ornamentals – mostly dogwoods and boxwoods – surround this home as
well, but unlike the landscaping of the country home, which cocoons the
house as if to protect it, these trees yield to the mansion as the dramatic
focal point, like attendants in a royal court. If you remain unconvinced
by the home's architectural theatricality, the historical marker out front
informs you that this is an Important Place: the home of Samuel Rumph,
the "father of Georgia's commercial peach industry," who originated a
peach called the Elberta at his Willow Lake Nursery "about three miles
outside of town." This is the home that Rumph built for his second wife,
Pearlie Reese, a home befitting her desire to live in town, her given name,
and the success he had won in the highly competitive New York City
produce markets. Together, the two homes tell a parable of horticultural
progress. Start in the country with some fruit trees; end in town in a
house that early twentieth-century newspaper articles routinely described
as "palatial."[1]

In 1885, the year after Berckmans's return trip to Belgium, the
Georgia State Horticultural Society met on Berckmans's adopted home
turf in Augusta for the first time. Samuel Rumph, for his part, intended
to arrive early. He was a young horticulturist, one of the society's brightest stars. He served as GSHS vice president of the Third Congressional
District, which included middle Georgia. In large part as a result of
Rumph's nursery and fruit business, the district had acquired a reputation as the foremost fruit growing region in the state. That year, Rumph
departed Willow Lake on Monday, July 27, with the peaches, apples,
pears, grapes, pomegranates, and quinces he intended to display at the

GSHS fruit exhibit, perhaps packed in the special refrigerated fruit car that he had designed himself. He intended to arrive in Augusta that evening. When he boarded the train, however, he discovered that his fruit would be detained, so he spent the night, with his fruit, in Macon. After his arrival Tuesday around four o'clock, the task of unpacking the fruit took up the entire evening. The next day, Rumph went to see Berckmans, with whom he expected to spend "the balance of the time" and to survey the fruit exhibit. Berckmans informed Rumph that he "must not leave until Friday evening" as Berckmans wanted him "on hand at his house on Friday" for the big society bash he planned to host there. This had not been Rumph's plan.

Indeed, the news heightened the tension between Rumph's two great loves: his wife and his fruit. So, the dutiful husband sat down that evening, pulled out a piece of office stationary – with the red engraved watermark of a Shockley apple and the letterhead introducing Samuel H. Rumph as the proprietor of Willow Lake Nursery in Marshallville, where he grew and dealt in "Fruit Trees and Fresh and Evaporated Fruit" – and wrote to his wife, Clara Elberta Moore Rumph. He had been married for almost eleven years; their daughter, Clara, was nine years old. "My Dear Little Wife," he began, using his customary salutation. He explained the situation with his fruit and Berckmans's request that he stay longer. He expected to be home Saturday morning, though he promised to write again if he decided to leave earlier. He seemed to feel bad about this, so he concluded with a preview of the fruit exhibit competition: "So far W. Lake has the best show of Apples & Peaches," he wrote, as if to say that his long absence was paying off in horticultural success. Then he apologized. "I am sorry to be compelled to stay so long from my little darling, but I think it would be best for me to spend Friday with Berckmans."[2]

As it turned out, Willow Lake's peaches and apples *were* the best that year. His fruit display dwarfed all the others, even Berckmans's, with fifty-eight peach varieties, forty-five apples, thirteen pears, ten grapes, two pomegranates, and one quince. On Thursday, the examining committee mentioned Rumph's exhibit first in each category, praising his "fine specimens" of Carter's Blue Elgin Pippin, Jewett's Best, and Red June apples; his Clapp's Favorite pear; and his large Elberta peaches.[3] The 1885 meeting was good for Rumph in other ways, too. He won not just the compliments of the fruit committee, but also the public approbation of Berckmans himself. In a Wednesday discussion of the relative merits of seedling and grafted peaches, Rumph spoke in favor of grafted peaches, provided that they were cultivated frequently. Berckmans was pleased with this defense of proper horticulture and, like a proud father, proclaimed that "Mr. Rumph had struck the real secret in the cultivation of his peaches."⁴ Little wonder then that Rumph's district report struck a high note, despite the wet spring and low quality harvest. "The interest taken in this immediate vicinity in fruit culture ... continues without abating," he declared. "This is destined to be the largest shipping point in the State."⁵

And in 1885 at least, Rumph's horticultural success did not prevent him from fulfilling his familial obligations. Berckmans had the society out to Fruitland on Thursday afternoon, so presumably Rumph returned to his "little darling" on Friday, ahead of schedule. And the meeting itself began with M. P. Foster's welcome, which exhorted the men to prove their masculinity with more attention to their homes. It was not just bad economics to buy what one could grow, said Foster; it was "a shame upon our manhood" and a "monstrous neglect" of their children. There were "acres immediately surrounding many homes, grown up in weeds, suffered to continue their noxious growth until they sap the vigor and strength of sturdy manhood, and steal the ruddy glow of health from the cheeks of the wife and children." Worse, the houses themselves were completely bare of flowers, the sacred "messengers between earth and heaven," yet not deemed precious enough by southern men to "increase their ever-increasing beauties."⁶ Foster in all his circumlocutory glory captured a sentiment close to the heart of the horticultural enterprise in the South: that the home was a primary front in the battle for southern civilization, and that the battle was essentially aesthetic.

Perhaps the best articulation of this sentiment was that of William Gilmore Simms, who was one of the nation's leading literary intellectuals in the nineteenth century. In 1870, shortly before colon cancer took his life, Simms's address to the Agricultural Society of South Carolina offered "the sense of the beautiful" – the capacity to "behold the latent beauties in the things we see, and to discover and to love the beautiful in the things we do not see" – as the one pathway to human flourishing in a land ravaged by war. And the careful study of flowers and fruits, according to Simms, trained the soul in this all-important "sense."⁷

As if fulfilling Simms's vision, the men of Prosper Berckmans's horticultural society provided one answer to the question of what should be done to rebuild the South. On the one hand, horticulturists embraced the language of beauty. They planted flowers. They nurtured fine fruits and delivered them to distant markets, delicate and fragrant like debutantes at a ball. On the other, they espoused the principles of business and science. They made money. They replaced tangled thickets of seedling fruits with orderly orchards of named varieties; they cleared away genetic anarchy with the hierarchical pronouncements of their annual *Catalogue*. Their association with fruit and flowers fell short of the rugged masculinity of the late 1800s, but they reclaimed their manhood by managing their fruit and flowers with scientific expertise and business acumen. The planter oversaw vast cotton plantations with the labor of his slaves; the horticulturist cultivated more intimate spaces with his own expert attention to detail.[8]

And so we move from the European nursery-estate of an aristocratic Belgian migrant, to the home life, plant breeding skill, and business sense of a middle Georgia native. In Samuel Rumph we see the incarnation of Prosper Berckmans's vision for the South. Rumph's story also reveals the New South campaign of the 1880s as more than a series of appeals for northern investment in southern industrialization. For the New South campaign was also *environmental*, articulating a rural aesthetic sketched out in general terms by boosters such as Henry Grady and lived out concretely by horticulturists such as Samuel Rumph. From the perspective of the countryside, horticulture represented a kind of third way between industrialism and the old plantation: by growing peaches, southerners could practice a progressive, urban-oriented agronomy without sacrificing their rural way of life.[9]

II

Samuel Rumph was a model not just of horticultural success but also of nonradical rural progress. It should not be surprising, then, that a set of stories developed around his rise that we might call the fable of Sam Rumph. The Rumph fable was, in turn, a kind of precursor to the twentieth-century development of a more full-fledged Georgia peach mythology. According to the fable, Samuel Rumph lost his parents when he was a toddler but benefited from the kindly attention of his grandmother, who gave him some peach pits she had been saving in an old work basket. Rumph planted them and tended them, the "honeybees and vagrant breezes" helped out, and the next generation of seedlings had among them a cultivar he would later name in honor of his wife, Clara Elberta.[10] The Elberta was a remarkable fruit: a peach with the firm flesh that separated easily from the pit (a "freestone") and could be "broken in half with the hands." Rumph grew and propagated the fruit and made

his reputation as both a fruit grower and a nurseryman on its wide adapt-
ability and commercial potential. "The story of the Elberta reads like a
romance," the USDA's chief pomologist wrote in 1908.[11]

Rumph's story was a kind of allegory for the rise of the New South,
revealing the hopes for an aesthetically pleasing rural New South as well
as an industrial and commercial one. That the fable coalesced and persisted as it did testifies in part to the paucity of sources on Rumph's life.
His 1885 letter to his wife, Clara Elberta Rumph, is one of only a few
surviving personal effects: a business card, a handful of similar letters, a
will, a desk, and the hand-hewn model of a refrigerated box car complete
the collection.[12] Contemporary accounts in newspapers and horticultural
society meetings provide some additional information, as do family memories, but unlike Prosper Berckmans, Rumph was a reluctant speaker. He
never gave formal addresses at horticultural society meetings, and his
newspaper interviews were coy. He seemed content to let others fill in the
details and meaning of his life. Rumph's successes might "read like a fairy
tale," said one correspondent for the *Atlanta Constitution*, "but they only
show the possibilities ahead of a man who has the vim to make them and
the intelligence to handle them."[13]

Contrary to the impression left by the fable, Samuel Rumph was not
alone. It is true that his brother, Edwin, only a year old, died the year (perhaps the day) of Samuel's birth, and that his father died a year later. The
Macon County administrator auctioned off Samuel Sr.'s real estate, two
slaves named John and Mary, and all his "perishable property." By January
1853, everything from his livestock to his shotgun belonged to someone
else. Before Samuel was ten years old, his mother, Caroline, had left as
well, to live with cousins in Copiah County, Mississippi.[14] But Samuel
Rumph's grandparents, Lewis and Maria, raised him, and their status
and history in middle Georgia gave him a solid start in life. The Rumphs,
along with a dozen other families – among them the Strothers, Hileys,
Murphs, Slappeys, Plants, Kaiglers, and Fredericks – had emigrated from
Germany and Holland in the 1730s and settled in Orangeburg District,
South Carolina. They governed Orangeburg as county officers and policed
it with local militias that became famous for daring exploits against
the Tories during the American Revolution.[15] Yet once middle Georgia
became available – once the Creek Indians had been forcibly removed –
they branched out readily. The first Orangeburg migrants arrived in 1821
or so; the Rumphs moved with another set of families in 1832.

Like the plantation landscape itself, then, Rumph's people were on the
move in the 1820s and 1830s. In Marshallville they grew cotton, and did so

successfully. Slaves made up more than a third of the population in the 1840s and 1850s.[16] By 1850, Samuel Rumph's grandfather, Lewis, one of the original settlers of Marshallville, was worth upward of thirty thousand dollars and owned sixty-four slaves. Unlike many of their contemporaries, however, who stopped in Georgia for a few years before going farther west for richer lands, the Orangeburg families' western fever seemed to dissipate in Georgia. They had abandoned Orangeburg together; once in the Marshallville area, they tarried together, too, and their names remain prominent in the area today, nearly two centuries later. Like immigrants from another land, the Orangeburg families intermarried, partnered in business, and generally strengthened the networks they took with them rather than remaking them in their new place. The noted agrarian and literary biographer John Donald Wade, a scion of one of these families (the Fredericks), later wrote that Marshallville in the 1860s seemed a "just launched extension of 1830 South Carolina, a South Carolina with its lands still unexhausted, its population still unbled by the great migrations."[17] As late as 1900, Wade reported, mixed marriages – in which one of the spouses was not of Carolina origin – met with resistance from the original families. When one of those old-timers was "utterly outdone but too pious to exclaim violently," he would comfort himself with the thought that "after all he was no longer in Carolina, and could not expect things to be just right elsewhere."[18]

Samuel Rumph grew up in the heart of this tight-knit community as a child of the cotton plantation. His grandfather, Lewis, was a major planter, one of the largest in middle Georgia. His great-grandfather, Jacob, had been a militia captain in Orangeburg and brigadier general of the South Carolina militia, and the family still took pride in his dramatic exploits on behalf of the Revolutionary Army. He came of age too late to make his mark militarily as his great-grandfather had, and in the meantime the slaves who had been the basis of his grandfather's wealth were suddenly free to stay or go as they wished. The question before him was how to live up to his paternal heritage. What was a young man of the postbellum South to do?[19]

Rumph used his family's wealth and prominence to his advantage. While many men of his age struck out for cities or western lands, Samuel Rumph dug in deeper in Marshallville. At age eighteen, he took the job of managing his grandfather's farm; by 1870 he was already personally worth eighty-five hundred dollars. He was surrounded by about seventy black farm laborers and domestic workers – including a family with the name Rumph.[20] The white Rumphs continued to employ the same

African American families who had served them as slaves. Abundant land and labor made Rumph's ascent possible, and family helped. His grandfather, Lewis Rumph, married again, late in life, this time to Samuel's *other* grandmother, Maria Kaigler. Lewis and Maria had two children. One of these, Lewis Adolphus, was raised practically as Samuel's brother, but he was actually Samuel's double half uncle – half brother to Samuel's father and his mother. If it were possible to confuse matters any further, the Rumphs appeared determined to do so: in 1874 Lewis Adolphus and Samuel Henry Rumph married sisters, Virginia Rebecca and Clara Elberta Moore, in a double wedding ceremony.[21] In making Marshallville a permanent home, the Rumphs and the other Orangeburg families provided a model of agrarian stability that the next generation would laud as the standard.

By staying put, Samuel Rumph also fulfilled the dreams of a generation of agricultural reformers. Contrary to twentieth century nostalgia, the plantation landscape was, as the historian Jack Temple Kirby observed, "temporary, in process, abandoned, repossessed … seldom pretentious, manicured, or lovely."[22] At a time when many farmers abandoned their plantations for the undiminished fertility of western lands recently taken from Native Americans and Mexico, reformers urged farmers to turn instead toward innovation and development, to manage smaller areas with greater care and attention. For W. B. Jones of Herndon, Georgia, the declining soils and "fast disappearing demoralized labor" had sounded the death knell of "that exhaustive, diffusive system of tillage." The future held promise only for "small areas, with intensive manuring and thorough cultivation." Jones and the horticulturists praised this new age of limits. This kind of cultivation would be "less risky and laborious, less wear and tear upon soil, human and brute muscle, promising more of the real comforts of a home living."[23] William Browne, a professor of agriculture and natural history at the state university, concurred. "The time is gone by when we can abandon our farms to overseers and negroes," he averred. "Yes, gentlemen, we must live upon our farms."[24]

According to the reformers, then, the first step in "improvement" – in making a civilization out of this late wilderness – was to remain in place. For how would the South develop unless people chose not to move on? A story told at the 1892 GSHS meeting illustrated this point. Garland Mitchell Ryals of Savannah was delivering a paper, "Truck Farming on the Coast Lands." Toward the end of his paper, having described the best practices of location, machinery, preparation, fertilizers, labor, seed, and shipping, Ryals told a story of traveling through Virginia (his birthplace) with his brother. Driving through rolling country, they arrived at a place "entirely different from anything we had seen," which turned out to be the property of "that crazy fellow Morepaw," as he was known locally. Morepaw, it seems, had determined to raise tomatoes and early crops in a countryside where no one did that, and everyone thought he was wasting his time. A few years later Ryals and his brother made the same trip. They arrived at a section "dotted with engines and immense boilers, with an air of thrift and enterprise about everything." Crazy old Morepaw had turned out to be a prophet, and now twenty-odd imitators had joined him in the truck and canning business. Then Ryals offered the story's moral:

Thus you see what one man accomplished in reference to canning fruit. He found land in abundance and labor cheap. He had sense enough to take in the situation. Those old moss-backs had sat down there and let things go to rack and ruin. When this man Morepaw came here with his new ideas he was despised of all. But in time he became the king bee of that country.[25]

Samuel Rumph was the "Morepaw" of Macon County, but as a fruit grower his story also conjured horticultural tradition. Truck farming expanded at the same time as peaches, but few truck farmers (Morepaw notwithstanding) grew famous with tomatoes or asparagus, which lacked the deep cultural resonance of peaches.[26] Peaches were from China, and the scientific name conjured up Persia, an association that fit nicely with the Americans' fascination with everything "oriental" in the late nineteenth century.[27] Though the fruit had been feral since the eighteenth century, horticulturists understood the significance of the Chinese Cling introduction and so frequently portrayed them as exotic. Atlantan Samuel Hape called the peach "the child of the East, thousands of miles from her native land," though the fruit was "nevertheless so pleased with her home in this beautiful, sunny Southland that occasionally she smiles on her new home and rewards with rich gifts her ardent admirers."[28]

On the other hand, fruit growing had distinctly European connotations, and orchards seemed to these reformers a necessary part of building a European-style civilization in newly opened American lands. Too, growing peaches for market required expertise that seemed unnecessary with corn and cotton, which any dirt farmer could grow. A peach grower would have to be literate, able to read the growing body of horticultural literature, and able to observe with scientific precision. For this reason, Berckmans called frequently for horticultural academies that would train boys and girls in the basics of good fruit and flower management. W. B. Jones held up an imaginary European civilization as an end goal of

this kind of education: "contented homes with a happy population, surrounded by gardens and orchards, as a means of economic and luxurious
living."[29]

III

Samuel Rumph's family and community life, then, promised to fulfill one
prong of the horticultural reform program. In order for the transformation of the southern landscape to take place, however, there would also
have to be new biological material, new fruit cultivars to bridge the gaps
among the Asian origins of the fruit, the cultured European civilizations
that had produced the older varieties, and the environmental characteristics of the local landscape. If Samuel Rumph was the embodiment of
the horticultural ideal as it related to home and family life, the Elberta
peach was the embodiment of the horticultural ideal as it touched on
plant life. Rumph's work with the Chinese Cling, along with the efforts
of Prosper Berckmans, Lewis A. Rumph, J. H. Hale, and Eugene Hiley,
made peaches into a national commodity. Just as early nineteenth-century
Belgian aristocrats had transformed the pear, so Rumph transformed the
peach. And just as the Belgians had created a fruit for their time – a
melting, buttery delicacy to be grown in gardens, ripened in fruit rooms,
and served as high society dessert – so Rumph produced a fruit for his: a
large, firm-fleshed freestone that could be picked green, packed quickly in
bushel baskets, sent to market hundreds of miles away, and still earn top
prices. Van Mons and company developed boutique pears; Rumph made
an industrial peach.[30]

    The making of "industrial" fruits and vegetables was the order of the
day. In California, the perfection of the Bartlett pear made it possible for
growers there to ship the fruit two thousand miles across the country.[31]
The Washington Navel had a similar catalyzing effect on the California
orange industry.[32] And in the South, Reuben F. Kolb, Alabama's commissioner of agriculture and one of the region's most famous progressive farmers, introduced the Kolb's Gem watermelon. At the time, most
southern watermelon growers had been raising Georgia Rattlesnake
watermelons, a sweet but relatively thin-skinned variety that had in turn
replaced the even more delicious Bradford watermelon. Kolb discovered
Kolb's Gem as a chance hybrid of Georgia Rattlesnake and Scaly Bark
watermelons and found that the thick, impervious rinds kept the fruit
marketable for several weeks after harvest, while its "convenient" oval
shape made it even easier to ship.[33]

The Elberta was a stupendous creation. Its fame spread rapidly after its introduction in the mid-1870s, so that by the early twentieth century more Elberta trees grew in the United States than any other fruit variety. By 1925 it was the most popular peach in every state but California, and from 1910 to 1930, when Georgia's peach industry led the nation, 40 percent of the state's massive production was 'Elberta.' In 1965 – then ninety years old – it was still among the top ten cultivars in Georgia.[34] And except perhaps for the 'J. H. Hale' (in the North) and the 'Georgia Belle,' it is the only peach anyone remembers by name. It was also the only variety to earn an ode.

> Your cheeks reflect the sunset glow,
>   Elberta!
> Your rounded outlines please me so,
>   Elberta!
> Your breath is sweet as summer dew;
> Your life blood richly flowing through
> Imparts a matchless charm to you.
>   Elberta, you're a peach![35]

And that was just the second of five breathless stanzas.

The Rumph fable included a rather far-fetched origin myth for the Elberta – some old peach pits left for years in a work basket. But the truth about the Elberta's origins may never be known with any precision. Geneticists are satisfied that the Chinese Cling was one parent, but the other parent remains unclear. How did the Chinese Cling, a white fleshed clingstone, produce a yellow fleshed freestone? Many assumed that the Elberta was a cross between Chinese Cling and Early Crawford, which would make sense, since the Early Crawford was a yellow-fleshed freestone. But peach genes are very difficult to pin down. A horticulturist trying to determine the genetic heritage of Elberta in 1923 discovered that out of some twenty-two hundred Elberta seedlings, none resembled Early Crawford, suggesting to him that the Elberta was a self-pollinated seedling and that the Chinese Cling carried recessive yellow flesh genes that emerged in the Elberta. Revisiting the issue in the 1980s, scientists knew that a clinging stone was a recessive trait and could not produce freestones without cross-pollination. Furthermore, the Chinese Cling produced almost no pollen and only rarely proved capable of self-pollination.[36] Samuel Rumph usually maintained the Chinese Cling x Early Crawford hypothesis, but not always. The state horticulturist, Thomas McHatton, lamented in 1914 that the Elberta was "a thing of mystery: its history is lost. Mr. Rumph never told the same story about it twice."[37] The fruit that made the southern peach industry was a horticultural love child, the product of a one-night stand with an unremembered suitor.

The Chinese Cling in the Rumphs' orchard continued to produce offspring after Elberta. Not long after Samuel Rumph had originated the Elberta, his double half uncle and brother-in-law, Lewis A. Rumph, also retrieved a seed from that Chinese Cling tree. The seedling became a prolific white-fleshed freestone that Lewis called the Belle, or Georgia Belle. (Supposedly, like Samuel Rumph, Lewis wanted to name it after his wife, Virginia, but did not want to give the impression of honoring that state. Belle was a suitable compromise.) A white fleshed freestone, Belle was for many years second only to the Elberta as the South's leading peach. And so it was that two "sisters" – offspring of the same tree – carried the banner of the horticultural New South into the next century.

Elberta and Belle were just two of many, many progeny of the Chinese Cling, which represented, as we saw in Chapter 1, the "second wave of peach introduction."[38] At the 1877 GSHS meeting alone, the Chinese Cling parented all seven of Berckmans's named seedlings. Along with the Elberta, the Georgia Belle, the J. H. Hale, and the Hiley all descended from the Chinese Cling. A 1989 study found the genetic imprint of Elberta and J. H. Hale – the Chinese Cling's firstborn children, so to speak – in more than 340 modern varieties.[39] The Chinese Cling and its descendants made the shipping peach industry not only in the South but throughout the United States.

The Rumph fable's portrayal of this process of selection and dissemination as an accident of evolution, or as an inexorable triumph of the Elberta's or Chinese Cling's natural advantages was also misleading. It is too simple to say that Samuel Rumph planted a seed, or that Robert Fortune found a peach in China, and the rest of the story followed from that point. Human judgment and decision making entered at every juncture. "Nature" played a role – it shaped what was possible – but people made the Georgia peach.

Samuel Rumph seems to have been more knowing than the mythology allows. Even if the story about finding the Elberta in his grandmother's work basket is true, he was the one who saw the fruit's potential when it began to bear. More likely his search for the Elberta was more painstaking than serendipitous. As another account had it, Rumph sifted through twelve hundred seedlings before he chose the Elberta.[40] After he selected it as a promising seedling, furthermore, he tested it for several years, trying its fruit on the northern markets, taking it to his elders in the horticultural society for their opinions, and then propagating it in his nursery and selling it around the Southeast.

Rumph acted not on his own, then, but as part of a horticultural community. Under Prosper Berckmans's watchful eyes, one of the society's most enduring contributions was the annual *Catalogue of Fruits*, which they published along with the record of their proceedings. Paper presentations varied from year to year, and even district reports were hit-or-miss, but the *Catalogue* was consistent. It was the central activity of the society. When Prosper Berckmans listed the society's eight goals in 1876, the first was "to compare the fruits from the various localities and zones of our State, with a view of determining their merits"; the fourth was the publication of the *Catalogue* in order to "simplify Fruit culture"; the fifth was "to adopt a correct nomenclature of fruits."[41] The goal of the GSHS, in other words, was not diversity, but reliability. The *Catalogue* was a winnowing tool: the efforts of the GSHS and other organizations yielded a shorter and shorter list of approved varieties each year. In 1876, the society had listed eighty-nine peach cultivars, thirty-two of which were deemed worthy of market production; by 1898, many growers limited their production to six varieties.[42] Some of this attrition resulted from discovering synonyms; some resulted from discarding unsuitable varieties.

Yet despite their confidence in the dawning light of science, horticulturists were far from grasping what went on inside the trees themselves. Fruit breeding was an exceedingly uncertain science, and efforts to classify *Prunus persica* into categories foundered on the shoals of the species's astonishing variability. White and yellow flesh, clingstone and freestone, bloom type and season were very difficult to explain, to say nothing of the "peach-monsters" (as Ulysses Hedrick labeled them) such as the Peento or flat peach, the cleft peach Emperor of Russia, the nippled peach Teton de Venus, the Perseque "with its teat-like protuberances," or the crimson-fleshed blood peaches.[43] Through the mid-nineteenth century, horticulturists generally classified peaches by whether or not the flesh clung to the pit – "clingstone" or "freestone" varieties, with nectarines (hairless peaches by way of mutation) as a separate category. In 1845, A. J. Downing introduced color as a category as well, finding that some peaches were "pale-fleshed" and others yellow-fleshed.[44] In 1887, a USDA agent named Gilbert Onderdonk introduced a classification scheme for peaches based on their region of origin and climatic suitability. According to Onderdonk and his follower R. H. Price, there were five "races" of the fruit: Persian, Northern Chinese, Spanish, Southern Chinese, and Peento. This classification system became enormously popular, but the system had serious limitations.[45] As Ulysses Hedrick complained in 1917, "we have wasted so much time and patience in attempting to group varieties according to Onderdonk and Price, and with so little success, that the Onderdonk classification seems to us to be cursed with the confusion of Babel."[46] In other words, it worked precisely contrary to its goal of conferring clarity on the muddled nomenclature of *Prunus persica*.

This general state of confusion may be one reason why horticulturists talked so much about naming in the nineteenth century.[47] National conferences gave plenty of space to often-contentious conversations about names. The American Pomological Society under the Boston horticulturist Marshall Wilder was obsessed. In the 1883 GSHS *Proceedings*, Berckmans reprinted the American Pomological Society's naming rules, along with what can only be described as a rant by Wilder.

> Let us have no more Generals, Colonels, or Captains … no more Presidents, Governors, or titled dignitaries; no more Monarchs, Giants, or Tom Thumbs; no more Nonesuches, Seek-no-furthers, Ne plus ultras, Hog-pens, Sheep-noses, Big Bogs, Iron Clads, Legal Tenders, Sucker States, or Stump-the-World. Let us have no more long, unpronounceable, irrelevant, high-flown, bombastic names to our fruits, and, if possible, let us dispense with the now confused terms of Belle, Buerre, Celebasse, Doyenne, Pearmain, Pippin, Seedling, Beauty, Favorite, and other like useless and improper titles to our fruits…

> Let us … give to the world a system of nomenclature for our fruits which shall be worthy of the Society and the country – a system pure and plain in its diction, pertinent and proper in its application, and which shall be an example not only for fruits, but for other products of the earth, and save our Society and the nation from the disgrace of unmeaning, pretentious, and nonsensical names, to the most perfect, useful, and beautiful productions of the soil the world has ever known.[48]

If Marshall Wilder and Prosper Berckmans had their way, then, cultivar names would be "simple," "plain," and "pertinent." Horticulturists could not fathom the mystery of their fruit trees' sexual habits, but they could cover the genetic unpredictability with solid, commonsense names, like planks across a pit of quicksand.

IV

With a variety worthy of commerce, Rumph plunged into the business of horticulture. By 1876 he was presenting fruits to the Georgia State Horticultural Society, which meant that he had been raising them for several years already. In 1878, the R. G. Dun Company recorded that he owned a "valuable nursery" and that he derived "a good profit from his orchard"; another correspondent estimated Rumph's income at eight to ten thousand a year and proclaimed him worthy of borrowing modest amounts. Unlike others, who drank heavily, or borrowed more than they could repay, Rumph was "Sober & attentive to business" and possessed a reputation as "an energetic bus[iness]man with "tem[perate] hab[it]s." In 1880 he was said to be "Thrifty and money mkg [making]" and "clear of any debts."[49] "Tell Sam," his father in law B.T. Moore wrote in 1882, "I see that he took the lead in Macon the other day in variety of fruits. I hope he will continue to do so it is now getting about time for him to make his luck."[50] Moore did not just wish young Sam well, nor merely hope he would be lucky at the fruit exhibit: no, Samuel Rumph was *making his luck*, manufacturing it with cross pollination, grafting, and savvy marketing.

This identity as a man of business seems to have been central to Rumph's self-assessment as well. Unlike many of his colleagues in the GSHS, he never presented formal papers or delivered stirring speeches. His participation was limited to the exhibits, reporting on conditions in the Third District, and commenting on specific varieties in the discussion of the annual *Catalogue*. In each case, he rarely missed an opportunity to allude to his commercial success. In discussions of varieties for the *Catalogue*, a member would name a variety for discussion, and growers with experience would debate ripening time, size, susceptibility to diseases, and so on, before making a motion to strike it from the list or put it in the *Catalogue* as an approved variety for one or more regions of the state. Rumph's contributions were littered with dollar signs; he could hardly speak without telling how much he had earned in the New York produce markets. In 1878, for example, he sold Fleitas St. John for $7.00 a bushel in New York, Crawford for $10.00, and the Chinese Cling for $10.50. Then as if concerned that they were not getting his point, Rumph boasted that by packing ripe peaches in live Spanish moss, he had "received from $3.00 to $5.50 more in New York than other Georgia shippers."[51]

What little survives of his personal correspondence betrays the same ambition to establish his reputation as a nurseryman and marketer of fruits. In 1882, on Willow Lake Nursery stationary, which both advertised that he was a "Grower and Dealer in Fruit Trees and Fresh and Evaporated Fruit" and featured colorful watermarks of Shockley apples, he wrote to his "dear little wife," Elberta, from the society's meeting in Macon, "So far I am ahead on Peaches and Apples."[52] Three years later, he wrote the same from the meeting in Augusta.[53] It was about this time that advertisements for the Willow Lake catalog began appearing in Georgia newspapers. "ONE MILLION Fruit Trees, Grape Vines, Strawberry Plants, Etc., selling low at Willow Lake Nursery," the text boasted, under an engraving of a peach.[54] In the preface to his 1887 catalog, Rumph thanked his subscribers for their "liberal patronage" and explained that he only sold those varieties "as are adapted to the Southern climate." He hoped, by producing first-class trees and selling them widely, not just to make money but to "greatly further the interest of Fruit growing."[55] His catalog that year offered apples, peaches, pears, quinces, grapes, plums, figs, mulberries, and strawberries. But an engraving of a well-endowed branch of Elbertas graced the back cover, and the description of the variety was twice as long as that for most other peach varieties: "Very large ... very fine grain, juicy, rich, sweet and splendidly flavored ... very prolific and ... handsome." The Elberta, Rumph said, was one of the "most successful" at market, "selling uniformly at higher prices than any other peach."[56] Similarly, the catalog section on peaches began with instructions on planting and cultivation, but transitioned quickly to a little superfluous praise. As if his readers were unfamiliar with the most common tree fruit in the state, he advised them:

Take it in its fresh, ripe state, and there is no fruit that so delights the eye or palate, and it not only appeals to the appetite but is highly conducive to health. It is also excellent for culinary purposes, either canned or evaporated. As to its market value none exceeds it.[57]

With the Elberta, Rumph not only followed Marshall Wilder's rules for naming – one word, a relative of the fruit's originator – but also paid homage to the domestic ideals of southern horticulture. Peach varieties were not always women. Berckmans had a Thurber and a General Lee, for example, memorials to a northern horticulturist and the archetypal southern military hero. Sometimes they simply took the name of their originator: the Slappey, the Hiley, the J. H. Hale. But for the Rumphs, the peaches were women, and members of the horticulturist's own household.

Pomological nomenclature thus reflected the gender dynamics of the late nineteenth-century South. Perhaps most obviously, the horticulturists feminized and racialized the fruits they discussed. They slipped easily into anthropomorphism. Peaches were feminine: soft, rounded, fragrant. They were white: blushing like the cheeks of a southern belle. The Elberta, said Samuel Hape, was "the acknowledged queen of midsummer varieties, with her golden countenance and blushing red cheeks, synonomous [sic] of health, beauty and wealth, the pride of Georgia and daughter of the South ... a most beautiful picture to contemplate."[58] This practice was nothing new, of course: one of Louis XIV's favorite pears was called Cuisse-Madame, or "Lady's Thigh."[59] But it was more than affectation. A horticulturist presented his fruit as he might present his daughter to society. Growing fruit and gathering flowers did not exactly exude manliness, but speaking of their fruits as if they were women allowed the horticulturists to stake a claim to masculine respectability.

Of course, fruit had an additional importance as food. Provision was not an abstract concept, and the visible, physical health of a man's family provided especially firm evidence of his ability to provide. A number of papers at GSHS meetings urged more consumption of fruits and vegetables, especially on farms where they were easily grown. Samuel Gustin believed that "the health and happiness of the people of Georgia would be promoted by a freer use of wholesome fruits and vegetables, and less fat bacon and poorly prepared bread." Poor southern dinners, in his opinion, frequently sent men to "the whisky shop for consolation."[60] W. B. Jones argued for a fixed relationship between climate and food that could not "be violated with impunity." For example, he cited an Englishman who stuck to his traditional diet of beef and mutton in the Tropics, but soon found "his skin clouded over with the sickly hue of climatic influence," susceptible to tropical diseases such as yellow fever. Meanwhile, Cuban men ate little meat but plenty of citrus and remained "active and wiry." The same was true of the South, Jones insisted. If one was going to thrive there, one had to eat the foods that naturally grew well in the climate, especially large quantities of fruits and vegetables. Better schools for southerners meant little "if feeble, degenerate men and women are to be the result." For how was a boy or girl to learn literature if he or she suffered from dyspepsia?[61] And how was a young man to make his way in the world who refused a table "filled with intelligently prepared dishes" simply because they were not the familiar meat "swimming in empyrematic oil"? In words that echoed Berckmans' own observations decades earlier, Jones argued that this sort of man shamed his community and condemned himself to "a limited sphere of enjoyment in life" and likely a limited span of life as well.[62] No father could raise his children this way and take pride in his legacy.

The members of the GSHS were intensely conscious of the presence of women at their meetings. Berckmans frequently credited the womenfolk of Georgia with the essential task of making homes lovely places that sons did not want to leave. The horticulturists needed "help from the women of Georgia," said Berckmans, in order to "create and encourage a taste for the cultivation of fruits and flowers," which could keep their sons at home in the countryside.[63] At Milledgeville in 1901 Berckmans extended a "cordial invitation" to the women in the audience to "grace our meetings with your presence." He patronized them with a promise that the sessions would "not be long" and that the men would "try to make them as instructive to you as possible."[64] Then he outlined his view of horticultural gender roles. "We men may look to the substantials of life but [women] look to the aesthetic ... we are inspired to day in our work by the grand and beautiful display which you have so artistically arranged in this hall."[65] And these were essentially the roles assigned to women: audience members who could "smile approvingly" at their men, and aesthetic experts who could create the domestic backdrop that would inspire male accomplishment and keep the children content at home.

The horticulturists of the late nineteenth and early twentieth centuries, then, held out the home as the battleground of civilization, the place where the future of the South would be won or lost. Perhaps this narrowing of the field of battle was, as some have suggested, a result of defeat in the Civil War – southern men had been cut off from the military and political sphere, and so it was in the management of their households that they reclaimed their manliness.[66] In any event, it made sense that southern agriculturists might turn from their plantations to their gardens, orchards, and homes. "We must live upon our farms," Professor Browne had said in 1882. And yet their homes were "generally the worst, the ugliest, the most dilapidated houses on the farms, unadorned by a single shrub, or tree or flower."[67] A man's front yard reflected his character, as Downing had instructed – but this had a particular resonance for the reconfiguration of southern masculinity following military defeat.

The *Atlanta Constitution* editor and New South booster Henry Grady captured this basic shift in a speech to farmers at Elberton, Georgia, in 1889. His description of a visit to a "country home" drew together rural aesthetics with gender roles, religiosity, and politics. First the rural aesthetics: it was a

modest, quiet house sheltered by great trees and set in a circle of field and meadow, gracious with the promise of harvest – barns and cribs well filled and the old smoke-house odorous with treasure – the fragrance of pink and hollyhock mingling with the aroma of garden and orchard, and resonant with the hum of bees and poultry's busy clucking – inside the house, thrift, comfort and that cleanliness that is next to godliness.

Then the evocation of gender:

Outside stood the master, strong and wholesome and upright; wearing no man's collar; with no mortgage on his roof and no lien on his ripening harvest... The good wife, true of touch and tender, happy amid her household cares, clean of heart and conscience, the helpmate and the buckler of her husband.

Then framed within proper gender roles, religion: As night fell the father gathered the family around the Bible to read the "old, old story of love and faith." And finally, politics, as Grady thought to himself, " 'Surely here [and not in Washington D.C.] – here in the homes of the people is lodged the ark of the covenant of my country. Here is its majesty and its strength...' The homes of the people; let us keep them pure and independent, and all will be well with the republic."[68]

In just a few words, Grady managed to articulate a new southern ideal to replace the antebellum lord of the manor: a humble, religious, literate man with a diverse set of agricultural skills and an adoring wife and family. In so doing, Grady touched on themes that had occupied Georgia's horticulturists for more than a decade already: that there might be a kind of "development" that was industrial in the quality of its work ethic as much as it was rural in its character; that was urban in its sophistication and scientific knowledge, but agricultural and human in its sensibility; that was masculine in its productivity and provisioning, but feminine in its refinement and beauty. He paid homage to a sort of progress in which rural folk turned tidy profits selling fruits to northern consumers without sacrificing their agrarian souls.[69]

Which takes us back to Samuel Rumph. Given all this concern for the home life of the farmer, it should be no surprise that Samuel Rumph's home earned a great deal of attention. His Willow Lake estate near Marshallville always won praise from visitors as "one of the loveliest in the country, surrounded by fruits and flowers of every species."[70] The house was a "fine, large, dwelling, with out buildings, all in the best style and in the most perfect order," wrote one reporter. "The perfect order and system of the establishment is at once apparent," wrote another. "Everything is as neat as a pin, from packing house to fruit crate."[71] A photograph of the house itself graced the front page of the *Sunny South* in August 1896, and the text praised it as a "model," what with its Spanish oaks shading the "gem" of a house, the front yard a "bower of shrub and flower." The article went on: "This is the residence of a man of culture, and a successful man withal, who has an eye to his home as well as to his business. The dwelling itself is supplied with the conveniences and appointments of a city home, while just in easy sight of the shady veranda there are 80,000 peach trees, flanked by picturesque fields of other growth."[72] Urban conveniences, rural charm: everything about Rumph's life seemed "picturesque" – like a picture (see Figures 3.1 and 3.2).

FIGURE 3.1. Samuel H. Rumph's home at Willow Lake, near Marshallville, Georgia. From the original caption: "The home of Mr. Samuel H. Rumph ... is a model... The front yard is a bower of shrub and flower and shows that this is the residence of a man of culture, and a successful man withal, who has an eye to his home as well as to his business."
Source: O. Pierre Havens, Photographer. In Pleasant A. Stovall, *Fruits of Industry: Points and Pictures along the Central Railroad of Georgia* (Savannah, GA: Central Railroad of Georgia, 1895).

And that is exactly how Rumph's life and story functioned for horticulturists and other New South boosters. He embodied what the visiting Connecticut horticulturist J. H. Hale praised about the GSHS in 1890: the "stimulus it gave to 'adorn' the home and provide the family with 'delicious food.' " The horticulturists were making money, Hale conceded, but it was not only about money in the end. "The real object is to make a happy home for himself and his family. I think the time will come when every home will be beautiful to look upon."[73] Samuel Rumph was the image of the South's future.

In Rumph's home at Willow Lake visitors saw beauty, but also order and control. A woman, his wife, Clara, inspired him, and her aesthetic instincts clearly ordered the interior of his home. But this was so under the auspices of his authority. He was master of this smaller but tightly controlled domain.[74] This smaller world – the attenuated circumstances that challenged postbellum southern masculinity – did not have the final word in Samuel Rumph's life. He found a way out through business. His second home, then, was the house that business built, but it was a business built from embracing rather than abandoning agriculture.

FIGURE 3.2. Samuel H. Rumph's "Suburban Fruit Farm" Packinghouse, near Marshallville, Georgia. The sign boasts of "43,000 Trees Planted Feb'y 1895." Both pear and peach trees are visible.
Source: Great Fruit Sections of the South: Views along the Lines of the Central of Georgia Railway (Savannah, GA: Central of Georgia Railway, 1898).

V

Despite the homage to homespun horticulture that filled newspaper columns and the meetings of the GSHS, southern pomology increasingly turned to northern investment. In the early 1890s, with the support of such horticultural luminaries as Rumph and Berckmans, middle Georgians hatched a scheme to attract this kind of outside interest: the Georgia Peach Carnival in Macon. It was three weeks of entertainment, food, orchard tours, and general merriment, scheduled for the peak of peach season in July 1895. There was nothing particularly original about this idea; this was the age of expositions, after all, Philadelphia in 1876, Atlanta in 1881, Louisville in 1883, New Orleans in 1885, Atlanta again in 1887, Chicago in 1893, Atlanta a third time in 1895, and Nashville in 1897.[75]

This crowded field notwithstanding, Peach Carnival boosters were enthusiastic. The organizing committee was composed mostly of up-and-coming Maconites, members of the Young Men's Business League, who embodied the "electric spirit of enterprise" that was needed to remake the South.[76] These energetic entrepreneurs had captured the support of

nearly every notable grower in the state. Their board of directors included
P. J. Berckmans, Samuel H. Rumph, J. B. James, W. H. Felton, Dudley
Hughes, and J. D. Cunningham, an Atlantan who planted his trees near
Kennesaw "in the very track of Sherman's desolating march to the sea," as
if pointing to a southern resurrection powered by peaches. The state horticulturist, Hugh M. Starnes, was on the board, and so was Berckmans's
fellow Belgian Dr. J. C. LeHardy, and the Dublin GSHS stalwart John
Stubbs. A group of northerners also served as board members: J. H. Hale
from Connecticut, and Ohioans N. H. Albaugh and F. W. Withoft. It was
veritable who's who of southern horticulture in 1895.[77]

As plans coalesced, the newspapermen grew giddy. "PEACHES AT
EVERY POINT," the *Macon Telegraph* trumpeted in June 1895. "The
Whole State of Georgia Is Full of Fruit of Every Kind to Take the Place
of Cotton," the headline continued: "The Georgia Peach Carnival Is on
Every Tongue in the Fruit Region and Fine Exhibits Will Be Sent In to
Advertise Their Resources. IT IS THE EVENT OF THE SUMMER."[78]
On the following page the paper boasted that the carnival's fame was
international: the reputable Parisian Spectacular Company of Ontario
had inquired about putting on one of their dramatic side attractions –
the "Burning of Moscow" perhaps, or the "Fall of Pompeii."[79] Evidently
news had at least reached the Pacific Coast: the *San Francisco Call* noted
that Georgia's peach carnival promised "big things."[80] The carnival
kicked off with a grand procession through downtown Macon, which
featured policemen, fire engines, local military, floral displays, ladies in
fine carriages, floats from Fort Valley and Hawkinsville, and a "watermelon brigade," followed by a "Rousing Address of Welcome" by the
mayor and several other eloquent speakers. Over the next three weeks,
the carnival held a baseball tournament; the "Great Interstate Gun
Shoot"; horse, bicycle, foot, and boat races; an athletic field day; dances;
an Independence Day celebration; a "harvest sermon"; balloon ascen-
sions; and even a medieval tournament featuring young men who rode
on horses as "gallant knight[s] of the days of chivalry" and then crowned
a young lady "as queen of love and beauty."[81]

But all of this was a backdrop for the carnival's main attraction: the
fruit display (see Figure 3.3). At the center of the main building of Macon's
Central City park, great eight-foot stands showcased – as the railroad
promoter Major Glessner later described it – "peaches twelve and fifteen
inches in circumference, brilliant with their red and gold, tempting to eye
and palate; plums in red, yellow and green, large as goose eggs; grapes in
purple, pink and amber, the bunches weighing a pound and over; pears and

FIGURE 3.3. The great fruit exhibit at the 1895 Peach Carnival in Macon, Georgia.
Source: O. Pierre Havens, Photographer. Pleasant A. Stovall, *Fruits of Industry: Points and Pictures along the Central Railroad of Georgia* (Savannah, GA: Central Railroad of Georgia, 1895).

apples in green, yellow and russet of all sizes and varieties; melons weighing from fifty to seventy pounds, with great red hearts of cooling juiciness."[82] And Glessner did not even mention the cantaloupes, tomatoes, cabbages, quinces, and other produce. Never mind that the carnival manager George Duncan later had to raise money to cover the costs of the fruit, because the growers did not just donate them as he assumed they would. The fruit exhibit was one to remember, a kind of Georgia State Horticultural Society meeting on artificial guano.

The Peach Carnival attracted attention to Macon as a progressive center of commerce and capitalized on the excitement leading up to the International Cotton States Exposition, which took place in October of the same year. But as in the latter exposition, the organizers of the Peach Carnival had in mind two specific outcomes: investment and immigration. As the advertisements inviting Georgians to the affair put it, the carnival was "Designed to Unfold to the Eye of Homeseekers and Investors still another page of Georgia's magnificent resources, and show where 'man and his opportunity have met in the paradise of the peach.'"[83] It was to be, as Glessner indicated, "a living, glowing illustration" of the advantages of middle Georgia for fruit culture, "a picture painted by the hand of the Great Master in nature's own colors."[84] Almost every day of the carnival, newspapers published tantalizing bits of information about visiting parties of northerners who were invariably wealthy, impressed with the state's agricultural potential, and sure to buy large parcels of land in middle Georgia. A group of South Dakotans toured lands in Jasper County; a prospector from New York perused the fruit exhibits; a young lawyer from Dayton, Ohio, represented an already organized colony of some two hundred families.[85] The carnival was attracting outside capital – the "one thing needful to make this part of the state the garden spot of the country."[86]

For the boosters who put on the Peach Carnival, however, northern and western investors represented more than just capital. Their presence would also make the cotton belt a progressive farming region. Having learned their trade in less productive regions, explained the *Telegraph*, these new Georgians would know all the best methods of "tillage and economy." They would practice this "improved husbandry" and teach it to their neighbors.[87] Before long the "waste places of Georgia would be settled by practical farmers," George Duncan predicted.[88]

This was all well and good; the idea of practical farmers colonizing wastelands sounded appealing enough. But for a few offhand remarks, the whole scheme might be taken as an innocent effort on behalf of the common good. Those offhand remarks, however, revealed a more disquieting vision. For example: Major Glessner was the immigration agent for the Georgia Southern and Florida Railroad, whose arranged excursions and pamphlets and articles were so crucial to the enterprise of attracting northern interest in southern fruit growing. In his retrospective on the carnival for the *Southern States* magazine, Glessner casually explained that the idea behind a midsummer fruit fair was to convince northerners that the South's hottest season was not only tolerable, but even less oppressive than July in the North. In his words, it was designed to "eliminat[e] the idea that the South is too hot for a white man to live and work in."[89] An editorial in the *Telegraph* on the effects of the carnival was even more explicit: "In time," it predicted, "white agriculturalists will reign in the fields of Georgia."[90] The picture thus becomes clearer: fruit farms would replace cotton plantations, which tended to be owned by whites but farmed by blacks. Assuming, as these boosters undoubtedly did, that the finer points of such progressive farming would be beyond the average rural black family – and in terms of start-up capital, it undoubtedly was – peach culture would make a place in the countryside for the white farmer, and one who was educated, urbane, and well capitalized to boot.

For these visionaries – though not necessarily for all horticulturists – fruit growing was a means of whitening the black belt. The New South rose in tandem with Jim Crow. Boosters such as Grady assured northerners that the "race question" was under control; meanwhile, the economic advancement of southern blacks shocked white supremacists, who, rather than recognize black equality, opted for segregation and lynching as a way to reiterate their superiority. Later, country-life reformers such as Clarence Poe and Hugh MacRae would argue for a restoration of a white civilization based again on the land, composed of smallholders rather than planters.[91] These visions of the southern future either insisted on a permanent black underclass or wrote them out of the picture altogether. Either way, segregation was the tragic but logical conclusion for gentle reformers and rabid racists alike.

Tellingly, the only role mentioned for black southerners in the great Georgia Peach Carnival was as members of the opening procession's "Watermelon Brigade." The policemen and soldiers and firefighters, with their prancing steeds and glinting steel, presented a picture of regimented strength; the floral displays, luxuriant orbits around beautiful maidens and fair ladies, offered the diversion of beauty. The watermelon brigade was "ridiculously funny." One hundred "little negroes" balanced watermelons on their heads as they marched through the street; when they arrived at the park, they had their hands tied behind their backs for the watermelon-eating contest. The winner was proclaimed "The Watermelon-Eating Champion of the World."[92] The "Georgia Watermelon Song" had just been published in the *Constitution* a few days prior:

> Oh de melon grow in de corner cool.
>   (Chillun, cl'ar de way!)
> En I fill de sack, en I load de mule.
>   (Chillun, cl'ar de way!)
> En I live en die in Georgy
> When de melon's ripe–oh my!
> I'll watch en pray
> Tell it's almos' day
> En I'll reach home by en by![93]

For the organizers of the carnival, then, black southerners represented an amusing sideshow.

But of course African Americans were much more crucial to the development of the South than this sort of demeaning nonsense allowed. A few months later, the International Cotton States Exposition in Atlanta would emphasize just how crucial. In a bit of hyperbole leading up the Peach

Carnival, the *Telegraph* and the *Atlanta Constitution* predicted that the Peach Carnival would be comparable, if not superior, to the International Cotton States Exposition, which would take place in Atlanta in October. This comparison was pure bluster; in an age of grand expositions, the Cotton States Exposition was one of the largest.[94] The bold-faced message of the exposition was one of industrial rather than agricultural development. But the industrial dream could not do without horticulture: the exposition grounds had to be landscaped. And on whom did the exposition call but Prosper Berckmans? In March 1895, Berckmans appeared before the exposition's planning committee and proposed a landscaping plan of 1,636 evergreens for $700. His son Robert and his foreman, Mr. Skinner, were also to be employed for eighteen days to transplant and arrange the grounds.[95]

And so Prosper Berckmans's Fruitland Nursery provided the greenery for the exposition in Atlanta – the scenic backdrop, as it were, for the drama of the New South that was to play out on that stage. In the midst of the noise and excitement of the Exposition, the horticulturists whispered that the South was not just an open space for the building of factories, but could also be a home. One could lead an aesthetically pleasing life, like that of Samuel Rumph at Willow Lake, with a small initial investment. Your money will go a long way here, they intimated. It will allow you to live like a gentleman. And like disaffected English nobility bound for Caribbean islands, northerners arrived. Not in great numbers, but with influence enough to change southern peach districts. The exposition conveyed the unmistakable message that the South was all set for industrial development, and horticulturists offered the corollary that development could also mean a more beautiful landscape.

The other important corollary to this message of industrial development was that blacks and whites were united in the cause. For the exposition also featured the famous speech by Booker T. Washington, which W. E. B. DuBois sneeringly dubbed "The Atlanta Compromise."[96] "In all things that are purely social, we can be as separate as the fingers," said Washington, "yet one as the hand in all things essential to mutual progress."[97] This quotation may be what Washington's 1895 speech is famous for now, but at the time listeners may have latched on to another phrase. "Cast down your bucket where you are!" Washington exhorted white southerners who looked to immigration for the South's renewal: "Cast it down among the eight millions of Negroes whose habits you know ... among these people who have, without strikes and labor wars, tilled your fields, cleared your forests, builded your railroads and cities, and brought forth treasures from the bowels of the earth, and helped make possible this magnificent representation of the progress of the South." Washington enjoined his fellow southerners to employ these loyal neighbors, all the while "helping and encouraging them as you are doing on these grounds, and to education of head, hand, and heart." Do these things, he promised, and "you will find that they will buy your surplus land, make blossom the waste places in your fields, and run your factories."[98]

Critics complained that with these words Washington sold his people, that he portrayed the black South as little more than dark-skinned brawn to power the South's industrial catch-up project. But a closer reading shows that Washington offered an alternative to visions such as that of the Peach Carnival organizers. Instead of filling middle Georgia's waste places with northern horticulturists – instead of expecting that "white agriculturalists" would "reign in the fields of Georgia" – Washington envisioned an economic development project that was of, by, and for the people of the South, both black and white. Couched in the language of subservient cooperation, he painted a competing future of eventual but real economic equality between the races. Of course, Washington was no stranger to the need to court northern capital – his own Tuskegee Institute depended on it – but at the exposition he addressed his exhortations to his fellow southerners, white and black. But white northerners, some of whom had just enjoyed the amusements of Macon's Peach Carnival, were also pleased with Washington's vision, or at least the half they readily grasped: blacks would work! And some of these northerners would cast down their buckets not where they were but where Washington was: Connecticut Yankees playing at business in King Cotton's Court.

For the great development project that was the New South campaign, it was crucial to find images and products that could attract outside capital and still honor the native productions of the South. Peaches fit the bill. The fruit were soft and sweet and blushing, like (so its promoters incessantly pointed out) white southern maidens. And because the Georgia peach was first to all the major markets, the fruit seemed somehow to belong to the state. But getting it to those markets required large temporary labor forces, entrepreneurial acumen, modern management methods, and, increasingly, cutting edge technology – all of which required capital, which in the late nineteenth and early twentieth centuries meant looking north.[99]

VI

Prosper Berckmans had some parenting advice for the society in 1886. He was talking about the problem of rural out-migration, the sad rejection by so many sons of their fathers' homes and occupations. Instead of deploring the immoral appetites of the young, as many did at this time, Berckmans pointed to the discontent of their elders. "If we are unsuccessful and consequently dissatisfied with our calling, our children cannot expect benefit or encouragement in following us," he argued. Which is where the business of horticulture came into view: for "if we derive comforts, contentment, happiness and financial success from our pursuit, there is an assurance that … their first training will decide this important question."

And how was one to train children to love rural life? Berckmans offered two general principles and then two specific words of advice. First, attend: "carefully study the peculiar drift of our childrens' minds" and encourage them in the sorts of husbandry for which they show aptitude. Second, delight: "a beautiful flower or a temptingly colored fruit," were "often more potent" than the "gaudy toy[s]" of urban spaces. Then he gave two bits of gender-specific counsel. Sons needed a piece of land stocked with well-chosen fruits, the advice of their fathers as they learned to grow the fruits, and "all the pecuniary returns from the sale of surplus fruits or vegetables" – an arrangement far superior to a simple allowance, for the earnings would "cause them to look with manly pride upon their efforts in earning it." But it was not just sons who needed this kind of hands-in-the-dirt education. Daughters "should not receive a lesser share of your attention," he urged. By nature, girls knew flowers, those "more refined products of Horticulture," for which there was a rapidly increasing demand in the cities. Let them raise flowers for their own enjoyment and sell the surplus in the towns.[100]

Thirty years later, as Samuel Rumph drew up his will, he may have been following this advice. In the original will, in 1914, he had bequeathed Willow Lake to his daughter, the house in town and the Suburban Fruit Farm to his second wife, and a three-story brick house in the city of Macon to his son. In 1920, though, he changed these instructions to simple liquidation and division of the proceeds. As this change suggested, Rumph's heirs did not continue in the fruit business. When he died two years later of central apoplexy, his descendants fanned away from farming.[101] His daughter, Clara, married an ambitious lawyer, Warren Grice, who became chief justice of the Georgia Supreme Court. His son, Samuel

Rumph Jr., moved away from the farm and died at the age of fifty-five near Atlanta, Georgia.[102] His great grandson, Samuel Rumph Grice, is also a lawyer and lives in the Atlanta suburbs.

At the end of his life, Samuel Rumph Sr. had "made his luck," and he knew it. He set aside fifteen hundred dollars for a gravestone "suitable to my circumstances and conditions in life," which remains a striking monument. He listed a remarkable number of personal possessions by name, including his "mahogany rollertop desk," his "marble top iron safe," and his "jewelry consisting of diamond rings and stud, watches and chains," which he left to his son by his second marriage. The picture that emerges in his will is of a man with wide-ranging and ample possessions, and acutely aware of it.[103] Having made his fortune by scrupulous management, he aimed to dispose of it in the same manner.

In the example of Samuel Rumph, then, horticulture became something less than the full-fledged program of reform envisioned by Berckmans and other horticulturists. He lived a beautiful life, bred a marketable fruit, and made a pile of money. But horticulture had become a path to wealth more than a path to agrarian permanence. What was a subtle shift in Rumph's lifetime became a yawning rift in the career of John Howard Hale. And all those words about the numerous, educable, loyal, easily satisfied, and – most importantly – hard-working southern blacks? The "ridiculously funny" entertainment they were supposed to offer?

Hale, it seems, took them very much to heart.

4

A Connecticut Yankee in King Cotton's Court

I

Prosper Berckmans envisioned a beautiful South, the offspring of European horticulture. Samuel Rumph embodied the horticultural dream of commercial diversification, originating a peach variety that captured big city markets and seemed to free southern farmers from cotton. John Howard Hale showed how to make the South *work*. He laid bare the mechanics of commercial fruit growing in a way that Berckmans and Rumph and their counterparts – with the sensibilities of European and southern gentility – would or could not. A self-described Yankee who ran his two-thousand-acre farm near Fort Valley as a factory, Hale also reveled in the novelty of his operation's southernness, especially its African American labor supply. Fort Valley offered Hale the chance to form an agricultural enterprise in his own image. You can see the imperial glint in his eye in Figure 4.1. Hale and his fellow northerners *made* the Georgia peach industry, both rhetorically and materially. He was, to paraphrase Mark Twain, a Connecticut Yankee in King Cotton's Court.[1]

Hale's arrival in Georgia coincided with the end of what the historian C. Vann Woodward called the "missionary and political phase of the North's Southern policy." What replaced it was not a laissez-faire retirement of government resources but a "policy of economic exploitation."[2] In the name of industrial development, southerners offered the northern investors every opportunity, especially in minerals, timber, railroads, and mills. Federal and state governments sold their public lands for sale on an unprecedented scale – millions of acres for a song.

Although "exploitation" may be the right word to describe northern activity in mining and timber, Hale's story suggests that "development"

FIGURE 4.1. "Profitable peach-growing depends more on the man than anything else." Caption from J. H. Hale, "Peach Culture and Marketing," in Western New York Horticultural Society, *Proceedings of the Annual Meeting* 46 (1901), 29. *Source:* J. H. Hale Lantern Slide Collection. Courtesy of Historical Society of Glastonbury, Glastonbury, CT.

is more appropriate for the work of northern horticulturists. They arrived with slightly higher ideals than other speculators, for horticulture included a language of beauty and cultivation that softened the harder edges of modernization.[3] They were planting trees and bushes, after all, not building factories. They were improving the landscape, teaching a worthy skill to a needy people, and freeing southerners from their bondage to one-crop agriculture. The South's mineral and forest wealth was literally carried off in steamships and railcars, but horticulture forced those who might otherwise exploit to attend to a place for a longer time. Trees had to be planted and tended for years before anyone reaped a profit from them. The landscape itself still demanded attention and care, even as, following the example of horticulturists such as John Howard Hale, southern horticulture became more aggressively commercial. Some of the aesthetic and cultural idealism of nineteenth-century horticulture followed it into the twentieth century, like aging chaperones struggling to keep up with an energetic adolescent. Peaches earned praise as a quintessentially southern product, and the quintessential Georgia peach cultivar may have been introduced by a southern gentleman, but the Georgia peach *industry*, as Hale's story makes clear, was a northern import.[4]

II

Before J. H. Hale raised Georgia peaches in Fort Valley, he had resurrected Connecticut peach growing. New England agriculture was at low ebb in the late nineteenth century. Sons and daughters fled the countryside for the big northern cities to hammer and shape in factories and clerk and stock in stores. Or they followed the setting sun as western lands gained their reputation for rockless, fantastically fertile topsoils. Abandoned farm homes multiplied. Rural New Englanders advertised these places as vacation houses for wealthy urbanites, made boardinghouses out of their working farms for extra cash, and later sponsored "Old Home Week," a celebration of the region's rural past aimed at jogging middle-aged memories: the old small town where you grew up, the narrow lanes and green pastures, the rocky fields, a nice place to visit, and maybe to retire.[5]

But Hale looked forward. He combined the old discipline of horticulture with the new techniques of turn-of-the-century capitalism and injected fresh life into the family farm and thereby New England farming more generally. Or at least this is the story that Hale told about himself. Like Samuel Henry Rumph, Hale grew up in a fatherless home. Unlike Rumph, who said little about his childhood and allowed newspapermen to fill in the meaning of his rise from rags to riches, Hale proclaimed his story himself. His nursery catalogs, in addition to selling fruit trees and strawberry plants, offered entertainment in the form of Hale's memoirs.[6] The 1896 edition, for instance, announced the essential arc of Hale's career: "From a Push-Cart to a Trolley Car." Inside Hale described his beginnings as a child battling quack-grass in the back lot in order to plant some strawberries, pushing that rickety cart to market, and gradually making enough to build up a fruit empire.[7]

Born in South Glastonbury, Connecticut, in 1853, J. H. Hale was the second son of John A. Hale, a farmer and insurance salesman who died while J. H. was young. Accounts vary as to how successful the father was. The *Hartford Courant* called him "general agent of the Aetna Life Insurance Company" and claimed that he had been "influential in the building up of that company."[8] Other accounts portrayed him as a failed farmer who became a traveling insurance man and still could not pay off the family's debts.[9] In any case, Hale claimed to have started with little but a set of shoddy tools – a "broken handled shovel, one short handled spade and a hoe," for transportation that inescapable pushcart, for capital the "skinned" and "run-down" family land, and for labor the "latent energies of two boys, anxious to carry their share of life's burdens."[10]

Along with these rather poor resources, Hale possessed a rich "love of fruits inherited from ancestors on both sides," a predilection that showed from his earliest days on the Hale family farm.[11] But with his father dead and a mortgage to pay, the Hale family was "kept hustling" to put food on the table. When J. H. was twelve, he worked for cash in a neighbor's cornfield, where he discovered "a seedling peach tree, right there in the corn field, loaded down with ripening fruit; rosy, red little peaches, sweet and delicious." Young Hale rested under the tree, "eating peaches and dreaming of the peach orchard I would have if ever I got money enough to buy the trees." His mind in thrall to this vision, he threw himself into his farmwork.[12] By the fall of 1868, Hale had saved nearly one hundred dollars, and it was time to begin. He dropped out of school – he was only attending the three coldest months out of the year anyway – and put all his horticultural reading into practice. He began with strawberries and raspberries, crops with fast turnaround, for as he said, "Quick returns must be had." They were had, and then reinvested, and his quarter-acre rapidly expanded to four.[13] In short order J. H. Hale, and to a lesser extent his brother, George, became not only sellers of strawberries but nurserymen and acknowledged strawberry experts. In 1882 Hale dueled rhetorically with formidable old Charles Hovey himself over the identity (and superiority vis-a-vis the famous Hovey Seedling) of the new Manchester strawberry that Hale Nurseries was promoting.[14] Hale became a respected peer of Charles Downing, Marshall Wilder, Patrick Barry, and Peter Henderson and gave frequent talks at horticultural societies and nurserymen's meetings on strawberry culture and nomenclature.[15]

As it turned out, strawberries were just the opening episode in a star-studded pomological career. Peaches beckoned him in 1877, or so he recalled in his 1896 catalog. From a remote fencerow those old peach trees called to him, like New England oracles:

See here boy! We poor neglected old trees have been here in the fence-corners for fifty years or more. We don't dress as well, in rich dark green, or put on as much style as our sisters down near the house, who are liberally fed with the best of everything, but we don't get sick and have the yellows... We are healthy, our buds are tough, and we have often had fruit to feed your tribe when our more favored sisters said it was too cold to work. If you are after money in fruit culture, and want to show the North a trick or two, try a peach orchard up here on the hills![16]

By presenting his decision to grow peaches in this way, Hale embedded an old agrarian argument in the pages of his self-promotion: rural New England's prosperity would result, as it always had, from its soil. Rugged New England peaches would be immune to "the yellows," a sickness then decimating old orchards in the Delmarva region and in Michigan. Not coincidentally, this picture of hardy half-wild trees from the New England hills mapped easily onto racial projections of the late nineteenth century, a moment when "hardy pioneer stock," especially from New England, seemed to many amateur racial theorists just the thing to combat the flood of "inferior" southern and eastern Europeans.[17]

As a good horticulturist, Hale listened to his trees, and by taking the temperature of his land at daylight discovered that the warmest spots were up on the hills.[18] He planted about ten thousand trees in two blocks on leased land that had the desired altitude. Five years later, when he could expect his first full crop, three severe winters in a row killed all the buds. His friends counseled pulling out before his debt mounted beyond his capacity to repay. Hale demurred. With "my hand to the peach plow I did hate to turn back," he explained, "and then, thinking how the Lord hates a 'quitter,' I began hustling to borrow more money."[19] A visit from Senator Joseph Hawley, *Hartford Courant* editor Charles Dudley Warner, and two other *Courant* editors occurred at a crucial time, for these "lovers of nature" were smitten with Hale's peach enterprise and "expressed great confidence in it." The loans appeared.[20] A few years later, Hale put his long-contemplated marketing plan into practice, thinning the trees of all but the largest fruit, making advance arrangements with specialty grocers, and then packing and delivering with scrupulous care. In 1887, he reaped a ten-thousand-dollar profit, enough to pay off his debts and expand; in 1889, he made twenty-four thousand dollars on only thirty-five acres of fruit.[21]

Hale did not leave his readers to form their own conclusions about his story. He spelled them out in capital letters: PUSH and CULTURE. The lesson of Push he claimed to have learned from his "little old push-cart," which he and his brother borrowed and then purchased from a neighbor for one dollar. Perhaps, Hale mused in 1896, that cart "had more to do with our success than we are aware of ... hanging back would not move it a peg, but pushing would, and to 'keep everlastingly at it' was the only way to get there."[22] Of course, Hale meant much more than physical effort. Push meant looking on the bright side, for "nothing so surely tends to success in any enterprise as to ignore the clouds and look for sunshine."[23] "Push" was a watchword of the late nineteenth century. Americans on the move pushed westward the boundaries of the nation, pushed Indians onto reservations, and pushed the decrepit Spanish empire back across the Atlantic. Inventors and engineers pushed past obstacles and failures to fashion a pulsing new world for the reconstructed nation. Entrepreneurs pushed their ideas and products onto a public with cash to spend. And, yes, it was a gendered concept. Push was something men were supposed to have and do. Women might persevere or sparkle with intelligence. Men pushed.

"Culture," the second lesson of Hale's life, drew on that intentional ambiguity in nineteenth-century horticultural usage of the term: the practices of raising plants ("peach culture"), refinement and taste ("men of high culture"), and the specific act of plowing and harrowing.[24] In Hale's teenage years, a severe drought and a nasty infestation of quack grass led him to a plan of "frequent culture" to save a large section of sweet corn. "I rode the old, bony horse probably thirty times up and down, out and across, every row in that corn patch during the awful heat and drouth of July and August, while my brother followed along holding the cultivator. It killed the quack-grass, and it nearly killed me, but the superb crop of corn … ground into me through the bones of that old horse's back a never-to-be-forgotten lesson in Culture."[25] Hale expanded on this thought in a promotional pamphlet he wrote for the Cutaway Harrow in 1900 – an early example of celebrity endorsement – titled, "Culture, Agriculture, and Orchard Culture. The Utility of Weeds." Hale believed that cultivating with a tool such as the Cutaway Harrow had the effect of fertilizing and irrigating the soil: "Tillage is manure," he said, for it mixed particles and freed latent chemicals in the soil that would otherwise be inaccessible to plants. Similarly, he maintained, "Tillage is moisture," presumably because it coaxed water to the surface, where plants could use it. For Hale, these lessons highlighted the "utility and blessings of weeds, those ever-true and constant friends of the farmer, without which I fear the lessons of culture would never have been fully learned by the most of us soil tillers."[26]

It should be clear that the lesson of Culture, like the lesson of Push, extended beyond commonsense agricultural practice. In fact, frequent cultivation could also lead to rapid erosion of soil fertility, as nutrients leached into the subsoil and topsoil washed quietly away. But aggressive culture made sense in an age of "push" because it meant that the farmer was always doing something. "You love to flirt with nature," a speaker told the members (including Hale) of the Connecticut Pomological Society in 1901, "to stroke her breast with the hoe, massage her with the harrow, and manicure her with the pruning knife, and feed her with fertilizers to see how she'll act."[27] Not content idly to pluck the fruits of nature, in other words, the cultivator with frequent plowing brought his strength to bear upon the earth. Hale's agricultural vision thus drew on the language of masculinity then in vogue. He wanted a strenuous life for the farmer and the farmed.[28]

Push and culture were ways of expressing a fundamental belief in the power of the individual to "make his luck" through very hard work. Hale's story mapped closely to the upward mobility trope of America's nineteenth-century middle class. Work hard, be smart, don't give up, and success will come your way, even if "the interests" are arrayed against you.[29] The fact that Hale achieved success through agriculture – in the provision of life's basic necessities – and not through land speculation or in service to a corporation only increased his appeal. By 1889 he was grand master of the Connecticut Grange, and in the 1890s he campaigned for the Democratic and People's Party candidate William Jennings Bryan and might have landed a cabinet post had Bryan won.[30] But Hale's classic Yankee work-hard success story also depended on the very hard work of very many others. And this was a lesson he learned in the South.

III

Hale's first visit to the South was in 1890. Officially, he was on a mission from the Census Bureau, for horticulture was finally earning federal attention. Contemplating a special section of the Census of Agriculture on fruits and flowers, the Census director invited Hale to make a national survey of nurseries, seed farms, floriculture, citrus and other tropical fruits, truck farming, and viticulture. Along with this special narrative section, the census for the first time counted production and acreage of individual fruits, not just "fruits and nuts," as a broad category. In surveying tropical fruits, Hale not only gave current production numbers but also estimated *potential* acreage in California and Florida by county. Hale and the Census Bureau were bullish on horticulture.

The census surveyor job was a plum position for Hale. It cemented his reputation as a national authority on fruits and nurseries. It also gave him a chance to satisfy his great curiosity about production practices in different parts of the continent, a license to spy on his competitors, and a first crack at any investment opportunities he discovered. In California he encountered a profusion of fruit unlike anything he had ever seen – forty miles of peach and apricot orchards on the way to Marysville in the Sacramento Valley, rapidly expanding citrus lands near Chico, roses by the bushel at Yuba City.[31] Near Spokane, Washington, he caught his breath at four-and-a-half-pound potatoes, eight-foot oat straw, and forty-ounce apples; in Walla Walla he toured large nurseries with ten-foot cherry trees only a year old; in Idaho's Snake River Valley he saw "exceptionally good fruit country," especially for peaches and pears; at the Dalles on the Columbia River he saw "splendid wheat country" and salmon fisheries that made the river seem "almost alive."[32]

These stupendous sights notwithstanding, the riches of California, Washington, and Idaho never really tempted him. Even years later, Hale declined an invitation from the USDA pomologist and leader of Sunkist G. H. Powell to make an easy fortune growing California citrus. "If you would move out of that country and come out to California to live," Powell wrote, "you would not have any trouble with frozen buds, and you would make more money in five years than you can make in a life time either in Connecticut or Georgia... The records are simply phenomenal." Hale was unmoved. "I note what you say about the splendid block of 750 acres of oranges and lemons at Corona," he wrote, "and there is a lot that is fascinating and tempting in California, but as the fellow said 'It is so far away' and I think I had rather live in little old New England and take the risk of climatic conditions."[33]

Middle Georgia was a different story. "I just lost my head" upon arriving there, he later said.[34] He wrote to his *Courant* readers in August 1890 that "some things he saw in the South" led him to think that he might live there part of the year. "I do like the people, the soil and the climate, and with these three essentials all right one can make a happy home, and if I mistake not that's what we are all aiming at."[35] Climate, soil, and people – these are indeed the characteristics that drew Hale and other northern investors to the South. His breezy description of these "essentials" making a "happy home" belied a much deeper understanding of what made the South – middle Georgia in particular – such a fine place for launching an agricultural business.

On a superficial level, Hale claimed to like the southern climate because it was not as hot as he expected. "When I left home I dreaded the heat of a southern summer," he wrote from North Carolina in early August, "yet since I wrote you last it has been delightfully cool and pleasant here." His readers, meanwhile, were undergoing a major heat wave. "My friends

here laughingly suggest that it will not be safe for me to go up into that
hot northern country for a month or six weeks yet."[36] More importantly,
the southern climate did not preclude a diverse and beautiful landscape.
He reported with relief that the lack of "fine grassy lawns, broad mead-
ows, and green pastures" was a cultural preference rather than an environmental limitation. For although timothy and clover would not grow
in the South, Hale thought Bermuda grass and Johnson grass to be suitable alternatives. A northerner could cultivate a decent lawn here, raise
a full crop of hay, maintain a pasture for his cattle and horses.[37] This
was a false impression. Southern grasses would never approach the nutri-
ent level of northern grasses, and while Bermuda and Johnson grasses
thrived, they also proved to be nearly ineradicable in crop fields.[38] Be that
as it may, a visit to Prosper Berckmans's Fruitland estate confirmed that
not only grasses but also a profusion of ornamental and edible plants
could thrive in the South. On the whole, Hale found southern agriculture
and culture lacking in refinement, but Berckmans and the other horticulturists of the Georgia State Horticultural Society proved that the climate was not to blame. Northern fears about their people or their plants
wilting and rotting in the southern heat and humidity were, according to
Hale, unfounded.[39]

In commercial terms, the climate also offered a crucial advantage. The
"fine late peaches" that earned good prices on the New York markets
ripened two to three months earlier in Fort Valley than in Delaware and
Connecticut, a feature that translated into even better prices. Why would
a discriminating consumer purchase a small peach from Delaware when
a big red Georgia peach was available?[40] Of course, Hale was not the
first to make this observation. Berckmans had predicted it; Rumph had
made his name with well-timed shipments of Elbertas in the 1880s; and,
even as Hale contemplated his own future in Fort Valley, other northern
fruit growers were moving in, one Ohio company having recently purchased a twelve-hundred-acre tract near Fort Valley. They understood
with Hale that middle Georgia marked the southern limit of peach production, though they may not have understood that commercial varieties
had need for a certain number of chilling hours, which were lacking in
southern Georgia and in Florida. Add to this the fact that Fort Valley was
within a thousand miles of "80 per cent of the consuming population of
the country" who lived in major cities from Denver to Boston, and middle Georgia seemed to be a perfect location for growing peaches.[41]

It was not just its location that made middle Georgia so attractive to
Hale, but also its elevation. "The land is high and dry," he reported to his

Courant readers.[42] Though it is not clear how thoroughly he had taken in the topography of the middle Georgia landscape in 1890 when he bought his farm, he learned from local growers that the Fort Valley region rarely lost a crop to a late freeze: only two from 1874 to 1894, and not one from 1900 to 1926. The reason was the same one that had led Hale to put his peaches on hillsides in Connecticut: cold air drifts downhill and, on still nights, settles in low places. Middle Georgia peaches grew mostly on what became known as the "Fort Valley Plateau," about seven hundred feet above sea level, the highest part of a ridge separating the Ocmulgee and Flint Rivers. This topographical advantage accumulated over time. Unlike other areas, which lost entire crops to late frosts every five years or so, Fort Valley growers made some money almost every year. And in years when competitors lost their crops, they made a lot of money. As local growers say today, "If anybody had peaches, *we* had peaches."[43]

Hale was, if anything, even more enthusiastic about the *soil* around Fort Valley.[44] He mentioned it every time he wrote about the place: "large, level fields of rich, brown, sandy, loamy soil" – later Hale would add "chocolate-colored." Presumably, Hale and his New England readers pictured their own small, sloping fields of rocky, gray dirt.[45] But what made middle Georgia's soil so "magnificent" was not just this fertile easy-to-work topsoil, but its red-clay subsoil, lying like an aquifer beneath the surface and giving life to Fort Valley's fruit culture. "It is a magnificent soil," Hale proclaimed, "and the peach trees going down into that red clay, it does produce fine colored peaches."[46]

Later soil surveys confirmed Hale's observations. Georgia can be divided into three geographic zones – mountains, piedmont, and coastal plain – which generally descend in elevation across the state northwest to southeast. The irregular shelf that separates piedmont from coastal plain – the former North American coastline – is known as the "fall line" because of a preponderance of waterfalls. Here the piedmont's red clay gives way to sand, forming sandy loams underlain by clay.[47] In 1903, the first federal soil survey found that loam underlain by clay was good for all crops, but especially peaches. "The yield, flavor, and general appearance of the fruit is superior to that grown on any of the other soils in the area," the authors wrote. Not surprisingly, by 1903, the soil was "in great demand" and "almost all clear and under cultivation."[48]

Hale saved his greatest enthusiasm for the third "essential": the people. On one hand, he was full of high praise for Berckmans and the "earnest workers" of the Horticultural Society. Georgia had become "the foremost horticultural state of the South," Hale maintained. He visited Prosper Berckmans at his "perfect Nursery and fruit farm" near Augusta and was astonished at the "high cultivation" and sheer variety of plant material on the nursery grounds. Berckmans, whom Hale called "the leading pomologist of America and of the world," spoke of the frequent visits and botanical mementos of Charles Downing, Marshall Wilder, Bayard Taylor, Asa Gray, Louis Agassiz, and others. As the head of both the American Pomological Society and the Georgia State Horticultural Society, Berckmans confirmed Hale's hope that high culture could be practiced in Georgia.[49] Hale was also pleased that the farmer's movement had picked up momentum in the South, since a "few leading families" had controlled southern political office for years. Though this southern People's Party seemed "crude" to him, he thought the populists meant well, and he believed that "in the end much good would come of" the movement in the South.[50] In 1892 Hale thought Tom Watson – Georgia People's Party founder and 1896 Vice Presidential candidate – a "bright fellow, with lots of pluck and energy," though up against a fearsome Goliath of a Democratic Party.[51]

On the other hand, Hale saw a lot of room for improvement. As it happened, the Georgia State Horticultural Society was also meeting in Fort Valley during Hale's visit in 1890. They elected him an honorary member of the club, offered the "right hand of fellowship," and then gave ear to his impromptu address "on horticultural topics." He presented his rambling remarks as disinterested advice, but they contained the germ of his own business plan. He made his criticisms gently, in part by using the pronoun "we," when he really meant the plural "you." We have it too easy, he said; we take things for granted. We "who work in the ground live so well and make a living so easily that we do not understand our business as well as we should." Knowing your business would take "some capital"; a cosmopolitan orientation, roving about the country "to see what others are doing in the same line of business"; and firsthand knowledge of the nation's "great fruit markets." Hale possessed all of these kinds of knowledge: he had investors backing him; he was in the midst of traveling around the country (and on the federal dime, too!); he had seen "peaches from Georgia that were nicely packed which brought good prices"; and he had also seen "others that didn't pay the freight." Hale concluded his speech with a rousing exhortation:

I have been looking over your peach orchards in Fort Valley. Nature has done a great deal for you; but I believe, if you want to make the greatest amount of money for the amount of capital and labor you have invested, you will have to give even more and better care than you have yet done in Fort Valley. Will you be satisfied with what you have done, or will you aim higher and take double prices and double your business? Do not rest where you are; for you have not got anywhere near the top.

And of course Hale was not resting where he was. He took his own advice. As he was dispensing it, in fact, he was formulating his own plans to "take double prices and double [his] business."[52]

To his *Courant* readers Hale was more pointed in his analysis of the southern peach growers. Most of the orchards belonged to southerners "who have not manured highly or given extra cultivation," he observed. Despite this lack of effort, however, some had made "great fortunes."[53] If they did so just throwing the trees in the ground and reaping the harvests, imagine what a thrifty northerner like him could accomplish! Echoing Alexander von Humboldt's comments on Mexico, Hale wrote that the South was "'cursed with too much,' a rich fertile soil and climate that will produce almost everything." And yet there were precious few "comfortable well-kept homes" like those of "thrifty New England." What good were all the South's "natural advantages" if a man was unable "to carve out as pleasant and attractive a home as others can and do" in other parts of the country?[54] According to Hale, what Samuel Rumph had done at Willow Lake, and Berckmans at Fruitland, were exceptions to the southern rule.

But to a man like Hale, poverty was opportunity, and the South offered a "better field of opportunity than any other part of the country." Indeed, Hale maintained, southerners, even the families of Old South planters, were so desperate for "industrious northern" men to make their home in the South that they were giving away land to attract them.[55] There was "a great desire" throughout the South that the "thrifty Yankee people should come among them and show them 'how to do things,'" Hale said, "for go where you will there is a wonderful respect for the thrifty, pushing Yankee."[56] In other words, just by being who they were, northerners could barge in with confidence in their salutary influence.

So when Hale claimed to like the southern people, he meant it in multiple ways. Some of them had earned his high regard with their progressive agriculture and sophisticated living. Others, the indolent and unimaginative who lacked "push" and "culture," had left open the field of development to thrifty, well-capitalized northerners like him. And to some extent, Hale was right: immigration campaigns and industrial expositions, with their fawning invitations to northern capital, attested to this welcoming attitude.

Hale's regard for southern whites, however, paled in comparison to his celebration of southern blacks. Initially, he saw African Americans as "happy and contented" people who stole constantly, worked carelessly, and spent profligately.[57] In other words, he adopted the lies white folks had told about black folks for decades – lies that justified black subjugation as a sort of kindly remedy for people who would be lost and helpless on their own. These were the self-deceptions that allowed well-meaning clergy such as Stephen Elliott to keep quiet about slavery; that painted the black-populated Reconstruction governments as inevitably corrupt and inept; that, in the minds of whites, refuted evidence of black educational and economic progress in the wake of emancipation with a new and aggressively policed color line.[58]

If Hale had continued parroting these self-serving lines about black inferiority and contentment, it would have been unsurprising and worthy of little comment. But his views underwent an unusual transformation. Once Hale had become a landowner in the southern black belt himself, he began praising black labor. In the summer of 1891, after he had purchased his old plantation but before he had put peaches in, he paid a visit to inspect progress on the cotton crop and discovered that his "negro hands" had plowed, fertilized, and cultivated the lands "in straighter rows and more cleanly cultivated than our own farm at home, where we have white labor and two owners to boss the job."[59] Looking back in 1901, Hale explained, "I went South with the idea that the negro was a rather stupid creature, and could be used only in the grosser lines of work, but I have learned different." In fact, he maintained, they were "the best agricultural labor in America to-day ... way ahead of our New England Yankee."[60]

Hale blamed cotton monoculture for the idea that "the negro could never become a skilled workman." The South, in devoting itself to that crop, had shackled its workers to poverty and ignorance.[61] But when they were given a chance to with other kinds of labor, such as the difficult and precise knifework of budding fruit trees, his African American workers exceeded all his expectations. As Hale boasted to a congressional committee, "we have been growing one to three million trees a year, and they have been propagated and grown by negro labor," some of whom could bud twenty-five hundred buds a day – just shy of premium New England nursery help, who would bud three thousand a day but earned four times the wages of southern blacks.[62] A story Hale liked to tell of laying out his orchard in Georgia made a similar point. He had hired a surveyor to lay out straight lines for the tree rows, for cultivation was easier with straight rows, and since he would be viewing the great expanse of trees from the cupola atop his packing shed, he wanted it to be in order (see Figure 4.2).

FIGURE 4.2. "Land was cheap, and good Negro labor abundant ... When I found the best plantation in all that region was for sale at a moderate price, and that its thousand acres would only be sold in one tract, I promptly took an option on it ... I could see that a large orchard could be handled much better and cheaper proportionately than a small one; so I borrowed the money, bought the whole tract, and undertook to organize a stock company to equip and run it." Caption from J.H. Hale, "Peaches: A National Product," *World's Work* 4.2 (June 1902), 2174.
Source: O. Pierre Havens, photographer. Pleasant A. Stovall, *Fruits of Industry: Points and Pictures along the Central Railroad of Georgia* (Savannah, GA: Central Railroad of Georgia, 1895).

But before the surveyor had finished the job, one of the "old plantation darkies" went to him and boasted: "Lulu and I can do it a heap sight quicker, and I reckon about as well as dat ar man wid de machine." And so Lulu the mule and Old Henry set to work with some poles. "The work was absolutely perfect," exclaimed Hale, "and now with more than 250,000 trees in what I am often told is the best arranged orchard in America, I give due credit to the darkey and the mule for the orderly way in which the trees are planted."[63]

Hale's acknowledgment of African Americans' horticultural skill did not lead him to stand against inequity. Instead, he made use of it. In 1892, he observed that a short crop combined with low prices had made it impossible for black tenants to "pay out," to cover the cost of their land rent, much less for the previous year's fertilizer and rations. With no means of buying food and clothing over the winter, and no chance of obtaining another loan until the February plowing season, they waited for the sheriff to take away "the only working capital most of the darky renters have," their mules, which had been mortgaged in the spring. Hale told this sad story to his *Courant* readers, but rather than lamenting the situation, he explained frankly what a stroke of good fortune it was. He had wanted to buy five or six mules, and had expected to pay the market rate of $125 or $150 each. But with conditions as they were among black tenants, and with cash scarce among even the more prosperous middle Georgians, he could buy his mules at the auction block for $30 to $50 apiece.[64]

In 1893, Hale printed a letter from Henry Belle, one of his "old plantation darkies," who served as an interim supervisor for the orchard. The letter described in detail the progress of their haying, barn building, plowing, and, most significantly, budding nursery stock. Hale boasted that many of his letters from New Englanders were not "half so intelligently written as this one, from an old time slave and a faithful, trusty man. Give the southern plantation darky a chance," he concluded, tellingly, "and he is a good deal of a man."[65] In saying so, Hale described his own changed views on African Americans: they were more manly, less childlike, than he originally supposed, and much more highly skilled in agricultural work. And whether or not Hale intended the double meaning in this particular line – *a good deal* – he certainly appreciated the fact that he could hire equal labor at quarter-rate pay. Georgia peaches commanded high prices in the northern markets; considering the going wage for labor in the cotton belt, the profits could be even higher. But Hale's comment also spoke to a deeper truth about the courage and tenacity of black southerners, who carried on in the face of the crushing disappointments and the daily indignities of life in the post-Reconstruction South.

The history of Fort Valley High and Industrial School (FVHIS) illustrates that courage and tenacity and offers a counternarrative to the story Hale told. Perhaps because of his experience with horticultural training for his black workers, Hale enthusiastically supported the establishment of FVHIS, a school for the industrial training of blacks along the lines of Tuskegee Institute in Alabama. Though African Americans technically ran and staffed FVHIS, for much of its early history it served the interests of the white southerners who tolerated it and the white northern philanthropists who funded it.

Hale had joined the board of FVHIS in 1895 and donated land and supplies to the school on a regular basis.[66] In 1910, he wrote to the

Courant's readers on behalf of what he called "A Little Tuskegee." Booker T. Washington was doing "splendid work," Hale acknowledged, but he knew of a "little Tuskegee" near his orchards that also needed the financial support of Connecticut residents. The school's principal, Henry Hunt, was "sacrificing his life and that of his family to this work when he could go it alone and make a fine living for himself," all for the sake of the "two or three hundred negro boys and girls" who desperately needed instruction in the "practical duties of life." Would the good people of Connecticut sacrifice a few good dollars for the sake of this good work? Hale then printed a letter to him from Hunt, which listed their "real and pressing need" for agricultural tools worth about $540. He expressed confidence that if Hale could "do anything to help us," he would.[67]

Hale framed his support for this particular incarnation of black education as a way for northerners to leave southern labor issues in the hands of southerners. "Help the negro to help himself in an industrial way," he wrote in 1895 after reading about Booker T. Washington's Atlanta Exposition speech, "and it seems to me the whole negro problem is settled." Washington had claimed southern whites as African Americans' best friends. Hale agreed. Look at the way southern whites fed and cared for former slaves too old to work, he argued: "They are not turned off to the poorhouse, or allowed to shift for themselves as are the laborers in many of our mills, factories or corporations."[68] Hale thus joined a chorus of northerners reassessing their opinion of southern whites in the 1890s. Whereas in the 1860s many northerners thought of themselves as the guardians of the freed people's destiny, a quarter-century later they were more pessimistic about the ability of blacks to "progress" and more willing to pay homage to the expertise of white southerners in handling "their" negroes. Such sentiment was part of a pervasive culture of what the historian Nina Silber calls the "whitewashed road to reunion."[69]

Hale's professed willingness to leave "the negro" in southern hands was disingenuous: he wrote as an outside observer when he was very much an interested party. For what Hale and other northerners discovered is that a political system that kept a large portion of the population in poverty was just fine for business. Sloughing off the nobler goals of Reconstruction was not just a matter of reform fatigue, then. It was a sly move toward maximizing returns on investment by keeping the cost of southern labor low. Northern philanthropy thus served the interests of northern investment, making a cheap workforce better without making it more expensive. As the historian James Anderson argues, northerners pushed for industrial education, not in deference to southern prejudice, but in accord with their own vision for the South's modernization.[70] They could not afford a more expensive or more politically empowered labor force.

Hale was not the only northerner attracted to this southern way of life, growing a high-value, sophisticated crop with the labor of people who were, because of their skin color and the southern political system, readily available. His Georgia orchard did well in 1895, and Hale continued to pursue expansion: a "fine large new hotel building" for his "leading workers," a "complete system of water works," and a spur track, courtesy of the Central of Georgia Railroad, which ran two miles from the trunk line, through the middle of Hale's orchard, and right up to his packing shed.[71] To celebrate these advances, and promote the quality of his product, he invited a number of railroad men, commission merchants, jobbers, and retailers for a tour of his operation. Always the consummate publicist, Hale also took along some journalists, including the president of New York City's *Fruit Trade Journal* and a representative from the Harrisburg, Pennsylvania, *Horticultural Catalogue*. These fruiterati set out by steamer for Savannah, Georgia, where they were met by representatives of the Central of Georgia Railroad and escorted to Macon by special train. In Macon, several other railroad executives coupled their own private cars to the train, and they went south toward Fort Valley and the new spur track, thousands of trees heavy with ripening fruit stretching out on either side. At the packing shed the group inspected the "scores of bright young men and women" who sorted and packed the fruit, the refrigerator cars, all of this "tending toward perfection."[72] Hale intended to make believers of the whole lot, and he apparently did. The Yankees who joined him in his orchard were "fully convinced that the half has never been told of Georgia," according to the *Macon Telegraph*. The "star of empire," they said, appeared to be "steadily moving southward."[73]

These northerners were, no doubt, impressed with the cheapness of the South's resources and labor and Hale's methodical use of such bounty, but they also professed admiration for southern culture and tradition. After visiting Hale, they rode down to Samuel Rumph's Willow Lake estate in Marshallville, where Rumph "extended them a cordial welcome" to his home. There on the "broad veranda" before the "spacious hallway," amid the botanical curiosities of Rumph's pleasure grounds ("None of them had ever seen a pomegranate and few of them a magnolia tree"), Rumph entertained in grand style. Willow Lake "fulfilled the expectations of the New Englanders of an ideal Southern home." Nature itself seemed hospitable: midway through their half-day visit, a mockingbird suddenly burst into "his most melodious roundelay," and the chatter quieted so the visitors could hear him as "a dozen or more sweet warblers joined in the chorus." It was as if the birds knew these well-heeled New Englanders had never heard such songs "in the freedom of their [the birds'] native home." Little wonder that "the party was wont to linger" at Willow Lake. Here was a prosperity founded on steel-ribbed connections to bustling northern cities and filthy northern lucre, yet Rumph's home was an idyllic country retreat. In an age of neurasthenia and hay fever and vague guilt about speculation and graft as a source of prosperity, southern horticulture must indeed have seemed an ideal business.[74]

And among these hallmarks of southern tradition – verandas, mockingbirds, magnolias – was, of course, the tradition of desperate labor. One night, Hale gathered his group of northerners at the old plantation's big house. And then Hale's description took on the air of a colonial expedition narrative:

> When the shades of the soft Southern night had fallen the visitors gathered upon the broad veranda of the farm home, enjoyed the plantation songs and "breakdown jigs" of the negro laborers, who had flocked in to do honor to our visitors. Later, when out among the fruit trees we sought our sleeping cars for a little rest, we were lulled to sleep by the quaint, low and sweet singing of the darkies, way off at some cabins, where they had congregated to talk over the events of the evening and wonder "what Marse Hale dun gwine to do next!"[75]

Here, then, was Hale's "New South": the representatives of northern business, ambling through the peach trees to their private cars, resting on railroad tracks that were the very sinews of national integration. The Old South aristocrat with his verandas and great fields, now resurrected as a Yankee entrepreneur. The "darkies" performing the old plantation melodies and jigging to the expectations of those northern authenticity hounds and then lulling them to sleep with their charming wonderment, their "sweet voices" signifying their willing submission to the new regime.

These idyllic scenes depended, at least indirectly, on distinctly unidyllic facts. Less than three years later and less than one hundred miles away, a crowd of approximately two thousand white middle Georgians – many of whom had traveled from Atlanta on special trains – participated in the lynching of an African American laborer named Sam Hose, who was accused of, but not tried for, murder and rape. They cut off his ears, sliced his body, doused him with oil, set him aflame, and then picked his bones, pieces of his liver, slices of his heart from the ashes as souvenirs. And Hose's was just one of the more gruesome of 27 documented lynchings that occurred in Georgia in 1899 – the state's most violent year in terms of mob violence – just one of the 458 lynchings in Georgia between 1880 and 1930, just one of the roughly 3,000 lynchings across the American South during the same period. The vast majority of victims were black men. And the perpetrators were frequently upstanding citizens; crowds often included women and children. The man who poured oil on Hose was a northerner who said he was "ready to do his part."[76] As Grace Hale argues, "Spectacle lynchings brutally conjured a collective, all-powerful whiteness even as they made the color line seem modern, civilized, and sane."[77] Whether or not Billie Holliday was thinking of peaches when she sang Abel Meeropol's haunting meditation on lynching, "Strange Fruit," some four decades later, the song offered a reminder that the color line that made the commercial peach possible was policed by violence of the most heinous kind. "Pastoral scene of the gallant South, / the bulging eyes and the twisted mouth, / scent of magnolia, sweet and fresh, / and the sudden smell of burning flesh." A "strange and bitter crop" indeed.[78]

IV

In the early twentieth century, Hale imported the labor management methods he learned in the South to his Connecticut operation. In 1906, Hale took a reporter from the *Hartford Courant* on a tour of his Glastonbury orchards, where they encountered dozens of Italians picking fruit, directed by Italian foremen. "These Italians are natural fruit lovers," Hale explained glibly. "They don't have to be taught how to handle the peaches." He had 150 working in his orchards at the season's height, he said, many of them waiters from fine New York City restaurants – Delmonico's, Sherry's, the Waldorf – who according to Hale saw their work in his Glastonbury peach orchards as a country vacation. They enjoyed the "healthy exercise" and the fruit-heavy diet. "They love to be near the fruit," Hale maintained, pointing to what he called the "Waldorf-Castoria," a "long, low shack" where the workers slept, as if he were running a summer camp for city kids.[79] As evidence of their happiness, the correspondent reported that every Italian they met "spoke to 'de boss' with great politeness." Hale, for his part, relished his role as lord of the manor. "Yes," he said, "I never employ any but Italians... They give a lot of satisfaction."[80]

In 1911, after a disastrous experience with New York City workers who had struck for higher wages under the purported influence of a "mobster," Hale ordered a steamship of sixty "young negroes" from his Georgia plantation, along with the Georgia plantation manager, John Baird, and the crew's elderly black foreman, Mr. Peevey. Many of them were college students earning money during their summer vacation. According to Joey Pero, the son of Hale's Italian foreman, Peevey ruled "those black boys with an iron hand, but still he was very kind to them and they loved him."[81] This time, no mobsters reminded the workers of their paltry pay and low treatment. Instead, "the hills rang with the voices of those negroes singing spirituals all day." And Pero joined a long tradition of presumption about the disposition of African American labor in arguing that the songs "proved they were happy."[82]

The *Hartford Courant* concurred. "Hale's Darkies a Merry Crowd," the headline announced, beneath photographs of the workers "Enjoying Themselves during a Period of Rest" and "Keep[ing] Busy While They Work." The presence of black men in Glastonbury was quite the novelty. The men picked peaches with great speed and skill – far better than any help Hale could get locally, said John Baird. And they sang and gossiped throughout the workday. For their part, the workers claimed amazement at the hilly, rocky landscape – they were "lost in wonder," said the *Courant*. Some gathered bags of "mineral formations" as keepsakes. The "best thing" about Connecticut, said one of the workers, was the ability to "go right into the woods anywhere and find nice ice water to drink. That's mighty good to us." They visited the Connecticut Fair and marveled at the lights, dancing, and music – "'Jes' Hebben,'" said one, "'or at least de secon' Hebben.'" And, the *Courant* reported with relief, they gave "no sign of possessing hookworms." If they ever had, they left "these little animals" back in Georgia.

Hale felt fatherly and sentimental at the sight. He remembered many of these strong young men as "pickaninnies," children and grandchildren of the slaves who had loyally remained on the plantation after emancipation (see Figure 4.5). These old men and women were still living there in 1890 when Hale purchased the Georgia plantation. And now their descendants walked uphill and down through his Glastonbury orchards, deftly harvesting his late season peaches. The *Courant* reporter undoubtedly repeated Hale's own words when he surmised, "They are part of the family"[83] (see Figures 4.3 and 4.4).

Hale had learned how to harness the energy of a marginalized class, and how to justify their marginalization with their "joy" in the kind of work he wanted them to do. Italians just loved fruit. "Darkeys" were born to labor in the fields, and only needed some direction from an authoritarian figure like Hale. And yet the paths of the two workforces

NOON HOUR AT STABLE YARD
HALE GA. ORCHARD CO.
FORT VALLEY, GA., JULY, 1898

FIGURE 4.3. "Bridal couples, both black and white; ministers, lawyers, editors, artists, doctors; magazine writers, students, school teachers and college professors; bright tramps who have been the world over; young people from the best plantation homes of the South; 'Georgia crackers' and blacks of all degrees, make up the forces of the farm in fruit season." Caption from J.H. Hale, "Peaches: A National Product," *World's Work* 4.2 (June 1902), 2176.
Source: Historical Photo Album. Courtesy Peach County Historical Society, Fort Valley, Georgia.

diverged sharply. The Italians – many of them at least – moved up. Today Hale's hometown of Glastonbury is an oasis in the midst of metropolitan sprawl, full of pruned and trellised fruit farms that lure New Englanders and New Yorkers in late summer to pick and purchase fresh cherries, blueberries, raspberries, apples, plums, apricots, peaches. This is an iconic New England landscape, but there is hardly a Yankee name among the orchards. Berruti, Botticello, Bussa, Carini, Dondero, Draghi, Preli: Glastonbury is a little Italy in central Connecticut. In the South, despite the efforts of black extension agents, institutions like FVHIS, and the year-after-year labor of sharecroppers, there was not much hope for moving up in agriculture.

After a long illness, John Howard Hale died in 1919, with his family about him. Hale Georgia Orchards passed to John Baird, its manager all these years, who, despite his New Jersey heritage, had adopted the planter's aristocratic mien.[84] Hale's homage to the home notwithstanding, his own home was in pieces. For years, he had carried on a not-so-secret

FIGURE 4.4. "Meals are furnished at cost, which is about twelve cents, for an abundance of wholesome food in variety ... and yet a majority of white people always prefer to bring their own cooks and provisions from home and rig up a little camp, while others form clubs, buy their provisions from the commissary on the place, and hire some old aunty to cook for them at her cabin at twenty-five cents a week for each person and 'de chillen take the leavins.'" Caption from J. H. Hale, "Peaches: A National Product," *World's Work* 4.2 (June 1902), 2163–2178.
Source: J. H. Hale Lantern Slide Collection. Courtesy of Historical Society of Glastonbury, Glastonbury, CT.

affair with his secretary, fathering a child with her, and at his death he left one of his Connecticut fruit farms to her. The family was outraged, and there was a messy court battle for control of the property. His children never did much with the fruit business – Stancliff died young, while Moseley had a reputation for fast living that led him away from the farm.[85]

Meanwhile, Hale's legacy was already fading from view. In 1903, an article in the *Fruit Trade Journal* praised the "Emancipation of the South," where "Cotton Is Not King." It was a striking interpretation of "emancipation," one that repurposed the word to fit the spirit of the times: North and South together in the cause of Progress, blacks out of the picture altogether. It was "the peach which emancipated the Georgia farmer," declared the article, for it "won him from cotton and poverty to fruit

FIGURE 4.5. "Mr. Hale explained that … some of their parents were slaves on the place before the Civil War … and many of the younger boys he remembered as little pickaninnies. They are part of the family." Caption from "Hale's Darkies a Merry Crowd," *Hartford Courant* (September 6, 1913), 11.
Source: J. H. Hale Lantern Slide Collection. Courtesy of Historical Society of Glastonbury, Glastonbury, CT.

and vegetables and prosperity." Then the article excerpted an essay by a railway agent, titled "The South at the Dawn of the Twentieth Century":

A new spirit has come over the dreams of the Georgia planter. Low prices in cotton year after year drove him to diversify. The large plantation was divided up into small farms, and these farms were closely and carefully cultivated. The growing order was reversed. Instead of great combinations and large systems, as followed in industrial lines, the farmer drew in his limits and commenced to build up his orchards, lay out his truck gardens and improve his wheat field. Fruit farms sprang up in beautiful profusion, and acres were planted with new and prolific varieties of peaches, pears, plums and strawberries, while vineyards developed as if upon the slopes of Italy or the sunny hills of France. From Atlanta to Fort Valley and far below, the fruit belt has been extended, and one hears very little about King Cotton, but a great deal about the all-conquering Elberta.[86]

The passive voice in the first part of the paragraph, intentional or not, is telling: *was divided up ... were closely and carefully cultivated ... was reversed ... were planted.* The author gave the impression that southerners had looked about them and begun to diversify of their own accord, with no need for northern capital or immigration. *Fruit farms sprang up in beautiful profusion.* The article was typical of southern claims on the Georgia peach, as folks like Hale faded into the background and folks like Rumph emerged as the face of the industry that had become the face of the South. The story of J. H. Hale's southern peach empire suggests otherwise. The peach industry depended on northerners to become what it was.

And wealthier northerners and southerners alike depended on black southerners to plant, prune, and pick their trees, just as they did to clean their floors, pick their cotton, nurse their children, drive their carriages. To adapt Booker T. Washington's famous formulation, whites had "cast down their bucket where they were" – but with the exception of people like Hale, rarely acknowledged the fact. Instead, they went on pretending that peach orchards had indeed sprung up out of the ground, as if called into being by the pronouncements of New South partisans.

More than a decade after Hale's death, *Fortune Magazine* sent a reporter down to Fort Valley. Predictably perhaps, the title claimed that "the peach ... has the complexion of Georgia." But the text was more astute. Observing that the southern peach grower was, unlike his California "industrialist" counterparts, a "planter," with its "chief servant ... still that uncertain mechanism, the Afro-American," the reporter then encapsulated and undermined the myth of the Georgia peach in a single sentence:

Under the trees in peach season burr-headed Negro pickers pass, and a day later the Georgia peach lands in New York at the Peach Dock, wearing just the complexion that every girl in Macon [Georgia] envies.[87]

And this formulation became the twentieth-century story of the Georgia peach: the peach as a white crop, with the complexion that Macon's *white* girls may have admired, but not southern black girls. Meanwhile, those southern black girls – and their mothers and fathers and sisters and brothers – remained partially hidden in the foliage, part of the scenery, until in the name of economic progress and civic equality they would pick no more.

5

Rot and Glut

In the early twentieth century, thanks to the changes set in motion by Berckmans, Rumph, and Hale, Georgia peach growing expanded rapidly. Northerners bought up land; southern growers made deals with railroads and commission merchants; urban consumers learned the Georgia peach by name; rural African Americans saw their options foreclosed and started moving away from the fields. John Howard Hale's own farm doubled in size from his original thousand-acre purchase. By 1904, the vastness of the place reduced a *Southern Cultivator* correspondent to a breathless series of numbers: "2160 acres, 350,000 trees, 43 miles of driveways, 250 cars shipped yearly, 800 employees encamped on the place."[1] And Hale-Georgia was not the only new orchard in middle Georgia. The Dayton, Ohio, businessmen N. H. Albaugh and F. W. Withoft each had 75,000 trees in Fort Valley; the Ohio Fruit Land Company had about 100,000; the Tivola Fruit Company had 80,000 and the Oak Ridge Orchard Company 40,000 trees; and four other northern-owned stock companies held from 10,000 to 30,000 trees each.[2] All of these individual farms added up to a major boom in peach planting. There were 2.8 million trees in the state in 1889, 7.7 million in 1899, and nearly 15 million by 1924 (see Table 5.1). And the expansion spread beyond middle Georgia, for as the lands around Fort Valley went up in price, northerners found other centers, especially around Rome in northwest Georgia and Habersham County in the northeast.[3] (See the expansion maps in Figures 7.1, 7.2, and 7.3.)

This precipitous rise was in part due to simple arithmetic. Georgia peaches could be extremely profitable, especially when compared with cotton. As Table 5.2 suggests, while middle Georgia cotton hovered

TABLE 5.1. *Peach acreage and farms in Georgia, 1890–1925*

Year	Peach acreage	Number of farms reporting peaches	Number of farms	Percentage of farms reporting peaches (%)
1890	27,875	n/a	171,071	n/a
1900	76,686	22,708	224,691	10.10
1910	106,090	33,278	291,027	11.40
1920	120,470	n/a	310,732	n/a
1925	149,690	92,656	249,095	37.20

Source: Compiled from U.S. Census Bureau, *Census of Agriculture*, 1890, 1900, 1910, 1920, 1925.

TABLE 5.2. *Potential value of peaches and cotton in middle Georgia,*
1909–1929

Year	Cotton			Peaches		
	Price/lb. (U.S.)	Production, lb.	Value/acre	Price/bu	Production, bu	Value/acre
1909	$ 0.139	47,343,000	$26.66	n/a	826,594	n/a
1919	$ 0.356	19,904,000	$36.44	$ 2.500	3,497,906	$156.33
1924	$ 0.226	20,016,000	$37.52	$ 1.010	4,456,427	$61.47
1929	$ 0.164	20,001,000	$24.36	$ 1.150	1,073,121	$45.72

Note: Middle Georgia here includes Bibb, Crawford, Houston, Jones, Macon, Peach, and Taylor counties. To calculate the value per acre for middle Georgia cotton, I multiplied the average yield per acre (145 pounds) by the average price per pound for that year. To calculate the value per acre for peaches, I multiplied middle Georgia production (in bushels) by average price per bushel in that year to yield a value of total production. I then divided that value of total production by the total middle Georgia peach acreage to get the value per acre. In 1919, for example, the value of total production was $8,744,765, for 55,938 acres (calculated at 100 trees per acre, since censuses reported number of trees instead of acreage). Because of obvious variations from farm to farm and year to year, these numbers are suggestive rather than determinative.
Sources: USDA *Yearbook of Agriculture*, 1919, 1923, 1930; U.S. Census Bureau, *Census of Agriculture*, 1920, 1925, 1930.

between $25 and $40 per acre in the early twentieth century, peaches could earn over $150 per acre.[4] Peaches cost much more than cotton to produce – especially since the grower had to consider the three or four years required for an orchard to begin production – but Fort Valley, at just $118.51 per acre (at least in 1926), had the lowest peach production costs in the country.[5] The returns on peaches in good years, moreover, were *much* higher than on cotton, where the average price beat out the average cost by just 0.6 cent per pound.[6] Increasingly, those who had the financial flexibility to do so added some peach trees to their cotton lands.

The rapid expansion of the peach industry was critical in the making of the peach myth, as we'll see in Chapter 6, but it also created a set of challenges. What growers called the "labor problem" would loom largest as the century wore on, but initially it was pests and diseases, and then markets, that presented the greatest challenges to Georgia peach growers. More *Prunus persica* trees – mostly Elbertas – attracted more pests and succumbed to them in more devastating fashion; more peaches at urban markets, harvested and shipped on a schedule that varied dramatically from year to year, meant more gluts and lower prices.

Not surprisingly, peach growers sought to control both environmental and economic forms of chaos, at first relying on their own capital and then seeking the financial and investigative support of state and federal agencies. But the case of the peach industry offers an interesting twist on the biological hazards of monoculture and the agricultural cooperative movements, both of which are well-traveled territories in agricultural and environmental history.[7] As in other cases, the new peach monoculture made growers more vulnerable to pests and diseases. But fighting those pests and diseases, in the southern case, was *less* environmental than it might seem: keeping San Jose scale and plum curculio at bay was an effort to control labor as much as nature. Ordering the economic connections of the Georgia peach, meanwhile, was *more* environmental than it might seem: the extreme perishability of fresh fruit revealed marketplaces to be *places*, with difficult-to-control climatological and biological characteristics.

In the end, southern peach growers did learn to manage the risks that accompanied the volatile southern environment, the perishable peach, and the distant markets. But although rationality and expertise played important roles, it was simple attrition that ultimately permitted the continuation of the Georgia peach industry. Growing peaches for commercial markets was an immensely complicated business: choosing varieties, nurturing orchards to bearing age, controlling increasingly aggressive pests, protecting the harvested fruit from decay, negotiating with harvesters and packers and transporters and marketers of the fruit, and surviving seasons of nearly complete loss. After peaking in the mid-1920s, the planting of new orchards slowed, and the number of growers dwindled. The remnant would be those with decades of family experience and the political connections, capital, and skill to manage pests, tame market vicissitudes, and maintain a consistent source of cheap labor.

FIGURE 5.1. "Then comes the spraying, for we do all that science and practice can suggest to check the ravages of insects and fungous pests, to the end that every specimen of fruit may be the best and most beautiful of its kind." Caption from J. H. Hale, "Peaches: A National Product," *World's Work* 4.2 (June 1902), 2163–2178.
Source: J. H. Hale Lantern Slide Collection. Courtesy of Historical Society of Glastonbury, Glastonbury, CT.

II

Labor-intensive agriculture survived in the South much longer than in other places, with the exception perhaps of the fruit and vegetable lands of California. So it should not be surprising that labor control has often been central in fights against insect infestations. In the Mississippi Delta, for instance, powerful planters realized that the key to fighting the boll weevil lay not in eradicating the insect, nor in protecting their cotton fields from it. "Instead," the historian James Giesen writes, "winning this latest war against nature meant *controlling* the fight against the boll weevil" – in particular, keeping the labor force of tenant farmers intact.[8] The control of labor was also crucial in the pest invasions of the Georgia peach industry, but more because the methods of defense depended on what J. H. Hale would call worker "armies" (see Figures 5.1 and 5.2).

It took just a decade of rapid expansion for the peach orchards of Georgia to face their first pest crisis: the San Jose scale, which Georgia

FIGURE 5.2. "It was a great sight to see the work going on. Such an 'outfit' (darkey, club and trap)... They started off like an army, two to each tree, then at the word 'go' the start was made, quick whack, whack, whack, from tree to tree, down the long line to the end, then a gathering in of the harvest, a drink of water, a little rest, and then a fresh attack on the enemy. Whack, whack, whack!" Caption from J. H. Hale, "Farm Life and Work," *Hartford Courant* (June 13, 1896), 12.
Source: J. H. Hale Lantern Slide Collection. Courtesy of Historical Society of Glastonbury, Glastonbury, CT.

growers first noticed in 1895. Appearing in California orchards in the 1880s, apparently as a stowaway with some Asian nursery stock, the scale had reached eastern apple and pear orchards by the 1890s. A USDA entomologist gave it the Latin name *Quadraspidiotus perniciosus*, as it was the "most pernicious scale insect known in this country."[9] It seemed alien and monstrous, "too small to be seen with the naked eye," and hiding "beneath a waxlike coating." The female was a "wingless, legless, and eyeless insect, having a long whip-like sucker, or mouth, which once fastened never leaves the bark of the tree." The male, mouthless, flew about the orchard mating; a pair could produce four billion offspring in a single season. Limbs, trees, then orchards of tens of thousands of trees succumbed rapidly to "such a formidable pest."[10] With its capacity to level entire orchards in two or three years, San Jose scale inspired such fear that one entomologist believed the bug had induced more legislation than all other insect pests together.[11] This legislation included the Plant Quarantine Act of 1912, which paralleled the antiimmigration movement of the 1910s by severely restricting foreign imports and giving search and seizure powers to the USDA.[12]

Once U.S. entomologists accepted that San Jose scale would not be eradicated, they worked to establish chemical controls of the pest. Some treated the scale with whale oil emulsions or with a kerosene–water mixture. But whale oil proved to be ineffective, since the scale could rapidly repopulate if not entirely exterminated. Kerosene, on the other hand, interacted with southern atmospheric conditions in unpredictable ways and seemed to be particularly damaging to peach trees. The recommended treatment, therefore, was fumigation with hydrocyanic gas: covering an infested tree with a conical tent twelve feet tall and ten feet in diameter, homemade with eight-ounce duck canvas and hoops of gas pipe, and, in order to make it "as near air tight as possible," sewn with close seams and painted with coats of linseed oil and lampblack. After placing the tent over the tree with a forked pole, an earthenware vessel with water and sulfuric acid was placed inside, and then cyanide ladled in under the edge of the tent, and then dirt immediately kicked over the edges of the tent. A four-man team could handle twelve to twenty such tents, but only after training in handling these chemicals, which were "deadly poisonous."[13]

In view of these difficult methods of extermination, Prosper Berckmans and the members of the GSHS proposed a stronger nursery inspection law to the Georgia state legislature, one that would give the entomologist more enforcement power and offer stronger protections to growers. In 1898, as they were discussing this proposal, Hale interjected his own strong opinion. Not surprisingly, he had little problem with such a laborious and expensive treatment regimen. He encouraged the GSHS not to "go too far" in pressing for state involvement in fighting insects, urging them instead to continue with their "campaign of education." Then, in the cavalier manner typical of his addresses, Hale argued that "these scales and 'fungcusses' and other 'cusses'" were "grand blessings to horticulture." He continued:

It is believed by some that you have only to plant trees and vines and get rich ... and the angel of goodness has brought along scales and blessed them, and said if you don't take care of your trees, we will wipe you off the face of the earth; so don't be worried by these scales and "fungcusses." Mr. President, they are blessings, just as weeds and grass are blessings. Many a farmer would not work half so hard to get rid of grass if it did not injure his crop. He would sit right down and do nothing, and I repeat that these things are blessings in disguise.[14]

But Hale's optimistic belief in what we might call an "economy of scales" did not earn the enthusiastic applause to which he was accustomed. John Stubbs, a Dublin-based lawyer for the Central of Georgia Railroad, would not countenance such talk from the biggest grower in the state, and a northerner at that. Calling it "good talk for the men who are able with their thousands to combat these evils," he began with a firm declaration of his own vantage point – "I was born a Georgian and expect to live and die a Georgian, and the life of horticulture is no new thing with me" – and continued with a hymn to the small farmer. "It is the small grower of Georgia that we should look out for," he said. "Wherever you find prosperity in any country, you find it among the countries with small farmers." He reminded listeners that hydrocyanic gas fumigation was beyond the reach of many fruit growers. "Men who are engaged in fruit culture with large capital have no right to monopolize horticultural interests in this State," he complained. "It should be open and put in reach of the humblest citizen in the State of Georgia." Sadly, he reflected:

A little close thought on this subject for a few years has taught me that a different state of affairs exists now among the fruit growers of Georgia than existed when this Society was organized. I have discovered a great deal of selfishness among the members. A great many people think his neighbor is trying to get the better of him... I have now for the first time in my life learned that a pest was a blessing, that we must not have any legislation to protect us.

Then, pointing to California's strict plant quarantine laws as an example, Stubbs urged members to lobby their legislators aggressively. "Let us get rid of [the scale]," he insisted. "We can get them back if we want them."[15]

In time, the San Jose scale crisis passed, as a seasonal routine of California-style lime-sulfur washes curbed the insect's destructive powers. The battle with pests brought on by the rapid expansion of peach acreage, however, had only begun. The plum curculio was the next attacker, and again J. H. Hale placed himself (at least rhetorically) on the front lines. And again, a labor-intensive, expensive treatment regimen became the standard.

The plum curculio (*Contrachelus nenuphar*) was a brownish gray weevil – "not unlike the cotton boll weevil," one horticulturist noted in 1919 – which, like the boll weevil, attacked the fruiting part of the plant. The curculio had a cosmopolitan taste in fruit, eating freely of native Chickasaw plums and apples, as well as peaches. In the Southeast, as peach orchards multiplied and the long growing season allowed for multiple generations, the curculio quickly became the primary fruit-feeding (as opposed to leaf- or bark-feeding) pest of peaches. The adult weevils, with their piercing mouthparts, made round puncture wounds as they fed on the fruit. Worse, they laid eggs in the fruit, creating a crescent-shaped oviposition wound, and releasing "yellowish-white, legless larvae," which tunneled into the fruit toward the pit.[16] In the late nineteenth century, growers called curculios "Little Turks" for the crescent-shaped (and thus vaguely Muslim) wounds they left in the fruit. High curculio populations meant heavy green fruit drop, followed by an unmarketable crop. "Wormy fruit" usually meant curculio-infested.

The first treatment for curculio was biological: swine. In the nineteenth century, pigs cleaned orchards of fallen fruit, consuming with the "drops" the curculio larvae and pupae hidden inside – a process that did not eliminate the curculio, but at least kept down the population of the next generation. "Turning hogs into the orchard is an economical way" of keeping the curculio at bay, Samuel Hape declared to the 1888 meeting of the GSHS.[17] Hogs were not practical on the great peach plantations of the 1890s, however, and while some growers tried lime-sulfur sprays, they were not effective enough to commend widespread adoption. In the 1890s, the only effective treatment for curculio was picking off the insects by hand. In 1896, when the Cornell horticulturist Liberty Hyde Bailey visited the GSHS at their annual meeting in Griffin, he recommended this method. "You say it is a good deal of work and expense," Bailey said. "I have yet to find a single insect who will come to you and ask to be killed." And curculios demanded not only the energetic shrewdness of the hunter but also the fanatical hygiene of the sanitation engineer: "You must pay attention to drainage, cultivation, and clean orchards."[18] Garland Ryals of Savannah replied emphatically – as if to make up for the disastrous impact of the curculio that year – that they were "going to fight these bugs to the finish." The Georgia "cracker holds his own in Wall street," he assured Bailey.[19]

Hale's approach to the curculio again surpassed the best efforts of his southern counterparts. He had noticed "some few" of the insects in 1895, and in consultation with his superintendent determined to "fight in the only sure way known at present," by manually destroying the insects. Workers placed two semicircles of sheeting around the base of the tree, like an inverted umbrella, and then "jarred" the tree with rubber padded clubs. The startled weevils played dead, fell into the sheeting, and the workers gathered the "critters" into buckets, which were in turn dumped into barrels at the end of the rows. A wagon hauled barrels to the "crematory," where they were boiled along with all infested fruit. It was a slow and expensive process, and Hale claimed to have endured the ridicule of other growers who thought it could not be done in an orchard of 100,000 trees. Undaunted, Hale set his "'bugologist' Bryan and his gang of 'white winged darkey angels'" to the task in late April, and this small "army" of forty to fifty people worked daily for seven straight weeks "at no small cost." But Hale thought it paid off: in neighboring orchards that year, curculios destroyed from 60 to 90 percent of the fruit.[20] In this case, rather than relying on the chemical expertise that thwarted San Jose scale, Hale used a small battalion of his vast army of workers (see Figure 5.2).

As these cases attest, the magnitude of the northerners' peach operations had begun to change the environmental dynamics of middle Georgia. The altered conditions created by the larger growers also favored them, for Hale and other big growers had the capital and the labor to combat the pest insurgency. In the end, though, Hale and other northerners attracted the attention and funding of the USDA and other state and federal agencies. Prosper Berckmans, for all his horticultural eminence, was unable to convince the Georgia state legislature to provide much in the way of funding for horticultural education, entomological investigations, or market research. But Hale, with his experience at the Census Bureau, with his access to the ears of folks like G. H. Powell, put Georgia peach orchards on the map. In 1921, the USDA established a peach research laboratory in Fort Valley to investigate plum curculio and oriental peach moth, among other pests.

John Stubbs's charges at the 1898 GSHS meeting, then, rang true: pests allowed growers with the capital to adopt the latest extermination technology and pick off the pests – and pick off the smaller producers. For larger growers especially, the best production years often produced little profit, while late frosts or insect infestations could yield handsome returns for those who still had some peaches on the market. Stubbs's thinly veiled sectionalism – blaming J. H. Hale and other northerners for the dissension among Georgia peach growers – may have been self-serving, but his analysis of horticultural dissension was prescient. Whether or not the growers were northern or southern, their rapidly increasing numbers made the competition among them that much more fierce. Slowly, the larger growers realized that if the smaller growers were not eliminated by the difficulties of pest control, they would need to be put under control at the marketplace. And so they started a cooperative.

III

For the first twenty years of Georgia's commercial peach industry, Georgia growers faced almost no competition in the eastern markets, at least early in the season. Georgia peaches had been celebrated and amply rewarded in northern markets; demand seemed automatic. Consequently, growers and their organizations had focused on production and transportation as their primary concerns (see Figures 5.3, 5.4, and 5.5). They were growers and shippers, not marketers, and market advice was simple and straightforward: send high-quality, unblemished fruit, and pick a reliable, honest merchant to sell your fruit. It was not until 1908 that growers understood the market for their fruit as a set of market*places* – locations with physical limitations. That season transported Georgia growers into the markets, especially the largest market in New York City, in a way that previous seasons had not, forcing them to peer into the places where their fruit changed hands.

The 1908 season, in other words, acquainted peach growers with what consumers, government agents, farmers, and muckrakers called "the problem of markets." Why were farmers getting such low returns? Why were housewives paying such high prices? What happened to food during transit? Underlying all these concerns were two fundamental convictions: first, that misdistribution and waste, not underproduction, were to blame; and second, that professionally-trained experts could analyze and fix those supply-chain inefficiencies and make sanitary, affordable food readily available to the entire population. In this sense, the effort to address the market problem was another manifestation of the progressive movement at high tide: the acknowledgment of inequality, hunger, and poverty as social ills, which with proper attention by properly trained physicians could be healed.[21]

For peach growers, the market problem began as a result of all that tree planting in the 1890s and 1900s: 1908 was their biggest production year yet. In April the *Constitution* cheerily predicted that the state's seven million trees, producing a crate each, at fifty cents a crate above expenses, would yield fourteen thousand carloads – nearly three times as much as the state had ever produced – and a collective profit of $3.5 million.[22] It was indeed a record crop, but it was a financial disaster. More than half of Georgia's peaches typically went to New York and Philadelphia, and these markets were simply overwhelmed. In about two weeks in late June and early July, New York City absorbed nearly 700 carloads of Georgia peaches, not to mention fruit from North Carolina, Virginia,

FIGURE 5.3. "White labor is used entirely in the packing house, and at two long tables running the full length of the great building stand the men and women who, under careful instruction, take the fruit from the field baskets and sort it into three sizes, placing in canvas trays in front of them ... Every hour through the day the tickets are taken to the office, and a record made of all picking, sorting and packing, so that at all times the superintendent and myself can know just how things are moving, and what each individual is doing." Caption from J.H. Hale, "Peaches: A National Product," *World's Work* 4.2 (June 1902), 2177.

Source: J.H. Hale Collection. Courtesy of Historical Society of Glastonbury, Glastonbury, CT.

FIGURE 5.4. "As soon as covers are nailed on the crates, they are rushed into the refrigerator car waiting alongside, and the five hundred and sixty or more crates that go in a car are so spaced that there is a circulation of cold air about each one at all times in transit." Caption from J.H. Hale, "Peaches: A National Product," *World's Work* 4.2 (June 1902), 2177.

Source: Historical Photo Album. Courtesy Peach County Historical Society, Fort Valley, Georgia.

Icing Cars, at Griffin, on the line of the Central of Georgia Railway.

FIGURE 5.5. "These cars are 'iced up' twelve to twenty-four hours before loading begins. The warm fruit starts the ice to melting fast, and in a few hours, when the fruit is cooled, from two to three more tons of ice are required to fill the bunkers. In the fifty hours running time to New York, the cars are re-iced three times."
Source: Great Fruit Sections of the South: Views along the Lines of the Central of Georgia Railway (Savannah, GA: Central of Georgia Railway, 1898).

and Arkansas.[23] More than 300 cars were unloaded in Manhattan in the course of two days. About 150 of those sold at transportation cost; the New York board of health condemned the rest as unsafe for consumption and dumped them into the bay.[24] Fifteen million once-lovely Georgia peaches bobbed in the dirty water of the Hudson River.[25] This image appeared several times in stories about the 1908 season, and it must have pained Georgia growers to imagine it. It was not just the condemned fruit – which only affected a few growers – but also the thoroughly mediocre prices that yielded a harvest of "depression" among growers, especially smaller ones.[26]

The larger growers, meanwhile, had been waiting for just such a season to demonstrate the necessity of organization. In September 1908, some two hundred growers gathered to organize the "Georgia Fruit Exchange." The two-day convention had the atmosphere of a religious revival. It featured a confession of their sins of disorganization: "The growers all told of the hardships undergone during the season just closed, by glutting the market." It provided a forum for their profession of their faith in the new organization: "They admitted that the exchange was the only solution of the problem."[27] And it produced a leadership committee of twenty-one major growers, who were sent out like evangelists to "canvass the state" for subscribers. This committee met in late September to plan and, as the crisp days of October and November signaled the coming winter and the need to provide for the coming season, rode the rails to meet with growers at depots and drum up pledges. By early November the committee claimed to have wrapped up 40 percent of the coming year's peach crop, and sent a packet – containing a letter, a leaflet describing the organization, and a pledge card with a stamped envelope – to known peach growers who had not yet signed up.[28]

The Georgia Fruit Exchange sought to make a business of the peach movement. Just as agricultural scientists had preached businesslike methods on the productive end of farming – record keeping, precision spraying, labor management – promoters of cooperatives held up business as the model for agricultural marketing as well.[29] Cooperative marketing, the American Farm Bureau representative Herman Steen would later write, replaced "dumping" with "merchandizing."[30] As an exchange president said in 1912, "individuals might have hesitated in taking advantage of a railroad's error, but the Georgia Fruit Exchange is a corporation, just as soulless as any railroad corporation."[31] It could fight hand to hand with railroads and other hard-hearted businesses; it had no soul to lose.

Actually, as its charter admitted, the GFE was more corporation than cooperative. "The object and purpose ... is pecuniary gain and profit to shareholders."[32] Members of the exchange spoke the language of cooperation – the exchange did "not exist for profit, but for service," a president claimed in 1916 – but occasionally a spokesperson made a revealing slip. After its first, successful season, the directors rather sheepishly agreed to reduce their cut of sales from 10 percent to 8 percent. They aimed, they said, "to make the organization more of a cooperative and less of a dividend-paying proposition."[33] In 1917, as if the exchange's success had rendered discretion unnecessary, a gushing editorial acknowledged, "While not essentially a mutual concern, there are so many special clauses in its contract in favor of the grower that it is virtually co-operative."[34]

From the 1840s – when some hand loom weavers in Rochdale, England, formed the first employee-owned modern cooperative – through the 1930s, cooperation was, as the historian Daniel Rodgers writes, "corporate capitalism's twin, its shadow, its progressive alternative."[35] As the phrase "virtually cooperative" suggests, the Georgia Fruit Exchange, like the cooperative movement at large, nodded simultaneously to the democratic producerist model of Rochdale and the no-responsibility-but-profit model of the modern corporation.[36] The former held to four tenets: at-cost services, democratic control, limited dividends, and patron owner-ship, thus converting "the private corporation into a public, nonprofit collective."[37] The latter inspired what became known as California-style cooperatives, most notably the California Fruit Growers' Exchange (Sunkist), which were often stock corporations that made no secret of their ambitions to monopolize crop sales. Proponents of California-style cooperation claimed that the methods of modern business – especially monopoly control – were the only way for farmers to maintain their inde-pendence in a market system that was stacked against them. Although the rhetoric of barn raising stayed with the movement, the means and methods rapidly shed whatever utopianism they originally had.[38]

Still, the Georgia peach cooperative movement had rather modest ambitions at first. Unlike the CFGE, which enforced standardization at the packinghouse and pooled fruit from all affiliated growers under the Sunkist brand, the GFE focused its efforts on distribution and sales. A grower who signed up with the GFE consigned his fruit directly to the exchange, which then shipped the fruit to the Potomac or Cincinnati yards and then reassigned it to whichever market seemed likely to have the best price at that moment. Once sold, the balance was returned to the individual grower, less the commission, which was split between the commission merchant and the exchange. If a commission house was not among those selected but still wanted to sell Georgia peaches, it had to purchase them "foot-on-board" (f.o.b.) directly from a Georgia grower, who then paid a 5 percent commission to the exchange for these f.o.b. sales. At the end of the season, the exchange paid dividends to its shareholders, put some money in reserve, and gave out rebates calibrated to the amount each grower shipped for the season.[39]

To keep up with all these calculations during the season, the Atlanta office was a busy hive. On a floor of the Atlanta, Birmingham, and Atlantic Building, the "transportation room" featured a large blackboard that somehow managed to contain information on all of the major mar-ket centers and amounts of fruit at shipping points, in transit, and in mar-kets. Too bad no photograph survives of the blackboard in the exchange's Atlanta transportation room. In a way, since the organization claimed information as its raison d'être, the blackboard *was* the exchange. Other organizations had emphasized fraud protection, by litigating with rail-roads and merchants, or keeping members in line with fines or even physical intimidation. But "the big, the distinctive thing" about the GFE was its "broad and intelligent scheme for collecting and classifying the information necessary to a sound and shrewd allotment of the crop" on a daily basis, even "when the rush of the shipping season is greatest." Before the first shipping season, Ian Fleming's envoys were already gathering data from every actual and potential market, in a "great statistical campaign" designed to provide just the right kind of knowledge for decision making in the "busiest moment of the actual crop-moving season." The information would keep flowing in during the season, and these "special reports from all the principal markets" would give the management "a daily bird's-eye view of the market situation the whole country over."⁴⁰ Here is a snapshot of how the process worked.

One of the office's many telephones rings. A grower from Fort Valley has a carload ready to ship; where should he send them? They look at the great blackboard in the transportation room. Supplies are low in Boston. Bill your car to the Potomac yards. The grower agrees, gives the operator the number of the car, which is dutifully entered on the blackboard. At each re-icing point – Atlanta, Charlotte, and Potomac yards – the car is inspected by a GFE representative, and the information goes up on the blackboard. Once the car reaches Potomac, the GFE staff reconsiders its destination on the basis of reports from its fifty market men, who inspect shipments and report on conditions – young men like W. H. Beckham, professor at the high school in Dallas, Georgia.⁴¹ That night, all this information collated, the GFE staff issues instructions to the railroad men at Potomac yards, using the telephone line that the GFE leases by the hour for this purpose. Fruit moves toward New York, Boston, Philadelphia, Newark, Providence, or Pittsburgh, in the wee hours of the morning, in order to be on time for market hour in the various cities.⁴²

In 1909, the plan worked beautifully: about 60 percent of the state's acreage shipped through GFE. Happily for the exchange, the crop was short and of rather poor quality, so they were able to distribute it easily. About 40 percent of the crop still went to New York, but for the first time, Georgia peaches went directly to smaller markets identified by the GFE, places such as Schenectady (six cars), Youngstown (one car), and Milwaukee (two cars). At the same time, track and orchard sales were on the rise. Fleming reported f.o.b. sales as early as mid-May, which indicated to him that money would be "in the hands of the growers before it leaves the shipping station." It appeared that the GFE's strategy of limiting consignments to only a few commission houses was having the desired effect: commission houses were "alarmed as to their source of supply" and were "flocking to Georgia" to buy up fruit on the track.⁴³ In one season, Georgia peach growers went from almost no track sales to nearly half: 1,012 cars of a crop of 2,062.[44] GFE-affiliated growers cleared $11,000 on the season.[45] Observers gleefully pointed out that the 1909 crop earned about as much ($1.5 million) as the 1908 crop, even though it was only one-third the size.[46]

Exchange advocates were ecstatic. They were putting the peach industry on an "established paying basis," the *Constitution* said. No more gambling, no more up-and-down speculation, just reliable returns year after year.[47] The muckraking journalist Forrest Crissey chose the GFE as an example of what he called "Cooperation Close to the Soil" – the solution to the problem of the corrupt commission merchants he had skewered in an earlier piece, "Robbing the Hand That Feeds." Finally, Crissey wrote, farmers were acknowledging their need to "get together and stand together!"[48]

But the GFE leadership knew that the participation of smaller growers was essential to the survival of the exchange, and the 1909 season closed with an ominous statistic: 30 to 40 percent of growers chose not to affiliate. The GFE director Ian Fleming could not understand the men who held back on such a progressive organization. They appeared to be "intelligent" and "broad-minded men," and they clearly benefited from the exchange's market research. But they refused to commit their crop or pay the fees.[49] "Such things might be business in this money-mad world," the *Southern Ruralist* scolded, "but the man who will take advantage of the good markets made by his neighbors ... and not help them in their organized effort is not to be considered the best citizen in the community."[50]

Underneath this good-neighbor rhetoric, of course, was large growers' desire for a predictable market. Writing fifteen years later, the cooperative advocate Herman Steen confirmed this analysis. "The big growers of Elberta peaches in Georgia once believed that they were big enough to develop their markets and hold them," Steen wrote. But the "grief encountered [in 1908] demonstrated that the volume of fruit from small growers was sufficient to smash the big growers' markets, and that disorganization would continue as long as Georgia peaches were dumped on a few markets."[51] There were more than four thousand growers in the state, but only a few hundred went to the initial meeting, and only six hundred joined the exchange in 1908.[52] These included Judge George C. Gober of Marietta, known as the "largest peach grower" in the world;[53] H. C. Bagley, who owned 250,000 trees; W. H. Harris, president of First National Bank in Fort Valley with 78,000 trees; C. J. Hood of Commerce with 20,000; J. M. Hunt of Round Oak with 30,000 trees.[54] A. M. Kitchen was "one of the largest growers in the north Georgia peach belt."[55] And, of course, J. H. Hale had some 200,000 trees and Samuel Rumph around 150,000. Tellingly, Fleming claimed that he would not really want the entire crop of Georgia peaches; 75 percent would allow him to control the market but preclude the necessity of marketing the crop of "the undesirable element who do not keep up their orchards and are careless in their packinghouse methods, and will always remain a menace and drawback to the progressive growers."[56] Georgia peach growers' search for order was less a universal cry for reform than a persuasive campaign run by one coalition of interests.

IV

The Georgia Fruit Exchange's star continued to rise through the 1910s.[57] In his 1918 annual report, the exchange president, W. B. Hunter, gleefully proclaimed that the larger-than-ever 8,025-car crop, complicated that year by a government takeover of railroads and an ice shortage, had been "distributed without a hitch." In the GFE's annual report, Hunter boasted that the exchange had finished 1918 "with the greatest record of its history, and demonstrated beyond peradventure its existence is absolutely necessary to the welfare of the industry of the State.[58] Self-promotion aside, Hunter had reason to be pleased. The 1918 season was, like 1908, unprecedented in terms of production. But unlike in 1908, a wider distribution and higher rate of f.o.b. purchases had earned the growers a tidy profit. In 1908, Georgia peaches had only gone to 40 cities; in 1918 the GFE had arrangements with 254 cities, and shipped to 191 of those. In 1908, f.o.b. sales were almost unheard of; in 1918 merchants purchased 76 percent of the crop "on Georgia soil," and in Cincinnati – a city that had up to 1917 purchased Georgia fruit on consignment only – the f.o.b. figure was closer to 100 percent.[59] The GFE could plausibly claim some credit for these fine figures: they had shipped 82 percent of the crop, or 6,615 cars.[60]

In 1920, perhaps hoping to emulate Sunkist's dramatic success with California oranges, the GFE tried a few advertisements in major market newspapers. "Peaches that fairly drip with JUICE!" crowed one such ad in the *New York Times*. A housewife smiled blithely in her apron as she split a wet mess of a peach with her delicate hands. The peach obligingly poured a puddle of juice onto a plate – "and such delicious juice it is," the text continued. "The luscious, distinctive juicy flavor found only in GEORGIA PEACHES ... the best for eating, the best for canning." In smaller print, a recipe told how "to Can Peaches without Sugar."

But remember, the advertisement urged, "the season doesn't last very long – so be sure to get YOURS at once." Then it reminded the consumer that Georgia peaches were grown by the members of the Georgia Fruit Exchange and sold, in New York, by only three produce merchants.[61]

The 1920 advertising campaign, however, appears to have been a rearguard attempt to shore up the GFE's waning power. The 1919 season had not built on 1918's success. Instead, heavy rains produced a better crop of curculios and brown rot than of peaches, so even though f.o.b. sales were high, the fruit "did not carry," and buyers lost money – and confidence. Feeling burned, in 1920 buyers added clauses to the contracts that the fruit must make it to market intact, and a warm winter and wet spring yielded a "main crop so full of worms and brown rot that it could hardly get out of Georgia before it was unsalable."[62] In 1922, with f.o.b. purchases declining, the GFE tried auction sales in New York City, which forced commission houses to compete with one another in the moment and thus drove up prices. Commission houses protested in a 1923 open letter to the *Constitution*, expressing outrage at the way the auction was "depressing private sales prices and causing the growers heavy losses."[63]

The GFE also faced increasing internal dissension. As the 1923 season came to a close, the GFE director J. G. Carlisle admitted that "a stronger organization is necessary," one that could provide "more protection in the marketing of their product."[64] Growers gathered on August 30 in Macon, where they proceeded to dissolve the GFE and reconstitute it as the Georgia Peach Growers' Exchange (GPGE). The new organization was a true cooperative, organized according to the requirements of the 1922 Capper-Volstead Act, which granted limited antitrust exemption to groups of farmers who marketed their products together.[65] Like the California Fruit Growers' Exchange, the GPGE included only peach growers and had full control of sales and distribution. Observers praised the move as yet another "new era" in the history of peach growing. "The peach industry is being revolutionized," W. B. Hunter proclaimed with characteristic bombast. "From now on dates the freedom of the Georgia peach growers."[66] The organizers embarked again on an energetic membership drive, exerting "tremendous pressure" on the state's growers – and signed up only 60 percent of the crop.

The season that followed, according to a later manager, was "disastrous in the extreme."[67] The GPGE tried its best. They launched a monthly journal, formulated a comprehensive marketing plan, arranged for government inspection at shipping points, adopted a standard six-layer peach pack, and engaged an Atlanta marketing firm to tell "the

story of the excellence and quality of the Georgia peach ... in every consuming center in the United States."[68] But the harvest of eighteen thousand carloads – 60 percent of that ripening in just twenty-one days –
was simply too much for the new organization to handle. For the first
time, the GPGE resorted to court injunctions to prevent its own members
from breaking contracts and selling directly to buyers. The postseason
meeting of the board of directors promised to be a "stormy session,"
the *Constitution* reported, with at least one director supposedly ready
to dissolve the organization.[69] The GPGE did not dissolve after that first
season, but the last few years of the 1920s saw larger and larger crops
and less and less profit.[70] Because of the "disastrous" 1924 season, many
growers found it necessary to seek financing from commission merchants
and other private distributors, which left a large portion of the crop in
private hands. In 1926 the GPGE controlled only 35 percent of the crop,
the rest divided among half a dozen marketing agencies and several hundred growers who marketed independently.[71]

By 1932, the GPGE director W. C. Bewley sounded positively bitter.
Look around, he pled in that year's annual report. The "wave of cooperative marketing is sweeping over the country," and "industries of
all kinds are being consolidated."[72] August figures in American politics,
business, and agriculture had endorsed cooperative marketing, Bewley
continued, quoting Calvin Coolidge, Herbert Hoover, Wells Sherman,
and other leaders; indeed, the "history of civilization has largely consisted
of attempts on the part of man to co-operate."[73] And would Georgians
find themselves outside this great history? Bewley hoped not. "Surely, our
people are as intelligent, as fair, and as unselfish as those in other sections," he reasoned.[74] Yet in Georgia "peach growers are worse divided
than ever before" and in "worse financial condition than ever before."[75]
Despite Bewley's pleading, the GPGE never regained the kind of influence
the GFE had known in the 1910s, though the cooperative continued to
operate until the 1960s.[76]

In explaining the organization's failure to fulfill its promise, GPGE
officials acknowledged two factors: nature and individualism. The GPGE
president, J. L. Benton, blamed the weather following the 1924 season,
which had caused the crop to ripen "over a shorter period than ever
known in the history of our industry." Hileys and Georgia Belles overlapped with the Elberta season, causing what Bewley called "a very
abnormal and excessive movement": more than eight thousand cars in
twenty-one days. Bewley protested that this was simply too much for
"the Exchange or any other human agency" to process adequately.[77] To

be sure, the peach crop of 1924 was larger than ever. But "abnormal" implied the existence of a "normal" season. There was no such thing. Variation was the rule in peach production.

Normal production was impossible to predict for at least three reasons. First, acreage expanded steadily from 1880 through 1930, so predicting the size of a crop year to year depended on precise knowledge of who had planted what in years past, how many trees would be coming into bearing that year, and how many would be nearing the end of their productive lives. The Census of Agriculture surveyed too infrequently (every ten years; every five starting in 1925) to be much help in this regard, and the Bureau of Markets cum Bureau of Agricultural Economics did not gather exhaustive statistics on peach production until 1926.

Second, even if such comprehensive numbers had been gathered, they would have had to account for geography. That is, it was not just that more peach trees began bearing each year, but also that more *regions* began bearing: north Georgia grew rapidly in the early decades of the twentieth century, and so did North Carolina, Arkansas, Texas, and, somewhat later, South Carolina. Nineteen twenty-four may have been an exceptionally productive year for Georgia, but it was also a good year for these other areas. And whereas in 1923 Georgia's crop had run its course by the time growers in other states began shipping, in 1924 they overlapped for four solid weeks.[78]

Which leads to the third obstacle to predicting the peach crop: the weather. Varieties ripened at different times and in varying quantities each year, according to the particular location and its particular weather patterns. As Figure 5.6 illustrates, the peak of car lot shipments could occur anywhere from early July to early August. Today scientists know much more about the need for a certain number of chilling hours for proper bloom and fruit development, but they still cannot predict the timing of blooms and harvest – especially in the Southeast, where winter and spring temperatures vary considerably year to year. It appears, though, that there is an exponential relationship between the amount of cold weather and the amount of warm weather needed for budbreak in a given season. A season with a lot of cold weather might, paradoxically, result in earlier blooms, if warming occurred suddenly in March. Blooming time varies by cultivar, of course, but also from top to bottom of a tree, and even on a single twig in the controlled environment of a laboratory refrigerator. *Each bud* has its own chilling and heating requirements.[79]

This intricate dance between peach trees and the local environment would have made the work of any grower organization difficult, but exchange advocates were even more concerned with the problem of grower individualism. In their view, the problem was not the unpredictability of the weather but the way that growers "played" the weather, using its capriciousness as the set of dice with which they challenged other growers. The Georgia Fruit Exchange had treated the question of grower independence with some delicacy. It was primarily an information agency, allowing growers to make their own arrangements if they sold f.o.b. When it came to the distribution of the crop, the GFE advised rather than controlled. But there was an inherent tension between their two strategies of reshaping distribution and increasing f.o.b. sales. Limiting the number of commission merchants who could sell on consignment pushed many merchants into the f.o.b. market. The growing f.o.b. market, in turn, undercut the exchange's powers of distribution by allowing speculators to glut markets. In order to control the Georgia peach market, in other words, the exchange would have had to control all sales, not just consignments.[80]

The GPGE was an effort to capture this kind of control – to sell all GPGE fruit as GPGE fruit – but Georgia growers were not prepared to relinquish their freedom to go their own way. And the grumbling of cooperative advocates such as Fleming and Bewley notwithstanding, selfishness and disloyalty do not fully explain the reluctance of growers to affiliate with the GPGE. Compared with California's fruit cooperatives, the GPGE lacked police power – it was unwilling or unable to force the compliance of small growers with violence.[81] And whereas in California the long distance to population centers made organization and standardization a precondition of commercial fruit growing, in Georgia advocates of organization ran into a deep-rooted culture of independence. Many – perhaps most – of Georgia's growers prided themselves on making their own arrangements. When pondering the structure of the original Georgia Fruit Exchange, the Fort Valley grower W. H. Harris insisted on preserving this autonomy. "I believe that the transactions between grower and merchant should be rigidly separated from any work of a central bureau," he told the *Constitution*. "The actual sale would be between the merchant and the orchardist."[82] Given this tradition in Georgia, pooled marketing represented a radical shift in practice. Joining with the GPGE meant surrendering one's reputation. And it was a short step from the sacrificing of one's reputation to the diminishing of one's manhood.

Here the example of Lamartine G. Hardman is instructive. As a medical doctor, hardware merchant, dairy farmer, owner of one of the South's largest cotton mills, and governor of the state of Georgia from 1926 to 1930, Hardman personified southern business progressivism. When he was in his sixties, in the 1910s, he planted or acquired several hundred acres of peaches and ultimately owned some ten thousand acres of orchard land in seven different counties. But peach growing was not a central part of his public persona. It was another business opportunity for a man whose appetite for such opportunities was well-nigh insatiable.[83]

Yet to judge by his correspondence with his New York commission house, Smith and Holden, Hardman devoted himself personally to the new enterprise. On the morning of July 23, 1923, he ordered a refrigerator car from the Southern Railway for his first shipment; the car was in place by 9:00 p.m. and loaded by midnight. The next morning Hardman telegraphed Smith and Holden in New York with the news that his first car was on its way to Potomac yards with 476 crates of Elbertas; Smith and Holden replied cheerily that they expected "a good healthy situation here tomorrow."[84]

Smith and Holden seemed to use comparisons with Hardman's neighbors to motivate him. On July 27, Smith wrote to Hardman that the peaches of C. J. Hood led all others in prices at $3 a crate. Hood lived in neighboring Habersham County; the two were undoubtedly acquainted personally. So it must have brought some color to Hardman's face when Smith and Holden rated his first carload as "better than most," but "not as good as the best" as a result of the presence of some mildew spotted fruit. They sold the largest fruit for $2.50 a crate and the majority of the car for $2.25: $0.50 to $0.75 less than Hood. Hardman was not pleased. He dashed off a letter to Smith and Holden on July 30. "The remainder of my peaches are going to be just as good as any on the market," he promised. "I certainly hope you will get a better price." And then, just to be sure Smith and Holden understood, he named names: "I do not believe that J. B. Hardman's nor C. J. Hood's peaches will bring any better price than mine."[85]

To elevate the reputation of his "mark," Hardman separated mildewed or otherwise subpar peaches and packed them in unmarked bushel baskets. In the crates stamped with his name, however, he packed only his best fruit – a practice in keeping with Smith and Holden's recommendations. In reply to Hardman's letter, the commission merchants observed that Hood's peaches had a fifteen year reputation behind them, while Hardman's 1922 crop had been only mediocre. "You have got to demonstrate to the buyer that you have something as good as the 'Other Fellow,' " they explained. "When you once accomplish that you have not as much trouble to induce him to pay the top price." Far from dismissing Hardman's concerns, Smith and Holden played to them. "We have unloaded here today the nicest car of peaches from you we have had this season," Smith wrote on August 1.

Before the season is over we hope to make your best Elbertas on some day at least outsell Hoods [*sic*] mark if we can. I might say that our dock manager was talking with Mr. Hood this morning and he apparently is not at all desirous of having your mark outsell his in any way. Perhaps what we want to accomplish as mentioned above may take place tomorrow or Friday. We will get there as soon as possible.[86]

Two days later, they did just that, outselling Hood by twenty-five cents on one lot. "I guess this is about all that you could expect of us," the firm wrote. "So we will not comment any further."[87] One can imagine a delighted Hardman picking up the phone or riding down the road to confront his rival with the news.

Given this highly competitive relationship between two men in the same district, it is not hard to imagine the difficulty that the GPGE experienced trying to recruit 85 to 90 percent of the crop each year. The GPGE publication, the *Georgia Peach*, reminded its readers incessantly of the cooperative tradition. Interspersed with advertisements for chemical sprays, bank financing, and crate and box companies, inspirational blurbs exhorted the reader to keep the faith. "The life of duty, not the life of mere ease or mere pleasure," they quoted Theodore Roosevelt; "that is the kind of life which makes the great man as it makes the great nation."[88] The next month they offered some original drivel: "Co-operation means standing with your neighbor, for your neighbor and sharing equally with your neighbor the burdens and blessings of life."[89]

But for peach growers, "sharing equally with your neighbor" sounded a lot like settling for the lowest common denominator. And sharing a reputation with the little guy down the road who employed his drunken cousin to supervise the harvest did not sound noble enough to make the consequences worthwhile. For growers to accept the terms of the exchange required great faith in the honesty and integrity of the system. It also required an acceptance of middling terms for the duration of their careers. It was a company job.

A story from a North Carolina grower memoir makes this point with particular clarity. In the early 1920s, the South Carolinians Clement and Catharine Ball Ripley bought land in the North Carolina sand hills in order to find a better life than the one of office work and bridge parties they knew in Charleston. They pinned their hopes on a tidy little peach farm. In 1931, they fled peach growing for good. Reflecting on their career as farmers, Catharine wrote: "I never happened to know a farmer in real life who genuinely loved the soil as they are supposed to do in fiction, but I knew plenty who loved the gamble of planting crops." The Ripleys had not found the "system of life" they sought when they bought their peach farm, but they did learn "to gamble, the pleasantist life in the world."[90] In the midst of the difficult process of extricating themselves from their unremunerative sandhill peach business, the Ripleys visited the farm that had inspired them nearly a decade earlier. As they watched the packing line run, the superintendent of that farm explained why he was still in peaches: "There ain't a thing to this peach business. Any God damn fool can raise 'em and it ain't worth a damn fool's time to do it," he said. "But I'll tell you something else, Clem. I'd rather stay here and go broke raising peaches than make a fortune not raising them. This way you get some excitement anyhow."[91]

And so, beset by environmental instability and internal dissension, the southern fruit cooperative movement fell back. But the marketing focus of the period from 1908 through the 1920s did produce some important changes. The exchange abetted a wider distribution than ever before, which may have cemented the national reputation of Georgia peaches. And the exchange's campaign for standardization eventually resulted in the creation of peach grades and government inspection, but only after the exchange had ceased to be an influential force in the industry. Instead, a government-sponsored marketing order brought it about.

V

The federal government barreled down the path pioneered by cooperatives like the GFE. In the nineteenth century, the USDA had been almost entirely focused on production: better pest control, better cultivation methods, better cultivars, all in the name of making "two blades of grass grow where only one grew before," to borrow a famous cliché from the time period. "The Department of Agriculture was conservative, even to the point of being reactionary, in its attitude toward the pressing problems of marketing and distribution," wrote the historian James Malin. "It was quite unprepared to assume leadership in this new field."[92] But "the problem of the markets" eventually became too pressing to ignore. This shift in the USDA – from teaching farmers how to produce to teaching them how to market – reflected the Department of Agriculture's embrace of the idea that a farmer should have a notion of "the economy" as a whole – economy as a self-contained system, instead of as a character quality synonymous with thrift or frugality.[93] Factory methods for production would be of little good without business methods for distribution and selling.

The new emphasis on markets within the USDA also reflected a direct tie to the experiences of the Georgia peach industry. When Senator Hoke Smith of Georgia helped to push through the law that created a "Market Division" within the USDA, he drew inspiration from the "recent disastrous experience of the peach growers of Georgia in attempting to market within a few weeks one of the largest crops which had ever been produced." Perhaps Smith saw in his mind's eye the millions of yellow-red orbs turning to mush in the dark waters of the Hudson. "The waste which takes place between the producer and the consumer is startling," Smith declared. If "properly studied by a department of the Government equipped for the work," some $2.76 billion could be saved annually.[94] As a result of the advocacy of Hoke Smith and many others, Congress appropriated $50,000 for a kind of Market Division pilot program, a study of the current situation and a prospectus for future activity. In May 1913, the USDA created the Office of Markets, under Charles J. Brand, who had cut his bureaucratic teeth in the USDA's program for cotton marketing. As an office chief, Brand reported directly to the secretary and so avoided some of the red tape that constrained the actions of divisions within bureaus. An office would be less "hampered by tradition and custom ... more flexible, more susceptible to readjustments, and therefore ... well adapted for the trying-out of this important line of work."[95] The next year Congress quadrupled the Office of Markets's appropriation to $200,000.[96] The marketing work grew rapidly. In 1915 Congress gave it $390,000, in 1917 nearly $1.2 million, and in 1918 $14.2 million. By then the office had been rechristened the Bureau of Markets, and, in addition to inspecting shipments and disseminating market news, had taken on the work of grain standards, warehousing, cotton futures, and the wartime distribution of nitrate of soda. It employed 2,289 workers at 108 permanent branch offices. In just five years, the Bureau of Markets became not just one of the largest bureaus in the department, but "probably ... the best known and most widely praised."[97] The Bureau of Markets sloshed around for a few more years with the Bureaus of Crop Estimates, Statistics, and Plant Industry; the Rural Organization Service; and the Office of Farm Management, until the Bureau of Agricultural Economics (BAE) emerged in 1922 as a sort of elephantine synthesis – "because," the former BAE chief Lloyd Tenny observed in 1947, "an elephant is rather unwieldy and sometimes does not know just where he is going."[98]

The mission of the Bureau of Markets and Bureau of Agricultural Economics, like that of the GFE, was information. They later offered services to growers – most notably, shipping point and terminal market inspections – but even these services were primarily forms of information. They piled study upon study; issued daily, weekly, monthly reports of car lot unloads; published immense tables; drew impressive charts and graphs; and provided an inspector at both ends of the shipment to sign off on the quality of the fruit. The Exchange still made shipping decisions and took responsibility for the product in transit and still made claims against railroads when negligence led to loss, but the information function became less central to the Exchange as the bureau grew. The bureau seemed to be addressing head-on what its chief, Charles Brand, called "the problem of articulation."[99]

Some of this research appeared in USDA circulars as efforts to apply the BAE's statistical acumen to the problems of the farmer. M. R. Cooper's and J. W. Park's 1927 "The Peach Situation in the Southern States," for example, took as its starting point "the difficulties encountered in marketing recent peach crops." It offered a series of graphs intended to answer questions about the future prospects and "most practicable things" to be done in order to "stabilize the industry in the shortest possible time."[100] One set showed rapidly increasing carload shipments from Georgia, Tennessee, Alabama, North Carolina, South Carolina, Arkansas, and Texas; another illustrated the overlapping seasons of the same states; a third compared the drastically reduced prices of the 1926 season with the nearly equal costs of picking and packing; a fourth projected future production levels based on the age of southern peach trees in 1925 (production peaked at eight to nine years and then dropped off quickly); several mapped the distribution of southern peaches (85 percent of Georgia peaches went to population centers of 100,000 or more); another showed the competition of southern peaches with other fruit such as apples and melons (it was getting worse); another illustrated how constant shipping and marketing charges made for exceedingly poor returns on poor quality fruit; and a final series of charts and tables showed how different varieties fared on the market (the Belle was near the bottom, the Elberta continued to hold its own, and early varieties were the best). By flipping through the bulletin and looking at the pictures, a grower could easily ascertain the thrust of its argument: the peach situation in the southern states was, in a word, bad. Any grower still standing after the 1926 season could have articulated this without the charts and graphs.

If circulars were the appetizers of the BAE, offering numbers in palatable quantities, technical bulletins were BAE main courses, a feast for the statistically astute. Harry S. Kantor's 1929 "Factors Affecting the Price of Peaches in the New York City Market" built on some of the same research as Cooper and Park, but it was a tabular tour de force, a display of unadulterated expertise. It featured twenty-nine pages of narrative interspersed with price curves and bar graphs of unloads, followed by thirty-five pages of "detailed tables." And again, the conclusion underwhelmed. Peach prices, Kantor affirmed, varied "from day to day, from week to week and from year to year, and for different lots on the same day" according to variety, size, condition, grade, and pack. Therefore, Grow "the most desirable varieties." Ship only the larger peaches. Pack them properly.[101] An almost word-for-word recitation of advice given to growers at GSHS meetings in the 1880s.

When standardization finally occurred in Georgia in 1942, it was in the form of a USDA-sponsored arrangement called a "Marketing Agreement and Order." The federal Marketing Agreement Act of 1937 gave nearly monopolistic powers to farmers, permitting them to control supply and quality with government backing.[102] In Georgia a group of growers known as the "Industry Committee" would set certain parameters on the size, quality, and maturity of Georgia peaches that were sold across state lines. To implement these guidelines, the secretary of agriculture would issue "an Order based upon the recommendations which has the force of law."[103] The USDA's Agricultural Marketing Administration's investigative division then enforced the order.[104]

The Marketing Order standards changed every year, with the committee meeting in the late spring to send their recommendation off to the USDA. In a high-production year, the standards were stricter; in a lower-production year, they were more relaxed. Whatever did not meet the standards set for interstate shipment – one government scientist estimated that 40 percent of peaches, on average, did not – was sold in-state, at roadside stands and canneries, wineries, and farmers' markets.[105] In this way, the Marketing Order achieved what generations of progressive growers had been urging on Georgia's peach growers: standardization. It gave a small class of growers control over the entire crop. Tellingly, they had to draw on the coercive power of the federal government to do so.

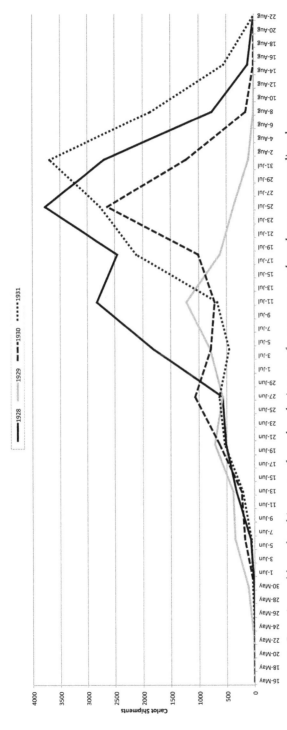

FIGURE 5.6. Georgia weekly carlot shipments of peaches during past four seasons and totals to corresponding dates.
Source: R. E. Keller, "Marketing the Georgia Peach Crop: Summary of the 1931 Season" (Washington, DC: Market News Service on Fruits and Vegetables, March 1932), 11.

TABLE 5.3. *Peach acreage and farms in Georgia, 1925–1950*

Year	Peach acreage	Number of farms reporting peaches	Number of farms	Percentage of farms reporting peaches (%)
1925	149,690	92,656	249,095	37.20
1930	92,200	66,075	255,598	25.90
1935	75,245	75,641	250,544	30.20
1940	85,870	77,506	216,033	35.90
1945	69,380	84,331	225,897	37.30
1950	53,360	49,003	198,191	24.70

Source: Compiled from U.S. Census Bureau, *Census of Agriculture*, 1925, 1930, 1935, 1945, 1950

The Marketing Order, by tightening standards for marketed fruit, increased the state's collective cull pile. It appears to have done the same for the growers themselves. For while the program was praised as an advance for the peach industry in terms of the national reputation of Georgia fruit, it also marked the beginning of a steady decrease in the number of growers in the state. The number of farms reporting peaches had ranged from 92,656 to 66,075 since 1925; in 1945 the census reported 84,331 farms with peaches. In 1950, the number was less than 50,000, not quite a quarter of all farms (see Table 5.3 and maps in Figures 7.2 and 7.3). Like the first sorter on the packing line, marketing standards took a rough cut out of the grower population in Georgia; in coming years, a restive labor force and a mysterious disease would take out most of the rest (see Chapter 7).

VI

To solve the problems of pests and diseases and unpredictable markets, peach growers and their allies imagined that information – and the labor force to act on that information – would be enough. J. H. Hale needed to know how much hydrocyanic gas to pump into his tree tents; the Fruit Growers' Express needed to know how many refrigerator cars to have ready for Lamartine Hardman on July 13; the commission merchants Smith and Holden needed to know whether Manchester, Georgia, was going to have a big crop this year, and when, and which grower had a reputation for wormy fruit; C. J. Hood needed to know whether prices were better in Youngstown or Bridgewater, whether the North Carolina sandhill growers had started shipping yet, and whether the W. L. Brown Co. would tell him the truth about conditions on the market. And the councils and bureaus and exchanges and offices and departments created to collect and disseminate this information did so with vigor. Numbers sped across telegraph wires, tumbled out of radios, scattered across bulletin boards. Production by state; shipments by state, district, county, billing station; monthly, weekly, and daily shipments and unloads by producing state and principal market; shipping point and jobbing prices: the data made a dizzying array.

But numbers alone could not solve the problems of pests and markets. In part the failure of information was a matter of the physical environment. A crop as perishable as peaches, grown in a climate as unpredictable as early twentieth-century Georgia's, shipped in the heat of summer – such a crop could not be made thoroughly reliable. Wheat poured together in a seemingly endless stream in Chicago's great elevators, where its particular place of origin ceased to make any difference. Fruit breathed and perspired. The mark on the crate, and the conditions under which the contents were grown, harvested, and packed, continued to affect the price until the day the fruit was sold.

One speaks today of "the market" as the disembodied meeting point of the abstract forces of supply and demand, a medium calling forth the ghosts of producers and consumers for parley. But space, time, and weather mattered a great deal in the marketing of peaches, and so did the biological processes of the fruit itself – growth, ripening, decay – each of which was often accompanied and abetted by other organisms. Miles and minutes and atmospheric conditions made perfect decision making impossible, though this limitation did not stop growers, marketers, and government agents from trying.

Market information was not just imperfect because weather was unpredictable, but also because human beings were too. Markets were personal places. Early twentieth-century marketing of perishables took on the character of its characters – it depended on the personalities of the housewife who haggled with the peddler, the merchant who hoodwinked the shipper, the grower who brought suit against the railroad. Prices were the product of relationships. Over the course of the twentieth century, prices became less personal, as the messy negotiation that once characterized each interaction in the supply chain gave way to a kind of order and control.

This movement toward standardization may seem inevitable to twenty-first-century eyes. But the fact that so many growers rejected the terms offered by the exchange – and voted with their lands after the Marketing Agreement set the standard for the industry – suggests that alongside the rhetoric of agrarian stability we must also place the language of the lottery.

The possibility of striking it rich in some sort of freakish year beckoned constantly to farmers, none more than those growing peaches, a crop for which freakish years were the norm.[106] Businesspeople, bureaucrats, consumer advocates, and sometimes farmers as well assumed that instability and disorder were obstacles to be overcome. But some growers – especially the smaller ones – welcomed the instability of sites of production and consumption alike.

In the 1910s and 1920s, the Georgia peach industry found itself caught up in a wider web of distribution and marketing agents. As Georgia peach growers sought by cooperation and business organization to make this wider world more predictable and amenable to their prosperity, they also turned their attention toward consolidating a stronger local identity and consolidating their power over a workforce that seemed more discontented with each decade.

6

Blossoms and Hams

I

The movement of Georgia peaches into more and more towns and cities across the eastern half of the United States in the early twentieth century had a kind of demographic echo in the movement of outsiders to Fort Valley. Increasingly, these outsiders arrived not to grow peaches, as J. H. Hale had, but to finance, analyze, market, and otherwise support the industry. Mabel and Frank Withoft were representative of this group. Though they had little to do with growing or picking peaches, the members of this "peach auxiliary" were, in some ways, more influential in the consolidation of the peach myth during the 1910s and 1920s. These decades were an era of intense concern about "the rural question," the problems of the countryside. This concern could be romantic and patronizing, as in some manifestations of the country life movement, a transatlantic campaign for rural revitalization with Irish, English, Danish, and American variants. It could be perceptive, as in the case of the Cornell horticulturist and Country Life Commission chair Liberty Hyde Bailey, who saw the deleterious effects of industrial capitalism on the social and ecological fortunes of the countryside. And it could be frankly exploitative, as it was with Bailey's student Edwin G. Nourse, who believed that agriculture needed to be modernized in order to feed the industrial and urban United States – whatever the human costs.[1]

Less well-known but equally important was the contemporaneous African American rural reform movement, which found spokespersons in the Tuskegee agriculturist George Washington Carver; the Fort Valley High and Industrial School president, Henry Hunt; and, at times, W.

E. B. DuBois. For the most part, this rural black movement has been overshadowed by the contemporary literary urbanism of the Harlem Renaissance and the later large-town–urban-amenity confrontations of the civil rights movement. Booker T. Washington died in 1915. George Washington Carver is a well-known figure in American history, but as Mark Hersey argues, his agrarian reform efforts have been overshadowed by his somewhat inflated reputation as the peanut chemist.[2] Carver spoke of fertility hidden in swamp muck, fabric dyed with old tomato vines, rugs made of corn shucks, livestock foraging on acorns, seasonal sweets from wild plums and pecans, and stunning wildflowers in the forests. He wrote, "We are richer than we think we are."[3] But that African American environmental tradition is only recently earning more attention.[4]

In the early twentieth century, Fort Valley was host to manifestations of both movements: two representative visions of how the world should be and two corresponding efforts to shape the surrounding landscape. For the Ohio transplant Mabel Withoft and her allies, the town was the center of Peachland, the "World's Peach Paradise," the seat of a "wonder county" that in March became a "sweet riot of pink beauty" and a "rosy sea."[5] Withoft was a central organizing figure for a decade-long campaign to create a new county named in honor of the fruit that had drawn her there. As a kind of poet laureate of Peach County, she made what was otherwise a rather mundane political goal into something divinely ordained and intimately tied to the progress of civilization itself: a politics of beauty.[6] For Henry Hunt and the friends of Fort Valley High and Industrial School, Fort Valley was the central point of a region where blacks outnumbered whites three to one, where "within a radius of 50 miles 200,000 colored people can be reached," or the "hub of a gigantic wheel, radiating its influence into a vast community of 300,000 Negroes."[7] It was a "spark in the dark hinterlands of the Black Belt of Georgia," or in the words of W. E. B. DuBois, "a lovely oasis, but Good Lord, the surrounding desert!"[8]

These images overlap and contradict. Was it a rosy sea or a black desert? The former had all the advantages of power and wealth, and ultimately triumphed over the latter. But it was impossible to have one without the other. "We simply cannot understand the form (or the meanings) of the landscape," the geographer Don Mitchell writes of California, "without attending closely to the relations of labor that were indispensable to its making."[9] In middle Georgia, likewise, those vast orchards of rosy trees – and the vision born of the wealth those trees generated for the area – mapped vast outlying areas of black poverty. There could be no rosy sea without a black belt.

II

Frank and Mabel Clare Withoft moved to Fort Valley from Dayton, Ohio, around 1908. A member of a prominent and well-connected Ohio family with investment properties in nearby Myrtle, Georgia, Frank became a partner in the Southern Brokerage Company, which supplied peach growers with crates and insecticides and sold peaches in northern markets. Mabel, for her part, was a volunteer dynamo and helped write the narrative of peach progress that justified the Peach County movement.

Born in 1873, in Newark, Ohio, Mabel was extraordinarily bright, even if the claim that she could "read from practically any book" at age three was exaggerated. Her mother died when she was seven. Burdened with a young law practice and his own grief, her father, John Swartz, sent Mabel and her sister to live with their grandparents in the Ohio countryside, until he remarried two years later.[10] She flourished in the reunited family, graduating from Granville Academy in 1889 (at age sixteen); teaching school in Pueblo, Colorado, for a year; then returning to Newark to teach Latin and German in the city high school. In 1894, she married the dashing Frank Withoft, a recent graduate of Denison University, where he had been a star athlete. Frank was the son of Frederick G. Withoft, a confidant of the Ohio governor James Cox and, as president of Ohio Fruitland Company, a Fort Valley peach grower.[11] The groom had also recently been offered a job as deputy treasurer of Montgomery County in Dayton, where he had already prepared a "handsome home" for his bride, who had received many "costly and handsome presents." Their son, John Frederick, was born less than a year later.

The apparently charmed life of the Withoft family lasted for six years. On February 13, 1902, Mabel bore a daughter, Alice Virginia. On February 14, 1902, Alice died. Mabel scrawled her grief in a prayer that was, for a devout Baptist, bracingly candid.

> Thou canst not know, dear God, just what it means
> To be a mother. Surely that one pang is sacred to
>   the human breast alone.
> Thou art the Father, only, of this race
> Born of Thy brain and will, not of Thy flesh –

Withoft described herself in the aftermath as "machine-like," unable to hold back her "scalding" tears, dwelling constantly on that dark

Valentine's Day. She cast one last accusing question – "Is it harder, Lord, /
To give one's child to die to save the world, / Than this, for nothing?" –
before concluding less darkly. For she had known the kindnesses of
friends; her soul had been "harrowed" – prepared for a new season of
planting – with sorrow. And strangely, she saw this apparent chastise-
ment as evidence of God's love:

> Oh, God, forgive me! Show me to be
> A woman fit for earth, and so for heaven.

So Mabel Withoft would dedicate her life to good work, to showing herself worthy of reunification with her little "angel."[12]

As it turned out, that good work would be bearing the light of civilization and intelligence to the rural South. Just a week or two after the death
of Mabel Withoft's daughter, the *Macon Telegraph* published her second
paean to the Georgia peach (her first was the Elberta poem highlighted
in Chapter 3) – perhaps written during a visit to Fort Valley during peach
season – which concluded:

> Under the moon of a southern sky,
>   Breathing the ocean's balm,
> Gazing afar on the sandy stretch.
>   Of live oak and pine and palm.
> Listening hushed, for the cuckoo's call,
>   Learning what love may teach.
> There's nothing – nothing – completes life's charm
>   Like the beautiful Georgia peach.[13]

The poem evoked a peaceful, lovely South, a place of refuge: *moon, balm,
hushed, love, charm*. Within two years, Mabel Withoft had moved to
Georgia permanently, as if to learn "what love may teach." She spent
her days in her new community in indefatigable volunteer work. At Fort
Valley First Baptist Church, she sang in the choir, taught the Marion
Reed Sunday school class, and directed the Young Women's Auxiliary,
the Girls' Auxiliary, and the Royal Ambassadors. She was president of
the Baptist Women's Missionary Society, superintendent of the Rehoboth
Association Women's Missionary Union, and vice president of the Baptist
Women's Missionary Union (BWMU) West Central District. For the
BWMU, she wrote a book, *Oak and Laurel*, about the Baptist mission
schools in the mountains of the Southeast which at least one reporter
thought would be "one of the most popular and most studied" missionary books.[14] She was a state officer of the Women's Christian Temperance
Union and president of the Fort Valley History Club, where she delivered

talks on (for instance) "Comprehensive Criticism" of new poetry.[15] She was chair of the better homes movement in Fort Valley and a member of the Literature Committee of the National Federation of Women's Clubs.[16] As president of the Fort Valley Women's Club – a local chapter of the national organization – she lobbied for better teacher pay.[17]

Tragedy struck again in 1919, when her son Frederick died of pneumonia fighting in France. She visited Arlington Cemetery and composed a poem, "Seeded Ground," that, true to form, turned a mundane horticultural warning on a sign she saw there ("Seeded Ground – Keep Off") into a prophecy for the postwar order:

> America, dear land, is seeded ground,
> That coming generations may have peace,
> We have sown men. Dear God, send harvest soon![18]

At that year's BWMU conference, though she was "not yet released from the burden, sacrifice, and grief of recent war," Withoft presented a resolution that the United States "act definitely and permanently as our God in heaven shall guide you, in making less armament and none of war, to secure for our dear land the peace which is the right of the followers of Jesus."[19] As a "Gold Star Mother" – one whose son had died overseas – Mabel Withoft became national president of the Service Star Legion in 1930.[20]

In the midst of this whirl of volunteer activity, Withoft also lent her considerable imaginative energy to the campaign to create Peach County. In the process, she supplied what would be almost the entire modern corpus of poetry honoring the Georgia peach. Withoft's lengthiest compositions were the pageants for Fort Valley's Peach Blossom Festivals of 1923–1926, which were performed in support of the campaign for Peach County. In these works Withoft spun a narrative of peach progress.

III

Fort Valley's elites presented the idea of Peach County as an innocent effort to make administration more efficient in middle Georgia. A new county, proponents argued, would make for better roads, more responsive government, and stronger schools. Houston County was simply too large to be administered effectively. In order to create their new county, they would need a constitutional amendment to pass in the General Assembly allowing for the creation of Peach County, and they would also need to win the battle at the popular level, convincing a majority of voters to approve the Peach County amendment. Their campaign did not proceed without controversy. The rural areas of old Houston and Macon Counties staged a determined countercampaign to keep the new county measure off the ballot and then to rally opposition to the measure when it went up for popular referendum (see Figures 6.1 and 6.2).

The Peach County campaign joined a long, almost humorous Georgia tradition of dividing the polity into ever tinier units. In 1832, Georgia had 89 counties; by 1875, there were 137. The new state constitution of 1877 prohibited the creation of new counties – until 1904, when the General Assembly amended the constitution to allow for 8 new counties. By 1924, the year Peach County was created, Georgia had 160 counties, more than any state in the union except Texas. Almost half of those had been created since the 1850s.[21] Georgia's county surplus was not necessarily a point of pride. Some complained that small counties were inefficient, and that Georgia's residents should be merging and consolidating, not subdividing. Others linked the "excessive number of lynchings in Georgia" to the "excessive number of counties," since public officials in small counties were more personally beholden to the county's residents and were therefore less likely to punish vigilantes.[22]

The Peach County campaign started with a 1914 meeting at the home of Alva B. Greene in Fort Valley. Many luminaries of the peach industry and of local politics were present, including A. J. Evans, D. C. Strother, Max L. James, J. E. Davidson, and C. L. Shepard. In sketching out the new county's borders, the group almost unanimously agreed to include as much of the "center of the great and growing peach industry" as possible. The new county's name would not honor a "favorite son or historic event in Georgia," therefore, but the product that had won them national fame: the peach.[23] In June 1916, Alva Greene and Emmett Houser set up office in Atlanta in order to lobby the state assembly at closer range.[24] In a letter to Governor Nat Harris on a Peach County letterhead emblazoned with a full color peach, Greene appealed to their shared friendship – an oblique reference, probably, to Greene's work on Harris's behalf in Fort Valley – but spent the majority of his letter defusing the argument that smaller counties were less efficient. New counties need not be a product of petty politics, he claimed. It was precisely in the interests of "good business judgment," not politics, that the Peach County campaign was organized. It was old Houston County that was inefficient, Greene argued. It had been laid out "years ago" as an "undeveloped territory," and Perry, the county seat, was situated near the center of the county. But northern Houston had developed so rapidly that now "10,000 people find

FIGURE 6.1. Middle Georgia before the creation of Peach County, with major railroads.
Source: Map prepared by Jennifer Bell, University of Georgia. Data courtesy of Minnesota Population Center, National Historical Geographic Information System: Version 2.0. (Minneapolis, MN: University of Minnesota, 2011).

FIGURE 6.2. Middle Georgia after the creation of Peach County, with major railroads.
Source: Map prepared by Jennifer Bell, University of Georgia. Data courtesy of Minnesota Population Center, National Historical Geographic Information System: Version 2.0. (Minneapolis, MN: University of Minnesota, 2011).

themselves so situated that they are at a great distance from the county seat, which can be reached only over a branch railroad twelve miles long, requiring a whole day for the trip there." Houston County was simply "too large to be handled in anything like a businesslike way," he wrote, complaining that "sections of the county have failed to have their roads worked for years at a time."[25] Elsewhere Greene called Houston a "vast empire," as though he hoped to associate it with the Ottoman realm then being dismantled in Europe.[26]

The new county, in contrast, would be a tidy, compact, businesslike proposition, purposely laid out with no resident more than eight miles from the Central of Georgia Railway (see the railroad routes in Figures 6.1 and 6.2). Furthermore, since the entire section was "devoted to the peach industry," the county government could be more responsive and aid the "further development" of the place. Houston County, once separate from Fort Valley, would also "advance with more substantial progress."[27] Citing no data to support his claim, Greene argued that new counties "immediately" produced "wonderful improvement. Better roads, better schools, lower taxes."[28] In an intriguing, handwritten postscript to his letter to Governor Harris, Greene clarified that he was not asking for an official expression of support "for manifest reasons" but only that the governor "help us in your own quiet way." And then a final plea: "Our needs for a new Co. are greater by far than Barrow Co. was. You know the situation."[29] Although it is not clear to what "situation" Greene referred, the fact that he felt the need to append this oblique appeal to personal knowledge suggests that the official reasons for the new county – greater administrative efficiency and more rapid economic development – did not tell the entire story.

Through public and private measures, opponents successfully kept the proposal off the legislative agenda until 1920, when it became the central debate in Houston County's legislative elections.[30] Once the new county faction won the local election, and the new representatives had successfully steered the proposal through the shoals of legislative procedure, the stage was set for a new and reinvigorated campaign in 1922. Confident in their cause, Peach County advocates "marked the roads entering the proposed new commonwealth with new and gayly [sic] signs that read 'Welcome to Peach County.'"[31] Mabel Withoft traveled to Atlanta to make the case for Peach County. "The facts on old Houston County's illiteracy and need of county health work, and the other complements of progress, are in reality but additional arguments for the organization of a new county," she said. "The people of the western half of Houston are eager to take all the forward steps possible to a progressive people;

but they have been held back and hampered by the conservation of their neighbors to the east." With the "steady tide" of business flowing through Fort Valley, the new county would be independently and well equipped, said Withoft.[32]

The debate in the House that August was bitter. Representative E. B. Dykes of Dooly County (which shared a border with south Houston) trotted out figures purportedly demonstrating that the new county would rob a majority of Houston's population and taxable property, leaving only, in Dykes's words, "swamps, niggers, and mules. You will cut off the cream of the county if you pass this measure," he protested. In an admission that Houston and the Peach County partisans did not get along, Representative Emmett Houser of Houston countered that the new county was the only way to reconcile the divided interests in middle Georgia. The measure passed by a bare two-thirds majority, giving way to a popular campaign that was even more rancorous.[33] In October, opponents held mass meetings in Perry, Marshallville, and Montezuma; a reporter predicted one of "the hardest fights ever staged in this state."[34] A week later, the "Citizens of Macon and Houston Counties" placed an advertisement in the *Constitution* urging Georgians, "Vote AGAINST 'Peach County.'" The authors first couched their opposition in familiar themes: new and smaller counties were inefficient, politically motivated, unbusinesslike, and all-too-common in Georgia. "The whole state is tired of new counties." But the ad went on to attack the new county advocates for their "unworthy motives" and "unworthy methods." It was a "pernicious" lobby that had "infested the halls of our legislature." Ultimately, the argument concluded, Macon and Houston residents – "we, whose ox happens to be gored at the present moment" – opposed the new county on behalf of the whole state. "FOR YOU," the ad intoned ominously, "MAY BE MARKED NEXT FOR THE SLAUGHTER." According to its opponents, then, the new county campaign was an attack on the southern ideal of self-determination. In the event of a Peach County victory, Houston would limp on, a mere "PART of a county. A COUNTY SHUT IN. A COUNTY WHOSE VITAL ROADS WOULD CROSS NEGLECTED CORNERS OF OTHER TERRITORIES. A county of a few white scions of the hardy folks who made it, and of a dominating multitude of their slaves' descendents." Thus appealing to the racial and economic fears of Georgia's white voters – of being shut off from commerce and dominated by a black majority – the "Citizens of Houston and Macon County" begged fellow citizens to "decree" the end of this campaign.[35]

A month later, Peach County advocates responded in kind, calling the anti-new-county campaign a "vicious lobby" full of "pernicious ... untruths." Those "wreckers of common justice" were trying to "destroy an enterprising community" fighting for "the right to grow and become something for the state." The new county opponents were standing in the way of progress. In a somewhat calmer tone, the authors then presented "the facts." Look, they soothed, Houston was still going to be a big county, greater in area, population, and tax values than seventy-five others. Macon County, meanwhile, had actually gained a few acres on the deal, since Houston had given it forty thousand acres earlier. Sure, Peach County would have more registered voters than Houston County (1,305 to 863), but that was only because Peach County women had taken advantage of their new suffrage rights and registered. In fact, more women (637) were registered to vote in Peach County than men (632). In Houston, on the other hand, only 89 women were registered. "As to negroes," they added, "Peach County will have more than old Houston; but we think the least said about this the better for boh [*sic*] sides."[36]

In the midst of the politicking, Peach County advocates added a more extravagant but less direct method to their repertoire of broadsides and letters to editors and legislators: the Peach Blossom Festival. The first festival was in March 1922, the year of the initial Peach County referendum. It featured an "Auto Ride through Pink Paradise of Houston County"; a parade of fanciful floats from local towns, counties, and companies; a ten-thousand-plate barbecue luncheon, addressed by "prominent Georgians"; and a "beautiful flower spectacle" created by the Fort Valley Community Service.[37] After lunch, with pulled pork and Brunswick stew swilling in their stomachs, an audience of about twelve thousand listened to Governor Thomas Hardwick praise the peach industry. "The one crop idea," he said, "had to be removed from the minds of the farmers if they were to go forward instead of backward in their battle for prosperity." Peaches had "done more in aiding crop diversification than any other one thing in the state." So much so, said Hardwick, that all Georgians were "indebted to the Fort Valley people" for the "great service they have rendered in this line."[38]

If audience members perused their souvenir programs, they saw a similar argument laid out on page 3. Fort Valley, they read, was already a bustling town of thirty-six hundred; with the "many profitable business possibilities in this section," that number was sure to grow. It had "a train service superior to any city of its size in the state." And its territory grew more than a third of Georgia's peaches, making it a "Mecca for the commission men" who handled peaches. Three-quarters of the peach commission agents who worked in Georgia made Fort Valley their seasonal headquarters. And since Fort Valley had the highest elevation of any point along the Central of Georgia Railway, its healthfulness was "unsurpassed."[39] This advertisement had multiple purposes; clearly one of them was, like that of Hardwick's address, to bolster their claims to independence. Roderick Houser, the *Constitution*'s emissary to the fête, described it as "a sight for the gods to see." He might have added: Yankees, too. License plates on some fifteen hundred automobiles showed diverse attendance: California, Illinois, Massachusetts, New York, Pennsylvania, Ohio, Virginia. One Chicagoan who had seen the Swiss Alps and the canals of Venice saved his highest praise for Fort Valley: "I really and truly believe that I saw the prettiest sight of my life when I looked on the peach orchards in full bloom just at sundown Tuesday afternoon."[40]

These pretty sights and clever advertisements notwithstanding, the Peach County campaign lost in 1922. Perhaps in reaction, the festival organizers determined to go bigger and bolder in subsequent years. In 1923, they sent invitations not only to residents of New York, New Jersey, Massachusetts, Indiana, Oregon, and Michigan, but also to President Warren Harding and his cabinet.[41] This year, rather than present a pageant written by an outsider, they composed their own, and it was Mabel Swartz Withoft who wrote the words that would define the peach blossom festivals. Withoft's 1923 effort, "Georgia's Crowning Glory: A Pageant of Peachland," was a historical panorama, featuring the "Spirit of Georgia," played by a local woman wrapped in the colors of the Georgia flag and carried on a litter by "Nubian" slaves. In 1924, the thirty-five thousand guests saw "Peach of the Word: A Pageant of Peach County." Whereas in 1923 the peach industry was Georgia's "crown of glory," in 1924 the middle Georgia peach industry was the zenith of global history. Born in China some two millenia before Christ, the story went, the peach visited Japan, India, and Persia; Greece, Italy, and France; England, Belgium, Holland, and Spain; and sixteenth-century Mexico, only to choose America (whose "red soil / Seems strangely homelike to the buried seed"), then Georgia (where "Each generation blossoms / Into some rarer, rosier, sweeter form"), then Fort Valley ("Diana-like, / Young, splendid, thrilling with fine enterprise") as her permanent home. Having portrayed the past and the present of the fruit, the pageant then unveiled the Future: a "rosy sea" of "pinky petals," in other words, the uninhibited expansion of peach growing, with the "brightness of eyes, the coloring of health" and other "delights" of civilization, courtesy of horticulture.[42] This year, the festival appeared in the *New York Times* "Rotogravure Picture Section." Alongside photos of Babe Ruth driving a golf ball off the mouth of his fellow Yankee Joe Bush; the new sheik of Turkey, Mustapha Fevsi; and an auction of the former crown prince of Germany's personal effects; a photograph of Miss Frances Felton as Miss Montezuma and Helen Hume as Queen of Peachland attested to the festival's widening reputation.[43] Hume wore a robe lent to her by the movie star Mary Pickford, a thirty-two-thousand-dollar pearl-inlaid outfit first used in the 1924 costume drama "Dorothy Vernon of Haddon Hall."[44]

In contrast to the 1895 peach festival in Macon, which was a harvest festival, the peach blossom festivals were festivals of *becoming*. The peaches, after all, were not yet in hand; the rosy sea only promised a bountiful harvest. The festival organizers and the Peach County partisans celebrated what lay ahead. As did F. Scott Fitzgerald's Jay Gatsby – as did many Americans in the 1920s – they "believed in the green light, the orgastic future," of the New World – or, in this case, a New County.[45] The pageant portrayed peaches as a progressive crop for a progressive place, but it stopped short of implying that agriculture must give way to industry. The state's "mightiest wealth" was in peaches. Its society would retain its rural character with the assistance of modern science. Horticulture offered the South a middle place between a fully agrarian society like the antebellum South and a fully industrialized society like the contemporary Northeast. Such a society had access to all the "delights of civilization" – including the expensive duds of movie stars – but on its own terms.

Whether because of the ornate winsomeness of the festivals or because of back room negotiating with Macon and Houston County opponents, the new county campaign finally triumphed in 1924. The prominence of women in the pageant – they made much of revolutionary war hero Nancy Hart, suffrage advocate Rebecca Latimer Felton ("Mistress Felton! Quite the peer of man"), and Wesleyan College in the 1923 pageant – may have been a sly way for Pauline Oak and Mabel Withoft to promulgate their political views, but it was also part of the Peach County campaign's official strategy.[46] In November 1924, when the amendment again went before the voters of the state, forty "women workers from the peach-raising area of Georgia" arrived in Atlanta to "plead their cause personally to the voters." The new county campaign was not an attack on Houston County, they promised. It was merely a matter of "good roads and good schools" and "the coming into the peach belt of manufacturing plants."[47] Georgia's voters agreed, apparently, approving the measure 77,952 to 31,211.[48]

The victory celebration was long and sustained. On a Tuesday evening, January 13, 1925, Fort Valley's elites gathered at the Harris House hotel for "Peach Products Day," a local celebration of the state-sponsored "Georgia Products Day." The mood was bright. Mabel Withoft had written a song for the occasion to the tune of "Maryland My Maryland." And so the victorious new county advocates filled the rooms of the Harris House with Peach County's praise:

> Oh long our hearts have sought for thee,
>   County Peach, my County Peach
> And truly have we wrought for thee,
>   County Peach, my County Peach
> We yearned for thy protecting care,
>   Desired thy lovely name to share,
> We longed to breathe thy perfumed air,
>   County Peach, My County Peach.[49]

The earnestness of the evening did not confine itself to the county anthem. The schools superintendent Ralph Newton addressed the audience on Peach County's "spirit." "Peoples in their collective capacities have souls," Newton declared, the new county of Peach no less than the nations of Europe. Other Georgia counties had been formed out of convenience, or out of dealings within the state legislature. But Peach County was a true democratic movement, "born of the desire of the whole people – a desire that rose stronger after each defeat – a desire that knew no limits of sacrifice."

The evening's other speaker, Jennie Vance, the sister of one of the festival organizers, took Newton's argument a step further. Peach County was "a living organism with a soul," she said, but one that must be trained and reared, a "veritable infant in arms!" Their dreams for this new county, she admitted, were "Utopian." They envisioned a polity "without graft or dishonesty," with officeholders elected on the basis of merit, a beautiful courthouse ("for we want nothing shoddy and inadequate"), a "small but modernly equipped jail," and – for Vance at least, the crown jewel of their plan – a "Kind Farm." Poor farms were usually shabby affairs, designed to stigmatize as well as provide some feeble support for the impoverished.[50] But Peach County's Kind Farm would live up to its name: "attractive looking buildings with the loveliest of lawns, flowers and vegetable gardens" tended by the inmates. In short, it would replace the "sting of shame" with the "happiness of a home." Vance concluded by warding off scoffers with fervent social gospel idealism: "Heaven is

FIGURE 6.3. Fruit dancers in the 1925 pageant, *The Trail of Pink Petals*.
Source: Rembrandt Studio Photograph, Local History Collection. Courtesy of
Thomas Public Library, Fort Valley, Georgia.

higher than the stars, more wonderful than the universe and far more
beautiful than our minds can conceive; nevertheless, that is the goal we
strive to attain."[51]

In keeping with the tone of triumph, the organizers of the 1925 Peach
Blossom Festival expanded the event to two days, running the same program both days in order to accommodate more visitors. They added
an evening fireworks show and planned to charge for admission to the
pageant and for the barbecue luncheon. *National Geographic* and several film studios sent photographers to the event.[52] An estimated sixty
thousand visitors attended, paying one dollar each to see a lavish victory
celebration for the new county campaign. The "Trail of Pink Petals" followed the Mount Olympus trope of 1924, with Pomona's five daughters
competing for the goddess's favor (see Figure 6.3). The Grape's "clinging
tendrils" and delicate fragrance seem graceful, but since "Bacchus claims
thee for his revels wild!," Pomona could not choose her. The Cherry fails
to charm completely. The Orange, the color of the sun, "dost compensate

our loneliness" in winter, but "alien art thou still." The Apple is "daintily demure" but carries from the Garden of Eden a besmirched reputation: "Eve's sore heart was never comforted / By wearing apple blossoms in her hair!"[53] And then comes the Peach:

> Thou darling of the gods!
> The sun has dowered thee with liquid gold;
> The singing rain prepared thy perfumed bath,
> And filled with nectar thy translucent bowl!

The Peach is, in fact, too lovely to remain at Olympus; she would surely arouse Juno's jealousy. Instead, the Peach would have to seek "a home upon the gracious earth."[54] So again the Peach sets off on a journey looking for her true home, though this year Pauline Oak and Mabel Withoft were careful to note the religious pluralism of her pilgrimage: Buddhist China, Hindu India, pagan Persia and Greece, Catholic Europe, Aztec Mexico. The Peach is amused by the attentions of these "foreign eyes" and eager to be taken by the next suitor whether "mighty Persian" or "resistless" Spanish Don. Finally, the peach arrives in America to choose a state and watches, unmoved, as they parade before her. And then, "rich Georgia, versed in rural art, / Knowing the longings of a Peach's heart," whispers in her ear of his "favorite son," whose home was "prepared for such a lovely bride," who would "cherish her through years of good or ill."[55]

"Behold!" Fort Valley: a tall twenty-four-year- old from Powersville named Arthur Vinson, clad in a blinding white suit and shoes, with Sam Rumph Jr. at his side as his best man. Wasting no time with flirtation, "with lovelight in his eyes," Fort Valley "woos and wins Pomona's richest prize!" And then that temperamental child of the gods, the Peach, "yields, – she blushes, – oh! how sweet is Spring! / She plights her troth with good Pomona's ring!" His conquest is final: the Peach would no longer be a sexual adventurer but a contented wife, "settled down in Georgia's happy state!"[56] Reading the "Aeneid of the Peach," it is easy to forget that Mabel Withoft was a devoted Baptist who approved the strict moral code of the denomination's mission schools.

The rhetoric of the new county advocates conjured a simple little community that wanted freedom from old imperial privilege. A more accurate picture, however, may be of Fort Valley trimming away its rural hinterland like a heavy garment, tailoring a government that fitted its own interests more closely. Indeed, the festivals that new county advocates staged in the midst of the Peach County campaign communicated a

TABLE 6.1. *Comparing Houston and Peach Counties in 1930*

	Houston County	Peach County
Total population	11,280	10,268
Black (%)	67.30	63.20
Female (%)	49.90	53.30
Urban (%)	0.00	44.40
Total number of families	2,574	2,392
White owners (%)	31.40	35.60
Black owners (%)	8.00	13.10

Source: U.S. Census Bureau, *1930 Census*, Social Explorer. Social Explorer Dataset (SE), Census 1930, Digitally transcribed by Inter-university Consortium for Political and Social Research. Edited, verified by Michael Haines. Compiled, edited, and verified by Social Explorer.

TABLE 6.2. *Houston, Macon, and Peach Counties peach and cotton acreage, 1889–1929*

	Houston cotton acreage	Macon cotton acreage	Peach cotton acreage	Houston peach acreage	Macon peach acreage	Peach peach acreage
1889	73,181	42,470	n/a	502	354	n/a
1899	62,022	35,764	n/a	6,383	1,842	n/a
1909	77,961	45,755	n/a	10,661	4,433	n/a
1919	43,728	42,297	n/a	26,119	13,765	n/a
1924	19,533	42,035	11,392	8,317	13,296	14,301
1929	25,333	48,048	13,244	4,071	4,784	6,055

Source: U.S. Census Bureau, *Census of Agriculture*, 1890, 1900, 1910, 1920, 1925, 1930. The cotton acreage is taken directly from the census reports, while the peach acreage is for trees of all ages (bearing and nonbearing) and assumes 130 trees per acre.

number of visual and textual arguments for the singularity of Fort Valley, but the overriding message was quite simple: We are rich and smart! The numbers from the first census after the split bolster this point. The new division did divide the black and white population approximately in half, as the Peach County campaign argued. Not surprisingly, they had more foreign-born whites (thirty-three in Peach, nine in Houston), and their rates of property ownership were slightly higher. The starkest difference is rurality: Peach County's population was almost half urban, living in towns of twenty-five hundred people or more (see Tables 6.1 and 6.2).

The observations of the sociologist Arthur Raper confirmed this portrayal of wealth separating from poverty. Raper was the author of a series of important and suggestively titled investigations of the rural South in the 1930s: *Preface to Peasantry, Tenants of the Almighty, Sharecroppers All.* Raper observed in 1936 that six of seven Georgia counties with the most overseers and farm managers were in middle Georgia. As overseers and managers were typically found only on the largest farms of five hundred or more acres, this statistic indicated an unusual concentration of wealth and power. Raper contended that this concentration was "accounted for largely by the peach, melon, asparagus, and pecan industries." Peach County, like Bleckley County in 1913, "was called into being ... by a group of large planters who wanted a county of their own." In fact, Raper noted, in 1925 only two Georgia counties exceeded Peach in the number of managers and overseers.[57]

And in Fort Valley, they managed and oversaw black labor, a point on which the peach blossom festivals were conspicuously silent. Local blacks appeared in the pageants as "Nubian" porters, carrying a princess in a litter; as Arabian grooms, tending to the festival king's horses; and as slaves, representing the harmony of the Old South. Their symbolic roles in the festival imagination were as foreign and historic curiosities. African Americans' actual roles in the festival were just as telling. The photographs in which blacks appeared most prominently were food-oriented. Black men, under white supervision, stand guard over vast barbecue pits and enormous cauldrons of Brunswick stew; black women peer at the camera over great pots of coffee.[58] White chroniclers of the festivals often cited the quantities served as points of pride – the Brunswick stew in 1924, for example, required six hundred pounds of salt, two cases of celery, four barrels of vinegar, sixty gallons of canned corn, eighty gallons of tomatoes, eighteen gallons of English peas, fifty pounds of onions, and twenty bushels of potatoes – but the labor that produced this feast earned no commentary. The humans sweating in the sun over smoking sides of pork and steaming vats of Brunswick stew made the photographs, but not the written accounts.

In the heat of the new county campaign, Peach County proponents had admitted that the new county's black population would be larger than Houston's. But "the least said about this," they wrote, "the better for boh [*sic*] sides."[59] The peach blossom festivals bore out this agreement of silence. They imagined the peach industry in escapist terms, as an exotic endowment from Persia or China, a gift of the gods and entirely apart from the ragged cotton culture that propelled Georgia's rural economy. But the organizers of the Peach Blossom Festivals could have acknowledged the presence of Fort Valley High and Industrial School; they could have praised that institution's own rural development campaign. Instead, as with so many early twentieth-century reform movements in the South, whiteness won out. Just as segregation appealed to southern progressives as a "clean solution" that allowed neither "disturbing private violence" nor "exceptions for individuals," the Peach Blossom Festivals scrubbed away the rural black population like the dark loam on which their prosperity depended.[60] Peach progress depended on both.

IV

The black rural improvement campaign was quieter and less ornate than the Peach County movement. The festivals emblematic of that campaign celebrated hams and eggs rather than flowers, solid sustenance rather than frothy potential. Henry and Florence Johnson Hunt arrived in Fort Valley just a few years before the Withofts to run the "little Tuskegee among the peach trees," Fort Valley High and Industrial School (FVHIS). Following the example and advice of Booker T. Washington, early twentieth-century cotton belt blacks such as Henry Hunt professed loyalty and exuded diligence. Meanwhile, they covertly pursued ambitions of transcending their disadvantages with an agricultural development program and a germ, at least, of agrarian subversion. Henry Hunt, along with the local extension agent Otis O'Neal, became national leaders of this black rural development program, and their story provides an important counternarrative to the peach myth as sketched out by Mabel Withoft and others.

According to the stories about him published during his lifetime, Henry Alexander Hunt Jr. was born in 1866 in a "little cabin that squatted on a red hillside" near Sparta, Hancock County, Georgia. There Hunt "chopped cotton, hoed potatoes, dropped corn and shelled peanuts" and thus "learned very early in life the hardships that beset 'darkies' on small, rundown farms." Hunt then worked his way through Atlanta University with odd jobs and carpentry until he landed at Biddle (later Johnson C. Smith) University in Charlotte, and then at FVHIS.[61] The casual reader was left to assume that Hunt was raised in a family newly freed from slavery. The shopworn respectability story of an African American climbing "up from slavery" via hard work – as Booker T. Washington had – was apparently irresistible.

In fact, Henry Hunt had risen up from freedom – and, in the curious local racial history of Hancock County, in a narrow space between white and black. His father, Henry Alexander Hunt Sr., was a white man, a tanner and a Confederate veteran who told the census takers year after year that he lived as a bachelor with his brother, J. M. Hunt, but whose store account records purchases of yards of silk and calico, needles and threads, white kid gloves, and pearl buttons. He also gave personalized porcelain cups to Henry Jr. and his four sisters and three brothers, and diamonds to the children's mother, "Cherokee Mariah Lilly" Hunt.[62] She wore her long, straight hair in a tight bun, and, as a child of one of Hancock County's finest homes, learned to play piano and organ at the whites-only Sparta Female Model School. Her mother, Susan Hunt, was the mixed-race mistress of Nathan Sayre, a prominent lawyer, legislator, state's attorney, and judge who kept in his library Alexander Walker's 1838 "precise rule" for racial amalgamation.[63] After Sayre's death in 1853, Hunt and her children moved a short distance away to "Hunt Hill," where they lived as part of a mixed-race community. While there is no official record of Mariah and Henry's marriage or cohabitation, the two apparently lived as husband and wife on a middling but prosperous farm until Henry Sr.'s death in 1889. So Henry Hunt Jr.'s supposed childhood of field labor seems an unlikely story. Henry Hunt Sr. had been a slaveholder prior to the war, and family members told the historian Adelle Logan Alexander "categorically that the white Hunts absolutely forbade [the Hunt children] to pick cotton because it was not considered an appropriate activity for anyone of their kin."[64]

A more accurate account of Henry A. Hunt Jr.'s childhood, then, would place him in an upwardly mobile middle-class family of rural origins. His sister Sarah taught elementary school in Tuskegee and was George Washington Carver's only documented love interest. His older sister, Adella Hunt, trained at Atlanta University, took a teaching job at Tuskegee Institute, married the institute's treasurer Warren Logan, and became a leading advocate for women's suffrage, public health, and black rights until December 1915, when she threw herself from the top floor of Tuskegee's main academic building, in full view of students, teachers, administrators, and two of her own children.[65] The youngest Hunt brother, Tom, also attended Tuskegee, graduated from the agricultural program at the University of Massachusetts, and worked as a professor of agriculture at Berkeley. Tom was apparently the only Hunt sibling who chose to pass as white.

The Hunts' unique ancestry gave them the privilege and the burden of choosing their race.[66] As W. E. B. Du Bois observed in an address at FVHIS after Henry Hunt's death, choosing whiteness would seem to be "perfectly natural" in view of what it had to offer: an escape from "the inhibitions, the caste laws, the prevalence of veiled or open insult, the problem of earning a living." But such a choice would have had its own kind of cost. For Henry Hunt, it would have meant severing himself from his siblings, unless they had all chosen to be white, in which case it would have meant disowning his mother.[67] Beyond the question of family, choosing to be Negro was, for Henry Hunt, also a matter of self-respect. It was a way of laying bare the absurdity of racial hierarchy: a society in which being of one-sixteenth African descent could trap an American in a lower caste, while being fifteen-sixteenths white was of no legal value. Being black, said W.E.B. DuBois, gave Henry Hunt a life of situations "where after having been treated as a man and a fellow he suddenly was subjected to ostracism or insult" when his racial self-identification was discovered.[68]

That life of purpose must have begun at home, growing up as he did in a family apparently devoted to the well-being of southern blacks, but it acquired focus when Hunt was a student at Atlanta University and a disciple of its founding president, Edmund Asa Ware.[69] After earning his B.A. in 1890, Hunt reportedly considered going to Africa to accept a position that awaited him – but decided instead to take on a directorship of a secondary school in Charlotte, North Carolina, and later the role of business manager and director of trades at Biddle University (soon to be Johnson C. Smith University), also in Charlotte. Perhaps he did so to be closer to the woman he had evidently fallen for at Atlanta University: Florence Johnson, who hailed from a middle-class black family in Raleigh. They married in 1893. For thirteen years, while Florence operated a boardinghouse for Biddle students, Henry worked to build the school's industrial program, organizing some of the state's first black farmers' conferences and quietly earning a reputation in the industrial school community of the turn of the century.[70] In 1904, the trustees of Fort Valley High and Industrial School came calling. Would Hunt be willing to take on the struggling institution?[71]

Hunt had grown up only a few miles away from Fort Valley, but he must have harbored concerns about this offer. FVHIS had been the brainchild of the Atlanta University graduate John W. Davison, who had cobbled together the school in 1895 from the ruins of a series of post-Reconstruction educational efforts.[72] For eight years, Davison kept the school running with his own money, the meager support of the local black community, and a few donors such as Anna T. Jeanes and John Howard Hale.[73] The school initially consisted of "one small shanty on four acres of land valued at $800, against which there was a mortgage of $1,000."[74] There were two teachers for about one hundred students, who attended for the four months out of the year when the planters did not require their labor in cotton fields.

But Davison's brainchild soon became the ward of northern philanthropy. In 1896, Davison hired James Torbert as assistant principal and financial agent. Torbert canvassed northern cities seeking monetary nourishment for their fledgling institution, sleeping in cheap hotels and Adirondack hay lofts, "trampling in the snow" of New York and Boston "without rubbers or even suitable shoes," and by 1900 was raising three thousand dollars to five thousand dollars per year.[75] He won the attention of some prominent northern industrialists, the most important of whom was George Foster Peabody. It was Peabody who, in addition to giving his own money to the school, attracted the attention of the Rockefeller Foundation's General Education Board (GEB). The members of the GEB were amazed by the absence of a Hampton–Tuskegee–style institution in Georgia, home to the largest black population in the South, and backed the FVHIS idea.[76]

But northern white philanthropy came with northern white strings. Among philanthropists and black leaders, there was broad agreement on the need for improved education for southern blacks, but not as to the nature of that education. Many blacks, most prominently W. E. B. DuBois, believed that liberal arts education was preparation for citizenship and equality, and that reformers ought to focus on the "talented tenth."[77] But to Peabody and other northern whites, and their allies such as Booker T. Washington, the liberal arts model seemed a wasteful extravagance. Why offer great books to southern blacks when they still lacked food and clothing? The northern philanthropic imagination was in thrall to the Hampton–Tuskegee model of industrial education. Then as now, there was a great deal of overlap between the ideals of personal advancement via "uplift" and the need for more reliable laborers.

Indeed, the FVHIS story suggests that northerners were even *more* adamant in their support for industrial education than southern whites. John W. Davison paid lip service to the Hampton–Tuskegee model because he knew that his northern supporters would approve, but the vocational component of FVHIS remained underdeveloped. When Davison failed to produce results even after they sent him to special training at the Hampton Institute, the FVHIS board – now stacked with northern industrialists, courtesy of Torbert's fund-raising efforts – pressured Davison to resign. It is not clear how much Henry Hunt knew of this back story when he agreed to work at FVHIS in 1904, but he pursued the GEB's agenda with vigor, firing teachers, replacing black trustees, and coercing

less-than-enthusiastic students to enroll in his industrial education programs. By 1907 the transformation was complete.[78]

Henry Hunt was no mere hatchet man or opportunist, though. FVHIS
was clearly in trouble. When Davison had resigned, the school only
remained solvent by renting out a room to a printing office and a hall as
a skating rink.[79] Moreover, the Hunts took on the work at FVHIS at great
personal cost. Charlotte, North Carolina, was no New York, but it was
at least four times the size of Fort Valley and in the midst of rapid economic and demographic growth.[80] For Florence Hunt, who had apparently never been to middle Georgia, the move bordered on the traumatic.
Her recollections of that moment, true to her medical training, took on
the air of a doctor checking off symptoms of economic, environmental
and social malaise.

> The rooms, so large, so empty and bare. Anna T. Jeanes Hall dormitory partially
> completed… The deep cellar surrounded by a three foot brick wall and filled
> with water. The beginning of another building. The school grounds, a sand bed,
> millions, billions, trillions of pebbles, but trees, shrubbery, lawns – where, oh
> where, were they! At night the croak of the frogs, the yell of the drinkers, gam-
> blers on the railroad banks, green slimy puddles of water, mosquitoes, malaria,
> typhoid. Summer-time, few gardens, green pork, no screened markets, flies, gnats,
> sore-eyed babies, no nurses, no colored doctors. Girls and boys loitering along to
> school eight, nine, ten o'clock any hour. Excused at noon to go home to carry din-
> ner. Four months, three, two, in school during the year. The new educated Negro,
> looked at so hard, so silently, with the eyes of suspicion, doubt, fear.[81]

Like George Washington Carver, who had arrived in Tuskegee from
Ames, Iowa, in 1896, the Hunts found themselves "in a strange land and
among strange people."[82] What would they make of the place?

V

"Will try to write more another time," Henry Hunt scrawled to a friend in
Atlanta a few months after he had arrived in Fort Valley, "but I need to get
to bed, it's nearly twelve and I was up later last night. You see I'm just 'getting a line on' things here and it takes pretty strenuous living."[83] In his first
years as president, Hunt not only lived strenuously himself but took it as
a watchword for the entire institution (see Figure 6.4). One of his first acts
was to issue a promotional pamphlet that captured the school's renewed
direction in its first word: *work*. On the cover was a photograph of blacks
in a peach cannery or packinghouse, with a caption explaining that many
students worked in the peach industry during their summer vacation. The

FIGURE 6.4. "President [Hunt] and matron in pantry, Fort Valley H and I School."
Original caption provided by source.
Source: Jackson Davis, photographer. Courtesy of Special Collections
Department, University of Virginia Library Jackson Davis Papers, 1906–1947,
Accession #3072, #3072-a. Online access: http://search.lib.virginia.edu/catalog/
uva-lib:330968.

photograph did double duty: it conjured associations with the nationally
known Georgia peach industry and signaled that Fort Valley's students
were comfortable with agricultural and other manual labor. Above the
photograph, boldfaced letters advertised the school's "Work in the Black
Belt of Southwest Georgia," where "Within a Radius of 50 Miles 200,000
Negroes Can Be Reached" with the school's message: "To Teach the Head
to Think, the Heart to Love, and the Hands to Work."[84] In addition to
being the first word in the title and occurring three times on the cover,
the word "work" and its variations appeared no fewer than twenty-nine
times in twelve pages of text. The leaflet explained that every student took
agricultural classes, since the school aimed to "take hold of the young men
and women from the country districts" and "to give to them the ability
and skill to cope with conditions as they exist." FVHIS was producing
the "real teachers and leaders" of the rural South. Images throughout the
leaflet showed students in fields, at sewing machines, on construction sites,
reading Bibles on the porches of poor tenants.

The pamphlet thus took a middle way between the two extremes of contemporary portrayals of black southerners. At one end, the photographs
of African American life assembled by W. E. B. DuBois for the 1900 Paris

Exposition highlighted the middle-class, even Victorian, character of "the Georgia Negro," with photographs of dapper mustached men in suits and light-skinned women in high collars and puff-sleeved shirtwaists.[85] At the opposite end of the spectrum, advertisements for Aunt Jemima flour products, Gold Dust Twins soap, Bull Durham tobacco, among others, became increasingly racist in their depictions of black characters.[86] In contrast to both of these portrayals, the FVHIS material suggested a dignified black populace – relegated to certain kinds of work.

This talk of rural revitalization through hard labor was more than donor-pleasing rhetoric for Henry Hunt. His classically oriented Atlanta University training notwithstanding, he appeared truly to believe, as the political scientist Willard Range indicated, that "agriculture was the only way out of distress for the Georgia Negro." In short, "The mantle of Booker T. Washington was upon him."[87] In the same way that Atlanta University's John Hope was "the Moses of the urban Negro of Georgia," Hunt sought to become "the patriarch of the rural masses."[88] Though his own background was in the trades, Hunt threw himself into agricultural education. He organized the first of many black farmers' conferences in July 1911, which earned praise from the *Atlanta Constitution* for having "awakened" rural blacks in middle Georgia.[89] In 1914, Hunt hired Otis Samuel O'Neal. Born in 1891 in Upson County, Georgia, O'Neal attended FVHIS from 1902 to 1908, taught briefly in the agricultural school at Forsyth, enrolled at Tuskegee Institute in 1910, and became the second black county agent in Houston County, and one of only two black male agents in the entire state.[90] Like his mentor, George Washington Carver, O'Neal started by coordinating his institution's biennial farmers' conferences.[91] And as Carver did, O'Neal believed in providing concrete examples. He held meat-curing demonstrations and encouraged "lead farmers" in local communities to display their homegrown eggs, cured meat, and canned fruit on their porches.[92]

The Ham and Egg Show followed logically from these demonstrations. O'Neal had puzzled for two years over the problem of rural blacks' low-protein diet before he hit upon a solution. "It came to me," he later explained, "that I could get all the farmers who had meat to bring it every year to one central place so that those who hadn't any could see and be inspired. People were having flower shows, horse shows and dog shows so that prettier flowers and better horses and dogs, would be raised; why not have a Ham Show?"[93] Initially a simple agricultural fair designed to demonstrate the black belt's "material progress," it later featured talks by extension specialists and, by the 1940s, concerts by blues musicians.[94]

The Ham and Egg Shows and the rural mission of FVHIS orbited around an eminently practical vision of rural development. O'Neal and Hunt hoped to establish a black yeomanry in the cotton belt, an educated class of small-holders with the roots of their prosperity firmly in the soil. With conferences, clubs, loans, education, O'Neal hoped to see his people "rise from almost starvation to home owners and comfort," as a later biographer put it.[95]

But of course all this agrarian development was in tension with the much-discussed phenomenon of the Great Migration. Leaving the rural South was not the solution to black poverty that Hunt wanted, committed as he was to making farmers and landowners of the rural masses, but he adroitly turned concern over the phenomenon to his advantage. In a 1916 article, he blamed out-migration in part on the desire of rural blacks for better schools. The *Constitution* republished his editorial and added their agreement: Georgia was "undoubtedly behind in the matter of negro education," the *Constitution* opined, "unfair in the matter of facilities, in the quality of teachers and instructors, and in the pay of those expected to impart proper instruction to negro children." And for the *Constitution*, this was a problem not just because it was unfair but because education "minimizes or removes" the "brutal instinct." Referring vaguely to the "list of outrageous crimes" committed by "illiterate negro brutes," the editorial argued that just as the "trained dog" makes a better animal, so "the right sort of education makes a better workman." A better funded, better run school system "would help both races" – not least, from the perspective of the *Constitution*, by keeping local blacks local, and ensuring a ready labor supply.[96]

Hunt's particular genius was to turn all kinds of opinions about the "negro problem" to the advantage of his cause, to use the incredibly tiny political space for a black spokesperson in the Jim Crow South to say something meaningful. Just as he used the prejudices of *Constitution* readers to make his case, he was equally astute when speaking to more racially liberal audiences. In a 1919 address on the "rural conditions of labor" to the NAACP's tenth anniversary conference in Cleveland, he acknowledged that widespread prejudice and the failure of black leaders had left the countryside's "common men" unaware of their "rights and privileges."[97] But the Great Migration was changing rural life for those who stayed, according to Hunt. The "scales are falling from the eyes," he argued. "Labor on account of its scarcity is becoming more and more free."[98] In 1921, representing the "community of Fort Valley," he was one of 113 delegates to the second Pan-African Congress in London and

Brussels, where he gave a talk on the "Negro problem" of the United
States in an international context. The DuBois-organized meeting – a
kind of international "talented tenth" according to the historian George
Frederickson – submitted resolutions to the League of Nations on the
self-determination of African nations and the treatment of African labor
under colonial rule.[99] If few tangible results emerged from the meeting,
it seemed to whet Hunt's appetite for international collaboration – a few
years later he would travel to Denmark to observe the success of rural
cooperatives there. In 1925 he was invited to give the opening address
at Atlanta University, where he argued: "The way men think is the most
practical concern in life."[100] Condemning the fatalism of assuming that
"ignorance, poverty and degradation" were theirs by "divine decree,"
Hunt urged the students to fight oppression and abuse by "straight thinking on the part of those who are the victims of crooked thinking."[101] For
all the talk of rank division between Booker T. Washington and W. E.
B. DuBois, Hunt's vision suggests that there was more common ground
than the professional jealousy of the two men seemed to permit.[102]

In 1927, Hunt gained an acolyte, Frank Horne, already a poet of
some renown for his "Letters Found near a Suicide," which won second place in a 1925 contest sponsored by *Crisis*. According to Horne, he
went to Fort Valley from Harlem determined to "discover a Lost Race;
to dig down amidst the roots from whence I sprang; to see black people
in the land that had risen from the labor of their hands; to see the streets
my mother knew; to see Negroes that were Negroes." No longer content
to dismiss the South as a "God-forsaken hinterland, the 'Sahara of the
Beaux Art,' the home of slavery and lynching and Confederate memorials, and benighted blacks who hadn't money nor sense enough to leave,"
Horne boarded a train to Georgia.[103] In Fort Valley, "the heart of peach
country," he found at FVHIS a "wonderful work ... enriching the lives of
an entire community." Seeing the students "learning to use their hands as
well as their hearts" his own heart filled with "a great peace and a great
hope."[104] At Fort Valley he coached track, took care of his ten-year-old
niece Lena Horne a few years before her rise to fame, and then became
academic director and later acting principal.[105] In 1930 Horne reported
to W. E. B. DuBois that his work had been "apparently successful and
very happy." He and Hunt had ambitions of making FVHIS "one of the
strongest preparatory schools in the South." And Hunt was "one of those
practical idealists with whom it has truly been inspiring to work."[106]

The African American elite found Hunt to be inspiring as well: the
NAACP named Hunt the 1930 Spingarn Medalist – a prestigious award

that had also been given to James Weldon Johnson, George Washington Carver, W. E. B. Du Bois, and Carter G. Woodson. Horne wrote a tribute in *Crisis* that called Hunt the "Civilizer of a Race!" and credited him with the fact that "the gleam of civilization has caught another spark in the dark hinterlands of the Black Belt of Georgia."[107] His "heroic" and "self-effacing" hard work had transformed a "barren wilderness" into a modern, beautiful, progressive campus. Local blacks were healthier because of the school nurse and hospital (a pet project of Henry Hunt's wife, Florence Johnson Hunt); they were better farmers because of Otis O'Neal's farm demonstration work; they were better educated because of the forty-five teachers and workers at FVHIS; they were even confident voters because of Hunt's "upright, fearless, straight-forward" approach to politics. Hunt, according to this article, had not only won over white residents, he had transformed a population of "ignorant, sodden, disinterested blacks" into "an upright, self-respecting, voting community."[108]

The *Atlanta Constitution* praised Hunt's accomplishments as well, though with the clear subtext that Hunt was teaching blacks to be productive *second-class* citizens. Hunt instructed middle Georgia's "ignorant, underfed, lazy-going, sleepy blacks" not how to stand up for themselves, said reporter Willie Snow Ethridge, but how to work. "A negro who has learned to be punctual, honest, and dependable is not ignorant," Ethridge wrote. "Though he does not know how to read and write, he is educated for he has mastered those subjects that count for most in life." For Ethridge, Hunt's influence in the black community was primarily moral rather than political or economic: he emphasized the presence of a "colored missionary" who went out to African American homes "on the peach orchards" in order to encourage Bible reading and church attendance. Ethridge also chronicled Hunt's efforts to "reach the young negro boys who hang around on street corners every summer between the closing of the peach season and the beginning of the cotton picking season," entertaining them with baseball and contests "so that their idle hands will not find evil work to do."[109] No voting or landowning here; indeed, it takes just a little reading between the lines to see Ethridge's portrayal as an attempt to calm white fears about mobs of "young negro boys" amid a generally restive black population.

As these two profiles of Henry Hunt and FVHIS suggest, the local nickname for the school – the "light in the valley" – could be taken in either of two ways, depending on how one defined the darkness. For local blacks, FVHIS appeared to represent a kind of quiet liberation from the oppressive darkness of white dominance. For local whites, FVHIS seemed to be about the business of training a "punctual, hard-working, honest and dependable" labor force.[110] This ambiguity seems to have been Hunt's precise aim: to work for black liberation while appearing to accept their subjugation. Frank Horne's description of Hunt as a *practical idealist* fit. For the moment, the idealistic work in the heart of the peach belt was making practical progress. As he described in 1930, "There are some who have something good the whole year through from their farms – eggs, chickens, and other fowls, vegetables, fruits, cane, oats, corn, peas, hogs, and a little cotton to supply his ready cash. They own their own farms and are happy." FVHIS was "making its students love the land and look to it for their support."[111]

VI

Henry Hunt and Otis O'Neal continued to pursue their dream of a black yeomanry. In the *Fort Valley Message*, a FVHIS publication, Hunt argued that "Negro farmers must be led to see for themselves that it is best to remain on the farm instead of having the information given to them by bitter experience in the crowded cities. They must be shown how they may succeed and attain a happy life such as they have not enjoyed before."[112] There is oblique evidence that Hunt helped to arrange for an expansion of the franchise among Fort Valley area blacks, perhaps as part of the Peach County campaign, i.e., in exchange for votes for the "new county" legislative ticket in 1920. According to Frank Horne, Hunt's bravery and sense of justice had earned the respect of whites and blacks alike. "Negroes," Horne wrote, "at first afraid to register, have gained with their organized votes a complete 9 room training school building and effected the administrative division of Peach and Houston counties."[113] Forty years after the new county campaign, the white Fort Valley druggist Homer Avera wrote to Senator Richard B. Russell that the voter registration campaign then under way in Fort Valley was proceeding peacefully. "They were allowed to register – and there were no incidents whatever," Avera averred, a little defensively. "Negroes have always been allowed to vote in Peach County."[114]

If Hunt's work on behalf of black suffrage was almost invisible – conducted, as it probably was, in private meetings with Fort Valley's leaders – his agrarian campaign was somewhat more public. In 1931, under the sponsorship of the Julius Rosenwald Fund, Henry Hunt traveled to Denmark to study rural cooperatives. His comments upon returning, in typical fashion, challenged the racial and economic order without overt confrontation. "There are practically no very wealthy people in Denmark and only a very few poor ones," he observed. "The Danes accepted many years ago the theory that the people of the country are happiest when there are few who have too much and fewer still who have too little."[115]

Hunt's rural expertise made him a candidate for a position in Franklin D. Roosevelt's so-called black cabinet – in this case, the director of special service for Negro farmers, an assistant to the governor of the Farm Credit Administration (FCA), Henry Morgenthau Jr.[116] The position grew out of the 1933 Amenia Conference in upstate New York, which sought to redefine the direction of the NAACP and afforded, among other things, an audience with Morganthau.[117] In their letter recommending Hunt to Morgenthau, W. E. B DuBois and Ira Reid observed, as if they feared that a New Yorker like Morganthau was unappreciative of this fact, that farming was "still the chief occupation of Negroes and also the occupation least removed from their former slavery, both by law and custom. The black farmer, either as laborer, share-cropper or owner, is very largely a serf and public opinion in the South has not yet been able to envisage him independent, intelligent and the recipient of a living income." Given the need to understand the nature of these problems from the ground up, Henry Hunt was the only person they could think of for the job. "Mr. Hunt knows intimately by personal visits and direct touch the situation of the Negro farmer," they wrote, but had also read and traveled widely. His school was private, giving him "greater independence" than state school officials, whose funding was dependent on legislators opposed to the New Deal, but he was also "known and well-thought of by the better class of white people in his state and in the South."[118] At the FCA, Hunt's primary task was to publicize the agency's programs – low-interest loans, primarily – to black farmers who might otherwise be unaware of it or reluctant to participate. As the agency reported directly to the president, it skirted the jurisdiction of the USDA, which was generally unfriendly to the cause of black farmers. According to the National Urban League's southern field director, Jesse O. Thomas, "the government, because of Hunt's close contact with affairs, is refusing but few farm loans to negro farmers on account of race."[119]

The Great Depression had fixed the nation's eyes on the countryside in ways of which the country life movement of previous decades had only dreamed. Documentary photographers for the Farm Security Administration such as Dorothea Lange and Walker Evans moved up and down the landscape making a case, as it were, for government relief for

FIGURE 6.5. "Peach pickers being driven to the orchards. They earn seventy-five cents a day. Muscella [*sic*], Georgia." Original caption provided by source.
Source: Dorothea Lange, July 1936. Courtesy of the Library of Congress, Prints and Photographs Division. LC-USF34-009452-E.

these wretched people (see Figure 6.5). John Steinbeck's *Grapes of Wrath* dramatized the plight of that American hero the independent yeoman farmer, still working in the fields, but homeless, landless, and powerless before the great factory farmers of California. Rural America was the proving ground of the American dream.[120]

But in the South, the fine progressive programs of the New Deal had to contend with the entrenched power of conservative white Democrats, and well-intended reforms often went awry. The best-known case is the Agricultural Adjustment Administration (AAA), which Jack Temple Kirby described as a "relief agency designed to raise the incomes of land-owning farmers."[121] Created by the Agricultural Adjustment Act of 1933, the AAA purported to stabilize crop prices by subsidizing farmers who reduced their acreage. In theory, these conservation payments would be

shared by the landowner and tenants, but in practice, the program provided the largest landowners with the financial flexibility to evict their
tenants. The Delta and Pine Land Company, which controlled thousands
of acres of cotton in Mississippi, received more than $318,000 from 1933
to 1935. In addition to low-interest loans through the Production Credit
Association, the AAA payments provided large landowners with the capital to diversify, mechanize, or otherwise modernize and consolidate their
operations. In 1935, southern tenancy began a sharp decline, accompanied by a more modest increase in wage labor. The changes set in motion
by the AAA amounted to what the historian Pete Daniel calls the "southern enclosure."[122]

By the mid-1930s, therefore, hopes that the New Deal might result
in genuine uplift for the most vulnerable rural southerners had dimmed.
Frank Horne, whom Hunt had left in charge of FVHIS while Hunt
worked in Washington and traveled the Southeast, grew increasingly
cynical about the potential for change. In 1934, Horne asked DuBois
for materials on "the practical principles of cooperative action," which
he thought might be pursued with success at Fort Valley. A few months
later, he invited DuBois to speak to the 350 "odd sisters" gathered at Fort
Valley for the summer session to seek "Inspiration and Enlightenment."
Would DuBois "say a word or two to these teachers for the good of their
souls"? Would he "stimulate" the agricultural teachers in particular "to
the realization of their real problems"? By the following spring, Horne's
budding sarcasm had blossomed into disenchantment. The National
Urban League's journal *Opportunity* had asked him for an article on
industrial schools for southern blacks, and he planned, he told DuBois,
"to tell them at least some of the unvarnished truth. Reflecting on the
potential backlash, he added: "if you need a good janitor, keep the job
open a while for me."[123] The editors of *Opportunity* divided the piece in
half and ran it in the May and June 1935 issues, with the understated
introduction: "The statements in this article ... will surprise many who
are seriously interested in the education of the Negro." From the opening sentence, Horne did not disappoint. "As factors in training Negro
youth to earn a livelihood in industrial America of today," he began,
"the industrial schools of the South, except in a few rare instances, could
practically all be scrapped without appreciable loss to any one."[124] Only
Hampton and Tuskegee – and only "possibly" – escaped his condemnation. The acting principal of FVHIS did not even spare his own institution.
In part, Horne contended, the failure resulted from the faulty premise
promulgated by Booker T. Washington and others: "Blessed would be

the meek and those who toiled would inherit the earth, *sans* vote, *sans* union, *sans* legal security."[125] Whereas there seemed to be progress in the first decades of the twentieth century, land loss and illiteracy had actually increased in the 1920s.[126] Horne also blamed the faulty practice that had followed that faulty premise. While the raison d'être of such schools was training in agriculture, carpentry, mechanics, leatherwork, plumbing, sewing, and nutrition, in fact the students were "attracted in droves by the questionable security of the teaching profession – *teachers* of agriculture, *teachers* of trades, *teachers* of home economics."[127] The schools "are poorly equipped, inadequately manned, pursue vague objectives, are over-ambitious in their offers, emphasize theory rather than practice... Too much farming is done in books and too much serving of meals on paper."[128]

Horne acknowledged that this gap between rhetoric and practice at industrial schools was not in most cases due to dishonesty, but rather to lack of funding, inability to keep up with rapid technological change, and demands of accrediting agencies for academic rather than vocational competence. But the effect was the same: "our most influential institutions [Tuskegee and Hampton] are after all but pin-points of flickering light in a surrounding chaos of darkness."[129] Horne then offered some suggestions for reform, but argued that the sharecropping system, legal discrimination, exclusion from unions, and the "abrogation of the franchise" would render even these reforms ineffectual. "Life, liberty and happiness go along with the vote," Horne concluded; "without it, all we have left is the pursuit."[130] Horne reinforced this point in "Dog House Education," an article for the *Journal of Negro Education* a year later. Without economic stability, suffrage, and legal protection, to talk about school reform was to discuss the "reorganization and redirection of the practically non-existent."[131] Recruited by Mary McLeod Bethune to work for the National Youth Administration, Horne left Fort Valley that year and never returned, though he went on to a distinguished career with the Federal Housing Administration. He had given up on rural reform, but not on racial uplift.

The black agrarian dream of Hunt and Horne had two final episodes in middle Georgia. The first was the effort to organize a cooperative community under the auspices of the Resettlement Administration (RA) in 1936.[132] At the invitation of an administrator at FVHIS, the RA had optioned several thousand acres in Peach County and initially projected a place called "Fort Valley Farms," which would settle "one hundred negro families on some of the finest land in the south and in a county that furnishes excellent educational facilities," resulting in an "ideal community project ... that will be of great economic and social benefit to the entire negro race."[133] Before building began, however, nearly fifty leading Fort Valley citizens – many associated with the peach industry – sent an urgent telegram to Tugwell. "Before proceeding further with your resettlement project in Fort Valley," they wrote, "we earnestly request that you investigate the feeling of the citizens of Peach County in regard to same. You will find serious and strong opposition."[134] Although the logic of such opposition was presumably explained only in face to face meetings, what survives in official correspondence suggests two potential explanations: fears about the "concentration of negro settlers" in such a project, and related concerns about the effect on wages and on the contentment of African Americans not chosen for the project.[135] The project was moved to Macon County, where despite an apparently fraudulent petition protesting the dangerous raising of expectations accomplished by such a project, Flint River Farms went into operation in 1937. There 106 black families owned and cooperatively farmed 10,653 acres for almost a decade.[136]

The second episode was the national attention paid to Otis O'Neal's Ham and Egg Show. Appearing in *Reader's Digest* and *Life* in 1943, the festival proclaimed, as usual, the importance of rural independence and agricultural diversification. *Life*'s profile noted the Ham and Egg Show's "usual carefree hours filled with laughing, singing, dancing and storytelling." But the magazine also observed how attuned the event was to the importance of food production during the war. A full-page photograph showed Otis O'Neal delivering the keynote address. He stood under a "Food for Victory" placard, behind a whole smoked pig, and completely surrounded by "more than 300 fine, meaty, juicy hams." The small farmer is vital to winning the war, O'Neal insisted, "pounding away" at his two main points: crop diversification and "the importance of farmers staying on their land," despite the temptation of high-paying jobs in wartime industries.[137]

The entertainment in 1943 offered a more compelling critique of conditions in the South. The special guest, Bus Ezell, belted out the show's theme song, "Roosevelt and Hitler (Strange Things Are Happening in the Land)," his eleven-stanza wartime hit that covered everything from Jesus's prophecies of earthquakes, to Franklin Roosevelt's reluctance to commit troops to fight Hitler, to the role of black soldiers.[138] But the song also contained a subtle critique of the nation's political economy.

We have read also of famines,
That shall come in this land.
But if you notice closely,
You can see and understand.
  Provisions are so high,
  'Til we can't hardly buy.
There are strange things a-happenin' in this Land."[139]

As if to underscore this contemporary application of biblical famine prophecies, a local 4-H troop dramatized the mission of the Office of Price Administration (OPA). Alphonsa Jessie, a young man dressed as Uncle Sam in stars and stripes and a top hat, gesticulated toward jumper-clad Emily Jones, who wielded a kitchen knife in one hand and a placard labeled "OPA" around her neck. Jones held her knife threateningly over a recalcitrant Pearlie Brown, who played the part of "Prices." Uncle Sam was giving the OPA the power to "slash" Prices.[140] The drama highlighted one solution to the lack of purchasing power occasioned by wartime inflation. The OPA, according to the historian Meg Jacobs, represented the zenith of twentieth-century "pocketbook politics," the alliance between a women-led consumer movement and labor unions. The OPA was itself a "radical model of management" that "challenged the right of private industries to set their own prices and sell their items freely." One could also argue, as did many in urban areas, that wages needed to increase as well.[141]

In rural areas, however, the solution to the rising cost of living presented by O'Neal and Hunt was to forgo buying in favor of raising provisions at home. And this was the burden of the Ham and Egg Festival: to convince farmers that they could be more self-sufficient. It was a campaign of progress by protein. As O'Neal explained in 1945: "Give a hard-working man a good slice of home-cured ham in a sandwich. Let him eat it and he can work all day and never get hungry and never need food. You can't do it with beef, you can't do it with fresh pork, you can't do it with lamb. But ham's got everything a man needs."[142] Nutritional self-sufficiency, in other words, made for better work. One could interpret O'Neal's explanation as an acceptance of low status for rural blacks, relegating them to the laboring classes, but such an interpretation would not do justice to the vision of O'Neal and Henry Hunt for African American self-sufficiency and landownership. The protein campaign was part of an overall agenda of allowing rural blacks to remain rural – and to flourish there.

The Ham and Egg Show's moment in the national spotlight was like a meteor burning its brightest just before extinguishing. For though the event continued for the next decade or so under the leadership of Otis O'Neal's successor Robert Church, and though the USDA honored O'Neal with a Superior Service Award in 1951, the festival's legacy was as much musical as it was agricultural.[143] Farming would *not* supply the answer for black progress. Better employment opportunities during and after World War II, the evolving strategies of the civil rights movement, and USDA policies that pushed black farmers off their land throughout the latter half of the twentieth century – all of these factors limited the power of the black agrarian vision of folks such as Henry Hunt and Otis O'Neal. But this foreclosure of the movement does not mean that we should read that irrelevance, teleologically, into the past. For a moment it offered a compelling alternative to the agricultural development campaigns like those represented by the peach auxiliary of Fort Valley.

VII

Henry Alexander Hunt died in Washington, D.C., on October 1, 1938. His body was transported back to FVHIS, where he was eulogized and buried. "It is hard for me to say anything that has meaning at your great bereavement," W. E. B. DuBois wrote to Florence Hunt a few days later. "You have at any rate the very great satisfaction of knowing that Henry Hunt at his death had finished a fine and beneficent work and after all what more could one ask?"[144] DuBois was in attendance at Hunt's memorial service in February 1939 in Fort Valley, where Paul Laurence Dunbar's "A Hymn" was read aloud.

> Through mist and cloud I grope,
> Save for that fitful spark,
> The little flame of hope.

Several notables spoke: Acting Principal and former Atlanta University professor and playwright George A. Towns, local attorney and chairman of the 1924 festival C. L. Shepherd, and white State Supervisor of Vocational Agriculture Alva Tabor. Then they sang Henry Hunt's favorite hymn:

> Sometimes I feel discouraged,
> And think my work's in vain...
> There is a balm in Gilead to make the wounded whole.[145]

The service was in keeping with the whole of Hunt's life: the diligent, painstaking effort to keep alive "the fitful spark." From the beginning of his time at Fort Valley to the very end, the deep sounding note of Hunt's life was *work*: his own toil in building up the school, the future employment of his students, and, of course, the labor of his neighbors in rural Georgia. They laid him to rest in the middle of campus, finally finding, perhaps, *a balm in Gilead.*

Within days of Hunt's memorial service, in the midst of a "mission study course" Mabel Withoft had been teaching in Macon, she took ill. On July 30, she died. At her memorial service, held just a couple of days later, the congregation sang "The Old Rugged Cross," and then the choir – of which Withoft had been a member for more than thirty years – sent her off with "Jerusalem the Golden," a favorite hymn and "one she had often said she wanted sung at her funeral."[146]

> Jerusalem, the golden!
>   I languish for one gleam
> Of all thy glory, folden
>   In distance and in dream.
> My thoughts, like palms in exile,
>   Climb up to look and pray
> For a glimpse of that dear country
>   That lies so far away.[147]

Then, a crowd of "sorrowing friends," from as far away as Macon and Atlanta, gathered at Fort Valley's train station and sent Mabel Withoft's coffin, along with Frank Withoft and two close friends, back to Dayton, Ohio, where she was buried. Frank would join her at his death nine years later.

Like Henry Hunt's, Mabel Withoft's life bore some resemblance to her favorite hymn. She strove always to weave her story – and the stories of the places she lived – into wider narratives, sweeping and romantic. As a girl in rural Ohio, she wrote original Gothic romances for the unappreciative children who shared the dusty little schoolhouse; later, she wrote that dark motherless time into a "picture of child life" that was almost a conversion narrative. As a young woman, she wrote ecstatic verse about southern fruit; later, she wrote epic poems that connected the mundane business of selling that fruit to classical narratives of longing and home: *All thy glory, folden in distance and in dream.*

Henry Hunt and Mabel Withoft are just two of the hundreds drawn to middle Georgia by the presence of the peach industry. Neither of them grew, picked, or packed fruit, but they nevertheless played crucial roles. Hunt was intimately involved with the welfare of the people who labored in the fields and made peach growing profitable; he spent most of his life working on behalf of the mostly unfulfilled aspirations of equality through landownership and agricultural acumen. Hunt's institution, FVHIS, would likely not have lasted without the peach industry, especially the more affluent brokers and merchants and investors, many of whom were from elsewhere and nurtured more "progressive" ideas about race relations. Mabel Withoft, meanwhile, moved to Fort Valley because of her husband's family connection and stayed because of his work with a produce brokerage. She typified the leading white citizens of Fort Valley, who believed in – or at least used – the idea of peach progress, the belief that animated the Peach County secession movement. All manner of good things were to follow in the train of Queen Peach: women's suffrage, efficient county administration, business investment, and agricultural development, and, not least, lives of beauty and purpose amid the southern pines.

These two campaigns for rural progress, black and white, proceeded with rough simultaneity, but their narratives have taken shape as parallel lines. And while parallel lines, by definition, never intersect, these stories did in Fort Valley. To tell the two stories *together*, as I have done here, is to lament the tragedy of separation. White problems and black problems in the rural South were intimately connected; teasing them apart in order to solve them separately was not to solve them at all.[148]

If Hunt's campaign for rural prosperity constituted, to adapt Frank Horne's formulation, a "practical idealism," the white-led campaign for Peach County represented what we might call "idealistic pragmatism" – a steel-fisted power grab under a lace glove of song, dance, and flowers. Hunt's idealism ultimately foundered on the shoals of the pragmatism of efforts like the Peach County campaign. A new war overseas created an overwhelming demand for labor; rural blacks followed the work and moved north. And so rural progress – at least in places like Fort Valley – became *white* progress.[149] With the labor leaving, white peach growers expanded their search to the Atlantic coast "migrant stream," and then, hemispherically, to Jamaica and Mexico, to keep their peach paradise afloat. Black southerners, meanwhile, decided it was about time for Jim Crow to die. And Richard Russell built a laboratory to make sure that the peach trees did not.

7

Under the Trees

In the middle of the twentieth century, middle Georgians looked out on the landscape and yet saw a "rosy sea" – visual evidence of rural progress that they had demarcated politically with a new county. Under the trees, though, in the soil that produced the nation's finest peaches and among the workers who picked them and sent them to market, matters were not so rosy. The 1950s and 1960s saw the emergence of new environmental problems for peach growers, in particular a new syndrome with the descriptive but imprecise title "peach tree short life" (PTSL). At the same time, the cheap agricultural labor that middle Georgia growers had taken for granted in the nineteenth and early twentieth centuries increasingly had other, more preferable employment options. Slowly, farmers transitioned away from the local, rural black labor that had sustained southern agriculture for generations, relying instead upon an ever-widening labor circuit: urban African Americans, World War II POWs, Caribbean migrants, undocumented Latinos, and, most recently, Mexican guest workers under the auspices of the federal H-2A program. In a fitting coda, these two stories joined in a movement for environmental justice in Fort Valley, where a local citizens' organization won an EPA-sponsored cleanup of the Woolfolk Chemical site.[1]

The historian Jason Sokol argues that the changes associated with the civil rights movement were felt just as deeply – if quite differently – by southern whites as they were by blacks. No, the movement insisted, black folks were *not* happy with "their place." No, they did *not* feel protected when white folks called them "our negroes." No, separate was *not* equal. Yes, traditions several generations old could shatter in just a few years. White southerners in the 1960s, Sokol writes, "felt the ground shift beneath their feet."[2] For peach growers facing the deterioration of their soil, and for Fort Valley residents looking for someone to take responsibility for fouling theirs, the ground shifted literally as well as figuratively. Environmental instability defined the fortunes of the Georgia peach industry in the latter half of the twentieth century, and, by extension, the civil rights movement in that corner of the world as well.[3]

The Peach Blossom Festivals had celebrated the future of peach culture – the flower, not the fruit – even as they ignored the very people who worked in the orchards to carry the fruit to market. There was a kind of poetic justice, then, in the way that PTSL cut down orchards in springtime, in the youth of a tree's life. For all their talk of permanence and beauty, the makers of the "world's peach paradise" built their orchard civilization upon a decidedly transitory and unattractive labor system. The Georgia peach, shining dream of the horticulturists, did not fall off the tree into the packing crate. It moved thanks to a swarm of the vulnerable: blacks, women, children, prisoners, undocumented immigrants, and state-sponsored "guests." For many years, this dependence was hard to see. But the combination of PTSL, mechanization of cotton, and African Americans' refusal to work in southern orchards made it painfully obvious.

II

The story begins with the simple fact that peaches are among the most delicate of commercial fruits and must be picked by hand. Though growers and researchers have investigated mechanical harvesters for decades now, human judgment and human hands have always been indispensable and will remain so for the foreseeable future. Unlike apples, peaches cannot be stored long even with modern refrigeration technology and must travel from orchard to market within days. The harvest season varies unpredictably from year to year and demands constant monitoring, for each variety has only a narrow window of ripeness and must be picked with all urgency. "To say that the shipping season is the most fervid time of a grower's year," wrote Inez Parker Cumming in 1947, "gives a dim picture of the actual color and whirl of activity that goes on in even the tiniest peach village – for the peaches are ready today, today, today, and tomorrow they will be past ready. Life moves at an amazing tempo for everybody."[4]

In certain cases, this perishability and unpredictability gave harvesters an unusual amount of leverage, for at the moment when a crop is ripe, *time* is more important to growers' profits than harvesting costs. In other times and places, workers used that leverage to strike for better wages or conditions.[5] If southern peach pickers used this harvest time strategy, I could not find it in the historical record; from the 1870s through the 1930s, southern peach growers only rarely complained about labor trouble. Workers lived close by, and, given the almost nonexistent alternatives for employment in between cotton tasks, worked quite willingly in the orchards. The peach labor system was what we might call neighbor labor: composed of local people and dependent on a core of tenants who lived on or near the land of the big growers. As long as the South had such a population, wages remained low; as long as wages remained low, African Americans picked cotton by hand; as long they picked by hand, the tenant system of production continued. And as long as the tenant system continued, the South had a seasonal labor surplus – that is, plenty of peach pickers.

Unlike Atlantic and Pacific perishable crops, then, it was not a migrant *stream* that powered the peach industry but – at the risk of flirting with what the historian James N. Gregory calls the migration scholar's addiction to water metaphors – a local *tide*.[6] Peach work took place nearly year round, with pruning the trees in January, thinning the small green fruit in April, and cleaning the orchard in late autumn. But June through August was the busiest season, and the workforce could balloon to as much as eight times its normal size. Rural folk from miles around flowed toward the peach farms, and then ebbed away as the season waned.

Pickers and packers alike worked long days. In the orchards, the pickers moved through the trees with bags or buckets or baskets, straining both their arms and their backs, since ripe fruit sometimes hung high on the tree and were supposed to be placed, not tossed, in the basket. The fruit ripened over the course of several pickings, meaning that the picker literally had to pick through the tree, not reap indiscriminately and thereby save time and mental effort. It was hot and humid, of course, but workers wore long sleeves and kerchiefs, or dusted themselves with talcum powder and flour, because peach fuzz mixed with sweat to create a maddening itch, like working with fiberglass insulation.[7]

Packing operations could be as simple as a few tables set up under an oak tree, but most middle Georgia farms of any size had their own shed. Early packing sheds were long, open-sided buildings, raised to wagon height off the ground to make unloading and loading less strenuous. On two tables,

one on each side of the shed, workers sorted the peaches by size and quality, culling green, overripe, or otherwise unmarketable fruit. Graders sorted
into containers, which were passed to the packers on the opposite side of
the table, who carefully placed the fruit in baskets (see Figure 5.3). The
packers arranged the baskets into crates and took them to inspectors, who
checked the quality and then nailed the crates shut. If the shed was large
enough to have its own spur track, workers loaded the crates onto a waiting
train car (see Figure 5.4). Sometime in late August or September, the harvest
ended. Year-round labor cleaned up while the seasonal help returned to
their homes. Growers and managers headed to the beach for an extended
vacation before cleaning and replanting work began in late autumn.

The seasonal needs of peach growing were critical to its success in
maintaining a labor force in the cotton belt. The seasonal tasks of the two
crops were perfectly aligned: Prune peaches; plant cotton. Thin peaches;
chop cotton. Pick peaches; pick cotton. "You had to diversify to keep the
labor," the Crawford County peach grower Bob Dickey explained. "You
had to pay 'em, I mean, a subsistence, so peaches were an obvious thing…
It was something for your labor to do year-round. That was the whole
concept."[8] From the perspective of landowners, peaches and cotton were
agricultural serendipity

The fruit also filled a crucial temporal niche in the communities where
it was grown commercially. Nick Strickland, whose father ran a store in
downtown Fort Valley, remembered peach season as the high point of the
year. "You could tell the difference," he declared. June, July, and August
could carry a storekeeper through the year. On Saturdays, his father woke
at 7:00 a.m. to open the store and kept it open till midnight to accommodate the farmers and mostly black farmhands from the rural areas arriving in town in their two-ton trucks. "During peach season, when those
people came into town, they had money in their pockets," Strickland
recalled. "If they made twenty-five dollars, they spent every damn cent of
it. I mean every penny." According to Strickland, peaches sustained the
dry-goods economy of the entire town: talcum powder, bandanas, glue,
brushes, Coca-Cola, Pepsi, Nu-Grape, chewing gum, tobacco. "Somebody
been smokin' a pack of cigarettes," Strickland explained, "peach season
get here he smokes two packs 'cause they could afford to buy it." Others
waited for peach season to put new tires on their cars. "It was something
that was tremendously noticeable," Strickland concluded. "Everybody
looked forward to it."[9]

In a world where most of the population worked with their hands
according to a seasonal rhythm set by cotton, peaches offered a precise

crossbeat. World War II dramatically increased the tempo, interrupting the rural cadence of southern life and offering some a ladder out of poverty. Southern farmers saw the flight of rural southerners, especially blacks, to wartime industries as an ominous indication that their labor-intensive ways could not continue indefinitely. Mechanization was an obvious solution, but, gripped by what one government official called "farm labor shortage hysteria," many worried that mechanization could not proceed rapidly enough to make up for the loss of workers.[10] From 1943 to 1945, as rural economies wrestled with one paradox of success – a revitalized national economy meant manpower shortages in some rural areas – the Allied forces wrestled with another, as their victories in the European theater left them with hundreds of thousands of German and Italian prisoners of war to feed and house. About four hundred thousand German and Italian POWs lived in the United States during World War II.[11]

Farmers needed labor; military officials needed to find the POWs something to do. These two problems merged into a solution. Despite widespread anti-German and anti-Italian sentiment among Americans, farmers and their allies eagerly sought these workers. Representative John S. Wood of the Ninth District in northeast Georgia explained to the provost marshal general that the citizens of this region – boasting some of the "largest peach producing plantations in the South" – had such an "acute manpower shortage" that they were willing to house the prisoners at their own expense, at sites with water, sewage, and electricity.[12] Prisoners of war represented an attractive option for farmers frustrated with high wartime wages, the headache of recruiting local workers, and the possibility of strikes and walkouts. The military would set wages, discipline unruly workers, and in many cases house and feed them as well. In all, about two-thirds of the prisoners of war who were stationed in the United States worked on southern farms.[13] And although POW labor teams were too few and short lived to offer a permanent solution to peach growers' labor needs, they may have suggested that impermanence *was* the solution. In any case, the use of POWs in agriculture set an important precedent: federal protection of agricultural employers from labor market fluctuations via temporary foreign labor.[14]

Compared to some places, such as the Mississippi Delta, middle Georgia used relatively few POWs in its fields and factories. The Peach County extension agent claimed in 1944 that only two peach growers needed POW labor, and these "used them very little." Local residents picked peaches as part of the war effort, and out of loyalty to growers, reported the agent. Taking advantage of dry weather to "get their own crops in good shape," local farmers left their work to help the peach growers. "A fine spirit of cooperation existed." Packing sheds opened at night to allow people who worked during the day to pitch in. The agent visited schools and asked for help from teachers and students: "there is no way to estimate the work done by school children," the agent wrote. "The majority of workers were children." And yet POW availability had "a tremendous psychological effect on local labor in this and surrounding counties," the agent said.[15] Prisoners represented the threat of replacement, but they were also working for lower wages. The commanding officer of Camp Wheeler, Lt. Col. Ralph Patterson, suspected that eighty cents a day was not really the "going wage" – it was only the cash amount farmers paid to their tenants, who also had access to land, housing, and "perhaps cows." The real rate of total compensation was probably close to two dollars a day, the inspector said. This observation apparently landed on deaf ears, as eighty cents remained standard for POW labor. Middle Georgia farmers were getting a fabulous deal.[16]

One such farmer was Dewey Bateman, who farmed approximately seven thousand acres across five middle Georgia counties. Along with peaches, he raised grain, cotton, sweet potatoes, peppers, pecans, cattle, and hogs; along with farming, he forayed into processing with a frozen food plant and a canning facility in Macon. "Peaches are a fascinating business," he once observed. "But you've got to be a philosopher to grow them."[17] His son Oliver remembered seeing him little during peach season: up before dawn and home after dark, often driving two hundred miles a day to and from the various farms. "The best fertilizer you can use are your footprints on the land," he said.[18] So it was no surprise to Oliver that, when he was home in 1945, on leave from his service in the European theater, Dewey wanted to take him driving. As they had in the past, father and son climbed in an old pickup truck and drove around the operation. They stopped at a store for bread and milk, and then his father pulled up to one of the tenant houses. Oliver assumed his father was taking food to a tenant laid up at home. Instead, a tall white man, apparently a trained carpenter, was repairing the cabin, and Dewey Bateman was providing his lunch. The man spoke little English, and his work clothes were emblazoned "P. W." "It always came as a shock to me when we came in there," Oliver remembered, "and here was this big, nice-looking German" – his erstwhile enemy.[19]

Two years later, the tall German wrote to Oliver's father. "Dear Mister Batemann!" he began. "I am Paul the joiner... Do you remember?"

After a long journey through several camps in the United States and in England, Paul Spieckermann was back in Germany with his wife and children, who were "in a state of good health." And as a joiner, furthermore, Spieckermann had "much to do" – but only because his land lay in ruins. "I can not say how old people look out here in Germany," he wrote. Spieckermann was "thinking of the good time in your factory of apricots" and thanked Bateman "for all what you had done for me."[20]

The letter was just one of a remarkable trove of missives from Bateman's former prisoner–workers, about twenty of whom worked in Bateman's fields, packinghouses, and frozen food plant. "Right now I'm thinking of our big time we had one year ago," Fritz Drüner wrote. "You remember the days in the Packing-house. Don't you? Wasn't it a wonderful time?" In a strangely poetic postscript, Drüner concluded: "Before my mind's eyes I see them peaches rolling. Oh! Why I cannot be there?"[21] A year earlier, Drüner and Werner Volkmann had presented Bateman with a photograph of thirteen members of the crew, posing in front of their barracks at Camp Wheeler. They stand in the midst of sunflowers and low shrubs, a garden meant to soften the camp's otherwise stark aspect. For prisoners living and working under armed guard, they seem relaxed, even content. One of the men holds a black-and-tan dog; another wears huarache sandals. They look steadily at the camera, or smile at each other. On the back of the photograph, Volkmann and Drüner wrote, "We never forget the 'Peach-Season.'"

This prisoner of war labor arrangement might seem to be another in a long line of particularly southern abuses of labor, from slavery to convict lease systems. Working under armed guard, forbidden to fraternize with locals, constantly scrutinized for signs of residual fascist sympathies, paid in camp canteen credit and a measly eighty cents a day, which they could take with them only upon release – from the workers' perspective, it was far from ideal. Yet in letter after letter, Bateman's crew detailed the *good* things they remembered about their time in his service. Matthias Jakobs had a "beautiful Panama hat" – given to him when Bateman named him supervisor of the prisoner crew – which he kept as a "dear souvenir."[22] Julius Winter, an Austrian postmaster, was apparently also an amateur naturalist: he returned to Vienna with the "chafer" – colorful scarab beetles common in Georgia – "and snakes" Bateman had given to him as a reminder of the "beautiful U.S.A."[23] What the former prisoners remembered most of all was the taste of Georgia. The "nice milk form [*sic*] the 'red oak' farm and the wanderful [*sic*] cake and coca-cola and all other things"; the "generous supper every night at 12 o'clock p.m.: sandwiches and a bottle of ice chocolate or milk … the peaches, peaches, peaches!

How many I ate I don't know: tons!"[24] "How was ist [*sic*] nice," Franz
Reitbaur remembered, "when the big crop was brought in and we had
everything we wished."[25]

Dewey Bateman later described this period as a time of "troubles,"
when he was "forced" to rely on POWs and transient laborers.[26] The system the POW workers represented, however, foreshadowed the solution
the industry would settle on some fifty years later, and pointed toward a
more direct reliance on federal labor recruitment. World War II drew not
only POWs to American agriculture but Mexicans through the Bracero
Program and Caribbeans through the British West Indies Temporary
Alien Labor Program (BWITALP).[27] The federal H-2A guest worker program, established in 1986, built upon these earlier efforts and paralleled
the POW system in some striking ways: the federal government's role as
labor padrone, the insulation of farm wages from the free market, and
the worker's circumscribed position.[28]

III

In the aftermath of World War II, after years of talk and trials, mechanization finally took hold in southeastern cotton production.[29] Middle
Georgia was home to just 534 tractors in 1939; by 1954, the number
had increased nearly fivefold, to 2,495. As cotton farming used less hand
labor, planters took over the operations of sharecroppers and other tenants. Georgia's 225,897 farms in 1944 had dwindled to 83,366 by 1964.[30]
In 1960, 10 percent of Georgia's cotton was harvested mechanically; by
1969, less than 10 percent was still hand-harvested.[31] The South's rural
workers had been finding other opportunities since the first wave of the
Great Migration in the 1910s; by the 1970s, cotton farmers no longer
needed these traditional hands.

If southern horticulture had been able to muster crops other than
peaches, this transition might have been somewhat easier for growers.
Although postwar peach production saw changes in the pesticides available and their method of application as well as more refined machines in
the packinghouse, peach harvests still required human hands and eyes.
In California, as Carey McWilliams and others have documented, a profusion of perishable crops sustained an extensive and nearly year-round
circuit for migrant workers, whom whites periodically kicked out "in
preference for some weaker racial unit," thus creating a succession of
what Cindy Hahamovitch calls "ethnic reserve armies": Chinese, then
Japanese, then Sikhs and Filipinos, then Mexicans.[32]

While some Georgia growers resorted to offshore labor to bring in the peach harvest as early as 1947 – when, according to one newspaper, there were some four hundred West Indians in the state, probably imported under the auspices of the British West Indies Temporary Labor Program – most still staffed their orchards with local African Americans.[33] But with the tenant system in decline and a smaller population on the land, growers turned to labor contractors they called "crew bosses" to do so.[34] As middle Georgia's black population grew increasingly urban, Macon became an especially important source of field crews.[35] "People would come and say, 'I can bring you a crew of twenty-five,' or 'I can bring you a crew of twenty,'" Bob Dickey recalled; in exchange, they were paid a commission above the normal wage. The best of these crew chiefs, according to Dickey, were black preachers who could talk their congregations – or at least the women and children within their congregations – into going to the fields.[36] Several growers furnished school buses to "highly reliable people," as Oliver Bateman remembered them, who "knew all the children, knew all the families."[37]

Growers recognized that this local contracting system reflected a loss of control. By the 1960s, some orchards around Atlanta let their peaches rot on the trees for what they called a lack of labor. "They stand in the streets, they won't work," a Jackson peach farmer groused. "They won't even come give it a try."[38] Another complained that adult workers waited until the trees were really heavy with fruit before going to the orchards to work. These "deadbeats ... only live for today and let tomorrow take care of itself," he declared, threatening to give up the business altogether.[39] In 1971, the Fort Valley grower Bill Wilson called the peach industry's dependence on crew bosses "one of our biggest problems."[40] Growers' buses filled with younger and younger workers, and Bateman remembered the contractors' complaining that adults refused to do the work, sending their children in their stead.[41] Where once the cotton season had made workers available for the orchards, now the school schedule did the same.

What these growers described, of course, was ordinary economic behavior. Unless one was fairly desperate for extra cash – as school-age children evidently were – the job offered few attractions. As the picker Rosa Mae Lucas told a reporter in 1984, "It ain't too much out here to like about it. It's too hot. It's just as bad as it looks."[42] And it made sense to pick only at the height of the season, when one could fill a bucket quickly and earn more money in a piece-rate system. Ultimately, of course, fewer and fewer African Americans had the *seasonal* availability that peach growers needed. Many participated in the Great Migrations of southern rural people to the cities of the North and West. But many also stayed home, finding work at Woolfolk Chemical (founded to produce agricultural chemicals in the 1910s), Blue Bird Bus Company (1935), Robins Air Force Base (built in nearby Warner Robins in 1942), or one of Macon's many factories.[43]

Hal Lowman's story is one among many along these lines. Lowman is a retired technician at the USDA research laboratory in Byron, where he worked for thirty-four years. In his eighties in 2009, when we spoke at the Thomas Library in Fort Valley, he walked with a limp and a slight stoop, the product, he told me, of arthritis in his ankle and a pinched nerve in his spine. But his eyes remained keen, and his delivery was decisive, opinionated, and abrupt. Did he ever work in the peach orchard? Only as a boy, he said. He never missed a day of school to do any kind of farmwork. His family never needed to pick peaches for anyone else. Instead, they set up a stand on their land along Highway 341 and sold fruit to tourists traveling south to Florida. Lowman and his five siblings all earned their educations, many from Fort Valley State College, and retired from professional jobs such as the postal service, nursing, and the USDA. Nine of their ten children graduated from college, and the tenth was taking courses. His eyes shining, Lowman told me that if a father never has to go to the morgue to identify his child, never to the jail to pick up his child, never to court to testify for his child, that he is blessed. And then, curious about his family's success and stability, as well as his knowledge of farmwork, I asked:

TO: So did you grow up on a farm?
HL: We owned our own.
TO: You had your own farm?
HL: Yes. My father had his own farm, so hallelujah! I never stayed out of school one day to work on nobody's farm. And I never plowed a mule.[44]

The Lowman family's stability, in other words, was rooted in the 250 acres of Crawford County soil they have owned since his enslaved grandfather managed to save enough to purchase it. Lowman's father inherited the land and raised "the usual things" such as cotton, although "one time they had peaches, hallelujah!" As several neighboring black families in Crawford County did, they held on to their farmland, even though it no longer supports them. For they also owe their success to hard work *off* the farm. Neither Lowman nor his siblings farmed for a living. As Lowman describes it, "Thirty-five cent an hour was a lot better than two or three dollars a day on the farm, you understand? ... There's something wrong with you if you don't want to do better."[45]

Of course, "doing better" for rural southern blacks meant more than simply earning a higher wage. Though the economic disadvantages of farmwork were quite apparent, there were deeper, generational reasons for leaving the fields and orchards. Agricultural labor carried with it centuries of chattel bondage and volumes of fatuous racial theorizing that justified that bondage. Fieldwork was demeaning. "When we were doing that work," Fort Valley City Councilman Marvin Crafter explained in 1993, "our prayers were that our children not have to be subjected to the 100-degree work of the peach orchard. Migrants are now doing what we no longer want to do."[46] As Frank Horne had foreseen in the 1930s, upward economic mobility could not be achieved without voting rights and legal protection – that is, without the recognition of basic human dignity that the long years of laboring on white men's farms had denied to African Americans.[47]

And so the movement away from farms accompanied a movement toward political equality. In 1963, angered by the murder of a black inmate and the banishment of a prominent black doctor for allegedly using obscene language in the presence of a white woman, Fort Valley African Americans organized the Citizenship Education Commission (CEC). Almost simultaneously, probably in response to the wave of sit-ins and other direct action campaigns across the South, Fort Valley's white leadership called for a formal "racial commission," to which the mayor appointed four whites and four blacks.[48] In 1969, the CEC, by then affiliated with the Atlanta-based Voter Education Project, published a weekly newsletter called "Information that Black Folk Should Know." Mimeographed on letter-sized paper, the newsletter eschewed the more traditional "Negro" for a capitalized "BLACK" and referred to white folks as "whitie." The lead editorial in the August 28, 1969, edition, for example, decried the continuing opposition of "some dark skin people (with white minds)" and called on readers to insist on being addressed as "Mr. and Mrs. _____ " by the white community, for the "the treatment given to the least of us BLACKS by whitie represents his true feelings for us all."

That summer, the CEC was spearheading a voter registration drive and a "Don't Shop Where You Can't Work" boycott of a local store, Young's Superfoods, which served a predominantly black population (80–90 percent) but did not employ African American cashiers. When the

CEC demanded that the proprietor, Marshall Young, hire a black cashier, he refused, claiming in his defense that his store was a family business, and that his wife and sister were the only cashiers. The CEC responded with a boycott – at the height of peach season, which would have been a key time for the store's overall profit margin. "It seems they would rather close their stores," the CEC wrote, "than let BLACK beautiful hands go in their cash registers." For six weeks, CEC volunteers picketed the store, followed the delivery truck to make sure it went to no black homes, published names and addresses of African Americans who ignored the picket, and disclaimed responsibility for "anything that happens to these people [or] their foodstuffs."[49] Young's Superfoods survived the boycott, not only because of these divisions within the black community, but also, according to Young, because of the solidarity of the white community. White patronage increased dramatically during the weeks of the boycott, more than making up for the lost sales to the black community, Young said. Fearing perhaps that this local movement might set a precedent across the county, whites from Fort Valley and neighboring towns went out of their way to shop at Young's Superfoods. "I've never had such good business," Young marveled.[50]

The Young's Superfoods campaign was part of a broader political mobilization in Fort Valley organized by professors and students at Fort Valley State College (FVSC).[51] Voter registration drives followed the 1965 Voting Rights Act, and Fort Valley elected its first black officials in 1970.[52] The many examples of "disturbances" throughout the South, along with a "Don't Shop Where You Can't Work" boycott led by the CEC, lit a fire under the white-led "racial commission." "Colored" and "White" signs above water fountains began to disappear; certain blacks ate in white restaurants; more worked in white-owned businesses and earned promotions. A 1969 survey conducted by FVSC students suggested that a sizable majority of blacks believed that whites should be welcomed in to live in black neighborhoods, join black churches, and visit in black homes. And yet when asked whether whites were "unfair in their dealings with Negroes," 81 percent of respondents said yes.[53] The political scientist Lois Banks Hollis, meanwhile, who studied Peach County in the early 1970s, discovered that federal Office of Economic Opportunity programs had begun to change social dynamics in the area, as black leaders became "brokers" of federal funding for their local economies.[54] Blacks who registered to vote need not fear, the CEC maintained: "Whitie will not cut off your welfare check or anything else, and by voting you can make sure that he doesn't think of telling you that, by electing BLACKS to the welfare board."[55]

Peach County blacks staged a slow, determined campaign for better electoral representation. The first black candidate ran for city council in 1964; thereafter, the CEC used funding from the Voter Education Project to run regular registration drives. In 1972, six blacks vied with eleven whites for various positions, including school superintendent, utilities commissioner, state legislator, and county sheriff. Two of the black candidates taught at Fort Valley State College, and four were alumni, and they counted on the votes of five hundred to one thousand of the school's students. In the end, only two of the black candidates won, but the election represented an ill omen for the white power structure of Peach County.[56] By 1976 nearly 48 percent of all registered voters were black; in 1980, Fort Valley elected Rudolph Carson as its first black mayor.

In a striking inversion of the previous forty years of desegregation litigation and apparently in reaction to this new display of power, Fort Valley whites sued for the desegregation of FVSC. Complaining that the "voting strength" of the "white minority electors" in Fort Valley had been "diluted" by the presence of FVSC – they insisted that Fort Valley's whites had been "substantially disenfranchised" – the suit called for an injunction requiring FVSC to admit no more African Americans than the University System as a whole, and to expedite plans for converting FVSC into a "racially unidentifiable school" and "to insure a meaningful white presence on the campus."[57] These were astonishing requests. African American enrollment in the University System then stood at 15 percent, thanks in large part to the three historically black colleges within the system. Only 26 of FVSC's 139 professors and 15 of its 2,300 students were white. To limit FVSC's black enrollment to 15 percent was tantamount to denying black Georgians admission to state institutions.[58] In the end, the court accepted a compromise plan presented by the Board of Regents, which maintained FVSC's racial identity while promising greater diversity in the student body and staff. But the suit served the larger purpose of discrediting the college and channeling a "wave of white resentment against the idea of sharing political power with blacks."[59] White Fort Valleyans followed up this desegregation suit with a voter registration campaign in the early 1980s, which combined with internal dissension in the black community to defeat Rudolf Carson.

Most peach growers claim no particular memories of activism in middle Georgia.[60] Their recollections about this period, however, betray a sense of their dwindling power. They petitioned the secretary of labor for special treatment: regulations on employment of minors were burdensome, they said, since "the perishable nature of the product and the shortness of the work season" made it "impossible to hire adults to perform all the activities necessary in the packing of peaches." Peach packing, they argued, should be treated as an agricultural pursuit rather than a processing operation. "Peach growers have traditionally been called upon to help each other out in times of emergency due to sudden ripening of peaches, or the breakdown of equipment," they argued, but these legal definitions meant that growers could no longer manage peach crises as neighbors and friends. "As soon as a grower packs any peaches for a neighbor or a friend ... he immediately comes under the provisions of the Wage and Hour Law and Child Labor Law."[61]

In addition to this lament over the loss of neighbor labor, growers seemed surprised and dismayed that workers were no longer willing to work long, hot hours for low pay. Government programs made payroll more complicated, they said: the payroll office could no longer be a sack of change in a pickup truck. Standards established by the Occupational Safety and Health Administration (OSHA) were an administrative headache. And they blamed the government's "War on Poverty" for making people lazy. "They didn't want to work," Bob Dickey remembered with exasperation, "and welfare came in, hell they started paying them to have children and all this kind of stuff."[62] The workers who depended on their government checks – who were "double dipping," to use Oliver Bateman's words – grew more reluctant to work lest their benefits be revoked.[63]

At a national level, peach growers were acutely aware of farm worker unionization campaigns. At annual conferences of the National Peach Council, growers from around the country portrayed themselves as humble farmers beleaguered by liberal "do-gooders." A representative from the American Farm Bureau Federation warned the National Peach Council that the AFL–CIO merger portended more unionization activity among farmworkers, and urged them to join other perishable crop growers in opposing unionization.[64] In 1968, the NPC passed a formal resolution opposing a farm labor relations bill then before the Senate. "Unionization of farm labor," they insisted, "could pose a possible death threat to the peach industry as we now know it."[65] The 1973 convention featured a talk on labor management by a Colorado grower who berated the "lazy portion of our society" and offered up a sarcastic prayer for the seasonal workers he employed: "for short term employment let me say

'Thank God for the wineo' [sic] or we wouldn't get our job done."[66] By 1975 many South Carolina growers were turning increasingly to migrant labor, mixed in with "all the local people we can employ."[67] And in 1981 a former United Farm Workers organizer – apparently now gone rogue – advised growers that they could forestall unionization with a simple maxim: "love your employees to death."[68]

When the *Atlanta Constitution* reporter Steve Oney visited Big Six Farms in 1979, the grower Al Pearson was not feeling much love. He described finding a woman in his orchard who dropped her peaches into the bucket, "bruising the hell out of them." When he instructed her to bend over and set the peach down gently, she sat down and quit, explaining that he was not paying enough for that kind of care. Pearson was appalled. His father would have been furious, he said, and "kicked all their butts off the place. But I can't just run 'em off," he protested. "Workers are harder to find now. The good ones end up in factories." He concluded, "I'm at their mercy. I'm at everyone's mercy."[69] Soon, as they had during World War II, Georgia's peach growers would cast themselves on the mercy of the state to bolster their labor supply.

By the late 1970s and early 1980s, the labor situation for peach growers was "just about impossible," and many turned to the East Coast migrant stream. Oliver Bateman, for instance, tried a Haitian crew who had been working for a timber company near Monticello, Georgia. When Bateman arrived the day they were to pick, he found that, as a result of a drunken brawl the night before, all of the workers had fled. He never employed Caribbean workers again.[70] For his part, Bob Dickey rued the day he was forced to use migrants. "Over half of them were derelicts," he lamented. "I mean they were alcoholics, and the crew chiefs that brought them, hell they would cheat us and cheat them. It was a terrible situation."[71] Dickey's peach-growing counterparts in Edgefield County, South Carolina, meanwhile, had become "rather notorious" for labor abuses. In the span of three years, the *New York Times*, the *Boston Globe*, the *Progressive*, and the *Atlanta Journal-Constitution* all ran exposés on the crew bosses employed by the growers of that county. Workers charged that crew leaders had cheated them of wages, beaten them, housed them in overcrowded tin shacks with no running water, sold them alcohol and crack cocaine, and held them in debt peonage for transportation, housing, and food expenses. One worker said his crew leader attacked him with a cement block when he complained.[72] This "Peonage for Peach Pickers," as the *Progressive* dubbed it, was a deeply disturbing image for those accustomed to thinking of the peach harvest as a festival.

IV

The combination of civil rights protest and economic opportunity changed the nature of rural life in the post–World War II South for growers as well as laborers. Where once peaches had been an ideal fit for the social system that underwrote the labor-intensive cotton economy, as well as for the climatic and geological characteristics of middle Georgia, increasingly the orchards stood alone in their dependence on large numbers of agricultural laborers. Because of this dependence, along with the routine challenges of unpredictable late freezes and a wide range of pests and pathogens, commercial peach growing shrank, by the late 1960s, to just a few counties around Fort Valley (see Figures 7.1–7.3 and Table 7.1). Labor troubles had always had an environmental dimension, tied as they were to the extreme seasonality of the work, and pests and diseases like San Jose scale and plum curculio periodically threatened production and raised expenses.[73] In the 1950s and 1960s, the advent of peach tree short life (PTSL) significantly raised the environmental stakes. And the campaign for federal research into causes and remedies threw into stark relief the crucial link between agricultural labor and civil rights in the old cotton belt.

Peach Tree Short Life – or the peach replant problem, or the peach longevity problem, as it was called at various moments – caused trees suddenly to wither and die, in the spring, at three to seven years old, at the beginning of their bearing lives. PTSL seemed to be worst in old peach land, and the area around Fort Valley was among the oldest in the Southeast. Growers and scientists had long recognized that fungal diseases persisted in the soil after the trees had been removed and had recommended either abandoning the land or fumigating the soil when an area was clearly infested. But a new kind of "replant problem" appeared in the 1950s in places where no "conspicuous disease" had been known: "Where peaches follow peaches there is frequently marked retardation of growth of the replants," wrote the Virginia plant pathologist A. B. Groves in 1958, "and in severe situations the replants may die."[74]

No one knew exactly what the trouble was, and each scientist saw it through the lens of his own expertise. E. F. Savage, the Georgia horticulturist at the Griffin (GA) experiment station, thought that the fungus *Clitocybe* (now *Amillaria*) *tabascens*, which was widespread in Georgia's peach belt, might be at least partly to blame.[75] Z. A. Patrick found that the breakdown of old peach roots, specifically the amygdalin contained therein, had laced the soil with toxins such as hydrogen cyanide,

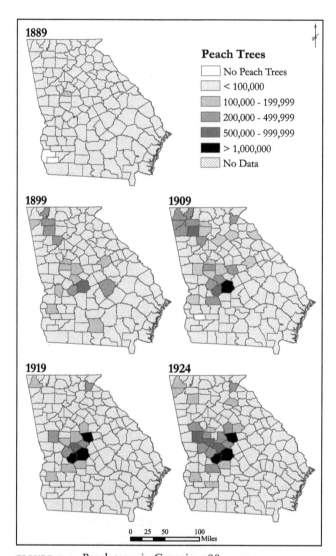

FIGURE 7.1. Peach trees in Georgia, 1889–1924.
Source: Map prepared by Jennifer Bell, University of Georgia. Data compiled by
the author from the Census of Agriculture and the National Agricultural Statistics
Service. Shapefiles courtesy of Dr. William M. Scholl Center for American History
and Culture, the Newberry Library, Chicago. Georgia Historical Counties Dataset
shapefile.

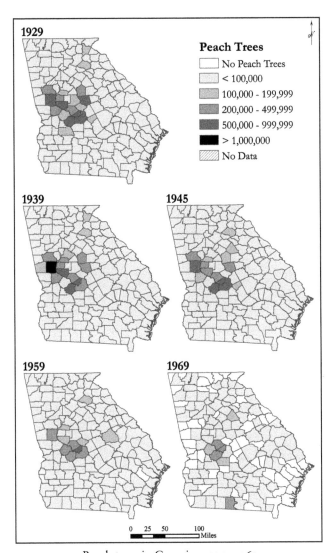

FIGURE 7.2. Peach trees in Georgia, 1929–1969.
Source: Map prepared by Jennifer Bell, University of Georgia. Data compiled by the author from the Census of Agriculture and the National Agricultural Statistics Service. Shapefiles courtesy of Dr. William M. Scholl Center for American History and Culture, the Newberry Library, Chicago. Georgia Historical Counties Dataset shapefile.

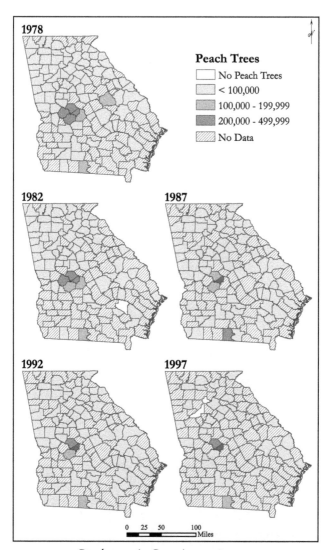

FIGURE 7.3. Peach trees in Georgia, 1978–1997.
Source: Map prepared by Jennifer Bell, University of Georgia. Data compiled by
the author from the Census of Agriculture and the National Agricultural Statistics
Service. Shapefiles courtesy of Dr. William M. Scholl Center for American History
and Culture, the Newberry Library, Chicago. Georgia Historical Counties Dataset
shapefile.

TABLE 7.1. *Peach acreage, production, and value, 1954–2012*

Year	Acres	Bushels	Crop value
1954	36,450	2,480,696	$11,400,000
1959	42,479	4,221,262	$10,080,000
1964	32,950	1,244,884	$7,120,000
1969	30,505	1,844,572	$12,802,000
1974	22,954	1,636,674	$8,055,000
1978	23,313	2,046,193	$18,720,000
1982	22,621	2,126,193	$22,460,000
1987	22,685	1,991,645	$17,758,000
1992	20,584	2,011,486	$26,714,000
1997	20,694	2,810,944	$35,235,000
2002	13,242	2,000,000	$32,148,000
2007	11,142	520,000	$45,169,822
2012	11,481	1,412,000	$33,867,850

Note: Acreage is calculated by dividing the number of trees by 100. The number of trees per acre has varied over the years, but 100 is a reasonable estimate. For later years, when peaches were reported by pounds instead of bushels, I have estimated that a bushel is equal to about 50 pounds of peaches. The value of peaches is derived from production and the season average price, except for 2007 and 2012, which are the reported farm gate values.

Sources: U.S. Census of Agriculture, USDA National Agricultural Statistics Service, Georgia Crop Reporting Service.

benzaldehyde, and benzoic acid.[76] Another trio of scientists found that liming the soil seemed to have a positive effect and concluded that soil pH was the primary cause; other scientists blamed the prevalence of root-knot, dagger, root-lesion, or ring nematodes; Groves thought it might also be related to spray chemical residues, the effect of which on "soil microflora" was at that point "wholly unexplored."[77]

For middle Georgia growers, concern about PTSL intersected fortuitously with an ongoing campaign for an expanded federal laboratory in Peach County, with Sen. Richard B. Russell Jr. as its chief legislative champion. Fort Valley's civic leaders had been loyal supporters of Senator Russell for almost his entire public career. As a young leader in the state house of representatives, Russell had played a key role in pushing through the new county proposal in 1924. The county had in turn gone his way for the governorship in 1930, and three years later for the U.S. Senate.[78] In 1949, the peach grower Bill Wilson wrote to Russell that the people of the "land of cotton" had "learned from bitter experience that they can not live on cotton alone." They needed better varieties of fruits, berries, and nuts, for "marketing in the north before northern crops are ready" and to "round out the diets of the people of the new Southland" – and not just peaches but Satsuma oranges, persimmon, feijoa, loquat, sapote, avocado, olive, jujube, bush cherries, dewberries, pistachio, quince, and twenty-one other fruits and nuts.[79] It was a striking revitalization of the nineteenth-century dream of southern horticultural diversity. If the proposal seemed outlandish to him – avocados in middle Georgia? – Russell did not let on and promised to take up the issue with Secretary Brannan.[80]

By 1962, when the growers finally appeared before the Senate Subcommittee on Agricultural Appropriations, which Russell chaired, PTSL (or, the peach longevity problem, as it was known then) was central to their campaign. The proposal featured tragic, poignant photographs. An aerial view of two orchards under the same management, the older orchard sparse and decrepit, decimated by short life; a close-up of bacterial spot; a landscape of shrunken, withered peach trees. "Why did these trees die? What can we do to prevent this loss?" read the plaintive caption. "We need research to find the answers."[81] The very existence of the industry was at stake, the growers said, and its demise would not only eliminate an essential fruit from the nation's diet (rich in vitamin A and only thirty-five calories!), but also send shock waves across the economy of the rural South. Banks would fire their agricultural finance specialists; small town druggists would close up shop; universities would lose revenue from students' summer work; manufacturers of pesticides and equipment would reconfigure their business or fail; freight carriers would be deprived of an enormous summer business.[82]

This economic argument was fairly predictable, common to any number of requests for federal funding in order to prevent a ripple effect across the economy. But the proposal for a peach laboratory also made much of the peach industry's importance in the lives of day laborers. Do not forget, the proposal urged, "the plight" of the rural labor force – nearly one million man-days over the course of the harvest season.[83] When growers went to defend their proposal to the agricultural appropriations subcommittee, they expanded upon this point. For while the peach growers' written proposal offered a long list of economic ramifications of the peach industry's decline, their oral testimony centered on just one. As Edgar Duke expressed it:

Practically every other farming operation in the South is now or shortly will be mechanized, so our unskilled farm labor must depend almost entirely on the growing and harvest season of fruit and nut crops for its livelihood. Take this away, and these people will be forced either to migrate or to turn to the already crowded offices of our welfare agencies.[84]

Save the peach industry, in other words, and you provide a "live-lihood" for the region's unskilled farm labor. You keep them out of northern cities and away from the welfare lines.[85] As Duke and Russell had probably observed, Georgia's farm population was in the midst of a rapid decline, shrinking by 50 percent in the decade from 1954 to 1964, while Georgia's nonwhite tenant farmer population shrank even faster, by nearly 82 percent.[86] Meanwhile, when African Americans tried to enter the peach business themselves, as did FVSC's head of agricultural education, Cozy Ellison, in 1957, they were rebuffed. Ellison found that local whites were hostile and packers unwilling to take his crop. The broker he ended up with, at the recommendation of whites, cheated him of his profits, leaving him to suspect that the "white power structure" had conspired to get him out of what they considered a "white man's crop."[87]

Senator Russell's support for the laboratory campaign was enthusias-tic. At several points, Russell helped the cause along with his own inter-jections. When a representative from the canning industry explained that they needed alternatives to the Elberta for canning, Russell protested: "When it comes to eating fruit, man has never yet developed anything which has as exquisite and delightful flavor as a tree-ripened Elberta peach." In another exchange, Senator Milton Young (R-North Dakota) agreed that there was a "great need" for research into the pests and dis-eases that threatened the industry. Then, in what seemed to be a complete non sequitur, he said: "I have been down in Georgia two or three times, but never during the summer. I would like to do that sometime." Russell joined him in reverie: "It is very beautiful. I would be glad to have you come down and see the peach trees when they are in bloom. There is no more beautiful sight than a peach orchard in full bloom."[88] The fact that peach trees bloom in spring, not summer, only underscores the point: it was the aesthetic character and the cultural resonance of the fruit that moved Russell.

Legislators, then as now, deal with a bewildering array of issues in short succession; their uneven voting records often render them weak presiden-tial candidates. But in this case the context of Russell's support for the laboratory is telling. The proposal passed the Senate subcommittee and, after what Russell later described as the most difficult negotiations in his thirty years as chair, the House as well; Congress authorized $500,000 for planning and construction of the lab.[89] Letters and telegrams of thanks poured into Russell's office. "I am amazed that you so willingly devoted your personal attention to our request," the prominent grower Edgar Duke wrote, "despite the extremely heavy demands being made on you by what, I must admit, are far more serious and important issues."[90] As Duke intimated, Senator Russell had more on his plate.[91] Two weeks earlier, James Meredith had registered for classes at the University of Mississippi – at the cost of an all-night battle between anti-integrationist protesters and federal marshals that left two dead and more than three hundred wounded.[92] Russell had publicly and angrily – and fruitlessly – denounced the use of federal troops to guard Meredith.[93] Despite his best efforts – he promised a southern audience in 1963 to "fight these outrageous measures with all the power of my being ... you will find me in the last ditch" – civil rights legislation went forward.[94] For Russell, blocking civil rights legislation and shoring up a branch of southern agriculture that depended on the manual labor of those who would benefit from that civil rights legislation went hand in hand.

Unlike Russell's stand against federally mandated integration, his work for the peach lab bore fruit in the fight against PTSL. Or perhaps I should say it bore roots: a new rootstock, which would eventually be released as Guardian™. Indeed, PTSL led to a kind of rediscovery of the importance of rootstocks. Commercial production had for decades been *grafted* production, with a tree bearing marketable fruit grafted on to a generic rootstock. Breeding and variety development had, since the time of Prosper Berckmans and Samuel Rumph, focused almost entirely on the fruiting plant. As late as the 1960s, most rootstocks were either Lovell or Elberta seedlings, but not, apparently, because of any particular root characteristics. Rather, Lovell was grown widely in California, and Elberta was frequently canned, making the seeds available in commercial quantities.[95] Canneries and driers had no use for the old pits, so they were cheap and abundant. For the first two-thirds of the twentieth century, peach rootstocks were essentially industrial by-products.

The "replant problem" became an outright crisis after the 1972–1973 season, when 500,000 young peach trees in North Carolina, Georgia, and South Carolina succumbed. That summer, representatives from the three states came up with the "Peach Tree Short Life" designation; a year later the Peach Tree Short Life Working Group outlined a ten-point program for the prevention of PTSL. Most of these points were just good commercial practices: liming soil to keep a balanced pH, subsoiling to break up hardpans, fumigating to kill nematodes, planting nematode-free trees, using Lovell rootstock, fertilizing, pruning late, practicing shallow cultivation, and removing and burning all dead and dying trees.[96] In words that replicated the problem itself, D. F. Ritchie and C. N. Clayton called PTSL "a complex of interacting factors."[97] The ten points would not solve the complex on their own, so in 1974, the working group initiated a new project to find or develop rootstocks resistant to PTSL.[98]

This rootstock testing program became even more critical after the EPA banned the soil fumigant dibromochloropropane (DBCP) in 1979. Widely used in California and elsewhere against nematodes, DBCP was one of the only effective treatments for lands afflicted with PTSL "In the Southeast, every chemical that has shown nematicidal activity and can be used without tree injury has been or is being tested," D. F. Ritchie and C. N. Clayton wrote in 1981. "So far none is comparable to DBCP."[99] But in the late 1970s, researchers discovered that many male workers at plants producing DBCP were sterile. Some peach growers had themselves and their workers tested, even as the National Peach Council proposed that the "elderly and young persons who did not want children could be recruited to handle DBCP."[100] In 1982, South Carolina growers, with the help of a Clemson University researcher funded in part by the DBCP manufacturer Amvac and the support of six of eight members of Congress, sought and received an emergency exemption from the EPA for the use of DBCP in South Carolina peach orchards. The South Carolina grower Larry Yonce explained: "We told Clemson that we needed control of the peach tree short-life problem, but not at the risk of anyone's health. The university advised that DBCP was the only thing available. We are caught in a crunch."[101]

Though researchers and growers did not yet know it, the seedling that would stay the advance of PTSL had already arrived. In the late 1970s, a researcher at Fort Valley State College visited the Byron research lab to survey the orchards and pick out some "interesting" material. The three seedlings he propagated included one known, inauspiciously, as B59452o-9. This seedling was the progeny of a cross made in the 1960s by Fort Valley's first peach breeder, John Weinberger, between Nemaguard and a seedling of S-37. Both parents were rootstocks selected in California for resistance to root knot nematodes. Since root-knot-resistant rootstocks survived poorly on PTSL sites, the researcher expected little of this line.

In 1983, when my father, Dick Okie, in collaboration with Clemson researcher David Cain and his assistant Billy Newall, set up a large test planting to screen exotic peaches for resistance to PTSL, B594520-9's seedlings were included. After nine years, sixty-nine of the original eighty-eight seedlings of B594520-9 survived – besting even Lovell, the former PTSL-tolerant favorite. Whereas 52 percent of Nemaguard seedlings had perished, and 44 percent of Lovell seedlings, only 9 percent of B594520-9 had died of PTSL. The researchers had found a gem.

Unfortunately, that gem no longer existed. As an economy measure some years earlier, my father had removed the only trees of the now wondrous B5942520-9, along with other parent trees not expected to resist PTSL. The sixty-nine surviving seedlings of B5942520-9 were used to produce seed released in 1993 as Guardian (TM) BY520-9. Later USDA-Clemson trials eliminated parents producing seed that germinated or grew poorly, and Guardian rapidly became the standard rootstock in the Southeast, with approximately a million seed sold every year.[102] And although much labor went into making Guardian, it was, like the Elberta, essentially a "found" variety.

V

In the same way that PTSL focused attention on the soil and the roots of the Georgia peach, the civil rights movement and the economic changes following World War II focused attention on the people laboring under the trees. In both cases, what had been taken for granted in the early twentieth century were matters of great anxiety by the 1970s. The attrition rate for growers was fairly high, as Figures 7.1–7.3 suggest. Those still in the business are family operations with decades of experience growing peaches, and they made two key changes to their operations: they planted Guardian trees and hired Mexican immigrants.

Although Mexicans and other Latinos have a long history of involvement in the Deep South, their numbers in Georgia have grown rapidly in the last thirty years, as Table 7.2 suggests.[103] In Florida, killing freezes every other year from 1981 to 1989 put citrus producers out of business and moved the industry's center of gravity southward toward Miami. Mexicans and Mexican Americans who worked in the orange groves suddenly found themselves jobless. In the midst of this climate crisis, Oliver Bateman received a call from a friend in Florida citrus. "I've got some Mexicans," the friend said, explaining that they were "fine people" without work because of the freezes. Would Bateman have a place for them

TABLE 7.2. *Hispanic population of Georgia and middle Georgia,*
1980–2007

Year	Georgia	Percent increase (%)	Middle Georgia	Percent increase (%)
1980	61,260		2,565	
1990	108,922	77.80	3,017	17.62
2000	435,227	299.58	7,212	139.05
2007	740,843	70.22	10,087	39.86

Note: "Middle Georgia" in this case includes Bibb, Crawford, Houston, Macon, Peach, and Taylor Counties.
Source: Georgia Statistics System, Time Series Analysis, available online at: www .georgiastats.uga.edu/timeseries1.html

in his peach orchard? Bateman agreed, and Robert Carrazco showed up in May with nine members of his family, ready to pick under two conditions: they did not want to work alongside African Americans, and they wanted to use picking bags.[104]

The desire of the Carrazcos and other migrants to work apart from blacks may have reflected their experience in the rough-and-tumble world of Florida migrant labor, where Mexicans and southern blacks mixed with West Indians, Cubans, and Haitians in unpredictable ways. When Bateman told this story nearly thirty years later, he made no comment on the Carrazcos' first request, though whether his reticence reflected ignorance or some deeper knowledge of the Carrazcos' reasons is impossible to know. But this Latino family also needed to demonstrate their superiority; they would have been acutely aware of their position as replacements. In later interviews with the sociologists John Studstill and Laura Nieto-Studstill, middle Georgia Latinos made four observations about race relations in the area. First, there was no overt hostility. Second, there may have been "some jealousy" at the closeness of the Latino crew leaders to the growers. Third, Latinos thought blacks were less willing to work at hard, sweaty, low-paying jobs. And, fourth, no Latino would work for a black man.[105] They did not elaborate on their reasons.

The Carrazco crew exceeded Bateman's expectations. They started at daylight, while it was still cool. They worked as an orderly unit, systematically going through the rows instead of scattering, as Bateman put it, "all over hell," randomly choosing and skipping trees. They were efficient: the nine of them picked two thousand bushels in the same amount of time it took forty-five of Bateman's local help. They selected good-quality fruit instead of leaving it to the graders to throw out half the pickings because they were too green or bruised. And they did not complain about the heat or the work. "It didn't take an idiot," Bateman concluded, "to see that [it] was a vast improvement." The next year he hired two crews and was just as pleased with the results. Thus, the Latino labor that began trickling haphazardly into the South in the early 1980s had by the 1990s almost entirely replaced black picking crews.

Local growers were universally enthusiastic. Chop Evans, who had some twenty-five hundred acres of peaches in the early 1990s, told an interviewer that the migrant laborers were the "key to success" for his company. He credited his crew leaders with the turnaround, as they had become more professional and legally astute.[106] The Big Six farms operator Bill McGehee summed up the sentiments of most growers in 1997, when he called Hispanic workers "the Michael Jordans of farm workers."[107] Growers abetted the new workers' acceptance in Peach County with "a concerted effort" to prevent misunderstandings. They explained their situation to the police chief and the Chamber of Commerce, introduced crew leaders to the Kiwanis Club and local churches, helped set up Sunday soccer matches with local parks and recreation officials, helped sponsor an annual health fair, encouraged banks to hire Spanish-speaking tellers and stores to stock Mexican food, and worked with the local Catholic Church to set up a migrant services center.[108]

Growers had reason to be so encouraging. In just a few years, they had regained control of the labor market, this time by importing a surplus from another nation. They claimed that they had no other options. One peach farmer assured Studstill and Nieto-Studstill that African Americans could make ten dollars an hour in local industries and were no longer interested in farm labor. Even student labor for the packinghouse was increasingly hard to find, the grower said. "No one around here wants to work in peaches anymore."[109] Some local African Americans agreed. Yet others viewed the transition to Mexican labor less sanguinely. "People will do the work," one local black man told a reporter for the *New York Times*. "I think [the growers] just want to find people who will do it cheaper."[110] Indeed, the trope of hard-working Mexicans and lazy blacks obscured the fact that local African Americans and migrant Mexicans worked in two different labor markets. Local workers lived in an economy keyed to much higher wages. For Mexicans, peach work was an extension of their extremely low-wage labor market at home, and was therefore relatively remunerative.

Whatever the availability of local labor, middle Georgia's peach grow-ers would make sure in coming years not to be dependent on it again. Only a few years into using undocumented Mexican migrant labor, the 1986 Immigration Reform and Control Act (IRCA) worried agricultural employers across the state. The law promised heightened border security, threatening to decrease the flow of undocumented workers. It offered amnesty to anyone who could prove five years of residency or ninety days of agricultural employment, which growers feared would spark a mass exodus from low-end agricultural jobs. It pledged tougher sanctions on employers, making it harder to replace the new "legals" with more illegal migrants.[111] And, as a sop to the farm lobby, IRCA expanded the guest worker program that had been in operation since the 1940s, a provi-sion that seemed too cumbersome to offer much aid to southern peach growers.

At least in public, Georgia's peach farmers had a simple strategy for dealing with the anticipated outflow of workers from agricultural jobs: provide better conditions. "The smart businessman is trying to upgrade his labor and get better productivity," Bill McGehee explained to a reporter. "What makes a consistent labor force is a guy who leaves at the end of the season happy with the way things went."[112] Indeed, at first it seemed the new law would help growers. Robert Carrazco joined 2.3 million fellow Mexicans in applying for legal status after the law went into effect.[113] His new status enhanced his capacity as a crew chief: he could now operate without fear of deportation, and he could cross the border to visit family and recruit more workers from his hometown of Tamazula, Jalisco. Many of Carrazco's counterparts did the same. Carlos Aguilar, a foreman for Big Six Farms, used his legal papers to visit his hometown every winter.[114] Not only did IRCA help the crew chiefs of middle Georgia's peach industry, it had little effect on the undocumented labor supply throughout the United States – if anything, illegal immi-gration increased. Instead of moving back and forth seasonally, workers arrived and stayed. And as they became permanent, they sought to have their families with them.[115] It seemed that IRCA had changed little.

Then, in June 1991, at the height of the picking season, the Immigration and Naturalization Service (INS) conducted a dramatic raid on Fort Valley's Lane Packing Company. The agency captured and deported 130 Mexicans, found what it described as fraudulent records, and arrested four Lane employees, all Latinos. Accusing the Lanes of running a "lit-tle bondage-type operation," the INS saddled them with a $1.1 million fine, the largest in agency history.[116] Despite the fact that only Mexican employees were arrested, the area director, Thomas Fischer, presented the Lane family, recognized pillars of the community, as the true international criminals. Together, he alleged, they had smuggled some 250 Mexican workers a month for at least two years, charging them hefty fees for illegal passage, paying them less than minimum wage, housing them in substandard dormitories, and encouraging them to buy from the company commissary. "Compared to the profits," Fischer maintained, "the penalties are a slap on the wrist. That's why many people get into this instead of drugs."[117] The raid would inhibit illegal employment activities in the Southeast, Fischer boasted to the *New York Times* and "cripple a major smuggling ring."[118] The loveliest product of southern orchards was again stained by an association with labor exploitation.

Yet aside from making area peach growers "as attentive as attentive can be," as one grower put it, the INS raid had few immediate consequences.[119] The fine was later negotiated to an undisclosed amount. Fischer, changing his tune, acknowledged in 1993 that the Lanes had been cooperating: "we now feel they will follow the letter of the law," he affirmed.[120] And Georgia growers continued employing undocumented workers. The middle Georgia peach industry had preserved its good standing in the community. The deported workers were not so fortunate.

The reprieve for growers was short-lived. In 1998, the INS staged Operation "Southern Denial" in the Vidalia onion fields of Tattnall and Toombs Counties. Although the agency had originally planned it as a ten-day, multistage operation, it halted the operation at the growers' request after the first day. INS agents apprehended only twenty-one workers, but growers complained that many workers never returned and that the onion harvest was severely disrupted.[121] The message was not lost on Georgia peach growers. "They swooped down on the Vidalia onion people while they were digging onions," Bob Dickey remembered with amazement, "and hell, they just scattered, I mean, ran in the woods!" As the onions "rotted in the field," middle Georgia peach growers considered what would happen if the INS conducted a similar raid in their orchards. "You couldn't bring them back the next day, and the peaches would rot on the trees," said Dickey. "So we decided to get a steady supply."[122]

Shortly thereafter, most Georgia perishable crop growers signed on with the government's H-2A guest worker program. Although available since 1986, most growers had deemed it too cumbersome and expensive to be useful. Fortunately for the Dickeys, Robert Dickey III was a good friend of then U.S. Representative Saxby Chambliss, a native of southwest Georgia and a friend of agribusiness.[123] With a skilled foreman in

FIGURE 7.4. A guest worker crew under the supervision of Robert Carrazco, Dickey Farms, Musella, Georgia, August 2009.
Source: Photograph by the author.

Robert Carrazco and the necessary political connections, the Dickeys' transition was smooth. The actual labor relations changed little, since many of the workers who came as undocumented workers continued to work under the H-2A program (see Figure 7.4).

The program seemed to be a good move for growers, as these Mexican migrants – temporary by definition – became the most stable workforce the peach industry had known for decades. For many growers, close to ninety percent of their workers returned each season. South Carolina grower Chalmers Carr, president of high-volume (and aptly-named) producer Titan Farms, testified to the U.S. House Committee on Agriculture that this low turnover rate translated into greater efficiency and a product that was "the best it has ever been." Carr believed that his workers took pride in their work and had developed "a feeling of ownership in Titan Peach Farms."[124] By his estimation, these workers, who hailed originally from the rural states of Hidalgo and Nayarit, had little interest in settling permanently. "They are happy," Carr insisted, "to have a safe means of travel to my farm, work for a limited period of time, [and] return to their homes."[125] The House Committee on Agriculture had to trust Carr on the happiness and the efficiency of his workers, because no Mexicans testified.

On one hand, growers correctly pointed to the low turnover rate as a great improvement. The same crews returned year after year, growing accustomed to working together. Furthermore, many of the same people did the pruning in January, then the thinning of early fruit in March and April, and finally the picking during the summer. This fact meant that workers wanted to prune and thin skillfully: their wages in the summer depended on the fruit's size, abundance, and accessibility on the tree. With the government's indispensable help, growers had discovered a highly-skilled horticultural workforce that had a stake in the success of the entire operation, not just the picking.

On the other hand, this labor force served at the growers' discretion. As subjects of a highly regulated federal labor program, guest workers' options were limited: they may have moved up within the farm operation (some pickers became tractor drivers, for instance), but they could not sell their dexterity and knowhow to the highest bidder. And then there was the question of motivation. Employers sometimes portrayed Hispanic workers as naturally suited to field labor, as people who just liked hard outdoor work. Whereas the local labor force was made up of teenagers and "derelicts" hired by the day, Mexican workers were more likely to be men in their twenties and thirties who had committed themselves not to a day of casual labor but to an entire season, since workers returned home early only at their own expense. But growers seemed reluctant to discuss the differences in motivation for the two labor pools. Agricultural labor rarely, if ever, offered southern blacks a chance for significant advancement, and in addition bore the stink of slavery and Jim Crow. For guest workers, however, seasonal jobs such as peach picking enabled many Mexicans to improve their status and living conditions at home. Temporary employment in the U.S. enabled workers to build bigger houses, pay for school fees, and purchase consumer goods such as radios and washing machines. Although we might question the long-term benefits for "sending communities," migration has often been worth the risk in the short run.[126] In this sense, the H-2A program did have some advantages over the undocumented alternative, especially in its stability and predictability. "Under H-2 contracts," anthropologist David Griffith notes, "workers at least know where they will be working, what they will be doing, and approximately how much money they will make."[127]

To acknowledge that the program had some relative advantages is a far cry from claiming that guest workers were "happy," however. While H-2A regulations made some pieces of this transnational labor arrangement more predictable, it still bore a strong resemblance to illegal forms.

Some of the irregularities came to light in a class action lawsuit brought by workers against the members of the Georgia Growers Association. The GGA contracted with Dan Bremer and his company AgWorks, Inc., who then hired Ricardo Rodriguez to "locate and recruit" H-2A workers. Rodriguez in turn hired his own agents to recruit workers from their home villages in Mexico. After paying Rodriguez' agents a "recruiting fee" in order to be selected, workers traveled to Monterrey at their own expense (about $50). There workers paid from $45 to $100 to the Mexican bank Banamex as a "visa reciprocity fee," another $100 to Ricardo Rodriguez for the U.S. Consulate's H-2A visa application, $35 for visa processing, and an additional $120 for transportation from Monterrey to Georgia. The suit charged that the growers never reimbursed the workers, which then caused their wages to fall below the legal minimum.[128] After a series of motions and counter motions, the parties reached an undisclosed settlement. Regardless of the outcome, the Duque-Tovar lawsuit suggests how labyrinthine – and how open to abuses – the H-2A system could be.

Furthermore, peach picking has always been unpleasant and poorly-paid work. For Angelo Surez, the job was his hardest in twenty-five years of field labor. "The sun is hot, and baskets get heavy after a while," Surez observed. "And the gnats fly in my mouth and up my nose."[129] Belying Mexicans' supposed preference for field labor is the second generation of "settled out" migrants and their career choices. Robert Carrazco's son graduated from the University of Georgia in 2008 with a business degree and now works in Atlanta.[130] Antonio Barajas hoped that his children would find something easier. "Picking peaches is hard work," Antonio's son Tony explained. "[My father] wants me to do something else."[131] In other words, once settled in the U.S., Latinos left the work for the same reasons African Americans abandoned it. Within the U.S. labor market, migrant farm work did not offer anywhere close to a living wage.

These ambitions notwithstanding, growers have implied that the stability of the Mexican workforce stemmed from the positive relations between crews and owners. Big Six farm operator Bill McGehee told *The Macon Telegraph* that he thought the peach growers had learned from past mistakes. "It's better for all of us," he explained, "if we take care of our workers."[132] In Fort Valley, according to local nurse Helen Hudson, growers established a reputation as leaders – at least in comparison to their counterparts among vegetable and tobacco growers of south Georgia – in offering decent living conditions. "The farmers value them here," Hudson maintained. "[The workers] will crawl to the field and

not miss work unless they absolutely have to."[133] Chalmers Carr pointed
to the invitations he and his family received every year to his workers'
hometowns to witness the benefits of working on his farm. "These workers," Carr declared, "have become part of my business and my life, as
I have become part of theirs."[134]

There is a subtle displacement at work when growers present this
labor system as a matter of personal relationships. For though growers
speak glowingly of their current workforce, their happiness hangs by the
thin thread of federal assistance. Indeed, with the exception of the POW
labor program, the federal government has never played a larger role
in the industry's labor relations. H-2A is a kind of immigration policy
loophole that allows employers to continue drawing from sending areas
of Latin America. And yet growers, like J. H. Hale and the planters before
him, use a strikingly personalist language – language that obscures the
structural dynamics at play – when discussing labor relations.

To point out this displacement is not to deny the sincerity of growers'
feelings toward their workers, nor even to dismiss the benefits experienced by some workers, but it does highlight the long history of this
approach to labor relations in the black belt. More than a century before
Chalmers Carr testified to Congress about his hard-working Latinos,
J. H. Hale made similar observations of the "splendid" faithfulness of
his African-American labor. In this light, *Fortune Magazine*'s lighthearted
portrayal of the Georgia peach grower as a "planter" was astute. For
peach growers shared much with their cotton-farming counterparts: they
managed expansive plantations, drew from the same impoverished labor
pool, and described their labor relations in terms of paternalistic responsibility rather than social and political power.[135]

VI

Ed Dunbar is a fourth generation landowner in the unincorporated
community of Dunbar, on the very northern edge of Houston County,
where one of the major arteries bears his family name. The Dunbars
have, since the nineteenth century, raised the usual things: cotton, corn,
wheat, sweet potatoes, cattle, and, for a few decades, peaches. Unlike
Rumph, Hale, Withoft, Duke, Pearson, and Dickey, the Dunbars ran a
modest operation – three hundred acres of fruit – but they had one of the
larger packing sheds outside of Fort Valley. As long as they could make a
profit packing their own peaches without much special equipment, they
stayed in the game. Once hydrocoolers and defuzzers and sizers became

standard, their enthusiasm began to wane. In 1955, a devastating freeze gave them the final impetus to get out of the peach business.[136]

Dunbar's voice has a corporeal quality, as if his words are forcing their way out of his solid frame, and the endings of words and sentences don't always quite make it through. He has already talked with me for several hours and driven me in an electric golf cart around his property, which includes several still-standing tenant shacks. He has a clear, if understated, affection for the land. He once tried to get Governor Sonny Perdue (2002–2010) to put in a forestry service unit at the USDA laboratory in Byron because of all the potential in the area for growing trees. Housing developments have sprung up all around him instead. "Houses we have got," he says, with emphasis. "There's some precious farmland covered up by houses."[137]

Resting in the shade of his porch, with the chatter of birds, the lowing of cattle, and the occasional braying of the pet donkey in the background, Dunbar tries to articulate his feelings about race and, in particular, the local civil rights movement. Growing up on a large farm, Dunbar had daily contact with black tenants and their children. "I loved them old boys," he insists. "If I needed something, they were there. They'd cut wood for me. That was my job, but they'd sneak up through the woods and cut wood while I smoked that rabbit tobacco." Dunbar laughs heavily. "But that hate come in, and that racial – that was political."

Dunbar refers several more times to "that racial," a phrase that seems to stand in for the civil rights movement, which in his mind oversimplified the historical narrative. "Yeah, there was a Ku Klux Klan," he says. "Yeah, there was wrong done. I can't do nothin' about that... I'm not trying to wash away any bad things that's done, because I *know* – I've *seen* – I just, *know* I've *seen* ..." His voice trails off, and then he concludes. "But the more you agitate something like that the more hate you get."[138] Jason Sokol's argument that the changes associated with the civil rights movement constituted a "revolution in a way of life," for whites as well as blacks, holds true in Dunbar's recollections.[139]

Ed Dunbar's memory of the civil rights movement is sharp and apparently painful. But he also recalls a story that unwittingly speaks to the economic opportunity that made the civil rights movement in the rural South possible. Sometime in the 1940s, a tenant named Arthur apologetically informed Ed Dunbar's father R. E. that he was taking a job at the Bursey flour mill in Macon. "'Mr. R. E.,' he said, 'I'll be makin' something like thirty dollars a week. You can't hold it against me now, that's pretty good money.'" Dunbar admitted that it was, and Arthur left, only to return two weeks later. "Mr. R. E., can I get my job back?" He explained that after paying for housing and electricity and food, he didn't have enough left to put anything by. "You done gone up there and got your belly full of that wasp nest bread," R.E. Dunbar rejoined. "You ain't no good" – and then he gave Arthur his house and job back anyway. For Ed Dunbar, this story is evidence for the decency of farm work. His father paid his tenants $15–$18 a week, bought the women snuff and the men tobacco and overalls; the tenants were "good to us and cried when they left." But the story also reflects the fact that many tenants were looking constantly for better work. The last tenants moved off the Dunbar place in the 1950s. "They'd come and go, you know."[140]

The advantages of H2A work for foreign workers are significant: a minimum wage keyed to local "going rates," legal protection from the worst abuses of the crew boss system, and consistent work for a prede-termined period of time. But the system also requires that workers give up their freedom to come and go – or rather, requires that they come and go at the will of the employer. Meanwhile, the growers have acquired a professional workforce without the burden of what Dunbar calls "that racial." They have replaced a laboring population with centuries of his-tory in the South with one only a generation old. Their efforts to welcome Mexicans and Mexican Americans to Fort Valley are good business prac-tice, since they depend on their labor to market their product. But those efforts may also represent what the historian Julie Weise calls "rural racial redemption" – making up for past racial sins with present generos-ity and kindness.[141] In either case, growers view their labor force with a new respect, not only for its evident skill but also – given the politics of immigration in the twenty-first century – for its fragility. "If today, I was prevented from using H2A, or illegal Hispanic labor," Al Pearson told me in 2008, "Tomorrow … I would push my trees up."[142]

Again, the peach harvest is an economic oasis, a welcome influx of cash into a rural economy – but this time it is so for the economies of Nayarit and Jalisco. And again the workers' have a home away from home: the labor camp. For some growers, worker housing has been a piecemeal affair. Bob Dickey bought some old houses and renovated a motel in Roberta, a few miles away from his packing shed in Musella. But at Lane Packing Company, the housing is part of the main complex and an integral piece of the farm tour. The jeep pulls the visitor trailer not only through the pecan and peach orchards but also through guest worker housing, where the recording assures visitors that all the workers are there legally.

Construction style has not changed much since the days of Camp Wheeler – long, low barracks like the 20x100 standard issue buildings at Wheeler, though with green metal roofs and the relative luxury of propane tanks and air conditioners. The few mountain bikes resting outside a building with a large screen porch suggest that these men have their own version of "limited parole." In place of a commissary, the Lane camp has a cinderblock building labeled "Mexican Cafe / Cafe Mexicano" – also run by Mexican immigrants so as to be sensitive to "national tastes" (see Figure C.2). The permanence of the South's signature product depends upon impermanence, a transfusion of rural Mexico into rural Georgia, a transitory repopulation of the rural South.

The federal investment represented by the Byron peach lab, meanwhile, shifted the local geography. As a boy, Ed Dunbar walked to baseball practice in Byron from his house, a straight shot along Dunbar Road. The laboratory started as a Navy Supply Depot in the 1940s, an enormous swath of land that bent Dunbar Road around it. And while few of the several hundred supply depot jobs went to locals, the laboratory that took over the property became an outpost dedicated to preserving the southern peach industry – and thus the way of life that had taken shape around it. The scientists who worked there have supported with their own careers and livelihoods this business of growing and selling peaches, as if the fruit were a public good. With the Guardian™ rootstock – not to mention the ongoing research into commercial cultivars, pest management, and plant pathology – they appear for the moment to have saved the Georgia peach.

VII

There is a coda to the history of agriculture and civil rights in the peach orchards of middle Georgia – a coda that ties together the threads of environment, peach cultivation, and civil rights while suggesting that the story has not yet reached its resolution.

Woolfolk Chemical occupied an eighteen-acre site on the southern edge of downtown Fort Valley, where for some seventy years it had quietly produced pesticides, herbicides, and fertilizer for the peach industry – and thoroughly contaminated over thirty acres in the mostly black neighborhood surrounding it. In the 1980s and 1990s, Fort Valley's African American community led a second civil rights movement, this time centered on an explicitly environmental kind of equality.

Marvin Crafter became the leader of this movement. He had grown up in the shadow of the first civil rights movement in Fort Valley, in one of the neighborhoods adjoining the Woolfolk site, where an open drainage ditch carried Woolfork pesticide sludge toward Big Indian Creek. "We knew the ditch well enough to sniff the air and guess what color the water was that day – yellow, green, milky-gray, white," Crafter recalled in 1998.[143] Probably in response to complaints from the parents of Crafter and the other children, a Georgia Water Quality Inspector tested the drainage ditch in 1966; complaints continued through the 1970s.[144] In 1980, the same year Fort Valley elected its first black mayor, Marvin Crafter won a city council seat; in 1983, the Georgia Environmental Protection Division closed the well that supplied Lizzie Chapel, a black church founded in the 1880s, because of leaching from the nearby Peach County landfill. In 1984, the Georgia Department of Natural Resources issued a notice of violation to Woolfolk, and the EPA began its investigation later in June.[145]

The EPA's findings were sobering: lead and dieldrin in the groundwater, arsenic dust in attics; arsenic, arsenic, lead, chromium, toxaphene, DDD, DDE, DDT, dieldrin, dichloroethane, and hexachlorocyclohexane (HCH) (commonly known as BHC) in the soil and sediment. The site itself had begun in 1910 as a lime-sulphur plant – likely for San Jose Scale and curculio prevention – before J. W. Woolfolk took over the factory in 1926 and began manufacturing a range of arsenic- and lead-based pesticides. In the 1950s, the plant expanded its production to DDT, lindane, toxaphene, and other chlorinated pesticides. Locals remembered unloading bags of arsenic from railroad cars, releasing clouds of the stuff into the air; the open drainage ditch carried sludge into Big Indian Creek; and other waste products seeped into the soil and groundwater. Mayor John Stumbo explained that the contamination was in part climatological: the heat of the Georgia summer meant open-sided buildings, which meant arsenic-laced dust blown into the air every time a moderate wind came up.[146] By 1990, the site was listed on the EPA's National Priorities List. Cleanup began in 1993.[147]

As head of the Woolfolk Citizen's Response Group (WCRG), Crafter became the movement's chief spokesperson, and, when the occasion demanded, its gadfly. This latter role was clear in a 1996 EPA-sponsored roundtable about superfund relocation that included Lois Gibbs of Niagara Falls, New York, whose campaign to clean up Love Canal was the key factor in the passage of federal superfund legislation.[148] After some opening pleasantries, the roundtable facilitator reminds participants of the "ground rules": be focused, be an active participant, and "don't take it personally." Crafter immediately objected: "People living in impacted communities don't have what it takes to not take it personally." The rest of the meeting proceeded in much the same way, Crafter relentlessly outspoken, ruthlessly pointing out inconsistencies in the EPA's approach – his anger bleeding through even the toneless prose of the meeting's stenographer. When the moderator sought to move the meeting on to a discussion of case studies, for instance, the minutes read: "Marvin Crafter noted his concern that the case study discussion was a waste of time, because everyone has already reviewed the case studies."[149] Crafter's refrain throughout the conversation was to call out racism. The EPA needed to "expand its definition of community to include 'colored folks' " he said, arguing that the EPA's willingness to move white folks away from "toxic dumps" did not seem to extend to black folks.[150]

Crafter expanded on this frustration in a 1998 interview with Sierra Club magazine *The Planet*, which profiled the collaboration of the WCRG with a similar group fighting for environmental justice in Nova Scotia. The EPA's initial testing and cleanup, Crafter said, focused only on arsenic and featured EPA representatives telling folks with arsenic-laced attics to "stay out of their attics, or else clean them up real good."[151] Federal recognition of a problem, in other words, was no guarantee of the problem's true resolution. The WCRG needed to keep pushing and prodding; ultimately, the black community also needed the local white community as well, joining what became known as the Woolfolk Alliance, to achieve full cleanup and redevelopment of the site.

In the end, the superfund cleanup was a moderate success. The EPA spent $32 million razing buildings saturated with arsenic, removing contaminated soil, and installing filtration systems on several groundwater wells. The city of Fort Valley won a redevelopment grant worth $1.8 million, and the Woolfolk Alliance met from the 1990s through the 2000s to plan how the site could be reused. They restored the nineteenth-century Troutman House as a Chamber of Commerce-run visitor's center, and built Thomas Public Library, where I conducted some of the research for this book, including the interview with Hal Lowman and the photographs of the peach blossom festivals. In 2012, Fort Valley Festival Park opened in the heart of the old Woolfolk site. And fittingly, in June every year, the park hosts the annual Georgia Peach Festival, featuring music, games, and, of course, the world's largest peach cobbler.[152]

Toward the end of the EPA's self-congratulatory video about the Woolfolk cleanup, "Life after Superfund," Marvin Crafter acknowledges: "We have not always" – and Crafter laughs before he can get out the rest

of his sentence – "We have not always – agreed."[153] Worlds of meaning
lay hidden in that simple statement: millennia of geologic history, centuries of racial history, decades of agricultural history, all playing out in a
few years of struggle in a southern town.

So go to Fort Valley in June. Eat cobbler made from peaches bred
by my father and grown on a rootstock discovered by a team of government scientists, picked and packed by Mexican migrants who are
"guests" of their employers and of the United States. Do so at a site
created by the peach industry's demand for chemical solutions to their
environmental problems, now recreated as a public amenity by a citizens' advocacy group trained in the civil rights movement of the 1960s.
Do so in a town that put on another set of festivals ninety years ago in
order to tell a parable of peach progress. Was that parable true? Could
all manner of human flourishing follow in the train of Queen Peach?
Well, no. Not everything is peaches down in Georgia. But perhaps, as
the writer Marilynne Robinson put it in 2008, "the distinctions available to us in this world are not arrayed between good and bad but
between bad and worse."[154]

In that case, don't just eat the cobbler at the Peach Festival. Enjoy it.

Conclusion

A Benediction

May the time soon come, when over the length and breadth of the land we shall find taste, beauty, ornament mingled with the necessities of life, and a glory of art corresponding in some measure with the glory of nature – when man shall aspire to imitate his Maker, and beautify rather than disfigure the great temple wherein he has placed us for worship, amid the richness of his own tracery and the grandeur of his own handiwork.
The Reverend Stephen Elliott Jr., 1851[1]

I

Just a few years after the Reverend Stephen Elliott Jr. breathed this benediction over southern agricultural reformers, Prosper Berckmans arrived in Georgia and established the nursery and the society that would make an earnest experiment of Elliott's prayer: a civilization built on gardens and orchards. Samuel Rumph provided the *Prunus persica* cultivar, the Elberta, that made peaches a viable commercial proposition. J. H. Hale led a cohort of northerners, flush with capital, to establish peach growing as an industry. Those northerners and their southern allies then created a series of cooperative organizations to try to impose order on the chaotic Georgia peach crop, and subsequently spearheaded a campaign to demarcate politically what they had already done physically, creating a county named for the myth of peach progress.

The second half of the twentieth century, with its rootstock epidemics and its "labor trouble," was hard on the notion that horticulture could usher in an era of human happiness in the South. The peach industry, winnowed to a handful of major growers, limped into the twenty-first century on skill inherited from generations of growing the fruit and on government support. Georgia peach acreage at the last agricultural census in 2012 was, at 12,318 acres, significantly less than South Carolina's (16,274), less than a quarter of California's (51,948), and just a twelfth of Georgia's acreage in 1925, when almost 40 percent of the state's farms grew peaches, boasting nearly 150,000 acres altogether (see Tables 5.1, 5.3, and 7.1, and Figures 7.1, 7.2, and 7.3).[2]

In Augusta, Berckmans' Fruitland Nursery is now the Augusta National, one of the most famous golf courses on the planet, hailed not only for its playability but also for its ornamental plantings and its holes named for Berckmans's work and vision here: Redbud, Pink Dogwood, Yellow Jasmine, Flowering Peach, Azelea, Camellia, Magnolia. You can watch the Masters on television in April, and it is all lucent greens, tall pines, bright azaleas, curving fairways, arched bridges over perfect water hazards, stately magnolias lining the avenue to the clubhouse. In other months, you can visit the tournament's Web site and download a Masters screensaver for your computer so that your unproductive moments at work can be redeemed with reminders of a place you will never be able to go without a stroke of luck. For the National, as it turns out, is one of the most exclusive clubs in the nation. Membership is by invitation only. The first African American joined in 1990; women were only allowed as guests until 2012, when the former secretary of state Condoleezza Rice and the South Carolina businesswoman Darla Moore were invited to join.[3] Even the professionals who play the Masters are not allowed inside except during the tournament, and only tournament winners are given honorary memberships.

The Augusta National pays tribute to Berckmans, but it is an incomplete tribute, and I cannot help but think that Berckmans would approach the place with some ambivalence. Not because it is inaccessible to the masses – Berckmans was an aristocrat, after all – but because it is an inedible landscape. He envisioned not just a more beautiful South but a more bountiful one, and given his views of American eating habits, I doubt the Zaxby's, Arby's, and Publix around the perimeter of Fruitland would do much to soften his disapproval. Although he might be heartened by the rise of North Georgia wine in the last decade or so, the just-launched Fruitland Distillery would likely only confuse him: a Japanese woman selling Kentucky-distilled Georgia-peach-flavored vodka from headquarters in Augusta, using his name and likeness and biography to do so. We have come a long way in a century and a half.[4]

It might seem that the Georgia peach, is, like the flavor in Fruitland Vodka, a mere essence, an ephemeral fancy, a myth in the most straightforward sense, that is, a lie told by the powerful to blunt challenges to their power. I have argued here that myths are better understood as stories embodying beliefs about the world, which can lead us into or away from what is true. And the truth is that peaches still grow in Georgia dirt. I recently took two tours to see them at the source.

II

The first tour was of Lane Southern Orchards in 2008. The place explodes out of the otherwise sleepy landscape with a sixty-foot sign advertising peaches, pecans, strawberries, sweet corn, and Indian River citrus; an imposing gate guarded by two man-sized fiberglass peaches; a rectangular pond with ducks and a fountain; and the two-story packing shed itself. This is more than a peach packing operation. It is an agritourism complex.

Inside, you can eat lunch with a chaser of soft-serve peach ice cream; buy peaches, pecans, peach wine, pecan brittle, and other seasonal goods; send your children to frolic at the playground lined with antique tractors; and tour the packinghouse and orchards. The Lanes run a high-tech operation, which you can survey from the catwalk that hovers above the packing line. Automatic conveyors move the fruit through washers, defuzzers, and waxers; a sizing machine uses digital photographs to sort the fruit into quarter-inch categories; another device applies a PLU sticker for use in supermarkets; yet another assembles cardboard boxes with hot glue.

Amid all this whirring machinery, people work. Unlike in some industries, the workers in this packing shed are not invisible but part of the attraction, enduring the constant stares of curious visitors. White, black, and Latino women sort the fruit into Ones and Twos – the best fruit will go to supermarket customers and the rest to local farm stands. Farther down the line, Latino men hand-pack every box of Lane peaches; a sign on the catwalk explains that packing by hand minimizes bruising and allows the company to customize orders (see Figure C.1).

If you sign up for the farm tour, an elderly man known only as "Red" drives your shaded cart through the migrant labor housing, while a pre-recorded voiceover emphasizes the workers' temporary, legal presence under the auspices of the federal H-2A guest worker program and their comfortable, clean housing, including their own lavandería and cafeteria (see Figure C.2).

Interspersed with informative explanations of the modern growing techniques used and advertisements for various delicacies back at

FIGURE C.1. The Lane Southern Orchards packing line, viewed from the tourist catwalk, Fort Valley, Georgia, July 2008.
Source: Photograph by the author.

the store, carefully selected songs drive home another point. Alabama's "Song of the South" takes you back to the singer's childhood as the son of a cotton farmer so poor they did not know that the stock market had crashed. "Gone, gone with the wind," they sing in the chorus. "There ain't nobody looking back again." This is followed up by Alan Jackson's "Where I Come From," in which a trucker tries to explain himself to a range of interlocutors from other places (New Jersey, California, Michigan). "Where I come from, it's cornbread and chicken," he sings, "a lotta front porch pickin'." The penultimate song is "Midnight Train to Georgia," a 1973 Motown number performed by Gladys Knight and the Pips. The song takes place in Los Angeles, where the female narrator

FIGURE C.2. The Lane Southern Orchards "Mexican Café," viewed from the farm tour, Fort Valley, Georgia, July 2008.
Source: Photograph by the author.

has fallen in love with a man from Georgia, who abruptly informs her that he is returning to his home, to find "what's left of his world … a simpler place and time." The tour closes out, naturally enough, with Ray Charles's famous rendition of "Georgia on My Mind," now the official song of the state of Georgia.[5]

Together the songs highlight the agrarian South, a "simpler place and time" lost to us moderns. But Lane Southern Orchards represents nothing so much as the modern, high-tech, multivocal South: the irrigation, the new varieties, the chemicals; the workers who do not live here; the new "partnership" with a company owned by the Banack and Hazel families, Indian River Citrus magnates of Vero Beach, Florida.[6]

The second visit takes place a year later, when Lawton Pearson, a fifth-generation peach grower, invites me to ride with him as he manages field operations for Pearson Farms. His truck is full of peaches, picked to examine for ripeness, or evidence of curculio, or stink bug, or mildew, and now overflowing the caddy in between the seats and clattering across the floor when we take a corner. Passing through an orchard where a

Mexican man with a backhoe is pushing up the trees (he has had a flat tire and Pearson is supplying him with a tube of silicon sealant) Pearson observes that what appeared to be a level field is actually full of dips and rises, which he can see now that the trees are gone. And that is why freezes would hit that cluster of trees harder, he explains, echoing J. H. Hale a century earlier: cold air sinks into the pockets. Later, he complains about infestations of stink bugs, the pest du jour, which descend upon orchards at random, and thus cannot be combated with spray schedules, and puncture the fruit in such a way that the wound only shows up as rot as the fruit speeds to market. "A bug you can't kill, making damage you can't see," Pearson shakes his head. "That's a nightmare." We stop at an orchard in the midst of a pecan grove, so it is well irrigated and almost junglelike, the trees planted more closely and allowed to grow taller. Pearson explains – in another echo of nineteenth-century peach cultivation – that this orchard in particular has had an infestation of feral hogs, which tear up the ground and eat some of the low-hanging fruit.

But late freezes, stink bugs, and hogs are not the Georgia peach grower's primary concern, according to Pearson: "The number one problem for growers today is labor." At one orchard Pearson hastily gathers *la muestra* – the sample – a dozen peaches that demonstrate the size and ripeness he wants that day. His field Spanish is rough but effective. "If you put me down in Mexico and told me to find a bathroom," he says, "I would be totally lost." After Pearson explains which peaches he wants, the foreman reiterates Pearson's instructions, and the workers snap on their picking bags and disappear into the lush foliage. They reappear frequently, one by one, to dump their half-bushels of peaches into the twenty-bushel bin, which is pulled slowly by a tractor through the orchard. These workers are being paid by the piece, so with each bagload, the picker bends his head to the checker, who rides the wagon with an electronic pen and scans the pen across the tag the picker has on his hat. This same crew has picked this orchard the whole season, so they pick carefully in order to earn more over the course of the season. At the end of the week, Pearson Farms cuts checks to the workers, who cash them at local banks. Pearson smiles. "If you are Hispanic, you could make a lot of money by cashing checks at local banks," since tellers do not routinely verify IDs.[7]

The workers are mostly picking a variety called July Prince, a large, delicious, and, so far, exceedingly reliable cultivar released by my father a few years ago, named (as most of his varieties are) for the breeder who preceded him in Byron, Victor Prince. At one of the orchards, a foreman approaches Pearson. "Una rama," he says, the workers echoing, "una rama!" Some of the pickers indicate a nectarine sport on one of the July Prince trees – a single branch (*rama*) producing fuzzless fruit. A large, delicious, reliable nectarine? The thought is tantalizing, and my father goes out to that tree later to gather some budwood.

It is common now to promote "Heirloom" varieties as if they were superior, across space and time, instead of treating them as historically contingent. The Elberta is an heirloom now – one of the only varieties you can still purchase by name at some farm stands – but in its day it was a remarkably adaptable and shippable innovation. And it is simply not true that older varieties always have superior qualities.[8] I have eaten both July Prince and Elberta, and the latter was an acidic, stringy mess in comparison to the former. Favorite peaches are a matter of taste, of course: some folks like the delicate sweetness of white fruit, others the more aggressive astringency of blood peaches.

But like the folks who grow and eat them, *Prunus persica* is a historical organism. It will continue to change in Georgia, helped along by government scientists who work increasingly at the molecular level, growers watching for marketing angles, workers on the orchard floor, as well as nonhumans such as stink bugs and microscopic *Armillaria* worms, late freezes and global warming. Horticulture – as nineteenth-century folks grasped readily – remains a dynamic set of relationships of people and land and plants. The Georgia peach, to paraphrase Walt Whitman, is large. It contains multitudes.

III

"The Peach Blossom Fountain" is a very old Chinese story written by T'ao Ch'ien (or T'ao Yüan-ming). T'ao was a disillusioned government official who lived during a time of instability between the great Han dynasty (200 BCE–200 CE) and the T'ang dynasty (600–900 CE). He relinquished a coveted magistrate position after only eighty-three days in office, returning home to write poetry, strum lutes, and cultivate chrysanthemums. "I want not wealth; I want not power; heaven is beyond my hopes," he wrote of his early retirement. "The times are out of joint for me, and what have I to seek from men?" Instead, he implored, "let me stroll through the bright hours as they pass, in my garden among my flowers; or I will mount the hill and sing my song, or weave my verse beside the limpid brook."[9]

"The Peach Blossom Fountain" tells of a fisherman who, wandering up the branch of a river in his boat, came upon a grove of peach trees in full bloom, carpeting both banks of the stream and extending into the distance on either side. "The beauty of the scene and the exquisite perfume of the flowers filled the heart of the fisherman with surprise," and he paddled into the grove to see how far it extended up the stream. In time, he discovered that the grove ended where the water emerged at the foot of a hill, and looking up, he "espied what seemed to be a cave with light issuing from it."[10]

Tying up his boat and clambering up to the cave to investigate, the fisherman found that the cave was actually a tunnel. Crawling to the other side, he discovered spread out before him "a new world of level country, of fine houses, of rich fields, of fine pools, and of luxuriance of mulberry and bamboo ... of crowing cocks and barking dogs." Although the garb of the people was strange, "young and old alike appeared to be contented and happy." An inhabitant – just as surprised as the fisherman – accosted him and, upon learning "whence he came," took the fisherman to his house and slaughtered a chicken and poured out wine. Soon all the people of that place arrived to see this curious visitor, and told him the story of how they came to be there. It seems that during the "troublous times" of the first emperor, some five centuries earlier, the people's ancestors had sought refuge in this place and had lived there, in complete isolation, ever since. The fisherman told them the story of the Han dynasty and the intervening years, and, hearing that of which they had been ignorant all these generations, "they grieved over the vicissitudes of human affairs."[11]

After visiting the inhabitants of this place for some time, the fisherman made ready to leave. "It will not be worthwhile," the people warned him, "to talk about what you have seen." But the fisherman proceeded immediately to the district governor of this "unknown region," and the governor sent the fisherman back with a group of men to find the place again. He failed. Later, a "famous adventurer" made another "desperate attempt" to "pierce the mystery; but he also failed, and died soon afterward of chagrin. No one else stepped forward to continue the search.[12]

On the face of it, T'ao's story explores the irretrievability of the "peach-blossom days" of one's youth. But like all good stories, it contains other truths. The grove of blossoming peach trees was the gate to a kind of utopia, where all were "contented and happy," where all enjoyed fine houses, rich fields, fine pools, mulberry, and bamboo. It was a land that offered refuge to people caught in the "troublous times" of the first emperor, when the fabric of traditional, local life in the land we now call China was torn apart for the sake of national political power. The land of the peach blossom fountain was a safe haven from the "politics of the day" and hence from the "vicissitudes of human affairs."[13]

Peach culture in the southern United States has likewise had the semblance of an occupation set apart from political and economic gain. The horticultural vision in the nineteenth century emerged as an alternative to the dirty, greedy, oppression-laden world of cotton culture. Even when peach growers were at their most overtly political – creating a new county, lobbying for a new research lab – the rhetoric was disinterested, nonpecuniary. We want to name our county after the fruit that has blessed us with prosperity, they said; we need a research lab to preserve this family work, this work that is clearly a benefit to the rural South, laborers included.

Of course, there was and is no refuge from politics. The "vicissitudes of human affairs" could not be escaped. Horticulturists found themselves making messy, imperfect decisions about whom to employ, how much to pay them, what to spray, and how to make a profit from an exceedingly delicate drupe. And so we have the Right Reverend Stephen Elliott praising the beauty of the southern landscape, opening schools for women and slaves; and Elliott the defender of a southern way of life that depended upon chattel slavery. We have John Howard Hale condescending to his black workers and taking advantage of their poverty; and Hale also helping to fund the creation of a black college that, however haltingly, planted the seeds of the civil rights movement in Fort Valley. We have Mabel Swartz Withoft making what she could of the middle Georgia landscape; and Withoft writing plays that naturalized African Americans as a lower caste. As an icon, the Georgia peach served as shorthand for southern beauty, hospitality, sweetness, and agrarian roots. But those roots sink deep into the messy racial politics of southern history, and as much as we have forgotten all but the highest and lowest points of that history, we need to hear it again in all the fear, anger, sorrow, and joy of the original experience. So that even our clichés, fuzz and all, have the aftertaste of truth.

"One of the penalties of an ecological education," Aldo Leopold once lamented, "is that one lives alone in a world of wounds."[14] It is an evocative and much-quoted passage that exemplifies why Leopold was such an important spokesperson for the environmental movement. But it also skews the experience of "ecological education" toward the suffering individual, when equally important consequences of ecological – and, I would add, historical – education are a sense of fellowship and delight.[15] You may live in a world of wounds, but you do not necessarily live alone. Instead, you might discover the kinship you already have, not just with Leopold's "land community," but also with the human community, past and present. Reading the past in a landscape is rather like meeting family members you did not know you had. You belong to these familiar strangers, and their lives and quirks and foibles explain parts of your own experience in ways you could not predict.

"Everything is peaches down in Georgia," wrote Grant Clarke, Milton Ager, and George Meyer in 1914. "Paradise is waiting there for you." It hardly needs saying, at this point, that everything was not peaches, that no paradise awaited anyone. The Georgia peach myth has been as inaccessible as the land beyond the peach blossom fountain. But that is not to say that these visions of paradise were altogether fraudulent or sinister. Perhaps we can allow ourselves to be at once compelled by and suspicious of such visions; perhaps we can pluck viable seeds from stinking manure; perhaps we can go beyond condemnation and learn to "grieve" over the "the vicissitudes of human affairs."

As for me, there is no return to the peach blossom days of youth. But like the Chinese fisherman, I have wandered up a branch of a river, pursuing the history of the Georgia peach, and caught a glimpse of those days. I have seen the peach dreams of generations past; and I understand a little more of the way in which stories can, to invoke Tim Ingold again, take us "into the world, deeper and deeper."[16] I am not just remembering what happened here, but touching, smelling, seeing, hearing "an environment that is itself pregnant with the past."[17] And of course, tasting too.

Would you care for a Georgia peach?

Notes

INTRODUCTION

1   Grant Clarke (Words), Milton Ager, and George Meyer (Music), "Ev'rything Is Peaches Down in Georgia" (New York: Leo Feist, 1918).

2   Luther Burbank, "Fuzzy Peaches and Smooth Skinned Nectarines," in *Luther Burbank: His Methods and Discoveries and Their Practical Application* (New York: Luther Burbank Press, 1914), 141. I am indebted to Pablo Lepegna for the Argentine saying.

3   T. S. Eliot, "The Lovesong of J. Alfred Prufrock," first published in 1915. Accessed 30 June 2014 at www.bartleby.com/198/1.html.

4   For more on Pink Lady apples, see Susanne Freidberg, *Fresh: A Perishable History* (Cambridge, MA: Belknap Press of Harvard University Press, 2009), 155–156.

5   Wallace Stevens, "A Dish of Peaches in Russia," *Poetry* (July 1939): 180.

6   The French gardener Christophe, quoted in Inez Parker Cumming, "Sweet with Bitter: Georgia's Peach," *Georgia Review* 2, no. 4 (December 1, 1948): 486.

7   David Mas Masumoto, *Four Seasons in Five Senses: Things Worth Savoring* (New York: W.W. Norton, 2003), 127–130.

8   "Following" has both academic and popular variants. For the former, see Arjun Appadurai, ed., *The Social Life of Things: Commodities in Cultural Perspective* (New York: Cambridge University Press, 1988); Jennifer L. Anderson, *Mahogany: The Costs of Luxury in Early America* (Cambridge, MA: Harvard University Press, 2012); Ian Cook, "Geographies of Food: Following," *Progress in Human Geography* 30, no. 5 (October 2006): 655–666, doi:10.1177/0309132506070183; Gregory T. Cushman, *Guano and the Opening of the Pacific World: A Global Ecological History* (New York: Cambridge University Press, 2013); Barbara Hahn et al., "Does Crop Determine Culture?" *Agricultural History* 88, no. 3 (Summer 2014): 407–439; Alison Hulme, *On the Commodity Trail: The Journey of a Bargain Store Product from East to West* (New York: Bloomsbury Publishing, 2015); Albert G. Way, "'A Cosmopolitan Weed of the World': Following Bermudagrass,"

Agricultural History 88, no. 3 (Summer 2014): 354–367. For the latter, see Mark Kurlansky, *Cod: A Biography of the Fish That Changed the World* (New York: Penguin Books, 1998) and Pierre Laszlo, *Citrus: A History* (Chicago: University of Chicago Press, 2008). My approach has more in common with the more place-oriented Jared Farmer, *Trees in Paradise: A California History* (New York: W.W. Norton, 2013); David Gentilcore, *Pomodoro!: A History of the Tomato in Italy* (New York: Columbia University Press, 2013); Douglas Cazaux Sackman, *Orange Empire: California and the Fruits of Eden* (Berkeley: University of California Press, 2005); and Steven Stoll, *The Fruits of Natural Advantage: Making the Industrial Countryside in California* (Berkeley: University of California Press, 1998).

9   Hoagy Carmichael and Stuart Gorrell, "Georgia on My Mind" (1930).
10 A myth, according to Webster's 1913 *Dictionary,* is a story that "embodied a belief regarding some fact or phenomenon of experience." Or as philosopher Mary Midgely puts it, myths are "imaginative patterns, networks of powerful symbols that suggest particular ways of interpreting the world. They shape its meaning." Stephen Hahn, in a similar vein, argues that black slaves used rumors as a "discourse of expectation and anticipation." More than mere wishful thinking, rumors played a powerful role in defining the political culture of rural African Americans. See Mary Midgley, *The Myths We Live By* (New York: Routledge, 2005), 1; Steven Hahn, *A Nation under Our Feet: Black Political Struggles in the Rural South from Slavery to the Great Migration* (Cambridge, MA: The Belknap Press of Harvard University Press, 2003), especially pp. 57–61. I part ways here with James C. Giesen, who defines myth as a "misrepresentation told and retold, wittingly and unwittingly, by people who can gain from it." See James C. Giesen, *Boll Weevil Blues: Cotton, Myth, and Power in the American South* (Chicago: University of Chicago Press, 2011), 178.
11 Louis E. Berckmans, "Pear Culture in the South," *Southern Cultivator* vol. 17, no. 10 (Oct. 1859), 312.
12 John T. Boifeuillet, "The Luscious Peach," *Atlanta Constitution,* July 5, 1896, 24.
13 Clarke, Ager, and Meyer, "Ev'rything Is Peaches Down in Georgia."
14 Taryn Winter Brill, "Georgia–South Carolina Peach War," CBS Early Show (CBS, August 15, 2011), accessed September 2011 at www.cbsnews.com/video/watch/?id=7376923n&tag=mncol;lst;5.
15 "Peach County peach trees make Olympic cut," *Macon Telegraph* (27 Jan, 1996), 1B.
16 Carrie Anne Allen, "The Georgia Peach," *The Grove Dictionary of American Music* (New York: Oxford University Press, 2013).This is by no means an exhaustive list. There are at least eight other songs with the title "Georgia Peach."
17 See Anna Clark, "Ty Cobb as Detroit," *Grantland,* July 27, 2011, accessed Aug. 9, 2016 at http://grantland.com/features/ty-cobb-detroit/; John Paul Hill, "Ty Cobb (1886–1961)," *New Georgia Encyclopedia,* September 25, 2014, accessed Aug. 9, 2016 at http://www.georgiaencyclopedia.org/articles/sports-outdoor-recreation/ty-cobb-1886-1961.

18 The Center for Agribusiness and Economic Development at the University of Georgia, *2014 Georgia Farm Gate Value Report* (Athens: University of Georgia, September 2015), accessed 17 November 2015 at www.caes.uga .edu/center/caed/pubs/annual.html

19 There were 1.38 million acres of cotton in Georgia in 2014. National Agricultural Statistics Service, "Quick Stats: Georgia," accessed 17 November 2015 at www.nass.usda.gov/Quick_Stats/Ag_Overview/stateOverview.php? state=GEORGIA

20 Donald Worster, *Dust Bowl: The Southern Plains in the 1930s*, 25th anniversary edition (New York: Oxford University Press, 2004). More recent work has called into question the extent to which farmers actually plowed up the plains and therefore "caused" the dust bowl. See Geoff Cunfer, *On the Great Plains: Agriculture and Environment* (College Station: Texas A&M University Press, 2005).

21 Craig E. Colten, *An Unnatural Metropolis: Wresting New Orleans from Nature* (Baton Rouge: Louisiana State University Press, 2006); Ari Kelman, *A River and Its City: The Nature of Landscape in New Orleans*, rev. ed. (Berkeley: University of California Press, 2006); Christopher Morris, *The Big Muddy: An Environmental History of the Mississippi and Its Peoples from Hernando de Soto to Hurricane Katrina* (New York: Oxford University Press, 2012).

22 Perhaps the most ambitious attempt to integrate American and environmental history is Mark Fiege, *The Republic of Nature: An Environmental History of the United States*, Weyerhaeuser Environmental Books (Seattle: University of Washington Press, 2013); the most widely used survey text is Theodore Steinberg, *Down to Earth: Nature's Role in American History* (New York: Oxford University Press, 2013); for the most recent assessment of the state of the field, see Paul S. Sutter, "The World with Us: The State of American Environmental History," *Journal of American History* 100, no. 1 (June 4, 2013): 94–119, doi:10.1093/jahist/jato95 and the response essays in the same issue.

23 William Cronon, "The Trouble with Wilderness: Or, Getting Back to the Wrong Nature," *Environmental History* 1, no. 1 (January 1996): 16, doi:10.2307/ 3985059. The essay eloquently provoked much debate at the time and remains controversial today. See, for instance J. Callicott and Michael Nelson, eds., *The Great New Wilderness Debate* (Athens: University of Georgia Press, 1998); J. Callicott and Michael Nelson, eds., *Wilderness Debate Rages On: Continuing the Great New Wilderness Debate* (Athens: University of Georgia Press, 2008); Daegan Ryan Miller, "Witness Tree: Landscape and Dissent in the Nineteenth-Century United States" (Ph.D., Cornell University, 2013); Paul Sutter, *Driven Wild: How the Fight against Automobiles Launched the Modern Wilderness Movement* Weyerhaeuser Environmental Books (Seattle: University of Washington Press, 2002); James Turner, *The Promise of Wilderness: American Environmental Politics since 1964*, Weyerhaeuser Environmental Books (Seattle: University of Washington Press, 2012).

24 The Agricultural History Society was founded in 1919 and is one of the oldest professional historical associations still in existence. For exemplars

of this more recent agroecological history, see William Cronon, *Nature's Metropolis: Chicago and the Great West* (New York: W. W. Norton, 1991); Brian Donahue, *The Great Meadow: Farmers and the Land in Colonial Concord* (New Haven, CT: Yale University Press, 2004); Andrew Duffin, *Plowed Under: Agriculture and Environment in the Palouse* (Seattle: University of Washington Press, 2010); Mark Fiege, *Irrigated Eden: The Making of an Agricultural Landscape in the American West*, Weyerhaeuser Environmental Books (Seattle: University of Washington Press, 1999); Linda Lorraine Nash, *Inescapable Ecologies: A History of Environment, Disease, and Knowledge* (Berkeley: University of California Press, 2006); Cindy Ott, *Pumpkin: The Curious History of an American Icon* Weyerhaeuser Environmental Books (Seattle: University of Washington Press, 2013); John Soluri, *Banana Cultures: Agriculture, Consumption, and Environmental Change in Honduras and the United States* (Austin: University of Texas Press, 2005); Sackman, *Orange Empire: California and the Fruits of Eden*; Kendra Smith-Howard, *Pure and Modern Milk: An Environmental History since 1900* (New York: Oxford University Press, 2014); Steven Stoll, *Larding the Lean Earth: Soil and Society in Nineteenth-Century America* (New York: Hill & Wang, 2002); Stoll, *The Fruits of Natural Advantage*; Ian R. Tyrrell, *True Gardens of the Gods: Californian-Australian Environmental Reform, 1860–1930* (Berkeley: University of California Press, 1999); Donald Worster, *Rivers of Empire: Water, Aridity, and the Growth of the American West* (New York: Pantheon Books, 1985); Worster, *Dust Bowl: The Southern Plains in the 1930s.*

25 Mart A. Stewart, "If John Muir Had Been an Agrarian: American Environmental History West and South," *Environment and History* 11, no. 2 (May 1, 2005): 148.

26 The list of southern agricultural environmental history is getting longer and longer. For a primer, see Paul Sutter and Christopher J. Manganiello, eds., *Environmental History and the American South: A Reader*, Environmental History and the American South (Athens: University of Georgia Press, 2009). Other studies, recent and classic, include Joshua Blu Buhs, *The Fire Ant Wars: Nature, Science, and Public Policy in Twentieth-Century America* (Chicago: University of Chicago Press, 2004); Joyce E. Chaplin, *An Anxious Pursuit: Agricultural Innovation and Modernity in the Lower South, 1730–1815* (Chapel Hill: Published for the Institute of Early American History and Culture, Williamsburg, Virginia, by the University of North Carolina Press, 1993); Albert E. Cowdrey, *This Land, This South: An Environmental History*, revised (Lexington: University Press of Kentucky, 1995); Avery Craven, *Soil Exhaustion as a Factor in the Agricultural History of Virginia and Maryland, 1606–1860* (Urbana: University of Illinois, 1926); Pete Daniel, *Breaking the Land: The Transformation of Cotton, Tobacco, and Rice Cultures since 1880* (Urbana: University of Illinois Press, 1985); Pete Daniel, *Toxic Drift: Pesticides and Health in the Post–World War II South*, Walter Lynwood Fleming Lectures in Southern History (Baton Rouge: Louisiana State University Press, 2005); Donald Edward Davis, *Where There Are Mountains: An Environmental History of the Southern Appalachians*

(Athens: University of Georgia Press, 2000); Brian Allen Drake, ed., *The Blue, the Gray, and the Green: Toward an Environmental History of the Civil War* (Athens: University of Georgia Press, 2015); Farmer, *Trees in Paradise: A California History*; Giesen, *Boll Weevil Blues*; Mark D. Hersey, *My Work Is That of Conservation: An Environmental Biography of George Washington Carver*, Environmental History and the American South (Athens: University of Georgia Press, 2011); Jack Temple Kirby, *Poquosin: A Study of Rural Landscape and Society*, Studies in Rural Culture (Chapel Hill: University of North Carolina Press, 1995); Jack Temple Kirby, *Mockingbird Song: Ecological Landscapes of the South* (Chapel Hill: University of North Carolina Press, 2006); Christopher J. Manganiello, *Southern Water, Southern Power: How the Politics of Cheap Energy and Water Scarcity Shaped a Region* (Chapel Hill: University of North Carolina Press, 2015); Lynn A Nelson, *Pharsalia: An Environmental Biography of a Southern Plantation, 1780–1880*, Environmental History and the American South (Athens: University of Georgia Press, 2007); Paul S. Sutter, *Let Us Now Praise Famous Gullies: Georgia's "Little Grand Canyon" and the Soils of the South*, Environmental History and the American South (Athens: University of Georgia Press, 2015); Mart A. Stewart, *"What Nature Suffers to Groe": Life, Labor, and Landscape on the Georgia Coast, 1680–1920*, Wormsloe Foundation Publications (Athens: University of Georgia Press, 2002); Claire Strom, *Making Catfish Bait out of Government Boys: The Fight against Cattle Ticks and the Transformation of the Yeoman South*, Environmental History and the American South (Athens: University of Georgia Press, 2010); Drew A. Swanson, *A Golden Weed: Tobacco and Environment in the Piedmont South* (New Haven, CT: Yale University Press, 2014); Albert G. Way, *Conserving Southern Longleaf: Herbert Stoddard and the Rise of Ecological Land Management*, Environmental History and the American South (Athens: University of Georgia Press, 2011).

27 Raymond Williams originally made this point – that culture has been a verb much longer than a noun, and is more material than esoteric – in his treatment of "culture" in *Keywords*. See Raymond Williams, *Keywords: A Vocabulary of Culture and Society*, revised (New York: Oxford University Press, 1983), 87–93.

28 This is especially true of agricultural modernization and development projects. See, for example, Nick Cullather, *The Hungry World: America's Cold War Battle against Poverty in Asia* (Cambridge, MA: Harvard University Press, 2010); Arturo Escobar, *Encountering Development* (Princeton, NJ: Princeton University Press, 1994); James Ferguson, *The Anti-Politics Machine: Development, Depoliticization, and Bureaucratic Power in Lesotho* (Minneapolis: University of Minnesota Press, 1994); Daniel Immerwahr, *Thinking Small: The United States and the Lure of Community Development* (Cambridge, MA: Harvard University Press, 2015); Tania Murray Li, *The Will to Improve: Governmentality, Development, and the Practice of Politics* (Durham, NC: Duke University Press, 2007); Timothy Mitchell, *Rule of Experts: Egypt, Techno-Politics, Modernity* (Berkeley: University of California Press, 2002); Tore C. Olsson, *Agrarian Crossings:*

Agrarian Crossings: Remaking the U.S. and Mexican Countryside in the Twentieth Century (Princeton, NJ: Princeton University Press, forthcoming); María Josefina Saldaña-Portillo, *The Revolutionary Imagination in the Americas and the Age of Development* (Durham, NC: Duke University Press Books, 2003); James C. Scott, *Seeing Like a State: How Certain Schemes to Improve the Human Condition Have Failed*, Yale Agrarian Studies (New Haven, CT: Yale University Press, 1998).

29 Stewart, "If John Muir Had Been an Agrarian," 156n10; T. H. Breen, "Back to Sweat and Toil: Suggestions for the Study of Agricultural Work in Early America," *Pennsylvania History* 49, no. 4 (October 1, 1982): 241–258. Breen's own superb effort to reconstruct the "tobacco mentality" – the relationship between crops and culture – is T. H. Breen, *Tobacco Culture: The Mentality of the Great Tidewater Planters on the Eve of Revolution*, 2nd ed. (Princeton, NJ: Princeton University Press, 2009).

30 See Daniel, *Breaking the Land: The Transformation of Cotton, Tobacco, and Rice Cultures Since 1880*; Drew Gilpin Faust, *James Henry Hammond and the Old South: A Design for Mastery* (Baton Rouge: Louisiana State University Press, 1983); Gilbert Courtland Fite, *Cotton Fields No More: Southern Agriculture, 1865–1980*, New Perspectives on the South (Lexington: University Press of Kentucky, 1984); Jack Temple Kirby, *Rural Worlds Lost: The American South, 1920–1960* (Baton Rouge: Louisiana State University Press, 1987); Kirby, *Poquosin*. Southern foodways scholarships – taking the perspective of the plate rather than the farm – is recently resurgent. See Jill Angela Cooley, *To Live and Dine in Dixie: The Evolution of Urban Food Culture in the Jim Crow South* (Athens: University of Georgia Press, 2015); Elizabeth Engelhardt, *A Mess of Greens: Southern Gender and Southern Food* (Athens: University of Georgia Press, 2011), Marcie Cohen Farris, *The Edible South: The Power of Food and the Making of an American Region* (Chapel Hill: University of North Carolina Press, 2014); Jessica B. Harris, *High on the Hog: A Culinary Journey from Africa to America* (New York: Bloomsbury Publishing, 2011), Frederick Douglass Opie, *Hog and Hominy: Soul Food from Africa to America* (New York: Columbia University Press, 2013); David S. Shields, *Southern Provisions: The Creation and Revival of a Cuisine* (Chicago: University of Chicago Press, 2015). There is also an older school of carefully researched and thoughtful southern agricultural history that deserves to be recovered, though sometimes – especially in the case of U.B. Philips' frankly racist defense of southern life – with caution. In addition to Breen, Daniel, Faust, Fite and Kirby, see James Calvin Bonner, *A History of Georgia Agriculture, 1732–1860* (Athens: University of Georgia Press, 1964); Craven, *Soil Exhaustion as a Factor in the Agricultural History of Virginia and Maryland, 1606–1860*; Lewis C. Gray and Esther Katherine Thompson, *History of Agriculture in the Southern United States to 1860*, Carnegie Institution of Washington Publication (Washington, DC: Carnegie Institution of Washington, 1933); Sam Bowers Hilliard, *Hog Meat and Hoecake: Food Supply in the Old South, 1840–1860* (University of Georgia Press, 2014 [1972]); Ulrich Bonnell Phillips, *Life and Labor in the Old South*, ed. John David Smith, Southern Classics Series (Columbia: University of South Carolina Press,

2007 [1929]); Willard Range, *A Century of Georgia Agriculture, 1850–1950* (Athens: University of Georgia Press, 1954).

31 Blain Roberts's new book on race and beauty is, among many other things, a study of the agriculture–beauty nexus in the twentieth-century South. She focuses on black and white women in pageants and beauty parlors and so tells a rather different story, but she does take beauty seriously. Blain Roberts, *Pageants, Parlors, and Pretty Women: Race and Beauty in the Twentieth-Century South* (Chapel Hill: University of North Carolina Press, 2014).

32 C. S. Lewis, *The Abolition of Man* (Grand Rapids, MI: Zondervan, 2001 [1943]), 81.

33 Eve Kosofsky Sedgwick, "Paranoid Reading and Reparative Reading; Or, You're So Paranoid You Probably Think This Introduction Is about You," in *Novel Gazing: Queer Readings in Fiction*, 22 (1997): 8. I am also indebted to Aaron Sachs, who first suggested the idea of reparative reading at the American Society for Environmental History's first "History Slam" in San Francisco, March 2013.

34 The point holds regardless of one's definition of beauty. Scholars in the social sciences (and the social science side of history) tend to talk about beauty mostly in the former, utilitarian sense, as a tool of dominance, a means of creating or perpetuating social inequality. And in some cases, beauty is clearly instrumental. But this is also a rather reductionist account of human experience, and I think there is also some merit in the older idea of beauty as the breaking in of the divine. See, for instance, the poetry and notebooks of Gerard Manley Hopkins, especially "The Principle or Foundation," in *Gerard Manley Hopkins: Poetry and Prose*, Everyman's Library Pocket Poets (New York: Alfred A. Knopf, 1995).

35 I am indebted to conversations with the historian Andrew Baker for this insight.

36 "The historical record is like the night sky: we see a few stars and group them into mythic constellations. But what is chiefly visible is the darkness." Roy Porter, *The Greatest Benefit to Mankind: A Medical History of Humanity* (New York: W. W. Norton, 1999), 13; C. S. Lewis, *Christian Reflections* (Grand Rapids, MI: Wm. B. Eerdmans, 2014 [1967]), 133.

37 I have in mind what James Scott calls "practical knowledge." See *Seeing Like a State: How Certain Schemes to Improve the Human Condition Have Failed*, 309–341.

38 David Boucher and Teresa Smith, eds., *R. G. Collingwood: An Autobiography and Other Writings: With Essays on Collingwood's Life and Work* (New York: Oxford University Press, 2013), 99.

39 The debate about objectivity and relativism is old and immensely complicated, but two points of departure for my own work are William Cronon, "A Place for Stories: Nature, History, and Narrative," *Journal of American History* 78, no. 4 (March 1, 1992): 1347–1376, doi:10.2307/2079346; and Tim Ingold, "Hunting, Gathering and Perceiving," in *The Perception of the Environment: Essays on Livelihood, Dwelling and Skill* (London: Routledge, 2011), 40–60. Cronon admits the difficulty of holding to any notion of correspondence between our stories and the actual past, but ends on the optimistic note that peer review keeps us honest, while Ingold observes that

stories can take us into a landscape, rather than separate us from it. See also Peter Novick, *That Noble Dream: The "Objectivity Question" and the American Historical Profession* (New York: Cambridge University Press, 1988); Aaron Sachs, "Letters to a Tenured Historian: Imagining History as Creative Nonfiction – or Maybe Even Poetry," *Rethinking History* 14, no. 1 (March 1, 2010): 5–38, doi:10.1080/13642520903515611.

40 Stevens, "Dish of Peaches in Russia." Many battles of the Civil War took place in the shadow of peach trees, which, in the quieter moments between volleys, must have reminded soldiers of home, agricultural work, "summer, dew, peace." Perhaps a few paused to appreciate the poignant loveliness of a landscape prepared for destruction, as Aaron Sachs has reminded us. A peach tree was, in this sense, what Daegan Miller calls a "witness tree," quietly affirming that violence might not be the last word. Miller uses the term – originally a tree marked by surveyors to "witness" the precise locations of property lines – to discuss the ways trees spoke to, laughed at, and criticized a rapidly modernizing nation in the nineteenth century. See Aaron Sachs, *Arcadian America: The Death and Life of an Environmental Tradition*, New Directions in Narrative History (New Haven, CT: Yale University Press, 2013), 137–209; and Miller, "Witness Tree," 8, 19–20.

41 Tim Ingold, "The Temporality of the Landscape," in *The Perception of the Environment: Essays on Livelihood, Dwelling and Skill* (London: Routledge, 2011), 57.

1 A WILDERNESS OF PEACH TREES

1 H. Huang, "History of Cultivation and Trends in China," in *The Peach: Botany, Production and Uses*, ed. Desmond R. Layne and Daniele Bassi (Cambridge, MA: CABI, 2008), 37–38.

2 Mark Swislocki, "The Honey Nectar Peach and the Idea of Shanghai in Late Imperial China," *Late Imperial China* 29, no. 1 (2008): 2.

3 Ibid., 9–13. Today, near the Shanghai satellite town of Yangshan, a version of the "honey nectar peach" still grows to enormous size. Workers wrap each one in newspaper to protect the delicate flesh from injury, and buyers consume them – slurp them over sinks – within twenty-four hours of harvest. China grows almost half of the world's peaches, with more than 1.7 million acres, or about six times the area in the United States. See Stan Sesser, "The Best Peach on Earth," *Wall Street Journal*, August 21, 2009, accessed Aug. 1, 2016 at http://online.wsj.com/article/SB100014240529702039469045 7430019208204098.html; Huang, "History of Cultivation and Trends in China." For contemporary statistics, see Food and Agriculture Organization, FAOSTAT, accessed Aug. 1, 2016 at http://faostat3.fao.org/.

4 Virgil, "The Second Eclogue, or, Alexis," trans. John Dryden (1697) accessed Sept. 22, 2016, at http://sourcebooks.fordham.edu/pwh/virgil-eclog2.asp

5 See U. P. Hedrick, *The Peaches of New York* (Albany, NY: J. B. Lyon, 1917), 2–3, 26–30, accessed Aug. 3, 2016 at http://archive.org/details/peaches ofnewyorkoohedr. For this etymological history, see the *Oxford English Dictionary*.

6 Susanne Freidberg, *Fresh: A Perishable History* (Cambridge, MA: Belknap Press of Harvard University Press, 2009), 130. Today in Greece, Italy, and Spain, large fruit companies ship peaches all over Western Europe, employing Romanies and other migrants to harvest the fruit in season. Spanish growers currently produce almost as many peaches and nectarines as the entire United States. Average production figures for 1993–2013 were as follows: United States 1,278,872 metric tons; Spain 1,104,142; Italy 1,566,772; China 6,537,927. See Food and Agricultural Organization, FAOSTAT, accessed Aug. 1, 2016 at http://faostat3.fao.org/.

7 Alfred W. Crosby, *The Columbian Exchange: Biological and Cultural Consequences of 1492*, Contributions in American Studies, No. 2 (Westport, CT: Greenwood, 1972).

8 John Mark Williams, "The Joe Bell Site: Seventeenth Century Lifeways on the Oconee River," (Ph.D. diss., University of Georgia, 1983), 427; Ulysses P. Hedrick, *The Peaches of New York*, 39–46.

9 Donald Edward Davis, *Where There Are Mountains: An Environmental History of the Southern Appalachians* (Athens: University of Georgia Press, 2000), 47; John H. Hann, *Appalachee: The Land Between the Rivers* (Gainesville: University of Florida Press, 1988), 133; Lewis C. Gray and Esther Katherine Thompson, *History of Agriculture in the Southern United States to 1860* (Washington, DC: Carnegie Institution of Washington (1933) 5, 7, 69; Ulysses P. Hedrick, *Peaches of New York*. In the Southwest, the fruit became a central part of the Navajo diet, and Navajo orchards dotted the Canyon de Chelly area of New Mexico into the twentieth century. See Stephen C. Jett, "History of Fruit Tree Raising among the Navajo," *Agricultural History* 51, no. 4 (October 1, 1977): 683.

10 Davis, *Where There Are Mountains*, 48.

11 John Lawson, *A New Voyage to Carolina*, Electronic ed., University of North Carolina, DocSouth Collection (London, 1709), accessed Aug. 1, 2016 at http://docsouth.unc.edu/nc/lawson/lawson.html, 110.

12 Ibid., 17.

13 In Oconee County, South Carolina, for example, Bartram found a "charming vale," which appeared to be "the remains of a town of the ancients, as the tumuli, terraces, posts or pillars, old Peach and Plumb orchards, &c. sufficiently testify." See William Bartram, *The Travels of William Bartram: Naturalist Edition* (Athens: University of Georgia Press, 1998), 333–334 (211); Davis, *Where There Are Mountain*, 48–49.

14 See, for example, the discussion of Indian peaches in the Georgia State Horticultural Society, *Annual Proceedings* 10 (1885), 38.

15 Lawson, *New Voyage to Carolina*, 164.

16 Ibid., 109–110. Lawson wrote, of course, in order to encourage settlement, and therefore wrote much as a car salesman talks.

17 See Steven Hahn, *The Roots of Southern Populism: Yeoman Farmers and the Transformation of the Georgia Upcountry, 1850–1890* (New York: Oxford University Press, 2006); Jack Temple Kirby, *Mockingbird Song: Ecological Landscapes of the South* (Chapel Hill: University of North Carolina Press, 2006).

18 Charles Ball, *Fifty Years in Chains*, ed. Philip S. Foner, Dover ed., Black Rediscovery (New York: Dover, 1970 [1837]), 51. Like many escaped slaves, Ball told his story to a northern writer, who published it to an increasingly sympathetic transatlantic audience. What Ball called Chinquapin was likely a shrub chestnut, *Castanea pumila* or related variety; the cedar was probably what we call eastern red cedar, *Juniperus virginiana*, which is actually a juniper. On Charles Ball's environmental imagination, see Thomas G. Andrews, "Beasts of the Southern Wild: Slaveholders, Slaves, and Other Animals in Charles Ball's Slavery in the United States," in *Rendering Nature: Animals, Bodies, Places, Politics*, ed. Marguerite S. Shaffer and Phoebe S. K. Young (Philadelphia: University of Pennsylvania Press, 2015), 21–47.
19 Ball, *Fifty Years in Chains*, 81.
20 Ibid., 81, 83. And yet despite these ill omens of his own future, Ball remained remarkably perceptive: he noted the "unrestrained luxuriance" of the vegetation and praised the magnificent groves of *Magnolia grandiflora* that he passed. His description of the latter was extraordinarily precise: "It rises in a right line to the height of seventy or eighty feet," he recalled; "the stem is of a delicate taper form, and casts off numerous branches, in nearly right angles with itself; the extremities of which, decline gently towards the ground." Ibid., 133.
21 Ibid., 68–69.
22 Ibid., 71.
23 Ibid., 81.
24 Ibid., 69.
25 Ball does not identify Hampton as his owner in the text, but his plantation on the Congaree River is one of the largest in the state, with 260 slaves, which fits Hampton, according to the historian John Blassingame. See Ball, *Fifty Years in Chains*, 137; John W. Blassingame, *Slave Testimony: Two Centuries of Letters, Speeches, Interviews, and Autobiographies* (Baton Rouge: Louisiana State University Press, 1977), xxiii–xxvi.
26 Ball, *Fifty Years in Chains*, 201.
27 Ibid., 205, 269.
28 Ibid., 399, 407, 409.
29 Mart Stewart, *"What Nature Suffers to Groe": Life, Labor, and Landscape on the Georgia Coast, 1680–1920* (Athens: University of Georgia Press, 2002), 50, 250; Jack Temple Kirby, *Poquosin: A Study of Rural Landscape and Society*, Studies in Rural Culture (Chapel Hill: University of North Carolina Press, 1995); *Mockingbird Song: Ecological Landscapes of the South* (Chapel Hill: University of North Carolina Press, 2006).
30 Ball, *Fifty Years in Chains*, 205, 269.
31 See Gray and Thompson, *History of Agriculture in the Southern United States to 1860*, 5, 7, 36, 69; James C. Bonner, "The Commercial Peach Industry in Ante-Bellum Georgia," *The Georgia Historical Quarterly* 31, no. 4 (December 1, 1947), 241; and Sam Bowers Hilliard, *Hog Meat and Hoe Cake: Food Supply in the Old South 1840–1860* (Carbondale: Southern Illinois University Press, 1972), 182.

32 See Andrea Wulf, *Founding Gardeners: The Revolutionary Generation, Nature, and the Shaping of the American Nation*, Reprint ed. (New York: Vintage, 2012).

33 George Washington, *Diaries*, 4 vols., ed. J. C. Fitzpatrick (Boston, 1925), quoted in U. P. Hedrick, *A History of Horticulture in America to 1860* (New York: Oxford University Press, 1950), 170, 172. Andrea Wulf has a lovely section on this preoccupation of Washington's in Wulf, *Founding Gardeners: The Revolutionary Generation, Nature, and the Shaping of the American Nation*, 13–15.

34 Letter to the marquis de Lafayette, Feb. 1, 1784, quoted in Library of Congress, "Washington's Diaries Available Online (October 2000)," *Library of Congress Information Bulletin*, accessed Feb. 6, 2014 at www.loc.gov/loc/lcib/0010/gwdiary.html.

35 Hamilton W. Pierson, *Jefferson at Monticello* (New York, 1862), quoted in Hedrick, *History of Horticulture in America to 1860*, 179.

36 Philip J. Pauly, *Fruits and Plains: The Horticultural Transformation of America* (Cambridge, MA: Harvard University Press, 2007), 13, 32.

37 Quoted in Hedrick, *History of Horticulture in America to 1860*, 181.

38 Pauly, *Fruits and Plains*, 2, 52–53. As Daniel Kevles has shown, the horticultural scene was led, on the one hand, by those whose fortunes were "made or accumulating" and so could turn to farming avocationally; and, on the other hand, by nurserymen who were only too happy to oblige the new craze. Daniel J. Kevles, "Fruit Nationalism: Horticulture in the United States – from the Revolution to the First Centennial," in *Aurora Torealis: Studies in the History of Science and Ideas in Honor of Tore Frangsmyr*, ed. Marco Beretta, Karl Grandin, and Svante Lindqvist (Sagamore Beach, MA: Science History Publications USA, 2008), 132. As Ian Tyrell and, more recently, Jared Farmer have shown, California occupied a special place in this period of horticultural experimentation. See Ian Tyrell, *True Gardens of the Gods: Californian-Australian Environmental Reform, 1860–1930* (Berkeley: University of California Press, 1999) esp. 36–55; and Jared Farmer, *Trees in Paradise: A California History* (New York: W.W. Norton, 2013), esp. xxiv–xxvi.

39 See Hedrick, *History of Horticulture in America to 1860*, 475–485; William Coxe, *A View of the Cultivation of Fruit Trees* (Philadelphia: M. Carey and Son, 1817); Thomas Green Fessenden, *The New American Gardener* (Boston: Carter & Hendee, 1832); C. M. Hovey, *Magazine of Horticulture, Botany, and All Useful Discoveries and Improvements in Rural Affairs* vol. 1 (Boston, 1835); Robert Manning, *Book of Fruits* (Salem: Ives & Jewett, 1838); William Robert Prince, *The Pomological Manual*, 2nd ed. (New York: T. & J. Swords, 1832); C. M. Hovey, *The Fruits of America* (Boston: C. C. Little and J. Brown and Hovey, 1848).

40 For more on this "horticultural revolution," see Hedrick, *History of Horticulture in America to 1860*; Kevles, "Fruit Nationalism"; Daniel J. Kevles, "Protections, Privileges, and Patents: Intellectual Property in American Horticulture, the Late Nineteenth Century to 1930," *Proceedings of the American Philosophical Society* 152, no. 2 (June 1, 2008): 207–213;

Abigail Jane Lustig, "The Creation and Uses of Horticulture in Britain and France in the Nineteenth Century" (Ph.D., University of California, Berkeley, 1997); Philip J. Pauly, "The Interpretation of Horticulture," *Raritan: A Quarterly Review*, no. 4 (2004); Pauly, *Fruits and Plains: The Horticultural Transformation of America*; Philip J. Pauly, "Mums as the Measure of Men: Horticulture and Culture," *Raritan* 27, no. 3 (Winter 2008): 1–25; Emily Pawley, "'The Balance-Sheet of Nature': Calculating the New York Farm, 1820–1860" (Ph.D., University of Pennsylvania, 2009); Aaron Sachs, "American Arcadia: Mount Auburn Cemetery and the Nineteenth-Century Landscape Tradition," *Environmental History* 15, no. 2 (April 1, 2010): 206–235, doi:10.1093/envhis/emq032; Aaron Sachs, *Arcadian America: The Death and Life of an Environmental Tradition*, New Directions in Narrative History (New Haven: Yale University Press, 2013); David Schuyler, *Apostle of Taste: Andrew Jackson Downing, 1815–1852, Creating the North American Landscape* (Baltimore: Johns Hopkins University Press, 1996); Eric Rutkow, *American Canopy: Trees, Forests, and the Making of a Nation* (New York: Scribner, 2012); Wulf, *Founding Gardeners*.

41 Fredrika Bremer, *The Homes of the New World: Impressions of America* (New York: Harper & Bros., 1853), 46.He was well known internationally, too, earning a surprised acclaim in England for the *Treatise*. J. C. Loudon, the most prominent landscape gardener in England at the time, called it a "masterly work," and the horticulturist John Lindley considered it superior to any other landscape gardening book in print. Downing received honorary diplomas from the Royal Prussian Gardening Society of Berlin and the Royal Botanic Society of London. See Schuyler, *Apostle of Taste*, 53, 55.

42 Andrew Jackson Downing, *The Fruits and Fruit Trees of America* (New York: Wiley and Putnam, 1845), v–vi; Andrew Jackson Downing, "Some Remarks on the Superiority of Native Varieties of Fruit," in *Transactions of the Massachusetts Horticultural Society*, vol. I (Boston, 1847), 30.

43 Pauly, "Mums as the Measure of Men," 2.

44 Andrew Jackson Downing, *A Treatise on the Theory and Practice of Landscape Gardening* (New York: G. P. Putnam, 1841), 18–19.

45 Ingold, "The Temporality of the Landscape," in *The Perception of the Environment: Essays on Livelihood, Dwelling and Skill* (London: Routledge, 2011), 194, 198.

46 Downing, *A Treatise on the Theory and Practice of Landscape Gardening*, x.

47 Ibid., x.

48 I am thinking here of Pierre Bourdieu's notions of misrecognition and symbolic violence. The latter David Swartz characterizes as "the capacity to impose the means for comprehending and adapting to the social world by representing economic and political power in disguised, taken-for-granted forms. Symbolic systems exercise symbolic power" via misrecognition: that is, "'only through the complicity of those who do not want to know that they are subject to it or even that they themselves exercise it'" (Bourdieu 1991c:164), cited in David Swartz, *Culture and Power: The Sociology of Pierre Bourdieu* (Chicago: University Of Chicago Press, 1997), 89.

49 Jenny Price, *Flight Maps: Adventures with Nature in Modern America* (New York: Basic Books, 1999), 122. See also Farmer, *Trees in Paradise: A California History*.

50 Sachs, *Arcadian America: The Death and Life of an Environmental Tradition*, 112; Dolores Hayden, *Building Suburbia: Green Fields and Urban Growth, 1820–2000* (New York: Pantheon Books, 2003), 34.

51 Kenneth T. Jackson, *Crabgrass Frontier: The Suburbanization of the United States* (New York: Oxford University Press, 1985), 64.

52 Downing, *Treatise on the Theory and Practice of Landscape Gardening*, 18–19; Price, *Flight Maps*, 119–121.

53 Price, Flight Maps, 123.

54 Mark Akenside, "The Pleasures of Imagination. Book III.," 1744, accessed Aug. 1, 2016 at http://spenserians.cath.vt.edu/TextRecord.php?action=GET& textsid=37339.

55 William Wordsworth, "Lines Composed a Few Miles above Tintern Abbey, On Revisiting the Banks of the Wye during a Tour. July 13, 1798," *Poetry Foundation*, July 13, 1798, accessed Aug. 1, 2016 at www.poetryfoundation .org/poem/174796.

56 See, for example, Crosby, *Columbian Exchange: Biological and Cultural Consequences of 1492*; Alfred W. Crosby, *Ecological Imperialism: The Biological Expansion of Europe, 900–1900*, Studies in Environment and History (New York: Cambridge University Press, 2004); Virginia DeJohn Anderson, *Creatures of Empire: How Domestic Animals Transformed Early America* (New York: Oxford University Press, 2004); Judith A. Carney, *Black Rice: The African Origins of Rice Cultivation in the Americas*, New ed. (Cambridge, MA: Harvard University Press, 2002).

57 Robert Fortune, *Three Years' Wanderings in the Northern Provinces of China*, 2nd ed. (London: J. Murray, 1847), 407–408; W. R. Okie, *Handbook of Peach and Nectarine Varieties: Performance in the Southeastern United States and Index of Names*, Agriculture Handbook 714 (Washington, DC: U.S. Department of Agriculture, Agricultural Research Service, 1998), 54. By comparison, commercial weight today is typically around seven ounces, though there are fruit upward of sixteen ounces. See Layne and Bassi, *Peach: Botany, Production and Uses*, 16.

58 *Soil of the South* I (March 1851), 36, quoted in James Calvin Bonner, *A History of Georgia Agriculture, 1732–1860* (Athens: University of Georgia Press, 1964), 64.

59 Herbert A. Keller, ed., *Solon Robinson, Pioneer and Agriculturist*, 2 vols. (Indianapolis, 1936), II, 378, 479, quoted in Bonner, *History of Georgia Agriculture*, 61–62.

60 Southern Central Agricultural Association of Georgia, *Transactions of the Southern Central Agricultural Society, from Its Organization in 1846 to 1851* (B. F. Griffin, 1852), 263.

61 The Agricultural Society of South Carolina was founded in 1795. See Joyce E. Chaplin, *An Anxious Pursuit: Agricultural Innovation and Modernity in the Lower South, 1730–1815* (Chapel Hill: Published for the Institute of Early American History and Culture, Williamsburg, Virginia, by

the University of North Carolina Press, 1993); Theodore Rosengarten, "The Southern Agriculturist in an Age of Reform," in *Intellectual Life in Antebellum Charleston*, ed. Michael O'Brien and David Moltke-Hansen (Knoxville: University of Tennessee Press, 1986), 279–294; Drew Gilpin Faust, "The Rhetoric and Ritual of Agriculture in Antebellum South Carolina," *Journal of Southern History* 45, no. 4 (November 1, 1979): 541–568, doi:10.2307/2207713.

62 Bonner, *History of Georgia Agriculture, 1732–1860*, 116–117.

63 Ibid., 112.

64 Ibid., 264.

65 *Soil of the South* III (Jan. 1853), 394, quoted in ibid., 72.

66 These reformers have earned a great deal of attention in recent years. See Benjamin R. Cohen, *Notes from the Ground: Science, Soil, and Society in the American Countryside* (New Haven, CT: Yale University Press, 2009); Philip Mills Herrington, "The Exceptional Plantation: Slavery, Agricultural Reform, and the Creation of an American Landscape" (Ph.D., University of Virginia, 2012); Kirby, *Poquosin*; Lynn A Nelson, *Pharsalia: An Environmental Biography of a Southern Plantation, 1780–1880*, Environmental History and the American South (Athens: University of Georgia Press, 2007); Edmund Ruffin, *Nature's Management: Writings on Landscape and Reform, 1822–1859*, ed. Jack Temple Kirby (Athens: University of Georgia Press, 2000); Steven Stoll, *Larding the Lean Earth: Soil and Society in Nineteenth-Century America* (New York: Hill and Wang, 2002). See also Bonner, *A History of Georgia Agriculture, 1732–1860*, chapters 4 and 5.

67 Southern Central Agricultural Association of Georgia, *Transactions of the Southern Central Agricultural Society, from Its Organization in 1846 to 1851*, 69. Andrews was a prominent planter in Wilkes; later he would run, and lose, as the gubernatorial candidate of the nativist Know Nothing Party. He served in 1859 in the Georgia House of Representatives, where he fought to preserve slavery and the union. See S. K. Rushing, "Garnett Andrews (1798–1873)," *New Georgia Encyclopedia*, December 9, 2013, accessed Aug. 1, 2016 at www.georgiaencyclopedia.org/articles/history-archaeology/garnett-andrews-1798-1873.

68 Southern Central Agricultural Association of Georgia, *Transactions of the Southern Central Agricultural Society, from Its Organization in 1846 to 1851*, 71.

69 Stephen Elliott Jr., "Address on Horticulture," in *Transactions of the Southern Central Agricultural Society, from Its Organization in 1846 to 1851* (Macon, GA: B. F. Griffin, 1852), 111–112.

70 Elliott, "Address on Horticulture," 112. Stephen Elliott Sr. published *A Sketch of the Botany of South Carolina and Georgia* in 1821. See Elliott, *A Sketch of the Botany of South Carolina and Georgia*, Vol. 1. (Charleston, SC: J.R. Schenck, 1821). On the bishop's support of slavery see his 1862 sermon, "Our Cause in Harmony with the Purposes of God in Christ Jesus" (Savannah, GA: Power Press of John M. Cooper, 1862), accessed Aug. 1, 2016 at http://docsouth.unc.edu/imls/elliott5/elliott5.html.

71 Elliott, "Address on Horticulture," 113.

72 Ibid.; Downing, *Fruits and Fruit Trees of America*, 1.

73 Elliott, "Address on Horticulture," 114, 115. Elliott apparently did not consider Indians a "permanent population"; nor did he mention (if he was aware of it) the sizable orchards of prominent Cherokees such as Major Ridge and John Ross.

74 Ibid., 115.

75 Ibid., 115, 116.

76 Ibid., 117, 118.

77 Ibid., 119.

78 Ibid.

79 Gavin Wright, *Old South, New South: Revolutions in the Southern Economy since the Civil War* (New York: Basic Books, 1986), 33–47.

80 S. Max Edelson, *Plantation Enterprise in Colonial South Carolina* (Cambridge, MA: Harvard University Press, 2006), 141–149.

81 Elliott, "Address on Horticulture," 123.

82 Ibid., 125.

83 Ibid., 127.

84 Ibid., 141.

85 Ibid., 149.

86 Herrington, "Exceptional Plantation: Slavery, Agricultural Reform, and the Creation of an American Landscape," 39–44.

87 Alexis de Tocqueville, *Democracy in America*, 3rd American ed. (New York, 1839), 1:359–360, quoted in ibid., 38–39.

88 See Southern Central Agricultural Association of Georgia, *Transactions of the Southern Central Agricultural Society, from Its Organization in 1846 to 1851*, xxi.

89 Michael Reynolds, "A History of Fruitland Nurseries, Augusta, Georgia and the Berckmans Family in America," *Magnolia* XVIII, no. 1 (Winter 2002–2003), 3.

90 Dennis Redmond, "Fruitland," *Southern Cultivator* 15, no. 8 (Aug. 1857), 242.

91 Herrington, "Exceptional Plantation: Slavery, Agricultural Reform, and the Creation of an American Landscape," 174–175.

92 On Gregg, Hammond, and Ravenel, see Tom Downey, *Planting a Capitalist South: Masters, Merchants, and Manufacturers in the Southern Interior, 1790–1860* (Baton Rouge: Louisiana State University Press, 2006), 204–205; Drew Gilpin Faust, *James Henry Hammond and the Old South: A Design for Mastery* (Baton Rouge: Louisiana State University Press, 1983); Tamara Miner Haygood, *Henry William Ravenel, 1814–1887: South Carolina Scientist in the Civil War Era* (Tuscaloosa: University of Alabama Press, 1987), 89–93.

93 "The Beautiful in Agriculture," *Southern Cultivator* (December 1856), 362–364, quoted in Herrington, "Exceptional Plantation: Slavery, Agricultural Reform, and the Creation of an American Landscape," 158.

94 Herrington, "Exceptional Plantation: Slavery, Agricultural Reform, and the Creation of an American Landscape," 144–145, 181.

95 Bremer, *Homes of the New World*, 328.
96 Thomas M. Hanckel, "Memoir of Rt. Rev. Stephen Elliott," in *Sermons* (New York: Pott and Amery, 1867), xiv.
97 See Edward E. Baptist, *The Half Has Never Been Told: Slavery and the Making of American Capitalism* (New York: Basic Books, 2014); Sven Beckert, *Empire of Cotton: A Global History* (New York: Knopf, 2014); Walter Johnson, *River of Dark Dreams: Slavery and Empire in the Cotton Kingdom* (Cambridge, MA: Harvard University Press, 2013); Seth Rockman, "What Makes the History of Capitalism Newsworthy?" *Journal of the Early Republic*, no. 3 (2014).
98 For a recent reappraisal of Bryant's poetry, see Norbert Krapf, "William Cullen Bryant's Roslyn Poems," in *Under Open Sky: Poets on William Cullen Bryant*, ed. Norbert Krapf (New York: Fordham University Press, 1986), 3–16.
99 Ball, *Fifty Years in Chains*, 201.
100 Hanckel, "Memoir of Rt. Rev. Stephen Elliott," xix.
101 Stewart, *What Nature Suffers to Groe*, 116–122; Steven Hahn, *The Roots of Southern Populism: Yeoman Farmers and the Transformation of the Georgia Upcountry, 1850–1890*.
102 Thomas Lunsford Stokes, *The Savannah* (Athens: University of Georgia Press, 1982), 219.

2 A BARON OF PEARS

1 As Walter Johnson evocatively suggests, agricultural literature "might be read as a set of extended efforts to translate [field hands'] practical knowledge ... into a set of visual terms" for their owners' eyes. Johnson, *River of Dark Dreams: Slavery and Empire in the Cotton Kingdom* (Cambridge, MA: Belknap Press of Harvard University Press, 2013), 166.
2 I am thinking of landscapes in Tim Ingold's terms: "an enduring record of – and testimony to – the lives and works of past generations who have dwelt within it, and in so doing, have left there something of themselves." Ingold, "Temporality of the Landscape," in *The Perception of the Environment: Essays on Livelihood, Dwelling and Skill* (London: Routledge, 2011), 189.
3 Prosper Jules Alphonse Berckmans, "Voyage en Amerique", 1850, 1, Berckmans Family Papers, MS 122, Hargrett Rare Book and Manuscript Library, University of Georgia Libraries.
4 Ibid., 2.
5 Ibid., 4.
6 Latour, drawing from Vinciane Despret, who in turn is drawing upon William James, writes: "to have a body is to learn to be affected, meaning 'effectuated', moved, put into motion by other entities, humans or non-humans. If you are not engaged in this learning you become insensitive, dumb, you drop dead." See Vinciane Despret, "The Body We Care for: Figures of Anthropo-Zoo-Genesis," *Body & Society* 10, no. 2–3 (June 1, 2004): 111–134, doi:10.1177/1357034X04042938; Bruno Latour, "How to Talk

about the Body? The Normative Dimension of Science Studies," *Body & Society* 10, no. 2–3 (June 1, 2004): 205, doi:10.1177/1357034X04042943.

7 Berckmans, "Voyage en Amerique," 6.

8 Ibid., 7.

9 George Magruder Battey, *A History of Rome and Floyd County, State of Georgia, United States of America, Including Numerous Incidents of More Than Local Interest, 1540–1922*, vol. 1 (Atlanta, GA: Webb and Vary, 1922), 355–356.

10 Berckmans, "Voyage en Amerique," 20.

11 Ibid.

12 Ibid., 21.

13 Berckmans, "Voyage en Amerique." I am indebted to my colleague Geert Voogt of Kennesaw State University for the translation of this portion of Berckmans's journal. As Berckmans was no doubt aware, the dinner was at least in keeping with *one* of the nineteenth-century French gastronome Jean Anthelme Brillat-Savarin's aphorisms: "A dessert without cheese is like a beautiful woman who has lost an eye." See *The Physiology of Taste; or Transcendental Gastronomy: Illustrated by Anecdotes of Distinguished Artists and Statesmen of Both Continents*, trans. Fayette Robinson, eBooks @ Adelaide (Adelaide: University of Adelaide Library, 2008 [1825]).

14 "There is no disputing about taste." Berckmans, "Voyage en Amerique." Berckmans's attitude toward mixing had echoes in the emerging "health food" literature of the mid-nineteenth century. See Sylvester Graham, *A Treatise on Bread, and Bread-Making* (Boston: Light & Stearns, 1837); Harvey A. Levenstein, *Revolution at the Table: The Transformation of the American Diet* (Berkeley: University of California Press, 2003), introduction, Chapter 3, Chapter 7; Helen Zoe Veit, *Modern Food, Moral Food: Self-Control, Science, and the Rise of Modern American Eating in the Early Twentieth Century* (Chapel Hill: University of North Carolina Press, 2013), 40–41.

15 Berckmans, "Voyage en Amerique." Here, Berckmans echoed Charles Dickens, who famously described Washington, D.C., as "the head-quarters of tobacco-tinctured saliva." See Charles Dickens, *American Notes for General Circulation* (London: Chapman and Hall, 1913), chapter VII, accessed Aug. 1, 2016 at www.gutenberg.org/ebooks/675.

16 Berckmans, "Voyage en Amerique."

17 Biographical Notes, Prosper Jules Alphonse Berckmans Collection, Cherokee Garden Library, Atlanta History Center, Atlanta History Center.

18 U. P. Hedrick, *The Pears of New York* (Albany, NY: J. B. Lyon, 1921), 15. Le Lectier listed 254 pears in 1628; Noisette listed 238 pears in 1833.

19 Ibid., 15, 19.

20 Ibid., 17.

21 See Pauly, *Fruits and Plains: The Horticultural Transformation of America*, 65–66.

22 A sluice box runs large quantities of water and gravel through a box with a screen that allows gold to sink to the bottom.

23 Downing, *Fruits and Fruit Trees of America* (New York: Wiley and Putnam, 1845), 7; William Kenrick, *The New American Orchardist*, 7th ed. (Boston: Otis, Broaders, 1844), 33; H. A. S. Dearborn, "Mr. Van Mons' Method of Raising Fruit Trees from Seed," *The Horticultural Register and Gardener's Magazine*, vol. II (June 1, 1836), 203–208.

24 Emily Pawley, " 'The Balance- Sheet of Nature': Calculating the New York Farm, 1820–1860" (Ph.D., University of Pennsylvania, 2009), ch. 4, especially p. 161; Pauly, *Fruits and Plains: The Horticultural Transformation of America*, ch. 3, especially p. 66.

25 Jean Baptiste van Mons, *Arbres Fruitiers: Leur Culture en Belqique et Leur Propagation par la Graine; ou, Pomonomie Belge, Expérimentale et Raisonnée* (Louvain, Belgium: L. Dusart et H. Vandenbroeck, 1835), 223.

26 Hedrick, *Pears of New York*, 18.

27 "Unnamed Article on Belgian Pomology," *Gardeners Chronicle and New Horticulturist* (Sept. 26, 1914): 220; Patrick Barry, "Editor's Table," *The Horticulturist, and Journal of Rural Art and Rural Taste* III, no. 3 (March 1853): 138. As of 2016, Arader Galleries in New York City was selling a rare first edition of the *Album* for $34,500. Accessed Aug. 9, 2016 at www .aradernyc.com/products/bivort-alexandre-joseph-desire-1809-1872-album-de-pomologie-bruxelles-deprez-parent-1847-1849-1850.

28 Charles Darwin, "Seedling Fruit Trees," *Gardeners' Chronicle and Agricultural Gazette* no. 52 (Dec. 29, 1855): 854.

29 Pauly, *Fruits and Plains: The Horticultural Transformation of America*, 65.

30 On the importance of labor and local knowledge to the practice of progressive, "scientific" agriculture in the antebellum South, see Benjamin R. Cohen, *Notes from the Ground: Science, Soil, and Society in the American Countryside* (New Haven, CT: Yale University Press, 2009).

31 Willard Range, "P. J. Berckmans: Georgia Horticulturalist," *Georgia Review* 6 (Summer 1952): 219–226.

32 Bernard A. Cook, *Belgium: A History* (New York: Peter Lang, 2002), 70; Herman vander Linden, *Belgium: The Making of a Nation* (Oxford: Clarendon Press, 1920), 301. Belgium saw little upheaval from the 1848 revolutions, but the nobility lost much of their influence.

33 Georgia State Horticultural Society, *Annual Proceedings* 1 (1876), 10–11.

34 Hedrick, *A History of Horticulture in America to 1860* (New York: Oxford University Press, 1950), 211.

35 Robert Manning, comments in business meeting in *Transactions of the Massachusetts Horticultural Society* (Boston, 1884), 127.

36 T. H. McHatton, "Memoir of Dr. P. J. A. Berckmans," in *Annual Proceedings*, Georgia State Board of Entomology Bulletin 35 (State Board of Entomology and State Horticultural Society, 1911), 9.

37 Charles Hovey, "Suburban Visits: Residence of L. E. Berckmans, Plainfield, NY," *Magazine of Horticulture* 22, no. 11 (November 1856): 518–520.

38 Essex County, New Jersey, "Prosper J. A. Berckmans, Declaration of American Citizenship" (United States of America, November 27, 1855), Prosper Jules Alphonse Berckmans Collection, Cherokee Garden Library, Atlanta History Center, Atlanta, GA.

39 Anne Berckmans, obituary of L. E. Berckmans, Jan. 14, 1997, in Rome Area Archives, Rome, GA; see also Range, "P. J. Berckmans: Georgia Horticulturalist."

40 Carl David Arfwedson, *The United States and Canada in 1832, 1833, and 1834* (R. Bentley, 1834), 410–411.

41 William N. White, "Georgia Pomological Society," *Southern Cultivator* 11, no. 8 (Aug. 1853): 243; Stephen Elliott, "American Pomological Society," *Southern Cultivator* 11, no. 9 (Sept. 1853), 273; William N. White, "Horticultural Department," *Southern Cultivator* 14, no. 9 (Sept. 1856), 283.

42 William N. White, "Horticultural Department"; White, "Report upon Grapes of the Committee ad Interim of the Pomological Society," *Horticulturist and Journal of Rural Art and Rural Taste* (Oct. 1, 1857), 457–461.

43 "Pomological Society of Georgia, L. E. Berckmans, President," *Southern Cultivator* 16, no. 9 (Sept. 1858), 286.

44 Georgia State Horticultural Society, *Annual Proceedings* 1, 8.

45 Dennis Redmond, "Fruitland Nursery, Augusta Ga.," *Southern Cultivator* 15, no. 4 (April 1857), 136. Redmond also had the assistance at this time of Robert Nelson, a Danish immigrant who had made his name as a nurseryman with his Troup Hill Nursery in Macon, Georgia. In January 1858, the firm was officially listed as under the management of "Redmond and Berckmans." Another advertisement trumpeted, "we are now prepared to furnish a complete succession of native Apples, Peaches, &c. from the earliest to the latest, and of unsurpassed quality. We have, also, a superior collection of Pear Trees, native and foreign – both dwarf and standard, and shall, hereafter, make the Pear one of our special objects of culture." See "Fruitland Nursery, Augusta, Geo." *Southern Cultivator* 16, no. 1 (Jan. 1858), 40; advertisement, *Southern Cultivator* 16, no. 1 (Jan. 1858), 34.

46 "Grapes for the South," *Southern Cultivator* 28, no. 6 (June 1860), 162; "Fruitland and Vineland," *Southern Cultivator* 28, no. 6 (June 1860), 190.

47 R. G. Dun and Company Credit Report Volumes, Georgia, Vol. 1b, Augusta-Richmond Co., Credit Report, R. G. Dun & Co. Collection, n.d., 161., Baker Library Historical Collections, Harvard Business School.

48 Ibid.

49 Ibid., 150.

50 "Editor's Table," *Horticulturist and Journal of Rural Art and Rural Taste* 8 (Feb. 1858), 89.

51 Dennis Redmond, "Report from the State of Georgia," *Southern Cultivator* 19, no. 3 (March 1861), 92.

52 Fruitland Nurseries, *1861 Descriptive Catalog of Fruit and Ornamental Shrubs, Vines, Roses, Evergreens, Bulbous Roots, Green House and Hedge Plants, &c. Cultivated and for Sale at the Fruitland Nurseries* (Augusta: James L. Gow, 1860), 3–5.

53 Fruitland Nurseries, *1861 Descriptive Catalog*, 3–5. William Summers ran Pomaria Nurseries in Newberry County, South Carolina, from 1852 to 1878, and specialized in apples; Thomas Affleck ran Southern Nurseries out of Washington, Mississippi. See Creighton Lee Calhoun, *Old Southern Apples: A Comprehensive History and Description of Varieties for Collectors, Growers,*

and Fruit Enthusiasts, 2nd ed. (White River Junction, VT: Chelsea Green, 2011), 8–9; South Carolina State Agricultural and Mechanical Society, *History of the State Agricultural Society of South Carolina from 1839 to 1845* (Columbia, SC: R. L. Bryan, 1916), 236–239; Thomas Affleck and Lake Douglas, *Steward of the Land: Selected Writings of Nineteenth-Century Horticulturist Thomas Affleck* (Baton Rouge: Louisiana State University Press, 2014).

54 Georgia State Horticultural Society, *Annual Proceedings* 3 (1879), 7–9.

55 Here I disagree with John D. Fair, who portrays southern horticulture as nationalistic, even autarchic. See "The Georgia Peach and the Southern Quest for Commercial Equity and Independence, 1843–1861," *Georgia Historical Quarterly* 86, no. 3 (Oct. 1, 2002): 372–397.

56 "Peach Culture," *Land We Love* III, no. 3 (July 1867), 257.

57 Joshua K. Callaway, *The Civil War Letters of Joshua K. Callaway*, ed. Judith Lee Hallock (Athens: University of Georgia Press, 1997), 51.

58 Georgia State Horticultural Society, *Annual Proceedings* 1, 9.

59 "The Labor Question," *Farmer and Gardener* (June 10, 1871), 4.

60 "The Labor Question in the Future – Immigration," *Farmer and Gardener* (Aug. 10, 1871), 4.

61 See Louis Kyriakoudes, "'Lookin' for Better All the Time': Rural Migration and Urbanization in the South 1900–1950," in *African American Life in the Rural South, 1900–1950*, ed. R. Douglas Hurt (Columbia: University of Missouri Press, 2011), 10–26.

62 On the failure of low country rice after emancipation, see Mart A. Stewart, *"What Nature Suffers to Groe": Life, Labor, and Landscape on the Georgia Coast, 1680–1920*, Wormsloe Foundation Publications (Athens: University of Georgia Press, 2002), 193–142.

63 William J. Towler Jr., "Biography of Armenius Oemler," from Savannah Biographies v. 19, Minis Collection, Lane Library, Armstrong Atlantic State University, Savannah, GA; A. J. Downing, "Notices on the State and Progress of Horticulture in the United States," (1834) in Andrew Jackson Downing, *Andrew Jackson Downing: Essential Texts*, ed. Robert C. Twombly (New York: W. W. Norton & Company, 2012), 313.

64 Towler, "Biography of Armenius Oemler," 4.

65 Armenius Oemler, *Truck-Farming at the South: A Guide to the Raising of Vegetables for Northern Markets* (New York: Orange Judd, 1883), 7–8.

66 Ibid.

67 James Henry Hammond, *Selections from the Letters and Speeches of the Hon. James H. Hammond of South Carolina* (New York: J. F. Trow, 1866), 168–169.

68 Du Bois, *Black Reconstruction*, 123, cited in Eugene D. Genovese, *Roll, Jordan, Roll: The World the Slaves Made* (New York: Vintage, 1976), 538.

69 Henry Bram, Ishmael Moultrie, and Sampson Yates, "Committee of Freedmen on Edisto Island, South Carolina, to the Freedmen's Bureau Commissioner [October 20 or 21, 1865]; the Commissioner's Reply, October 22, 1865; and the Committee to the President, October 28, 1865" (Freedmen and Southern Society Project, 1865), accessed Aug. 9, 2016 at www.freedmen.umd.edu/ Edisto%20petitions.htm.

70   An intriguing exception occurred in 1891, when the GSHS met in Quitman. Among the local exhibitor was a man named Sherard Williams of with an "extra good" plate of LeConte pears and a woman named Maggie Vickers with a plate of peaches. Both were denoted as "colored," with no other comment. Georgia State Horticultural Society, *Annual Proceedings* 16 (1891), 32, 34.

71   This post-emancipation "enclosure" phenomenon is explored by Steven Hahn in "Hunting, Fishing, and Foraging: Common Rights and Class Relations in the Postbellum South," *Radical History Review* 1982, no. 26 (Oct. 1, 1982): 37–64, doi:10.1215/01636545-1982-26-37.

72   William Robinson, Interview by Charles Hardy, interview by Charles Hardy III, 1984, Atwater Kent Museum, Philadelphia, accessed Aug. 1, 2016 at http://historymatters.gmu.edu/d/63/.

73   Manuscript Census of the United States, Richmond County, Georgia, 1860, roll M653-135, Family History Library Film 803135, (Provo, UT: Ancestry. com Operations, 2009).

74   Manuscript Census of the United States, Richmond County, Georgia, 1870, roll M593-172, Family History Library Film 545671 (Provo, UT: Ancestry. com Operations, 2009).

75   Manuscript Census of the United States, Richmond County, Georgia, 1910, roll T624_210, Family History Library Film 1374223 (Provo, UT: Ancestry.com Operations, 2006).

76   The WPA interviewer says grandmother, but seems to have meant Smith's mother. Works Progress Administration, "Interview with Wesley Smith," in *Slave Narratives: A Folk History of Slavery in the United States from Interviews with Former Slaves*, vol. IV, Georgia Narratives, Part 4 (Washington, DC: Library of Congress, 1941), 230–235.

77   Ibid.

78   See Grace Elizabeth Hale, *Making Whiteness: The Culture of Segregation in the South, 1890–1940* (New York: Pantheon Books, 1998); Micki McElya, *Clinging to Mammy: The Faithful Slave in Twentieth-Century America* (Cambridge, MA: Harvard University Press, 2009).

79   R. G. Dun and Company Credit Report Volumes, Georgia, Vol. 1b, Augusta-Richmond Co., 260. The 1880 census also estimated Berckmans' worth at $25,000.

80   Range, "P. J. Berckmans: Georgia Horticulturalist," 221, 223.

81   Berckmans never discussed his vested interests in the horticultural society. More interest in fruits, vegetables, and flowers would certainly have meant more business for nurseries like Fruitland, but it seems unlikely that he was not also motivated by a sincere love for horticulture and a belief in its transformative power.

82   Georgia State Horticultural Society, *Annual Proceedings* 1, front matter.

83   Ibid., 10.

84   Ibid., 11, 12.

85   Ibid., 11.

86   L. E. Berckmans, "Renovation of Old Trees," *Southern Cultivator* 17, no. 7 (July 1859), 217.

87   Which is not to say that southern wine culture was dead in the water. Nicholas Herbemont of South Carolina was a widely recognized expert on wine in the early nineteenth century. Nicholas Herbemont, *Pioneering American Wine: Writings of Nicholas Herbemont, Master Viticulturist*, ed. David S. Shields (Athens: University of Georgia Press, 2009). On the nineteenth century American wine industry more broadly, see Erica Hannickel, *Empire of Vines: Wine Culture in America* (Philadelphia: University of Pennsylvania Press, 2013).

88   Redmond, "The Pomological Resources of the South," 17, no. 10 (Oct. 1859), 314.

89   The biographical material comes from a transcript of a news article, Donald Harper, "The Hermit of Alto," dated 1888; Louis E. Berckmans, and an obituary by great granddaughter Anne Berckmans, dated June 14, 1997; both in Rome Area Archives, Rome, GA.

90   L. E. Berckmans, letter to Robert and Allie Berckmans, 10 February 1880. Rome Area Archives, Rome, GA.

91   L. E. Berckmans to Robert and Allie Berckmans, 13 April 1882. Transcript in Rome Area Archives, Rome, GA.

92   L. E. Berckmans, letter to Robert and Allie Berckmans, 6 November 1882. Rome Area Archive, Rome, GA.

93   L. E. Berckmans letter to Robert and Allie Berckmans, 11 August 1880. Rome Area Archive, Rome, GA.

94   L. E. Berckmans to Robert and Allie Berckmans, 13 April 1882, Rome Area Archives, Rome, GA.

95   Ann Berckmans, "Dr. Louis Mathieu Eduard Berckmans," 27 April 1969, Rome Area Archives, Rome, GA.

96   McHatton, "Memoir of Dr. P. J. A. Berckmans," 8.

97   Ibid., 10.

98   Ibid., 11.

99   Georgia State Horticultural Society, *Annual Proceedings* 35 (1911): 11.

100 Ibid., 14.

101 Ibid., 16–17.

102 Ibid., 21.

103 Ibid., 5–6.

104 David Robinson, letter to P. J. Berckmans Co., 21 October 1911, in Folder 5, Berckmans/Fruitland Nursery Papers, 1835–1947, Reese Library Archives, Georgia Regents University, Summerville, Georgia.

105 Range, "P. J. Berckmans: Georgia Horticulturalist," 224.

106 Prosper Jules Alphonse Berckmans, Jr., "Trip Diary 1884," (Prosper Jules Alphonse Berckmans Collection, Cherokee Garden Library, Atlanta History Center, Atlanta, GA) 6.

107 Ibid.,13.

108 Ibid., 5.

109 Ibid.

110 Ibid., 5, 7.

111 Ibid., inside cover.

3 ELBERTA, YOU'RE A PEACH

1 "MARSHALLVILLE, GA," *Atlanta Constitution* (Jan. 11, 1903), B8.
2 Samuel H. Rumph to Clara Elberta Moore Rumph, July 29, 1885. Deanna and Sam Grice Personal Collection, Snellville, Georgia.
3 Georgia State Horticultural Society, *Annual Proceedings* 10 (1885): 49–50.
4 Ibid., 10:39.
5 Ibid., 10:35.
6 Ibid., 10:27–28.
7 William Gilmore Simms, *The Sense of the Beautiful* (Charleston, SC: Agricultural Society of South Carolina, 1870), 6. On Simms, see David Moltke-Hansen, ed., *William Gilmore Simms's Unfinished Civil War: Consequences for a Southern Man of Letters* (Columbia: University of South Carolina Press, 2012) especially essays by Sara Georgini and John D. Miller.
8 The period during and immediately following Reconstruction was a crucial one for the forging of national gender ideals, but especially so for the defeated South. See, for example, Gail Bederman, *Manliness and Civilization: A Cultural History of Gender and Race in the United States, 1880–1917*, Women in Culture and Society (Chicago: University of Chicago Press, 1995); Laura F. Edwards, *Gendered Strife and Confusion: The Political Culture of Reconstruction* (Urbana: University of Illinois Press, 1997); Glenda Elizabeth Gilmore, *Gender and Jim Crow: Women and the Politics of White Supremacy in North Carolina, 1896–1920* (Chapel Hill: University of North Carolina Press, 1992); Kristin L. Hoganson, *Fighting for American Manhood: How Gender Politics Provoked the Spanish–American and Philippine–American Wars* (New Haven, CT: Yale University Press, 2000); Nina Silber, *The Romance of Reunion: Northerners and the South, 1865–1900*, Civil War America (Chapel Hill: University of North Carolina Press, 1993); LeeAnn Whites, *The Civil War as a Crisis in Gender: Augusta, Georgia, 1860–1890* (Athens: University of Georgia Press, 1995).
9 For a sampling of the New South literature, see Edward L Ayers, *The Promise of the New South: Life after Reconstruction* (New York: Oxford University Press, 1992); Don Harrison Doyle, *New Men, New Cities, New South: Atlanta, Nashville, Charleston, Mobile, 1860–1910*, Fred W. Morrison Series in Southern Studies (Chapel Hill: University of North Carolina Press, 1990); Louis A. Ferleger and John D. Metz, *Cultivating Success in the South: Farm Households in the Postbellum Era*, Cambridge Studies on the American South (New York: Cambridge University Press, 2014); Paul M Gaston, *The New South Creed: A Study in Southern Myth-Making* (New York: Vintage Books, 1973); C. Vann Woodward, *Origins of the New South, 1877–1913*, History of the South, vol. 9 (Baton Rouge: Louisiana State University Press, 1971); Gavin Wright, *Old South, New South: Revolutions in the Southern Economy since the Civil War* (Baton Rouge: Louisiana State University Press, 1996).
10 Medora Field Perkerson, *White Columns in Georgia* (New York: Rinehart, 1952), 294.

11 Col. G. B. Brackett, "The Peach Industry in Georgia," in Georgia State Horticultural Society, *Annual Proceedings* 27 (1908): 16. For a sampling of this "Sam Rumph fable" literature, see J. W. Frederick, "History of the Elberta Peach-Tree," in *Selections for Arbor Day in the Schools of Georgia*, ed. W. B. Meritt (Atlanta: Georgia Department of Education, 1904), 11; Inez Parker Cumming, "Sweet with Bitter: Georgia's Peach," *Georgia Review* 2, no. 4 (December 1, 1948): 480; Perkerson, *White Columns in Georgia*, 292–298; Pleasant Alexander Stovall, "Land of the Fruit Growers," *Macon Telegraph* (August 8, 1895), 4; "Peach and Grape," *Atlanta Constitution* (April 28, 1895); "The Georgia Peach," *Atlanta Constitution* (July 5, 1896), 16; "Some Inside Facts about Georgia's Fruit Industry," *Atlanta Constitution* (June 28, 1908), A2.

12 I am indebted to Deanna and Sam Grice for sharing their personal collection of Rumph ephemera with me.

13 "Peach and Grape."

14 William M. Haslam, "Announcement," *Macon Telegraph* (July 12, 1853), 3; Manuscript Census of the United States, Copiah County, MS, 1860, roll M653_580, Family History Library Film 803580 (Provo, UT: Ancestry.com Operations, 2009).

15 Alexander Samuel Salley et al., *The History of Orangeburg County, South Carolina: From Its First Settlement to the Close of the Revolutionary War* (R. L. Berry, printer, 1897), 471f.

16 Louise Frederick Hays, *History of Macon County, Georgia* (Spartanburg, SC: Reprint Co., 1979), 157. The numbers in 1845 were 5,194 total and 1,870 slaves.

17 John Donald Wade, "Marshallville," in ibid., 219.

18 John Donald Wade, *The Marshallville Methodist Church from Its Beginning to 1950* (n.p., 1952), 7.

19 This is a question addressed eloquently by Stephen William Berry, *All That Makes a Man: Love and Ambition in the Civil War South* (Oxford: Oxford University Press, 2003).

20 Manuscript Census of the United States, Houston County, Georgia, 1870, roll M593_158, Family History Library Film 545657 (Provo, UT: Ancestry. com Operations, 2009).

21 See Louise Frederick Hays, *The Rumph and Frederick Families, Genealogical and Biographical* (J. T. Hancock, 1942).

22 Jack Temple Kirby, *Mockingbird Song: Ecological Landscapes of the South* (Chapel Hill: University of North Carolina Press, 2006), 99. On the expanding cotton South, see James David Miller, *South by Southwest: Planter Emigration and Identity in the Slave South* (Charlottesville: University of Virginia Press, 2003); Joshua D. Rothman, *Flush Times and Fever Dreams: A Story of Capitalism and Slavery in the Age of Jackson* (Athens: University of Georgia Press, 2012); Steven Stoll, *Larding the Lean Earth: Soil and Society in Nineteenth-Century America* (New York: Hill and Wang, 2002); and Conevery Bolton Valencius, *The Health of the Country: How American Settlers Understood Themselves and Their Land* (New York: Basic Books, 2002).

23 W. B. Jones, "Growing Vegetables and Seed for Home and Distant Markets–New Industries in the Agriculture of Georgia," Georgia State Horticultural Society, *Annual Proceedings* 8 (1883): 19–20.

24 William M. Browne, "Address on Ornamental Gardening," Georgia State Horticultural Society, *Annual Proceedings* 7 (1882): 20.

25 Georgia State Horticultural Society, *Annual Proceedings* 17 (1892): 29.

26 This was true despite the fact that truck farming could be quite profitable. See James L. McCorkle, "Moving Perishables to Market: Southern Railroads and the Nineteenth-Century Origins of Southern Truck Farming," *Agricultural History* 66, no. 1 (1992): 42–62; James L. McCorkle Jr., "Southern Truck Growers' Associations: Organization for Profit," *Agricultural History* 72, no. 1 (1998): 77–99; James L. McCorkle, "Agricultural Experiment Stations and Southern Truck Farming," *Agricultural History* 62, no. 2 (1988): 234–243; Oemler, *Truck-Farming at the South;* David S. Shields, *Southern Provisions: The Creation and Revival of a Cuisine* (Chicago: University of Chicago Press, 2015).

27 See Kristin L Hoganson, *Consumers' Imperium: The Global Production of American Domesticity, 1865–1920* (Chapel Hill: University of North Carolina Press, 2007).

28 Samuel Hape, "Peach Culture," Georgia State Horticultural Society, *Annual Proceedings* 14 (1889): 55.

29 W. B. Jones, "Fruits and Vegetables a Hygienic Necessity in Our Climate," in Georgia State Horticultural Society, *Annual Proceedings* 9 (1884): 18–20.

30 For more on plant breeding, see Noël Kingsbury, *Hybrid: The History and Science of Plant Breeding* (Chicago: University of Chicago Press, 2011); Alan L. Olmstead, *Creating Abundance: Biological Innovation and American Agricultural Development* (New York: Cambridge University Press, 2008); Edmund Russell, *Evolutionary History: Uniting History and Biology to Understand Life on Earth* (New York: Cambridge University Press, 2011); Sackman, *Orange Empire: California and the Fruits of Eden;* Susan R. Schrepfer and Philip Scranton, *Industrializing Organisms: Introducing Evolutionary History*, Hagley Perspectives on Business and Culture (New York: Routledge, 2004); Shields, *Southern Provisions;* Steven Stoll, *The Fruits of Natural Advantage: Making the Industrial Countryside in California* (Berkeley: University of California Press, 1998).

31 Stoll, *Fruits of Natural Advantage: Making the Industrial Countryside in California*, chapter 3; Susanne Freidberg, *Fresh: A Perishable History* (Cambridge, MA: Belknap Press of Harvard University Press, 2009).

32 Douglas Cazaux Sackman, *Orange Empire: California and the Fruits of Eden* (Berkeley: University of California Press, 2005), chapter 2.

33 Once Kolb began marketing the melons in 1882, the demand for seeds turned his melon business primarily into a seed-growing enterprise: by 1889 he had some 200 acres in watermelon at a time when 20 acres seemed excessively risky. He grew around 200,000 melons a year for their seed. See William Warren Rogers, "Reuben F. Kolb: Agricultural Leader of the New South," *Agricultural History* 32, no. 2 (April 1958): 111–112; Shields, *Southern Provisions*, 203–204; Jill Neimark, "Saving the Sweetest

Watermelon the South Has Ever Known," *Salt*, May 19, 2015, accessed Aug. 3, 2016 at www.npr.org/sections/thesalt/2015/05/19/407949182/saving-the-sweetest-watermelon-the-south-has-ever-known.

34 U. P. Hedrick, *The Peaches of New York* (Albany, NY: J. B. Lyon Company, 1917), 169; Stephen C. Myers, William R. Okie, and Gary Lightner, "The 'Elberta' Peach," *Fruit Varieties Journal* 43, no. 4 (1989): 130–138; Allen G. Waller and Harry B. Weiss, "'The Peach Industry in New Jersey: A Statistical and Economic Study," *New Jersey Agricultural Experiment Station Bulletin*, no. 452 (September 1927): 15; "The Peach ... Has the Complexion of Georgia," *Fortune* (February 1932).

35 Mabel Swartz Withoft, "The Elberta," *American Florist* (September 26, 1903), 338.

36 Myers, Okie, and Lightner, "'Elberta' Peach," 131–132; E. F. Palmer, "Solving the Fruit Grower's Problems by Plant Breeding,"*American Society for Horticultural Science Proceedings* 19 (1923): 121.

37 Georgia State Horticultural Society, Georgia Breeders' Association, and Georgia Dairy and Livestock Association, *Annual Proceedings*, vol. 38, Bulletin of the Georgia State College of Agriculture, vol. 2, no. 12 (Athens: Georgia State College of Agriculture, 1914), 22.

38 Daniele Bassi and René Monet, "Botany and Taxonomy," in *The Peach: Botany, Production and Uses*, ed. Desmond R. Layne and Daniele Bassi (Cambridge, MA: CABI, 2008), 2.

39 Myers, Okie, and Lightner, "'Elberta' Peach."

40 Dorothy Nix, "1870 Dream Led to Famous Georgia Peach," *Atlanta Journal and Constitution* (April 30, 1967), 6; H. E. Van Deman, "The Elberta Peach," *Sunny South* XXII, no. 1129 (October 16, 1897), 3. The account actually says 12,000 seedlings, but this appears to be a typo, as other accounts have it as 1,200 seedlings. See Russell G. Snow, "Wonderful Growth and Promise of Peach Industry in Georgia," *Atlanta Constitution* (Dec. 4, 1910) D12B; and Col. G. B. Brackett, "Peach Industry in Georgia."

41 Georgia State Horticultural Society, *Annual Proceedings* 1 (1876): 8–9.

42 Georgia State Horticultural Society, *Annual Proceedings* 22 (1898): 12; Georgia State Horticultural Society, *Annual Proceedings* 1 (1876): 24–26.

43 Hedrick, *Peaches of New York*, 95.

44 Downing, *Fruits and Fruit Trees of America*, 469–470.

45 Price's work showed up many places. See, for instance, R. H. Price, "Classification of Varieties of Peaches," *American Gardening* (August 6 1898), 560; "Classification of Varieties of Peaches," *Annual Report of the State Horticultural Society of Missouri* 40 (Dec. 1897): 364; R. H. Price, "Classification of Varieties of Peaches," Association of American Agricultural Colleges and Experiment Stations, *Annual Proceedings* 8 (1894): 82; R. H. Price, "Classification of Varieties of Peaches," American Pomological Society, *Annual Transactions* 25 (1897): 110; Hugh N. Starnes, "Some Peach Notes," *Georgia Experiment Station Bulletin* 42 (Nov. 1898): 231.

46 Hedrick, *Peaches of New York*, 93.

47 On the cultural and economic implications of naming, see Emily Pawley, "'The Balance-Sheet of Nature': Calculating the New York Farm, 1820–1860" (Ph.D., University of Pennsylvania, 2009), 175–179.

48 Georgia State Horticultural Society, *Annual Proceedings* 8 (1883): 29–30.

49 1860 and 1870 Federal Census; R. G. Dun and Company Credit Report Volumes. Georgia, vol. 20, Macon County, 1852–1880. Credit Report. R. G. Dun & Co. Collection, Baker Library Historical Collections, Harvard Business School.

50 B.T. Moore to Mr. L. A. Rumph, August 3, 1882. Deanna and Sam Grice Personal Collection, Snellville, Georgia.

51 Georgia State Horticultural Society, *Annual Proceedings* 2 (1878): 8.

52 Samuel H. Rumph to Clara Elberta Moore Rumph, August 1, 1882. Deanna and Sam Grice Personal Collection, Snellville, Georgia.

53 Samuel H. Rumph to Clara Elberta Moore Rumph, July 29, 1885. Deanna and Sam Grice Personal Collection, Snellville, Georgia.

54 "Display Ad 4 – No Title," *Atlanta Constitution* (February 4, 1887).

55 Willow Lake Nursery, "Descriptive Catalogue of Fruit Trees, Grape Vines, Strawberry Plants, Etc.," (1887–1888): 2. Gilbert Seed Catalog Collection, National Agricultural Library Special Collections.

56 Ibid., 12.

57 Ibid., 10.

58 Hape, "Peach Culture," 55.

59 Roger Haden, "An Age Old Love Affair with the Pear," *Adelaide Review* (2004).

60 Samuel Gustin, "Kitchen Vegetables," in Georgia State Horticultural Society, *Annual Proceedings* 3 (1879): 22.

61 W. B. Jones, "Fruits and Vegetables a Hygienic Necessity in Our Climate," 18–20.

62 Ibid., 20.

63 Georgia State Horticultural Society, *Annual Proceedings* 3 (1878): 6.

64 Georgia State Horticultural Society, *Annual Proceedings* 25 (1901): 15.

65 Ibid., 25:13.

66 Whites, *Civil War as a Crisis in Gender*, 142; William Gilmore Simms, "Ellet's Women of the Revolution," *Southern Quarterly Review* I, no. 2 (July 1850): 314–354.

67 William M. Browne, "Address on Ornamental Gardening," Georgia State Horticultural Society, *Annual Proceedings* 7 (1882): 20.

68 Henry Grady, "The Farmer and the Cities," *The New South: Writings and Speeches of Henry Grady* (Savannah, GA: Beehive Press, 1971): 83–84.

69 He painted this image, furthermore, in an effort to drive people away from populism as one of those "great movements that destroy the equilibrium and threaten the prosperity of my country." Henry Grady, "The Farmer and the Cities." Charles Postel, drawing on Richard Hofstadter's classic, makes a similar point about the populist movement. See Charles Postel, *The Populist Vision* (New York: Oxford University Press, 2007), 6–7; and Richard Hofstadter, *The Age of Reform* (New York: Vintage, 1960), 23–59.

70 "From Georgia Soil," *Atlanta Constitution* (Aug. 9, 1886), 2.
71 W. E. Brown, "Rumph's Peaches," Letter to the Editor, *Atlanta Constitution* (Nov. 21, 1888): 2; "By Field and Lane: A Fair Section – Under Vine and Fig Tree – Old Days," *Atlanta Constitution* (Mar. 26, 1885), 2.
72 "The Great South," *Sunny South* XXII, no. 1068 (August 8, 1896, Atlanta), 1.
73 Georgia State Horticultural Society, *Annual Proceedings* 15 (1891): 16.
74 I echo here Stephanie McCurry, *Masters of Small Worlds: Yeoman Households, Gender Relations, and the Political Culture of the Antebellum South Carolina Low Country* (New York: Oxford University Press, 1997).
75 Woodward, *Origins of the New South, 1877–1913*, 124. See also See Bruce G. Harvey, *World's Fairs in a Southern Accent: Atlanta, Nashville, and Charleston, 1895–1902* (Knoxville: University of Tennessee Press, 2014); William A. Link, *Atlanta, Cradle of the New South: Race and Remembering in the Civil War's Aftermath* (Chapel Hill: University of North Carolina Press, 2013); Theda Perdue, *Race and the Atlanta Cotton States Exposition of 1895* (University of Georgia Press, 2011); Robert W. Rydell, *All the World's a Fair: Visions of Empire at American International Expositions, 1876–1916* (Chicago: University of Chicago Press, 2013).
76 John T. Boifeuillet, "Peaches and Cream," *Atlanta Constitution* (June 16, 1895), 2.
77 "The Peach Carnival," *Atlanta Constitution* (June 10, 1895), 7.
78 "Peaches at Every Point," *Macon Telegraph* (June 16, 1895), 6.
79 "A Voice from Canada," *Macon Telegraph* (June 16, 1895), 7.
80 *San Francisco Call* (June 24, 1895), 6.
81 John T. Boifeuillet, "Hail Queen Peach," *Atlanta Constitution* (July 7, 1895), 17.
82 Major Glessner, "Georgia Fruit Fairs," *Southern States* (Aug. 1895), reprinted in "The Carnival Illustrated," *Macon Telegraph* (Sept. 1, 1895), 9.
83 "Turn Your Face to the Sunrise" advertisement, *Atlanta Constitution* (June 23, 1895), 22.
84 Glessner, "Georgia Fruit Fairs."
85 "Carnival Still On," *Atlanta Constitution* (July 15, 1895), 3; "The Carnival as an Object Lesson," *Macon Telegraph* (July 10, 1895), 6.
86 "Peaches at Every Point," *Macon Telegraph* (June 16, 1895), 6.
87 "The Carnival and Its Effect," *Macon Telegraph* (July 21, 1895), 4.
88 "Well Pleased with the Carnival – Major Duncan Makes a Report on the Peach Celebration," *Atlanta Constitution* (July 26, 1895), 3.
89 Glessner, "Georgia Fruit Fairs."
90 "Peach Carnival and Its Effect"
91 Andrew Baker, "Race and Romantic Agrarianism: The Transnational Roots of Clarence Poe's Crusade for Rural Segregation in North Carolina," *Agricultural History* 87, no. 1 (Jan. 1, 2013): 93–114, doi:10.3098/ah.2013.87.1.93; Hale, *Making Whiteness: The Culture of Segregation in the South, 1890–1940; Jumpin' Jim Crow: Southern Politics from Civil War to Civil Rights* (Princeton, NJ: Princeton University Press, 2000); Gilmore,

Gender and Jim Crow: Women and the Politics of White Supremacy in North Carolina, 1896–1920.

92 "Formal Opening Georgia Peach Carnival" *Macon Telegraph* (July 2, 1895), 6; "Peach Is Queen Now," *Atlanta Constitution* (July 3, 1895), 3.

93 "Just from Georgia," *Atlanta Constitution* (June 29, 1895), 6.

94 The Cotton States Exposition of 1895 was especially significant, even amid the exposition-mad world of the Gilded Age. See Theda Perdue, *Race and the Atlanta Cotton States Exposition of 1895* (University of Georgia Press, 2011).

95 C. A. Collier to P. J. Berckmans, March 21, 1895, Series 2: Fruitland Nurseries, 1858–1967, folder 4: Correspondence, Prosper Jules Alphonse Berckmans Collection, MSS 961, Cherokee Garden Library, Atlanta History Center, Atlanta, GA.

96 William Edward Burghardt DuBois, *The Souls of Black Folk: Essays and Sketches*, 2nd ed. (Chicago: A. C. McClurg, 1903), 42.

97 Booker T. Washington, "Speech before the Atlanta Cotton States and International Exposition," September 18, 1895, accessed May 29, 2012, at http://teachingamericanhistory.org/library/index.asp?documentprint=69.

98 Ibid.

99 As Gavin Wright has argued, the emancipation of slaves left southern landowners without their primary measure of wealth; southern planters, tied as they usually were to a single cash crop (cotton, especially), struggled to maintain cash flow year-round. For this reason, large investments were often provided by northern financiers. See Wright, *Old South, New South*; see also Pete Daniel, *Breaking the Land: The Transformation of Cotton, Tobacco, and Rice Cultures Since 1880* (Urbana: University of Illinois Press, 1985); Joseph P. Reidy, *From Slavery to Agrarian Capitalism in the Cotton Plantation South: Central Georgia, 1800–1880*, The Fred W. Morrison Series in Southern Studies (Chapel Hill: University of North Carolina Press, 1992); Harold D. Woodman, *King Cotton and His Retainers: Financing and Marketing the Cotton Crop of the South, 1800–1925*, Southern Classics Series (Columbia: University of South Carolina Press, 1990); Woodward, *Origins of the New South, 1877–1913*.

100 Georgia State Horticultural Society, *Annual Proceedings* 11 (1886): 14.

101 Samuel H. Rumph Death Certificate, Death Certificates, Vital Records, Public Health, RG 26-5-95, Georgia Archives.

102 State of Georgia, Indexes of Vital Records for Georgia: Deaths, 1919–1998 (Provo, UT: Generations Network, 2001), accessed May 21, 2012, at www.ancestry.com.

103 Rumph, Samuel H. Will. Oglethorpe, GA, n.d. Macon County Probate Court, Montezuma, GA.

4 A CONNECTICUT YANKEE IN KING COTTON'S COURT

1 Hank Morgan, the protagonist of *A Connecticut Yankee in King Arthur's Court*, was a fictional creation of Mark Twain, who lived about twenty miles north of Hale in the Nook Farm suburb of Hartford. There he was

a neighbor of Charles Dudley Warner, with whom he had coauthored *The Gilded Age.* Warner was an editor of the *Hartford Courant,* which published Hale's agricultural column. So Twain may have read Hale as he worked on *A Connecticut Yankee* in the 1880s; Hale seems to have read Twain. There is strong evidence that Twain was envisioning the South when he described Camelot. See "Colonel Sellers," *Hartford Courant* (Dec. 14, 1893), 5; Mark Twain, *A Connecticut Yankee in King Arthur's Court* (New York: Oxford University Press, 1996 [1889]); Twain, *Life on the Mississippi* (Boston: James R. Osgood, 1883), 468–469; Henry Nash Smith, *Mark Twain's Fable of Progress: Political and Economic Ideas in "A Connecticut Yankee"* (New Brunswick, N.J.: Rutgers University Press, 1964), 36, 69.

2   C. Vann Woodward, *Origins of the New South, 1877–1913,* A History of the South, v. 9 (Baton Rouge: Louisiana State University Press, 1971), 114.

3   This tension among labor management, profits, and cultivation is what David Vaught seeks to capture in the California case. See David Vaught, *Cultivating California: Growers, Specialty Crops, and Labor, 1875–1920* (Baltimore: Johns Hopkins University Press, 1999).

4   Hale's own writings tell much of this story, but, courtesy of the Historical Society of Glastonbury (CT), we also have the advantage of a set of lantern slides that Hale used when he talked to northern audiences about his big Georgia peach farm. The present and the following chapters, like one of those evening talks, are punctuated photographically by Hale's own collection.

5   Howard S. Russell and Mark B. Lapping, *A Long, Deep Furrow: Three Centuries of Farming in New England* (Greater Lebanon, NH: University Press of New England, 1982), 316.

6   In 1906 he ran an advertisement for his free catalog that promised the "full story" of the "lifetime experience of largest fruit-grower in America." J. H. Hale, "Advertisement: Double the Strawberry Crop," *Youth's Companion* (1827–1929) 80, no. 7 (1906): III.

7   G. H. and J. H. Hale and Hale Georgia Orchard Company, "From a Push-Cart to a Trolley-Car in Fruit Growing" (South Glastonbury, CT: G. H. and J. H. Hale, 1896), cover.

8   "John Howard Hale, Peach King, Dead," *Hartford Daily Courant* (October 13, 1917).

9   Lee Jay Whittles, "John Howard Hale: Peach King" (Speech presented at the Historical Society of Glastonbury, Glastonbury, CT, May 19, 1955), 1.

10 J. H. Hale et al., *Culture, Agriculture, Orchard Culture and the Utility of Weeds* (The Cutaway Harrow Company, 1895), 5; "A Talk about Peaches," *Hartford Courant* (February 6, 1888); Whittles, "John Howard Hale: Peach King," 1; G. H. and J. H. Hale and Hale Georgia Orchard Company, "From a Push-Cart to a Trolley-Car in Fruit Growing," 1.

11 J. H. Hale, "Peaches: A National Product," *World's Work* (June 1902), 2164. The most detailed version of Hale's story appeared in this article for *The World's Work,* a journal edited by North Carolinian Walter Hines Page – who, incidentally, also went into peaches in the early twentieth century.

12 Ibid.

13 Ibid., 2166.

14 Charles Hovey, "'Hovey's Seedling' and the Manchester Strawberry," *Massachusetts Ploughman and New England Journal of Agriculture* 41 no. 46 (Aug. 12, 1882), 1; J. H. Hale, "Manchester Strawberry vs. Hovey Seedling," *Ohio Farmer* 62, no. 4 (July 29, 1882): 54.

15 G. H. and J. H. Hale and Hale Georgia Orchard Company, "From a Push-Cart to a Trolley-Car in Fruit Growing," 3.

16 Ibid., 4.

17 See Matthew Frye Jacobson, *Barbarian Virtues: The United States Encounters Foreign Peoples at Home and Abroad, 1876–1917* (New York: Hill & Wang, 2001); Helen Zoe Veit, *Modern Food, Moral Food: Self-Control, Science, and the Rise of Modern American Eating in the Early Twentieth Century (Chapel Hill: University of North Carolina Press, 2013)*, chapter 6.

18 Hale, "Peaches: A National Product," 2166.

19 Ibid., 2168.

20 Ibid., 2169.

21 Ibid., 2169, 2171–2172.

22 G. H. and J. H. Hale and Hale Georgia Orchard Company, "From a Push-Cart to a Trolley-Car in Fruit Growing," 1.

23 Ibid.

24 As Philip Pauly wrote, horticulturalists were "immersed in an old and rich linguistic compost redolent with sexuality, primitive religion, and primal group consciousness... From the early nineteenth century onward, horticulturalists argued that high culture, producing exquisitely flavored fruits, fancy camellias, and smooth greenswards, would lead to higher culture – to the refinement of public taste." See Philip J. Pauly, *Fruits and Plains: The Horticultural Transformation of America* (Cambridge, MA: Harvard University Press, 2007), 6.

25 G. H. and J. H. Hale and Hale Georgia Orchard Company, "From a Push-Cart to a Trolley-Car in Fruit Growing," 2.

26 Hale et al., *Culture, Agriculture, Orchard Culture and the Utility of Weeds*, 6.

27 J. Clarence Harvey "The Connecting Link between Fruit Growing and Fruit Selling" Connecticut Pomological Society, *Report of the Connecticut Pomological Society*, vol. 10 (Harrisburg, PA: Mount Pleasant Press, 1901), 49. The CPS secretary merely noted that "Mr. Harvey's very interesting and unique address was much enjoyed by all present."

28 Theodore Roosevelt is the most well-known representative of this masculinist discourse. See Theodore Roosevelt, *The Strenuous Life: Essays and Addresses* (New York: Century Co., 1900); for more on masculinity at the turn of the century, see also Gail Bederman, *Manliness and Civilization: A Cultural History of Gender and Race in the United States, 1880–1917*, Women in Culture and Society (Chicago: University of Chicago Press, 1995); Kristin L. Hoganson, *Fighting for American Manhood: How Gender Politics Provoked the Spanish-American and Philippine-American Wars* (New Haven, CT: Yale University Press, 2000).

29 The question of the era was whether the common man could win out versus "the interests." See, for example, Lawrence Goodwyn, *The Populist Moment: A Short History of the Agrarian Revolt in America* (New York: Oxford University Press, 1978); Christopher Lasch, *The True and Only Heaven: Progress and Its Critics* (New York: W. W. Norton, 2013); Meg Jacobs, *Pocketbook Politics: Economic Citizenship in Twentieth-Century America* (Princeton, NJ: Princeton University Press, 2005); Heather Cox Richardson, *West from Appomattox: The Reconstruction of America after the Civil War* (New Haven, NH: Yale University Press, 2007); Henry Nash Smith, *Mark Twain's Fable of Progress: Political and Economic Ideas in "A Connecticut Yankee."*

30 "National Grange Excursion," *Hartford Courant* (Oct. 16, 1889); M. A. Farber, "An Industry in Glastonbury," *Hartford Courant Magazine* (Aug. 8, 1965), 5.

31 Hale, "Among the Roses," *Hartford Courant* (Dec. 3, 1889) 3.

32 Hale, "Out on the West Coast," *Hartford Courant* (Nov. 6, 1890), 2.

33 G. H. Powell to J. H. Hale, April 23, 1907; and Hale to Powell, May 1, 1907; Records of the Bureau of Plant Industry, Soils, and Agricultural Engineering, Record Group 54, National Archives, College Park, MD.

34 J. H. Hale, quoted in Georgia Department of Agriculture, *Georgia: Her Resources and Possibilities* (Atlanta: G. W. Harrison, State Printer, 1896), 234.

35 J. H. Hale, "Notes from the South," *Hartford Courant* (Aug. 22, 1890), 2.

36 J. H. Hale, "Journey in the South," *Hartford Courant* (Aug. 7, 1890), 3. The cool weather was also in the black belt, where he would buy his farm: "It has been cool and comfortable now for some days," he wrote from Birmingham in July. See J. H. Hale, "Some Days in Alabama," *Hartford Courant* (July 30, 1890), 3.

37 J. H. Hale, "Notes from the South," *Hartford Courant* (Aug. 22, 1890), 2.

38 On grasses and southern agriculture, see Paul S. Sutter, "What Gullies Mean: Georgia's 'Little Grand Canyon' and Southern Environmental History," *Journal of Southern History* 76, no. 3 (2010): 607. See also Mark D. Hersey, *My Work Is That of Conservation: An Environmental Biography of George Washington Carver*, Environmental History and the American South. (University of Georgia Press, 2011); Lynn A. Nelson, *Pharsalia: An Environmental Biography of a Southern Plantation, 1780–1880*, Environmental History and the American South (Athens: University of Georgia Press, 2007); Paul S. Sutter, *Let Us Now Praise Famous Gullies: Georgia's "Little Grand Canyon" and the Soils of the South*, Environmental History and the American South (Athens: University of Georgia Press, 2015); and Albert G. Way, "'A Cosmopolitan Weed of the World': Following Bermudagrass," *Agricultural History* 88, no. 3 (Summer 2014): 354–67.

39 This conversation about climate and southern distinctiveness has a rich literature. See, for starters, Ulrich Bonnell Phillips, *Life and Labor in the Old South*, ed. John David Smith, Southern Classics Series (Columbia, S.C.: University of South Carolina Press, 2007 [1929]); A. Cash Koeniger, "Climate and Southern Distinctiveness," *The Journal of Southern History*

54, no. 1 (February 1988): 21, doi:10.2307/2208519; Mart A. Stewart, "'Let Us Begin with the Weather?': Climate, Race, and Cultural Distinctiveness in the American South," in *Nature and Society in Historical Context*, ed. Mikulas Teich, Roy Porter, and Bo Gustafsson (Cambridge University Press, 1997), 240–56.

40 J. H. Hale, "Notes from the South," *Hartford Courant* (Aug. 22, 1890), 2.

41 J. H. Hale, "Notes on Peach Culture," USDA Division of Pomology Circular 3 (1894) 1.

42 Hale, "Notes from the South" *Hartford Courant* (Aug. 22, 1890), 2.

43 J. H. Hale, "Notes on Peach Culture"; Ralph A. Graves, "Marching through Georgia Sixty Years After," *National Geographic Magazine* 50, no. 3 (September 1926), 274; Al Pearson, interview with the author, Fort Valley, Georgia, Feb. 21, 2008; Hale, "Life and Work on the Farm," *Hartford Courant* (July 15, 1893), 5.

44 See also Hale, "A Short Run Down South," *Hartford Courant* (July 17, 1891), 3; and "On the Way to Florida" *Hartford Courant* (Mar. 2, 1891), 3.

45 Hale, "Notes from the South" (Aug. 22, 1890), 2; J. H. Hale, quoted in Georgia Department of Agriculture, *Georgia: Her Resources and Possibilities* (Atlanta: Georgia Department of Agriculture, 1896), 234.

46 J. H. Hale, quoted in Georgia Department of Agriculture, Georgia, 234. Though peaches do not suck up red color from the soil, there is evidence that the absence of iron in the soil can delay ripening and produce smaller fruit, and therefore decrease the redness in the fruit's skin. See Ana Álvarez-Fernández et al., "Effects of Fe Deficiency Chlorosis on Yield and Fruit Quality in Peach (Prunus Persica L. Batsch)," *Journal of Agricultural and Food Chemistry* 51, no. 19 (September 1, 2003): 5738–44, doi:10.1021/jf034402c.

47 Kathryn C. Taylor, "Peaches," *New Georgia Encyclopedia*, accessed March 25, 2008 at www.georgiaencyclopedia.com/nge/Article.jsp?id=h-962&hl=y.

48 William G. Smith and William T. Carter Jr., "Soil Survey of the Fort Valley Area, Georgia," in Milton Whitney, USDA Bureau of Soils, Field Operations of the Bureau of Soils 1903 [Fifth Report] (Washington, DC: Government Printing Office, 1904), 322.

49 Hale, "Journey in the South," *Hartford Courant* (Aug. 7, 1890), 3.

50 Hale, "Notes from the South," *Hartford Courant* (Aug. 22, 1890), 2.

51 Hale, "On His Georgia Farm," *Hartford Courant* (Oct. 28, 1892), 7;

52 Georgia State Horticultural Society, *Annual Proceedings* 15 (1890), 15–17.

53 Hale, "On the Way to Florida," *Hartford Courant* (Mar. 2, 1891), 3.

54 Hale, "Notes from the South," *Hartford Courant* (Aug. 22, 1890), 2.

55 Ibid.

56 Hale, "Journey in the South," *Hartford Courant* (Aug. 7, 1890), 3.

57 Ibid.

58 The literature on racism in the South is vast, but see, for starters Eric Foner, *Reconstruction: America's Unfinished Revolution, 1863–1877* (New York: Harper Collins, 2002); Grace Elizabeth Hale, *Making Whiteness: The Culture of Segregation in the South, 1890–1940* (New York: Pantheon Books, 1998);

Winthrop D. Jordan, *White Over Black: American Attitudes toward the Negro, 1550–1812*, 2nd ed. (Chapel Hill: The University of North Carolina Press, 2012); Leon F. Litwack, *Trouble in Mind: Black Southerners in the Age of Jim Crow* (New York: Knopf, 1998); Mark M. Smith, *How Race Is Made: Slavery, Segregation, and the Senses* (Chapel Hill: The University of North Carolina Press, 2008).

59 Hale, "Short Run Down South," *Hartford Courant* (July 17, 1891), 3. It is likely that a white overseer supervised the hands, but Hale's willingness to give credit to his black employees is nevertheless striking.

60 "Testimony of Mr. J. H. Hale," in *Report of the U.S. Industrial Commission on Agriculture and Agricultural Labor*, vol. 10 (Washington, DC: Government Printing Office, 1901), 382.

61 Hale, "Farm Life and Work," *Hartford Courant* (Oct. 8, 1895), 11.

62 They wanted three dollars to four dollars a day, in comparison to the average black wage of sixty cents to one dollar a day. See "Testimony of Mr. J. H. Hale," 383.

63 Hale, "Peaches: A National Product," 2174.

64 Hale, "On His Georgia Farm," *Hartford Courant* (Oct. 28, 1892), 7.

65 Hale, "Life and Work on the Farm," *Hartford Courant* (Nov. 9, 1893), 4.

66 Donnie D. Bellamy, *Light in the Valley: A Pictorial History of Fort Valley State College since 1895* (Virginia Beach, VA: Donning Company, 1996), 13, 155. See also Franklin E. Frazier, "A Community School: Fort Valley High and Industrial School," *Southern Workman* 54 (Oct. 1925): 46; Joseph T. Porter, "The Fort Valley High and Industrial School," *Colored American Magazine* 11 (June 1906): 423–425; J. H. Torbert, "The Fort Valley High and Industrial School," *Colored American Magazine* 12 (June 1907): 447–457; W. T. B. Williams, "Fort Valley High and Industrial School," *Southern Workman* 14 (Nov. 1910): 627–631.

67 Hale, "Letters from the People: A Little Tuskegee," *Hartford Courant* (Apr. 22, 1910), 8.

68 Hale, "Farm Life and Work," *Hartford Courant* (Oct. 8, 1895), 11.

69 Nina Silber, *The Romance of Reunion: Northerners and the South, 1865–1900*, Civil War America (Chapel Hill: University of North Carolina Press, 1993), chapter 5.

70 See James D. Anderson, *The Education of Blacks in the South, 1860–1935* (Chapel Hill: University of North Carolina Press, 1988).

71 J. H. Hale, "Small Beginnings and Results Up to Date," Annual Catalogue of J. H. Hale Nurseries, 1897, 3.

72 Ibid., 4.

73 "New Englanders Gone," *Macon Telegraph* (July 2, 1896), 5.

74 Ibid.

75 Ibid.

76 Leon F. Litwack, *Trouble in Mind*, 280–283; E. M. Beck and Stewart E. Tolnay, "Lynching," *New Georgia Encyclopedia*, 2015, accessed Aug. 2, 2016 at www.georgiaencyclopedia.org/articles/history-archaeology/lynching; "Sam Holt, Murderer and Assailant, Burned at the Stake at Newman," *Atlanta Constitution* (Apr. 24, 1899), 1.

77 Hale, *Making Whiteness*, 203.
78 Abel Meeropol, "Strange Fruit," copyright Edward B. Marks Music Company, 1939, in *International Journal of Epidemiology* 35, no. 4 (August 2006), 902, accessed Aug. 1, 2016 at http://ije .oxfordjournals.org/content/35/4/902.full.
79 Joseph G. Pero, *Joey: My Mother's Favorite Son* (self-published ca. 1980), 17–19.
80 "From New York to Pick Peaches," *Hartford Courant* (Aug. 13, 1906), 11.
81 Pero, *Joey: My Mother's Favorite Son*, 17–19.
82 Pero, *Joey: My Mother's Favorite Son*, 23.
83 "Hale's Darkies a Merry Crowd," *Hartford Courant* (Sept. 6, 1913), 11.
84 "Ramblings of a Horticulturalist," *American Fruit Grower* (Aug. 1947): 28; Pero, *Joey: My Mother's Favorite Son*, 30–32.
85 Pero, *Joey: My Mother's Favorite Son*, 31.
86 Quoted in "Where Cotton Is Not King: The Emancipation of the South Emphasized Nowhere More Than in Georgia and Eastern Alabama," *Fruit Trade Journal* (Dec. 19, 1903): 34.
87 "The Peach … Has the Complexion of Georgia," *Fortune* (February 1932).

5 ROT AND GLUT

1 W. L. Hunnicutt, "The Nurserymen's Convention," *Southern Cultivator* 62, no. 14 (July 15, 1904), 1. During the busiest week of all, more than nine hundred workers were on the payroll. See "Hale's Big Crops of Fine Peaches," *Hartford Courant* (Aug. 10, 1904), 6.
2 "The Peach Carnival," *Atlanta Constitution* (June 10, 1895), 7.
3 "Hale's Big Crops of Fine Peaches," *Hartford Courant* (Aug. 10, 1904), 6.
4 Growing cotton in the early twentieth century, a Georgia farmer could gross anywhere from $12 (1899) to $52 (1918) an acre; the five-year (1914–1918) average for the state was $34.48 per acre. See USDA, *The Yearbook of Agriculture, 1918* (Washington, DC: Government Printing Office, 1918), 533; Allen G. Waller and Harry B. Weiss, "The Peach Industry in New Jersey: A Statistical and Economic Study" *Bulletin* 452 (Brunswick: New Jersey Agricultural Experiment Station, September 1927), 37.
5 By way of comparison, peach production cost $189.31/acre in New Jersey. Fort Valley growers produced an average of 100 bushels/acre, which was quite low compared to other peach growing sections; southern New Jersey averaged 170, and Sandhill, North Carolina 175 bushels per acre. See Waller and Weiss, "Peach Industry," 37.
6 Cotton costs varied widely – anywhere from 8 to 59 cents per pound of lint in 1927, depending on soil fertility, the flatness of the land, the size of the plantings, and how much the farmer chose to fertilize and cultivate. Higher costs per acre usually produced higher yields, meaning lower costs per pound and hence potentially greater profits. Across the South in 1919, the average price (35.6 cents per pound) just barely beat the average costs (35 cents per pound). According to the USDA, about half the South's cotton farmers

failed to break even that year, and, relatively speaking, it was a good year for cotton prices. See USDA *Yearbook*, 1928, 1049; and A. M. Agelasto, C. B. Doyle, G. S. Meloy, and O. C. Stine, "The Cotton Situation" in USDA, *The Yearbook of Agriculture, 1921* (Washington, DC: Government Printing Office, 1921), 357–365.

7 On monocultures and pesticide use, see Pete Daniel, *Breaking the Land: The Transformation of Cotton, Tobacco, and Rice Cultures since 1880* (Urbana: University of Illinois Press, 1985); Pete Daniel, *Toxic Drift: Pesticides and Health in the Post-World War II South*, The Walter Lynwood Fleming Lectures in Southern History (Baton Rouge: Louisiana State University Press, 2005); Frederick Rowe Davis, *Banned: A History of Pesticides and the Science of Toxicology* (New Haven, CT: Yale University Press, 2014). Mark Fiege, *Irrigated Eden: The Making of an Agricultural Landscape in the American West*, Weyerhaeuser Environmental Books (Seattle: University of Washington Press, 1999); Deborah Kay Fitzgerald, *Every Farm a Factory: The Industrial Ideal in American Agriculture*, Yale Agrarian Studies Series (New Haven, CT: Yale University Press, 2003); James C. Giesen, *Boll Weevil Blues: Cotton, Myth, and Power in the American South* (Chicago: University of Chicago Press, 2011); James C. Giesen, "'The Truth about the Boll Weevil': The Nature of Planter Power in the Mississippi Delta," *Environmental History* 14, no. 4 (October 1, 2009): 683–704, doi:10.1093/envhis/14.4.683. David Kinkela, *DDT and the American Century: Global Health, Environmental Politics, and the Pesticide That Changed the World* (Chapel Hill: University of North Carolina Press, 2011); Linda Lorraine Nash, *Inescapable Ecologies: A History of Environment, Disease, and Knowledge* (Berkeley: University of California Press, 2006); Adam M. Romero, "'From Oil Well to Farm': Industrial Waste, Shell Oil, and the Petrochemical Turn (1927–1947)," *Agricultural History* 90, no. 1 (2016): 70–93, doi:10.3098/ah.2016.090.1.70; Adam M. Romero, "Commercializing Chemical Warfare: Citrus, Cyanide, and an Endless War," *Agriculture and Human Values* 33, no. 1 (February 27, 2015): 3–26, doi:10.1007/s10460-015-9591-1; Richard Clark Sawyer, *To Make a Spotless Orange: Biological Control in California*, Henry A. Wallace Series on Agricultural History and Rural Life (Ames: Iowa State University Press, 1996); John Soluri, *Banana Cultures: Agriculture, Consumption, and Environmental Change in Honduras and the United States* (Austin: University of Texas Press, 2005); Steven Stoll, *The Fruits of Natural Advantage: Making the Industrial Countryside in California* (Berkeley: University of California Press, 1998); Adam Tompkins, *Ghostworkers and Greens: The Cooperative Campaigns of Farmworkers and Environmentalists for Pesticide Reform* (Ithaca: ILR Press, 2016); David Douglas Vail, "Guardians of Abundance: Aerial Application, Agricultural Chemicals, and Toxicity in the Postwar Prairie West" (Ph.D., Kansas State University, 2012). On cooperatives and markets, see Hal S Barron, *Mixed Harvest: The Second Great Transformation in the Rural North, 1870–1930*, Studies in Rural Culture (Chapel Hill: University of North Carolina Press, 1997); William Cronon, *Nature's Metropolis: Chicago and the Great West* (New York: W. W. Norton, 1991). Tracey Deutsch, *Building a Housewife's*

Paradise: Gender, Politics, and American Grocery Stores in the Twentieth Century (Chapel Hill: University of North Carolina Press, 2010); Fiege, *Irrigated Eden: The Making of an Agricultural Landscape in the American West*; Susanne Freidberg, *Fresh: A Perishable History* (Cambridge, MA: Belknap Press of Harvard University Press, 2009); Douglas Cazaux Sackman, *Orange Empire: California and the Fruits of Eden* (Berkeley: University of California Press, 2005); Stoll, *The Fruits of Natural Advantage: Making the Industrial Countryside in California*; Helen Tangires, *Public Markets and Civic Culture in Nineteenth-Century America*, Creating the North American Landscape (Baltimore: Johns Hopkins University Press, 2003); Victoria Saker Woeste, *The Farmer's Benevolent Trust: Law and Agricultural Cooperation in Industrial America, 1865–1945*, Studies in Legal History (Chapel Hill: University of North Carolina Press, 1998); Suzanne Wasserman, "Hawkers and Gawkers: Peddlers and Markets in New York City," in *Gastropolis: Food and New York City* (New York: Columbia University Press, 2010), 153–173.

8   James C. Giesen, "'Truth about the Boll Weevil,'" 685.

9   C. L. Marlatt, "The San Jose Scale: Its Native Home and Natural Enemy," in *Yearbook of the Department of Agriculture* (Washington, DC: Government Printing Office, 1902), 156.

10   "State Fruit Growers," *Hartford Courant* (July 2, 1901), 7.

11   C. L. Marlatt, "The San Jose Scale: Its Native Home and Natural Enemy," 155.

12   In a dramatic demonstration of this sentiment, the Bureau of Entomology chief, Charles Marlatt, inspected a lot of cherry trees from Japan – a diplomatic gesture from Japan to the U.S. government – and had the entire shipment destroyed. See Philip J. Pauly, "The Beauty and Menace of the Japanese Cherry Trees: Conflicting Visions of American Ecological Independence," *Isis* 87, no. 1 (Mar. 1, 1996): 51.

13   Georgia State Horticultural Society, *Annual Proceedings* 22 (1898), 71.

14   Ibid., 22:82.

15   Ibid., 22:82–84.

16   Dan Horton, "Insects and Mites," in Desmond R. Layne and Daniele Bassi, *The Peach: Botany, Production and Uses* (Cambridge, MA: CABI, 2008), 477–479.

17   Samuel Hape, "Apples at the South," in Georgia State Horticultural Society, *Annual Proceedings* 13 (1888), 27.

18   Georgia State Horticultural Society, *Annual Proceedings* 20 (1896), 39.

19   Ibid.; see also the District Reports, pp. 73–75, which noted the bad infestation of curculio.

20   Hale, "Farm Life and Work," *Hartford Courant* (June 13, 1896), 12.

21   The literature on progressivism is much too large to cite here, but for a sampling see Samuel P. Hays, *Conservation and the Gospel of Efficiency: The Progressive Conservation Movement, 1890–1920* (Pittsburgh: University of Pittsburgh Press, 1999); Richard Hofstadter, *The Age of Reform* (New York: Vintage, 1960); Meg Jacobs, *Pocketbook Politics: Economic Citizenship in Twentieth-Century America* (Princeton, N.J.: Princeton University Press,

2005); Jackson Lears, *Rebirth of a Nation: The Making of Modern America, 1877–1920* (New York: HarperCollins, 2009); Michael McGerr, *A Fierce Discontent: The Rise and Fall of the Progressive Movement in America* (New York: Simon & Schuster, 2010); Robyn Muncy, *Creating a Female Dominion in American Reform, 1890–1935* (Oxford: Oxford University Press, 1994); Daniel T. Rodgers, "In Search of Progressivism," *Reviews in American History* 10, no. 4 (December 1, 1982): 113–132; Daniel T. Rodgers, *Atlantic Crossings: Social Politics in a Progressive Age* (Cambridge, MA: Belknap Press of Harvard University Press, 1998).

22 Peach Crop May Break Record," *Atlanta Constitution* (April 25, 1908), 9.

23 "'Thumbs Up!' or 'Thumbs Down!' for Development of Georgia's Great Peach Growing Industry," *Atlanta Constitution* (Aug. 9, 1908), 7.

24 Forrest Crissey, "Cooperation Close to the Soil," *Everybody's Magazine* (September 1909), 408.

25 I calculated this number by estimating 200 peaches per crate (which varied, of course, by the size of the peach), 500 crates per railcar, and 150 cars.

26 "Georgia Fruit Crop," *Wall Street Journal* (Oct. 7, 1908), 6.

27 "Georgia Fruit Exchange Organized by Growers," *Atlanta Constitution* (Sept. 11, 1908), 1.

28 "Fruit Growers Plan Campaign," *Atlanta Constitution* (Sept. 26, 1908), 2; "Peach Crowers Respond to Call," *Atlanta Constitution* (Nov. 9, 1908), 5.

29 The importance of business forms and language in creating the factory model of agriculture is central to the argument of Deborah Kay Fitzgerald, *Every Farm a Factory: The Industrial Ideal in American Agriculture*, Yale Agrarian Studies Series (New Haven, ct: Yale University Press, 2003).

30 Herman Steen, *Coöperative Marketing: The Golden Rule in Agriculture* (New York: Doubleday, Page, 1923), v.

31 "Georgia Fruit Exchange Saves Its Members $80,000," *Atlanta Constitution* (Jan. 18, 1912), 3.

32 Georgia Fruit Exchange, *Charter and By-Laws* (Atlanta: Georgia Fruit Exchange, 1917), 4.

33 "Fruit Growers Name Officers," *Atlanta Constitution* (Nov. 9, 1909), A2.

34 "Georgia Fruit Exchange Proves Boon to State's Peach Growers," *Atlanta Constitution* (Sept. 26, 1917), 68.

35 Rodgers, *Atlantic Crossings: Social Politics in a Progressive Age*, 326.

36 Scholarly portrayals of agricultural cooperatives run the gamut from radical, quasi-socialist to slick precursors to modern agribusiness. See, for instance, the divergence between Lawrence Goodwyn, *The Populist Moment: A Short History of the Agrarian Revolt in America* (New York: Oxford University Press, 1978), and Charles Postel, *The Populist Vision* (New York: Oxford University Press, 2007).

37 Sackman, *Orange Empire: California and the Fruits of Eden*, 195–197; Stoll, *The Fruits of Natural Advantage: Making the Industrial Countryside in California*, 75–76; Woeste, *Farmer's Benevolent Trust: Law and Agricultural Cooperation in Industrial America, 1865–1945*, 20.

38 Woeste, *Farmer's Benevolent Trust: Law and Agricultural Cooperation in Industrial America, 1865–1945*, 32–33.

39 Steen, *Coöperative Marketing: The Golden Rule in Agriculture*, 72.

40 Crissey, "Cooperation Close to the Soil," 410.

41 "Will Inspect Georgia Fruit," *Atlanta Constitution* (May 30, 1909), 4.

42 "Fine Organization to Market Peach," *Atlanta Constitution* (June 26, 1910), E5.

43 "State Growers to Meet Here," *Atlanta Constitution* (May 17, 1909), 1.

44 "Peach Growers Here in Atlanta," *Atlanta Constitution* (Sept. 19, 1909), B3.

45 I. M. Fleming, "The Benefits Which Have Been Derived from the Work of the Fruit Exchange," in Georgia State Horticultural Society, *Annual Proceedings* 33 (1909), 92–93; "Dividend Paid to the Growers," *Atlanta Constitution* (Sept. 9, 1909), 5.

46 Georgia State Horticultural Society, *Annual Proceedings* 33 (1909), 10.

47 "State Growers to Meet Here," *Atlanta Constitution* (May 17, 1909), 1.

48 Crissey, "Cooperation Close to the Soil," 416. Crissey wrote for the *Saturday Evening Post*, *Everybody's Magazine*, and *Harper's* from 1901 through the 1930s. He was also the author of several books, including *The Story of Foods* (1917) and *Tattlings of a Retired Politician* (1904).

49 Ibid., 410; Fleming, "The Benefits Which Have Been Derived from the Work of the Fruit Exchange," 94.

50 "Georgia Fruit Exchange," *Atlanta Constitution* (Oct. 20, 1909), 8.

51 Steen, *Coöperative Marketing: The Golden Rule in Agriculture*, 71.

52 The number 4,000 is taken from "Growers Meet to Sell Stock," *Atlanta Constitution* (Sept. 21, 1908), 3. The full list of 21 growers: H. C. Bagley, chair, A. O. Murphy, Barnesville, A. M. Kitchen, Baldwin, P. J. A. Berckmanns Jr., Augusta. Judge George F. Gober, Marietta, J. O. Booton, Marshallville, J. W. Frederick, Marshallville, W. H. Harris, Fort Valley, Judge W. H. Felton, Macon, F. A. Ricks, Reynolds, E. M. Heard, Middleton, J. H. Hale, Fort Valley, J. T. West, Thomson, J. Scott Davis, Cave Springs, A. J. Evans, Fort Valley, W. F. Summerour, Dalton, E. Rumble, Goggins, J. H. Baird, Fort Valley, Mr. Veatch, Adiarsville, Ed McKenzie, Montezuma, W. W. Stevens, Mayfield. See "Million Trees in the Bureau," *Atlanta Constitution* (Oct. 11, 1908), A5.

53 "Georgia Fruit Exchange Organized by Growers," *Atlanta Constitution* (Sept. 11, 1908), 1.

54 "Peach Growers Hold Meeting," *Atlanta Constitution* (Mar. 24, 1908), 7.

55 A. M. Kitchen, "'Organization,' Keynote to the Peach Industry," *Atlanta Constitution* (Aug. 13, 1908), 3.

56 Fleming, "The Benefits Which Have Been Derived from the Work of the Fruit Exchange," 95.

57 Steen, *Coöperative Marketing: The Golden Rule in Agriculture*, 71–72.

58 W. B. Hunter, *Annual Report of the Georgia Fruit Exchange* (1918), 3.

59 Ibid., 9.

60 Thomas Hubbard McHatton, "The Peach Industry of Georgia" (Ph.D., Michigan State University, 1921), 42. McHatton lists the following figures: 1915 4,468 cars total; GFE 2,997 or 67.1%. 1916 3199 cars, GFE 2278 or 78.2%, 875 sold in East, 12% in West, and 1% in South. 1917 3869 cars, GFE 2789 or 72%, 134 towns, 28% to West and 72% to East. 1918

8052 cars, GFE 6615 or 82%, 191 markets and 76% f.o.b. 1913–1917 GFE averaged 61% of crop, so this was a banner year. 1919 7403 cars, GFE 5429 or 73%. 1920 6087 cars, GFE 4553 or 75%, f.o.b. 65%.

61 Display Ad 42 – No Title, *New York Times* (July 16, 1920), 8.

62 McHatton, "Peach Industry of Georgia," 47–48.

63 "New York Fruit Dealers Protest Peach Auctions," *Atlanta Constitution* (June 10, 1923), 2.

64 "Peach Growers Seek Protection," *Atlanta Constitution* (Aug. 26, 1923), 3.

65 USDA Rural Business and Cooperative Development Service, "Understanding Capper-Volstead," *Cooperative Information Report* 35 (June 1985).

66 "Georgia Peaches to Be Marketed Cooperatively," *Atlanta Constitution* (Aug. 30, 1923), 7.

67 W. C Bewley, *Georgia's Twenty-Five Million Dollar Peach Industry* (Macon, GA: 1932), 6.

68 "What's the Use of Standardization?" *Georgia Peach* (June 1924), 3; "Necessity of High Quality Grade and Pack," *Georgia Peach* (July 1924), 3, 4; "Serving the Consumer through Co-Operation," and "Less Fruit but More Money," *Georgia Peach* (August 1924), 5, 10; "Plan to Coordinate Marketing of Peach Will Be Developed," *Atlanta Constitution* (Mar. 23, 1924), 16; "Peach Growers Adopt Standard for 1924 Packing," *Atlanta Constitution* (May 20, 1924), 4.

69 "Peach Exchange Appeals to Law," *Atlanta Constitution* (Aug. 3, 1924), 9.

70 "Millions Brought to Peach Growers as Season Ends." *Atlanta Constitution* (July 26, 1925) 9.

71 Bewley, *Georgia's Twenty-Five Million Dollar Peach Industry*, 7; E. F. Savage, "History of the Georgia Peach Industry," (Griffin, GA, 1984), 130.

72 Bewley, *Georgia's Twenty-Five Million Dollar Peach Industry*, 7.

73 Ibid., 17.

74 Ibid., 16–17.

75 Ibid., 8.

76 Savage, "History of the Georgia Peach Industry," 130.

77 Bewley, *Georgia's Twenty-Five Million Dollar Peach Industry*, 7; "Peach Exchange Appeals to Law," *Atlanta Constitution* (Aug. 3, 1924), 9.

78 M. R. Cooper, "Findings of the Peach Survey in Georgia," Address delivered at the Nineteenth Annual Farmers Week, Georgia State College of Agriculture, Athens (Jan. 28, 1926), 6.

79 William R. Okie and Bryan Blackburn, "Interactive Effects of Light and Chilling on Peach Flower and Leaf Budbreak," *HortScience* 46, no. 7 (2011): 1056–1062.

80 Steen, *Coöperative Marketing: The Golden Rule in Agriculture*, 72.

81 See Cletus E Daniel, *Bitter Harvest, a History of California Farmworkers, 1870–1941* (Berkeley: University of California Press, 1982); Carey McWilliams, *Factories in the Field; The Story of Migratory Farm Labor in California* (Boston: Little, Brown, 1939); Sackman, *Orange Empire: California and the Fruits of Eden*; Woeste, *Farmer's Benevolent Trust: Law and Agricultural Cooperation in Industrial America, 1865–1945*.

82 "Marketing Peaches by a Game of Guess," *Atlanta Constitution* (Aug. 16, 1908), 7.

83 David Chapman, "Lamartine G. Hardman," *New Georgia Encyclopedia*, accessed July 21, 2011 at www.georgiaencyclopedia.org/nge/Article .jsp? id= h-2133.

84 L.G. Hardman, Telegraphic Car Order to Southern Railway System, July 23, 1923; Southern Railway System Inspection Report, July 23, 1923; L.G. Hardman to Smith and Holden, July 24, 1923; Smith and Holden to L.G. Hardman, July 25, 1923; all in Series II, Box 69, Folder 3, Lamartine Griffin Hardman Papers, Richard B. Russell Library for Political Research and Studies, The University of Georgia Libraries.

85 Smith and Holden to L. G. Hardman, July 27, 1923; L. G. Hardman to Smith and Holden, July 30, 1923; both in Series II, Box 69, Folder 3, Lamartine Griffin Hardman Papers, Richard B. Russell Library for Political Research and Studies, The University of Georgia Libraries.

86 L. G. Hardman to Smith and Holden, July 30, 1923; Smith and Holden to L. G. Hardman, Aug. 1, 1923; both in Series II, Box 69, Folder 3, Lamartine Griffin Hardman Papers, Richard B. Russell Library for Political Research and Studies, The University of Georgia Libraries.

87 Smith and Holden to L. G. Hardman, Aug. 3, 1923, Series II, Box 69, Folder 3, Lamartine Griffin Hardman Papers, Richard B. Russell Library for Political Research and Studies, The University of Georgia Libraries.

88 *Georgia Peach* (July 1924), back cover.

89 *Georgia Peach* (Aug. 1924), 17.

90 Katharine Ball Ripley, *Sand in My Shoes* (New York: Brewer, Warren & Putnam, 1931), 331, 330.

91 Ibid., 331.

92 James C. Malin, "The Background of the First Bills to Establish a Bureau of Markets, 1911–12," *Agricultural History* 6, no. 3 (July 1, 1932): 128.

93 Timothy Mitchell points out that the notion of "the economy" was an invention of the new discipline of econometrics in the 1930s and 1940s. See Timothy Mitchell, "Fixing the Economy" *Cultural Studies* 12, no. 1 (1998), 82–101.

94 Hoke Smith, Market Division for Farm Products Speech of Hon. Hoke Smith, of Georgia, in the Senate of the United States, Feb. 27, 1913 (Washington, DC: Government Printing Office, 1913), 4.

95 Caroline B. Sherman, "History of the Bureau of Markets (As Traced through Official Publications)" (Mimeograph, Bureau of Markets, 1920), reprinted in Wells Alvord Sherman, *Merchandising Fruits and Vegetables: A New Billion Dollar Industry* (Chicago: A. W. Shaw, 1928), 157.

96 Ibid., 158.

97 Ibid., 159–161.

98 Lloyd S. Tenny, "The Bureau of Agricultural Economics: The Early Years," *Journal of Farm Economics* 29, no. 4 (Nov. 1, 1947): 1017, doi:10.2307/1232732.

99 Wells A. Sherman, "Report on Market News Service," 1919, 15. Records of the Bureau of Agricultural Economics, Record Group 83, National Archives, College Park, MD.

100 M. R. Cooper and J.W. Park, *The Peach Situation in the Southern States*, USDA Circular 420 (Washington, D.C.: U.S. Government Printing Office, 1927), 1.

101 Harry S. Kantor, "Factors Affecting the Price of Peaches in the New York City Market" *USDA Technical Bulletin* no. 115 (April 1929), 29–30.

102 Ben C. French, "Fruit and Vegetable Marketing Orders: A Critique of the Issues and State of Analysis" *American Journal of Agricultural Economics* 64, no. 5, Proceedings Issue (Dec. 1982), 916.

103 Georgia Peach Industry Marketing Order, *Annual Report* (1942), 1.

104 Savage, "History of the Georgia Peach Industry," 41.

105 Ibid., 39.

106 Mark Fiege makes a similar point about risk and control in agriculture in his study of Idaho potato and alfalfa farmers. See Fiege, *Irrigated Eden: The Making of an Agricultural Landscape in the American West*, 161–163.

6 BLOSSOMS AND HAMS

1 On the "rural question" – and Bailey and Nourse in particular – see Steven Stoll, *The Fruits of Natural Advantage: Making the Industrial Countryside in California* (Berkeley: University of California Press, 1998), 8–16; Daniel T. Rodgers, *Atlantic Crossings: Social Politics in a Progressive Age* (Cambridge, MA: Belknap Press of Harvard University Press, 1998), 318–366; see also Liberty Hyde Bailey, *Liberty Hyde Bailey: Essential Agrarian and Environmental Writings*, ed. Zachary Michael Jack (Ithaca, NY: Cornell University Press, 2008); William L. Bowers, *The Country Life Movement in America, 1900–1920*, National University Publications, Series in American Studies (Port Washington, NY: Kennikat Press, 1974); David B. Danbom, *The Resisted Revolution: Urban America and the Industrialization of Agriculture, 1900–1930* (Ames: Iowa State University Press, 1979); Scott J. Peters and Paul A. Morgan, "The Country Life Commission: Reconsidering a Milestone in American Agricultural History," *Agricultural History* 78, no. 3 (July 1, 2004): 289–316. The South had its own variant of rural progressive reform. See Jack Temple Kirby, *Darkness at the Dawning; Race and Reform in the Progressive South*, Critical Periods of History (Philadelphia: Lippincott, 1972); Andrew Baker, "Race and Romantic Agrarianism: The Transnational Roots of Clarence Poe's Crusade for Rural Segregation in North Carolina," *Agricultural History* 87, no. 1 (January 1, 2013): 93–114, doi:10.3098/ah.2013.87.1.93.

2 On Carver, see Mark Hersey, "Hints and Suggestions to Farmers: George Washington Carver and Rural Conservation in the South," *Environmental History* 11, no. 2 (2006): 239–268; Mark D. Hersey, *My Work Is That of Conservation: An Environmental Biography of George Washington Carver*, Environmental History and the American South. (University of Georgia Press, 2011).

3 George Washington Carver, "How to Live Comfortably This Winter," Experiment Station Circular (1916), 7–8, quoted in Hersey, *My Work Is*

That of Conservation: An Environmental Biography of George Washington Carver, 143.

4 On the black rural environmental experience, in addition to Hersey, see Dianne D. Glave and Mark Stoll, eds., *"To Love the Wind and the Rain": African Americans and Environmental History* (Pittsburgh: University of Pittsburgh Press, 2006); Mark Schultz, *The Rural Face of White Supremacy: Beyond Jim Crow* (Urbana: University of Illinois Press, 2007); and, for a literary experiment with a southern rural aesthetic, Jean Toomer, *Cane* (New York: Liveright, 1923). For the civil rights period see Pete Daniel, *Dispossession: Discrimination against African American Farmers in the Age of Civil Rights* (Chapel Hill: University of North Carolina Press, 2013); for the nineteenth century, see Steven Hahn, *A Nation under Our Feet: Black Political Struggles in the Rural South, from Slavery to the Great Migration* (Cambridge, MA: Belknap Press of Harvard University Press, 2003); David Sehat, "The Civilizing Mission of Booker T. Washington," *Journal of Southern History* 73, no. 2 (May 2007): 323–362.

5 "The World's Peach Paradise," Peach Blossom Festival Program (1926), Thomas Public Library Local History Collection, Fort Valley, Georgia; Homer J. Avera, "The Peach County Program," *Fort Valley Leader–Tribune and Peachland Journal* (Mar. 19, 1925), 11; Lucy Hamilton Howard, "The Peach Blossom Festival," *Fort Valley Leader-Tribune and Peachland Journal* (Mar. 19, 1925), 9.

6 Rural beauty is perhaps most obviously associated with California, though of course New Hampshire, Vermont, and Maine have also staked a claim to the rural idyll as tourist attraction. See, for instance, William Francis Deverell, *Whitewashed Adobe : The Rise of Los Angeles and the Remaking of Its Mexican Past* (Berkeley: University of California Press, 2004); Richard William Judd, *Common Lands, Common People: The Origins of Conservation in Northern New England* (Cambridge, MA: Harvard University Press, 1997); Phoebe S. Kropp, *California Vieja: Culture and Memory in a Modern American Place* (Berkeley: University of California Press, 2006); David M. Masumoto, *Epitaph for a Peach: Four Seasons on My Family Farm* (New York: HarperOne, 1996); Douglas Cazaux Sackman, *Orange Empire: California and the Fruits of Eden* (Berkeley: University of California Press, 2005); David Vaught, *Cultivating California: Growers, Specialty Crops, and Labor, 1875–1920* (Baltimore: Johns Hopkins University Press, 1999). But the South has had its own set of aesthetic claims. See for example, Jack Temple Kirby, *Mockingbird Song: Ecological Landscapes of the South* (Chapel Hill: University of North Carolina Press, 2006); J. Drew Lanham, *The Home Place: Memoirs of a Colored Man's Love Affair with Nature* (Minneapolis, MN: Milkweed Editions, 2016); Janisse Ray, *Ecology of a Cracker Childhood*, Reprint (Minneapolis: Milkweed Editions, 2000); Blain Roberts, *Pageants, Parlors, and Pretty Women: Race and Beauty in the Twentieth-Century South* (Chapel Hill: University of North Carolina Press, 2014); and Toomer, *Cane*.

7 Fort Valley High and Industrial School, *Work in the Black Belt of Southwest Georgia*, Leaflet no. 4 (Fort Valley, GA: Fort Valley High and Industrial

School, 1904); Frank Horne, "Henry A. Hunt, Sixteenth Spingarn Medalist," *The Crisis*, (August 1930), 261. Originally a private institution affiliated with the Episcopal Church, Fort Valley High and Industrial School (FVHIS) merged with another institution and joined the University System of Georgia as Fort Valley State College (FVSC) in 1939. In 1996, the institution became Fort Valley State University (FVSU).

8 Horne, "Henry A. Hunt, Sixteenth Spingarn Medalist"; W. E. B. DuBois, "The Perfect Vacation," *The Crisis* (August 1931).

9 Don Mitchell, *The Lie of the Land: Migrant Workers and the California Landscape* (Minneapolis: University of Minnesota Press, 1996), 8.

10 Mabel Withoft would later publish a novel based on this experience, a "coming-of-age" story called *Little Misery* that profiled a bookish and sickly little girl and her transformation into a kind and energetic young woman under the tutelage of a Yankee farmhand named Jule and the environment of rural Ohio. See Mabel Swartz Withoft, *Little Misery: A Picture of Child Life*, 2013 ed. (Dayton, OH: United Brethren, 1906); Megan Evans Daniels, "Foreword," in *Little Misery: A Picture of Child Life*, 2013 ed. (Dayton, OH: United Brethren, 2013); Megan Evans Daniels, "Fleshing Out the Fiction in Mabel Swartz Withoft's *Little Misery*, 1906" (Granville, OH: Granville Historical Society, November 12, 2013).

11 Benjamin Harrison, *Speeches of Benjamin Harrison*, ed. Charles Hedges (New York: United States Book Company, 1892), 484; F. G. Withoft biography, Dayton Metro Library Special Collections; "Shock of Flood News Fatal," obituary for Frederick G. Withoft, Mar. 27, 1913.

12 Mabel Swartz Withoft, "Afterward," unpublished poem, c. 1902, hand copied from the original by Virginia Sutton (Mrs. William F.) of Macon, Georgia, who owns the original document. My thanks to Megan Evans Daniels for sharing this document.

13 Reprinted in the *Newark Advocate* (Feb. 28, 1902), 4. The cuckoo's call here was presumably that of the yellow-billed cuckoo, or "rain crow" (*Coccyzus americanus*), so called because of its "pounding note, dolefully sounded" in advance of rain. See Maurice Thompson, "Cuckoo Notes," *Library Magazine* (July 1885), 2.

14 "Beloved Fort Valley Woman Passes Sunday," *Fort Valley Leader Tribune* (Aug. 3, 1939), 1; Mabel Swartz Withoft, *Oak and Laurel: A Study of the Mountain Misson Schools of Southern Baptists* (Nashville, TN: Sunday School Board of the Southern Baptist Convention, 1923); "Mrs. Withoft Returns," *Macon Weekly Telegraph* (Nov. 2, 1922).

15 Fort Valley History Club Program, 1920–1921, in Local History Collection, Thomas Public Library, Fort Valley.

16 Mabel Claire Swartz Withoft, Biographical File, Georgia Archives, DOC-7365, 004-02-046, 060.

17 "Teachers of Our Children Must Be Paid, Say Women." *Atlanta Constitution.* Atlanta (July 20, 1913), sec. F.

18 "Fort Valley Soldier Is Dead in France," *Atlanta Constitution*, Atlanta (Mar. 16, 1919), a12; M. S. Withoft, "Seeded Ground," *The Delineator* (May 1922), 11.

19 "Baptist W.M.U. in Annual Convention in Macon," *Atlanta Constitution* (Nov. 20, 1921).

20 "Mrs. F. W. Withoft to Be Honored." *Atlanta Constitution* (Oct. 14, 1930).

21 Ed Jackson, "A Brief History of Georgia Counties," GeorgiaInfo, the Digital Library of Georgia, 2012, accessed 4 August 2016 at http://georgiainfo .galileo.usg.edu/countyhistory.htm. See also John H. Long, ed., "Georgia: Consolidated Chronology of State and County Boundaries," in Georgia Atlas of Historical County Boundaries (Newberry Library, 2010), accessed Sept. 27, 2016 at http://publications.newberry.org/ahcbp/documents/GA_ Consolidated_Chronology.htm#Consolidated_Chronology.

22 William B. Ahlgren, "Responsible for Lynching Evil," *Atlanta Constitution* (July 16, 1916), B4. The *Constitution*'s editorial staff agreed. "If we would only throw off the new county menace and base the county organization upon purely business principles, making for efficiency," the editorial concluded, "it would greatly contribute to the state's institutional progress." "New County Madness!" *Atlanta Constitution* (July 16, 1916), B4.

23 Mrs. C. N. Rountree, "With Creation of Peach, Georgia Has 161 Counties," *Atlanta Constitution* (Jan. 1, 1925); Ned McIntosh, "Capitol Gossip: New County Now Proposed to Bear the Name 'Peach,'" *Atlanta Constitution* (June 2, 1916), 3.

24 "Boosters Work Hard for "Peach" County," *Atlanta Constitution* (June 18, 1916), 11.

25 Alva B. Greene, letter to Gov. Nat E. Harris, June 10, 1916, Gov. Nat Harris Collection, Record Group 001, Georgia Archives, Morrow, GA.

26 A. B. Greene, "Says Peach County Comes under the Exceptional Classification," *Atlanta Constitution* (July 18, 1916), 8.

27 Greene, letter to Gov. Nat E. Harris, June 10, 1916.

28 Greene, "Says Peach County Comes under the Exceptional Classification."

29 Greene, letter to Gov. Nat E. Harris, June 10, 1916.

30 "Mass Meeting at Perry Opposes 'Peach' County," *Atlanta Constitution* (June 10, 1916), 10; "Planned To Give to Macon County Strip of Houston," *Atlanta Constitution* (June 17, 1916), 7; "Peach County Will Be Strongly Urged at Regular Session," *Atlanta Constitution* (Mar. 22, 1917), 9; "Denny Withdraws from Presidency Race," *Atlanta Constitution* (June 26, 1917), 12.

31 "Proposed New County Big Issue In Houston," *Atlanta Constitution* (May 25, 1920), 18; Fuzzy Woodruff, "Flivver Trip thro' Georgia Is Like Liberal Education," *The Atlanta Constitution* (July 24, 1921), C6; "Bill to Create County of Peach Meets Setback: Jules Felton, of Montezuma, Declares Georgia Is Opposed to Addition of Counties" *Atlanta Constitution* (July 21, 1921), 1.

32 "Mrs. F. W. Withoft Points Out Reasons for Supporting Peach," unnamed Atlanta newspaper (1922), clipping in Megan Evans Daniels personal collection.

33 "Victory in House Won by Friends of Peach County: Notice Is Given, However, That a Reconsideration of Measure Will Be Sought Next Week," *Atlanta Constitution* (Aug. 12, 1922), 1.

34 "Mass Meetings Oppose Forming County of Peach" *Atlanta Constitution* (Oct. 18, 1922), 20.
35 Opponents alleged that the insidious "Whisky Lobby" was planning to add three more counties after Peach. Display Ad 6 – No Title, *Atlanta Constitution* (Oct. 23, 1922), 5. A week later, a similar advertisement used the term "Big Lobby" to explain the presence of the proposal on the ballot. "Whisky Lobby" apparently referred generally to government corruption, the ability of wealthy parties to buy the votes of otherwise good men, which had beset Georgia politics "since the golden days of liquor." "Vote AGAINST 'Peach County,'" *Thomasville Times-Enterprise* (Oct. 31, 1922), 6.
36 Display Ad 10 – No Title, *Atlanta Constitution* (Nov. 6, 1922), 8.
37 Souvenir Program, Annual Peach Blossom Festival (1922), 4. Thomas Public Library, Local History Collection, Fort Valley, Georgia.
38 Governor Thomas Hardwick, speech given at First Annual Peach Blossom Festival (Mar. 14, 1922), quoted in Roderick Houser, "Peach Festival Draws Thousands to Fort Valley: Visitors from Many States See First King and Queen Crowned amidst Celebration," *Atlanta Constitution* (Mar. 15, 1922), 7.
39 Souvenir Program (1922), 3.
40 Roderick Houser, "Peach Festival Draws Thousands to Fort Valley: Visitors from Many States See First King and Queen Crowned amidst Celebration."
41 "President and Cabinet May Attend Celebration," *Atlanta Constitution* (Feb. 26, 1923), 3.
42 Peach Blossom Festival Program (1924). Thomas Public Library, Local History Collection, Fort Valley, GA.
43 "Rotogravure," *New York Times* (Apr. 6, 1924), RP2.
44 "Wielding a Sceptre of Peach Blossoms," *Atlanta Constitution* (Mar. 30, 1924), 12A; Deborah Nadoolman Landis, *Dressed: A Century of Hollywood Costume Design* (New York: HarperCollins, 2007), 40.
45 F. Scott Fitzgerald, *The Great Gatsby* (New York: Scribner, 2004), 180.
46 Peach Blossom Festival Program (1923). Thomas Public Library, Fort Valley, GA.
47 "Forty Women Workers Will Advocate New Peach County at Atlanta Polls Today," *Atlanta Constitution* (Nov. 4, 1924).
48 C. N. Rountree, "With Creation of Peach, Georgia Has 161 Counties," *Atlanta Constitution* (Jan. 1, 1925).
49 Mabel Swartz Withoft, "My County Peach," *Fort Valley Leader-Tribune and Peachland Journal* (Mar. 19, 1925), 19.
50 On the history of poor farms in the context of American welfare policy, see Michael B. Katz, *In the Shadow of the Poorhouse: A Social History of Welfare in America*, 10th anniversary edition (New York: Basic Books, 1996).
51 Mrs. Frank Vance, "Our Aims: Ever Upward, Fair, without Spot or Blemish," *Fort Valley Leader-Tribune and Peachland Journal* (Mar. 19, 1925), 19. Practically, according to the local druggist Homer Avera, the "Peach County Program" was fourfold: better schools, good roads, industrial and agricultural development, and commonsense county government. Peach County

would be, if not a little slice of heaven on earth, at least a Progressive era "wonder county." Homer J. Avera, "The Peach County Program," *Fort Valley Leader-Tribune and Peachland Journal* (Mar. 19, 1925), 11.

52 Marilyn Neisler Windham, *Peach County: The World's Peach Paradise*, Images of America (Dover, NH: Arcadia, 1997), 85–91.

53 Mabel Swartz Withoft, "The Aeneid of the Peach," *Fort Valley Leader-Tribune and Peachland Journal* (Mar. 19, 1925), 7.

54 Ibid.

55 Ibid., 21.

56 Ibid.

57 Arthur Franklin Raper, *Preface to Peasantry: A Tale of Two Black Belt Counties*, Southern Classics Series (Columbia: University of South Carolina Press, 2005), 107. See also Arthur Franklin Raper and Ira De Augustine Reid, *Sharecroppers All* (Chapel Hill: The University of North Carolina Press, 1941); and Arthur Franklin Raper, *Tenants of the Almighty* (New York: Macmillan, 1943).

58 Windham, *Peach County: The World's Peach Paradise*, 71.

59 Display Ad 10 – No Title, *Atlanta Constitution* (Nov. 6, 1922), 8.

60 Mark Schultz, *The Rural Face of White Supremacy: Beyond Jim Crow* (Urbana: University of Illinois Press, 2007), 68. On southern progressivism and segregation, see Grace Elizabeth Hale, *Making Whiteness: The Culture of Segregation in the South, 1890–1940* (New York: Pantheon Books, 1998); Kirby, *Darkness at the Dawning; Race and Reform in the Progressive South*; William A Link, *The Paradox of Southern Progressivism, 1880–1930* (Chapel Hill: University of North Carolina Press, 1992); George Brown Tindall, *The Emergence of the New South, 1913–1945*, vol. 10, History of the South (Baton Rouge: Louisiana State University Press, 1967); C. Vann Woodward, *The Strange Career of Jim Crow*, New and rev. ed (New York: Oxford University Press, 1957).

61 Willie Snow Ethridge, "Amazing Achievement of Prof. H. A. Hunt, Winner of Coveted Spingarn Medal, 1930," *Atlanta Constitution* (July 6, 1930). When fellow African Americans wrote about him, they told a similar story. See, for example, Frank Horne, "Henry A. Hunt, Sixteenth Spingarn Medalist."

62 Adele Logan Alexander, *Ambiguous Lives: Free Women of Color in Rural Georgia, 1789–1879* (Fayetteville: University of Arkansas Press, 1991), 125–126, 129. Adele Logan Alexander, a member of the Hunt clan herself, has written two other books unearthing the remarkable history of families like the Hunts who demonstrate the "enduring (in)significance of melanin," as she puts it. See also *Homelands and Waterways: The American Journey of the Bond Family, 1846–1926*, 1st edition (New York: Pantheon, 1999); *Parallel Worlds: The Remarkable Gibbs-Hunts and the Enduring (In)significance of Melanin* (Charlottesville: University of Virginia Press, 2010).

63 The full title was *Intermarriage; or The Mode in Which, and the Causes Why, Beauty, Health and Intellect, Result from Certain Unions, and Deformity, Disease and Insanity, from Others* (London: John Churchill, 1838). Though officially unmarried, Hunt and Sayre lived together for more than two decades, raising three children in a house specifically designed,

with secret passageways and a private three-room compartment, to accommodate the black family of a respected white man. Alexander, *Ambiguous Lives: Free Women of Color in Rural Georgia, 1789–1879*, 67–72.

64 Alexander, *Ambiguous Lives: Free Women of Color in Rural Georgia, 1789–1879*, 158.

65 Gary Nash, "Forbidden Love," 1999, accessed Aug. 9, 2016 at www.pbs .org/wgbh/pages/frontline/shows/jefferson/mixed/nash.html; Gary R. Kremer, *George Washington Carver: A Biography* (Santa Barbara, CA: ABC-CLIO, 2011), 68–69; Linda O. McMurry, *George Washington Carver: Scientist and Symbol* (New York: Oxford University Press, 1981), 48; Terrance D. Smith and Sally J. Zepeda, "Adella Hunt Logan, 1863–1915: Educator, Woman's Suffrage Leader, and Confidant of Booker T. Washington," in *The Varieties of Women's Experiences: Portraits of Southern Women in the Post-Civil War Century* (Gainesville: University Press of Florida, 2009), 166; Alexander, *Ambiguous Lives: Free Women of Color in Rural Georgia, 1789–1879*, 194. W. E. B. DuBois memorialized Adella Hunt Logan in his 1920 *Darkwater* as the "Princess of the Hither Isles," whose "pale-gold" face was as "beautiful as daybreak," and who, "very, very lonely, and full weary of the monotone of life," peered into a "chasm wide as earth from heaven," and "leapt." W. E. B. DuBois, *Darkwater: Voices from Within the Veil* (Project Gutenberg, 2005), accessed Aug. 9, 2016 at www.gutenberg .org/ebooks/15210.

66 William Edward Burghardt DuBois, *The Souls of Black Folk: Essays and Sketches*, 2nd ed. (Chicago: A. C. McClurg, 1903), 3.

67 As Du Bois explained, one could not "lightly cast off this enveloping and intriguing bond of love and affection" – particularly when his older sisters and brothers had already identified themselves as black. William Edward Burghardt DuBois, "The Significance of Henry Hunt," *Fort Valley High and Industrial School Bulletin* I, no. 2 (October 1940): 6–7.

68 DuBois, "Significance of Henry Hunt."

69 An 1863 graduate of Yale and a member of a solid middle-class New England family, Ware moved to Atlanta in 1866 as one of the more prominent "soldiers of light and love" intent on the uplift of former slaves. He stayed until his death nineteen years later. Ware lived poorly, especially while single, and devoted himself to the cause of black education. Hunt, as his colleague Frank Horne stated, "lit his torch at the white flame of the devotion of Asa Ware" – and became a professing Christian at the same time. Jacqueline Jones, *Soldiers of Light and Love: Northern Teachers and Georgia Blacks, 1865–1873* (Athens: University of Georgia Press, 1992), 33–34; Willard Range, *The Rise and Progress of Negro Colleges in Georgia, 1865–1949* (Athens: University of Georgia Press, 1951), 10; Horne, "Henry A. Hunt, Sixteenth Spingarn Medalist."

70 Fred R. van Hartesveldt, "'My Days of Labor': Georgia's Florence Johnson Hunt, an African American of Impressive Accomplishments," in *The Varieties of Women's Experiences: Portraits of Southern Women in the Post–Civil War Century* (Gainesville: University Press of Florida, 2009), 174.

71   D. D. Bellamy, "Henry A. Hunt and Black Agricultural Leadership in the New South," *Journal of Negro History* 60, no. 4 (1975): 464–465; Ethridge, "Amazing Achievement of Prof. H. A. Hunt, Winner of Coveted Spingarn Medal, 1930."

72   Range, *Rise and Progress of Negro Colleges in Georgia, 1865–1949*, 182.

73   According to Willard Range, Davison helped inspire Jeanes's interest in black education, which led to the establishment of the Jeanes Fund and rural schools throughout the South and in Africa as well. See *Rise and Progress of Negro Colleges in Georgia, 1865–1949*, 182–183; on the Jeanes Fund, see also James D. Anderson, *The Education of Blacks in the South, 1860–1935* (Chapel Hill: University of North Carolina Press, 1988), 152–153; Bonnie J. Krause, "'We Did Move Mountains!' Lucy Saunders Herring, North Carolina Jeanes Supervisor and African American Educator, 1916–1968," *North Carolina Historical Review* 80, no. 2 (April 1, 2003): 188–212; Linda B. Pincham, "A League of Willing Workers: The Impact of Northern Philanthropy, Virginia Estelle Randolph and the Jeanes Teachers in Early Twentieth-Century Virginia," *Journal of Negro Education* 74, no. 2 (April 1, 2005): 112–123; Mildred Williams, *The Jeanes Story: A Chapter in the History of American Education, 1908–1968* (Oxford: University Press of Mississippi, 1979).

74   Anderson, *The Education of Blacks in the South, 1860–1935*, 115. Much of the account of FVHIS that follows relies on Anderson's, with additional information from Bellamy, *Light in the Valley: A Pictorial History of Fort Valley State College since 1895*.

75   Henry S. Enck, "Black Self-Help in the Progressive Era: The 'Northern Campaigns' of Smaller Southern Black Industrial Schools, 1900–1915," *Journal of Negro History* 61, no. 1 (Jan. 1, 1976): 74, doi:10.2307/3031534.

76   Anderson, *Education of Blacks in the South, 1860–1935*, 118.

77   For a fictionalized version of DuBois's vision, see "Of the Coming of John," in *The Souls of Black Folk: Essays and Sketches* (Chicago: H. C. McClurg and Co., 1903). See also James D. Anderson, "Northern Foundations and the Shaping of Southern Black Rural Education, 1902–1935," *History of Education Quarterly* 18, no. 4 (Dec. 1, 1978): 371–396, doi:10.2307/367710; Anderson, *Education of Blacks in the South, 1860–1935*; Enck, "Black Self-Help in the Progressive Era"; Donald Spivey, *Schooling for the New Slavery: Black Industrial Education, 1868–1915* (Trenton, NJ: Africa World Press, 2006); William H. Watkins, *The White Architects of Black Education: Ideology and Power in America, 1865–1954* (New York: Teachers College Press, 2001).

78   Franklin E. Frazier, "A Community School: Fort Valley High and Industrial School," *Southern Workman* 54 (Oct. 1925):46; Joseph T. Porter, "The Fort Valley High and Industrial School," *Colored American Magazine* 11 (June 1906): 423–425; J. H. Torbert, "The Fort Valley High and Industrial School," *Colored American Magazine* 12 (June 1907): 447–457; W. T. B. Williams, "Fort Valley High and Industrial School," *Southern Workman* 14 (Nov. 1910): 627–631.

79 Range, *The Rise and Progress of Negro Colleges in Georgia, 1865–1949*, 183.

80 Charlotte grew from 18,091 people in 1900 to 34,014 in 1910. Thomas W. Hanchett, "The Growth of Charlotte: A History," Charlotte-Mecklenburg Historic Landmarks Commission, accessed Dec. 18, 2014, at www.cmhpf .org/educhargrowth.htm.

81 Florence Johnson, "Memoirs of Twenty-Five Years," (c. 1938) quoted in van Hartesveldt, " 'My Days of Labor': Georgia's Florence Johnson Hunt, an African American of Impressive Accomplishments," 178; and Range, *Rise and Progress of Negro Colleges in Georgia, 1865–1949*, 184.

82 George Washington Carver, "A Gleam on the Distant Horizon," unpublished typescript, George Washington Carver Papers, Box 65, Tuskegee University Archives, Tuskegee, AL, quoted in Hersey, *My Work Is That of Conservation: An Environmental Biography of George Washington Carver*, 2011, 83.

83 Henry A. Hunt, "Letters to 'Dick' and W. B. Matthews," 1904, Fort Valley High and Industrial School Letters, William B. Matthews Papers, Archives Division, Auburn Avenue Research Library on African-American Culture and History, Atlanta-Fulton Public Library System.

84 Fort Valley High and Industrial School, *Work in the Black Belt of Southwest Georgia; Within a Radius of 50 Miles 200,000 Negroes Can Be Reached*, 1.

85 See the photographs at the Library of Congress's online exhibition at Library of Congress, "African American Photographs Assembled for 1900 Paris Exposition," accessed Aug. 9, 2016 at www.loc.gov/pictures/collection/ anedub/; see also David Levering Lewis and Deborah Willis, *A Small Nation of People: W. E. B. Du Bois and African American Portraits of Progress* (New York: Harper Paperbacks, 2005); Shawn Michelle Smith, *Photography on the Color Line: W. E. B. Du Bois, Race, and Visual Culture* (Durham, NC: Duke University Press Books, 2004).

86 For more on advertisements, see Hale, *Making Whiteness: The Culture of Segregation in the South, 1890–1940*, 121–198.

87 Range, *Rise and Progress of Negro Colleges in Georgia, 1865–1949*, 185.

88 Quoted in Donnie D. Bellamy, *Light in the Valley: A Pictorial History of Fort Valley State College since 1895*, 28.

89 "Negro Farmers' Congress," *Atlanta Constitution* (July 18, 1911), 2. The following year, the conference attracted some four hundred participants, 15 percent landowners, 52 percent renters, 27 percent sharecroppers, and 6 percent wage hands. "Along the Color Line," *Crisis* (June 1912), 62.

90 W. B. Mercier, "Extension Work among Negroes, 1920," *USDA Circular No. 190* (Washington, DC: Government Printing Office, 1921), 7.

91 "White Educators Address Negroes," *Atlanta Constitution* (Mar. 2, 1913), 14.

92 Jettie Irving Felps, *The Lost Tongues* (Corpus Christi, TX: Christian Triumph Press, 1945), 83. On Carver's approach to demonstration, see Hersey, *My Work Is That of Conservation: An Environmental Biography of George Washington Carver*, 114–119.

93 Quoted in Bellamy, *Light in the Valley: A Pictorial History of Fort Valley State College since 1895*, 34–35.

94 Ibid., 35.

95 Felps, *Lost Tongues*, 87.
96 "Urges Better Educational Advantages Should Be Given Negroes of South," *Atlanta Constitution* (Dec. 2, 1916), 6; "Would Help Both Races," *The Atlanta Constitution*, (Dec. 2, 1916), 6.
97 D. D. Bellamy, "Henry A. Hunt and Black Agricultural Leadership in the New South," 473.
98 Quoted in William Anthony Aery, "Nationwide Organization of Negroes," *Southern Workman* XLVIII, no. 9 (Sept. 1919), 430. See also Mary G. Rolinson, *Grassroots Garveyism: The Universal Negro Improvement Association in the Rural South, 1920–1927* (Chapel Hill: University of North Carolina Press, 2007), 168.
99 Ramla Bandele, "Pan-African Congress in 1921," *Global Mappings: A Political Atlas of the African Diaspora, 1900–1989* (Evanston, IL: Institute for Diasporic Studies, Northwestern University), accessed Jan. 9, 2015 at http://diaspora.northwestern.edu/; George M. Frederickson, *Black Liberation : A Comparative History of Black Ideologies in the United States and South Africa* (New York: Oxford University Press, 1995), 151. See also documents in the W. E. B. DuBois Papers such as "93 Delegates to the Pan-African Congress by Countries, 1921," and Pan African Association, "The Second Pan-African Congress, 1921," W. E. B. Du Bois Papers (MS 312), Special Collections and University Archives, University of Massachusetts Amherst Libraries, accessed Aug. 9, 2016 at http://credo.library.umass.edu/view/collection/mums312.
100 Henry A. Hunt, "Opening Address," *Atlanta University Bulletin* II, no. 61 (November 1925): 7.
101 Ibid., 8, 9, 12.
102 For the outlines of the Washington-DuBois debate, see the special issue of *The Crisis*, starting with Charles P. Henry, "Who Won the Great Debate-Booker T. Washington or W.E.B. DuBois?," *The Crisis*, no. 2 (1992): 12–22. See also Mark Bauerlein, "Washington, Du Bois, and the Black Future," *The Wilson Quarterly (1976-)* 28, no. 4 (October 1, 2004): 74–86; Mark Bauerlein, "Booker T. Washington and W.E.B. Du Bois: The Origins of a Bitter Intellectual Battle," *The Journal of Blacks in Higher Education*, no. 46 (December 1, 2004): 106–14, doi:10.2307/4133693; Pero Gaglo Dagbovie, "Exploring a Century of Historical Scholarship on Booker T. Washington," *Journal of African American History* 92, no. 2 (Spring 2007): 239–64; Louis R. Harlan, *Booker T. Washington; the Making of a Black Leader, 1856–1901* (New York: Oxford University Press, 1972); Louis R. Harlan, *Booker T. Washington: The Wizard of Tuskegee, 1901–1915* (New York: Oxford University Press, 1983); Manning Marable, "History, Liberalism, and the Black Radical Tradition," *Radical History Review*, no. 71 (Spring 1998): 19; Jan Miller, "Annotated Bibliography of the Washington-Dubois Controversy," *Journal of Black Studies* 25, no. 2 (December 1, 1994): 250–72, doi:10.1177/002193479402500208; Jacqueline M. Moore, *Booker T. Washington, W.E.B. Du Bois, and the Struggle for Racial Uplift* (Lanham, MD: Rowman & Littlefield, 2003); David Sehat, "The Civilizing Mission of Booker T. Washington."

103 Frank S. Horne, "I Am Initiated into the Negro Race," *Opportunity* (May 1928), 136. Horne was alluding to H. L. Mencken's infamous takedown of the Deep South, "The Sahara of the Bozart," first published in 1917. See Mencken, "The Sahara of the Bozart," in *The American Scene: A Reader*, ed. Huntington Cairns (New York: Alfred A. Knopf, 1920), 157–68.

104 Ibid., 137.

105 Lena Horne lived with Frank Horne from 1927 to 1929. In 1933, she began performing in New York City's Cotton Club; in 1942 she began appearing in MGM films.

106 Frank Horne, "Letter from Frank Horne to W. E. B. Du Bois," June 3, 1930, W. E. B. Du Bois Papers (MS 312), Special Collections and University Archives, University of Massachusetts Amherst Libraries, accessed Aug. 8, 2016 at http://oubliette.library.umass.edu/view/full/mums312-b185-i402. In 1929, Horne published a second round of his poem, "Letters Found near a Suicide," in which he included one addressed "To Henry," which read in part: "You and I have studied / Together / The knowledge of the ages / And lived the life of Science / Matching for discovery -- / And yet / In a trice / With a small explosion / Of this little machine / In my hand / I shall know / All / That Aristotle, Newton, Lavoisier, and Galileo / Could not determine / In their entire / Lifetimes ... / And the joke of it is, / Henry, / That I have beat you to it.... ." Frank S. Horne, "More Letters Found Near a Suicide," *The Crisis* 37.1 (December 1929): 413. See also Frank Horne, *Haverstraw* (London: P. Breman, 1963).

107 Horne, "Henry A. Hunt, Sixteenth Spingarn Medalist."

108 Ibid.

109 Willie Snow Ethridge, "Amazing Achievement of Prof. H. A. Hunt, Winner of Coveted Springarn Medal, 1930," *Atlanta Constitution* (July 6, 1930), 13A.

110 Ibid. In 1935, blacks worked 61,681 acres on 772 farms in Houston County – and owned about 10 percent (7,081 acres (11.4%) on 70 farms (9.1%). In Peach County they owned 1,874 acres on 25 farms (5.1%), out of 10,027 acres (18.7%) of 492 farms that they operated. Together, blacks of the two counties owned just 12 percent of the land they farmed and only 7.3 percent of the farms. See Asa H. Gordon, *The Georgia Negro: A History* (Reprint Co., 1937), 236. On black landownership in the South, see Schultz, *Rural Face of White Supremacy: Beyond Jim Crow*, 45–56; Loren Schweninger, *Black Property Owners in the South, 1790–1915* (Urbana: University of Illinois Press, 1990); Adrienne Petty, *Standing Their Ground: Small Farmers in North Carolina since the Civil War* (New York: Oxford University Press, 2013).

111 H. A. Hunt, "Staying on the Farm," *Fort Valley Message* III, no. 1 (October 1930), 4.

112 "Staying on the Farm," *Fort Valley Message* vol. III, no. 1 (October 1930), 4.

113 Horne, "Henry A. Hunt, Sixteenth Spingarn Medalist."

114 Homer J. Avera, letter to Richard B. Russell, Sept. 20, 1965, in Subgroup C. series VI. Box 90, folder 7, Richard B. Russell Jr. Papers, Richard

B. Russell Library for Political Research and Studies, University of Georgia Libraries, Athens.

115 "Denmark's Co-Operative Movement Wins Praise of Professor H. A. Hunt," *Atlanta Constitution* (Oct. 6, 1931), 6.

116 "Service for Negro Farmers," *New York Times* (Nov. 8, 1933). Morgenthau almost immediately left to take over the U.S. Treasury.

117 Eben Miller, *Born along the Color Line: The 1933 Amenia Conference and the Rise of a National Civil Rights Movement* (New York: Oxford University Press, 2012), 135–136.

118 William Edward Burghardt DuBois and Ira De Augustine Reid, "Letter to Henry Morganthau," Aug. 30, 1933, W. E. B. Du Bois Papers (MS 312), Special Collections and University Archives, University of Massachusetts Amherst Libraries, accessed November 26, 2014 at http://oubliette.library .umass.edu/view/pageturn/mums312-b068-i104/#page/1/mode/1up.

119 Jesse O. Thomas, "Urban League Weekly Bulletin," *Atlanta Constitution* (January 20, 1935).

120 See, for example, Stuart Cohen, *The Likes of Us: America in the Eyes of the Farm Security Administration* (Jaffrey, NH: David R. Godine Publisher, 2009);Jess Gilbert, "Eastern Urban Liberals and Midwestern Agrarian Intellectuals: Two Group Portraits of Progressives in the New Deal Department of Agriculture," *Agricultural History* 74, no. 2 (April 1, 2000): 162–180; Jess Gilbert, *Planning Democracy: Agrarian Intellectuals and the Intended New Deal*, Yale Agrarian Studies (New Haven, CT: Yale University Press, 2015); Jess Gilbert and Carolyn Howe, "Beyond 'State vs. Society': Theories of the State and New Deal Agricultural Policies," *American Sociological Review* 56, no. 2 (Apr. 1, 1991): 204–220, doi:10.2307/2095780; Linda Gordon, *Dorothea Lange: A Life Beyond Limits* (New York: W.W. Norton, 2010); Jason Michael Manthorne, "As You Sow Culture, Agriculture, and the New Deal" (Ph.D., University of Georgia, 2013); Tore Carl Olsson, "Agrarian Crossings: The American South, Mexico, and the Twentieth-Century Remaking of the Rural World" (University of Georgia, 2013); Sarah T Phillips, *This Land, This Nation: Conservation, Rural America, and the New Deal* (New York: Cambridge University Press, 2007); Anne Whiston Spirn, *Daring to Look: Dorothea Lange's Photographs and Reports from the Field* (Chicago: University of Chicago Press, 2008).

121 Jack Temple Kirby, *Rural Worlds Lost: The American South, 1920–1960* (Baton Rouge: Louisiana State University Press, 1987), 60.

122 Ibid., 63–68; Pete Daniel, *Breaking the Land: The Transformation of Cotton, Tobacco, and Rice Cultures since 1880* (Urbana: University of Illinois Press, 1985), ch. 8.

123 Frank S. Horne, "Letter to W. E. B. Du Bois," Feb. 24, 1934, W. E. B. Du Bois Papers (MS 312), Special Collections and University Archives, University of Massachusetts Amherst Libraries, accessed November 16, 2014 at http://oubliette.library.umass.edu/view/full/mums312-b070-i426; Frank S. Horne, "Letter to W. E. B. Du Bois, June 15, 1934," June 15, 1934, W. E. B. Du Bois Papers (MS 312), Special Collections and University Archives,

University of Massachusetts Amherst Libraries, accessed November 16, 2014 at http://credo.library.umass.edu/view/full/mums312-b070-i431; Frank S. Horne, "Letter to W. E. B. Du Bois," Feb. 4, 1935, W. E. B. Du Bois Papers (MS 312), Special Collections and University Archives, University of Massachusetts Amherst Libraries, accessed November 16, 2014 at http://credo.library.umass.edu/view/full/mums312-b074-i339.

124   Frank Horne, "The Industrial School of the South," *Opportunity*, May 1935, 136.

125   Ibid.

126   Ibid., 137.

127   Ibid.

128   Ibid., 139.

129   Frank S. Horne, "The Industrial School of the South: A Program for the Future," *Opportunity* (June 1935), 180.

130   Ibid., 181.

131   Frank S. Horne, " 'Dog House' Education," *Journal of Negro Education* 5, no. 3 (July 1, 1936): 360, 364, doi:10.2307/2292108.

132   Robert Zabawa and Tash Hargrove, "Flint River Farms Resettlement Community," *New Georgia Encyclopedia*, October 27, 2015, accessed Aug. 9, 2016 at www.georgiaencyclopedia.org/articles/history-archaeology/flint-river-farms-resettlement-community.

133   R. W. Hudgens, memorandum to R. G. Tugwell, May 25, 1936, National Archives and Records Administration. I received these documents from the late Jason Manthorne and do not have a precise locator. They seem to be from Record Group 96, Farmers Home Administration.

134   Fort Valley citizens, telegram to R. G. Tugwell, July 2, 1936, in National Archives and Records Administration, Record Group 96.

135   W. W. Alexander, letter to Walter E. Packard, Mar. 9, 1937. National Archives and Records Administration, Record Group 96.

136   Donald L Grant and Jonathan Grant, *The Way It Was in the South: The Black Experience in Georgia* (Secaucus, NJ: Carol, 1993), 349–350.

137   "Ham and Egg Show," *Life* (Mar. 22, 1943), 20–21.

138   Ibid.

139   Raper, *Preface to Peasantry: A Tale of Two Black Belt Counties*, 107; "Roosevelt and Hitler," *The Peachite* Vol. 2, No. 2, Folk Festival Number (March 1944), 5, Accessed Dec. 12, 2011 at http://memory.loc.gov/cgi-bin/query/r?ammem/ftvbib:@field(DOCID+@lit(msso59)).

140   "Ham and Egg Show," *Life* (Mar. 22, 1943), 21. On the OPA's role during World War II, see Meg Jacobs, *Pocketbook Politics: Economic Citizenship in Twentieth-Century America* (Princeton, NJ: Princeton University Press, 2005), 179–220.

141   Jacobs, *Pocketbook Politics*, 180.

142   Paul Warwick, "Ham and Egg Show Again Big Success," *Atlanta Constitution* (Mar. 11, 1945), 4.

143   The Superior Service Award was the USDA's second highest honor, which had, prior to 1951, been given to only two African Americans. Jessie Parkhurst Guzman, Lewis W. Jones, and Woodrow Hall, eds., *Negro Year*

Book: A Review of Events Affecting Negro Life (New York: Tuskegee Institute, 1952), 374 and plate XV, accessed Aug. 9, 2016 at http://archive .org/details/negroyearbook52tuskrich.

144 William Edward Burghardt DuBois, "Letter to Florence Hunt," Oct. 6, 1938, W. E. B. Du Bois Papers (MS 312, Special Collections and University Archives, University of Massachusetts Amherst Libraries, accessed Aug. 9, 2016 at http://oubliette.library.umass.edu/view/full/mums312-b085-i419.

145 "Balm in Gilead," *Folk Songs of the American Negro*, vol. I (1907), no. 31, accessed Dec. 5, 2014 at www.hymnary.org/hymn/FSAN107/31.

146 "Beloved Fort Valley Woman Passes Sunday," *Fort Valley Leader-Tribune* (Aug. 3, 1939), 1.

147 J. R. Murray, "Jerusalem the Golden," *New Christian Hymn and Tune Book* (Cincinnati, OH: Fillmore Brothers, 1882), no. 614, accessed Dec. 5, 2014, at http://www.hymnary.org/hymn/NCHT1882/614.

148 This is a point made more fully by Mark Schultz, *The Rural Face of White Supremacy: Beyond Jim Crow*, 9–11.

149 This is a story all too well evidenced in Daniel, *Dispossession: Discrimination against African American Farmers in the Age of Civil Rights.*

7 UNDER THE TREES

1 On the role of the federal government as labor padrone, see Cindy Hahamovitch, *The Fruits of Their Labor: Atlantic Coast Farmworkers and the Making of Migrant Poverty, 1870–1945* (Chapel Hill: University of North Carolina Press, 1997); Cindy Hahamovitch, *No Man's Land: Jamaican Guestworkers in America and the Global History of Deportable Labor*, Politics and Society in Twentieth-Century America (Princeton, NJ: Princeton University Press, 2011).

2 Jason Sokol, *There Goes My Everything: White Southerners in the Age of Civil Rights, 1945–1975* (New York: Alfred A. Knopf, 2006), 10.

3 The literature on the civil rights movement is vast, but for a sampling of that which deals with rural life in the South, see Charles S. Aiken, *The Cotton Plantation South since the Civil War*, Creating the North American Landscape (Baltimore: Johns Hopkins University Press, 2003); Charles M. Payne, *I've Got the Light of Freedom: The Organizing Tradition and the Mississippi Freedom Struggle* (Berkeley: University of California Press, 1995); Mark Schultz, *The Rural Face of White Supremacy: Beyond Jim Crow* (Urbana: University of Illinois Press, 2007); Sokol, *There Goes My Everything*. This chapter joins other recent calls to trace the environmental threads in the civil rights movement. It was a struggle not just over ideals and rights but also place, pollution, and dirt. See Robert D. Bullard, *Dumping in Dixie: Race, Class, and Environmental Quality*, 3rd ed. (Boulder, CO: Westview Press, 2000); Pete Daniel, *Dispossession: Discrimination against African American Farmers in the Age of Civil Rights* (Chapel Hill: The University of North Carolina Press, 2013); Mark Fiege, *The Republic of Nature: An Environmental History of the United States*, ed. William Cronon

(Seattle: University of Washington Press, 2013), 318–357; Eileen McGurty, *Transforming Environmentalism: Warren County, PCBs, and the Origins of Environmental Justice* (New Brunswick, NJ: Rutgers University Press, 2009); Ellen Griffith Spears, *Baptized in PCBs: Race, Pollution, and Justice in an All-American Town* (Chapel Hill: The University of North Carolina Press, 2014); Ellen Griffith Spears, *The Newtown Story: One Community's Fight for Environmental Justice* (Atlanta: Center for Democratic Renewal and Newtown Florist Club, 1998).

4 Inez Parker Cumming, "Sweet with Bitter: Georgia's Peach," *The Georgia Review* 2, no. 4 (December 1, 1948): 484.

5 The most famous of these strikes was the Wheatland hop riot in 1913. See Cletus E. Daniel, *Bitter Harvest, a History of California Farmworkers, 1870–1941* (Berkeley: University of California Press, 1982); Carey McWilliams, *Factories in the Field: The Story of Migratory Farm Labor in California* (Boston: Little, Brown and Company, 1939), 152–158; David Vaught, *Cultivating California: Growers, Specialty Crops, and Labor, 1875–1920* (Baltimore: Johns Hopkins University Press, 1999), 130–142. For similar stories among eastern farmworkers, see Hahamovitch, *The Fruits of Their Labor: Atlantic Coast Farmworkers and the Making of Migrant Poverty, 1870–1945*, especially pp. 3–7.

6 James Noble Gregory, *The Southern Diaspora: How the Great Migrations of Black and White Southerners Transformed America* (Chapel Hill: University of North Carolina Press, 2005), 18.

7 Steve Oney, "Peaches: Picking through Facts and Fantasies about Georgia's Famous Fruit," *The Atlanta Journal and Constitution Magazine* (July 1, 1979), 10–12; Nick Strickland, interview with the author, July 9, 2009, Fort Valley, Georgia; Tom Okie, "Georgia Fuzz: Weather, Workers, and the World's Peach Paradise, Part I," *Southern Foodways Alliance Blog*, July 13, 2015, accessed Aug. 3, 2016 at www.southernfoodways.org/georgia-fuzz-weather-workers-and-the-worlds-peach-paradise-part-ii/; Tom Okie, "Georgia Fuzz: Weather, Workers, and the World's Peach Paradise, Part II," *Southern Foodways Alliance Blog*, July 20, 2015, accessed Aug. 3, 2016, at www.southernfoodways.org/georgia-fuzz-weather-workers-and-the-worlds-peach-paradise-part-ii/.

8 Robert Dickey, Jr., interview with the author, July 28, 2008.

9 Nick Strickland, interview with the author, July 9, 2009, Fort Valley, Georgia.

10 T. G. Standing to Conrad Taeuber, 12 May 1942, box 243, Farm Labor, Louisiana, General Correspondence, 1941–1946, Records of the Bureau of Agricultural Economics, quoted in Pete Daniel, "Going among Strangers: Southern Reactions to World War II," *The Journal of American History* 77 (December 1990), 889.

11 Jason Morgan Ward, "'Nazis Hoe Cotton': Planters, POWs, and the Future of Farm Labor in the Deep South," *Agricultural History* 81 (Fall 2007), 471–472. See also Robert D. Billinger, *Hitler's Soldiers in the Sunshine State: German Pows in Florida*, The Florida History and Culture Series (Gainesville: University Press of Florida, 2000); Lewis H. Carlson, *We Were Each Other's Prisoners: An Oral History of World War II American and*

German Prisoners of War (New York: Basic Books, 1997); Louis E. Keefer, *Italian Prisoners of War in America, 1942–1946: Captives or Allies?* (New York: Praeger, 1992); Allen V. Koop, *Stark Decency: German Prisoners of War in a New England Village* (Hanover, NH: University Press of New England, 1988); Michael R. Waters, *Lone Star Stalag: German Prisoners of War at Camp Hearne* (College Station: Texas A & M University Press, 2004).

12   John S. Wood, to Provost Marshal General, 25 April 1945, Records of the Provost Marshal General, Record Group 389, National Archives, College Park, MD.

13   Ward, "'Nazis Hoe Cotton,'" 471–472.

14   Ibid., 471.

15   Peach County Extension Agent, *Annual Report* (1944), reprinted in Virginia Greene, "Survey of Peach County and Fort Valley Georgia," a Term Paper for Huntingdon College. Thomas Public Library Local History Room, Fort Valley, Georgia.

16   Earl L. Edwards, Inspection, September 10, 1943, Records of the Provost Marshal General, Record Group 389, National Archives, College Park, MD.

17   Dewey Bateman, quoted in Willard Neal, "When Georgia Peaches Pay Off," *The Atlanta Journal Magazine* (July 11, 1948), 22.

18   Oliver Bateman II, interview with author, 22 February 2008, Macon, Georgia.

19   Ibid.

20   Oliver Bateman, interview with the author, July 29, 2008, Macon, GA; Paul Spiekermann to Dewey Bateman, January 14, 1948, Oliver Bateman Private Collection. I cannot say for certain that Spieckermann was the carpenter Bateman saw during his visit home, but the details fit.

21   Friedrich Drüner to Dewey Bateman, February 23, 1947, Oliver Bateman Private Collection.

22   Matthias Jakobs to Dewey Bateman, January 21, 1947, Oliver Bateman Private Collection.

23   Julius Winter to Dewey Bateman, January 16, 1946, Oliver Bateman Private Collection. Bateman may or may not have shared his fascination with beetles and reptiles, but in any event he sent Winter a C.A.R.E. package.

24   Matthias Jakobs to Dewey Bateman, January 21, 1947; Julius Winter to Dewey Bateman, January 16, 1946; Rûdolf Bergmaier to Dewey Bateman, March 29, 1947, Oliver Bateman Private Collection.

25   Franz Reitbaur to Dewey Bateman, September 10, 1947, Oliver Bateman Private Collection.

26   Dewey Bateman, quoted in Neal, "When Georgia Peaches Pay Off," 22.

27   David Craig Griffith, *American Guestworkers: Jamaicans and Mexicans in the U.S. Labor Market*, Rural Studies Series (University Park: Pennsylvania State University Press, 2006), 32. See also Hahamovitch, *No Man's Land: Jamaican Guestworkers in America and the Global History of Deportable Labor*.

28   See Hahamovitch, *The Fruits of Their Labor: Atlantic Coast Farmworkers and the Making of Migrant Poverty, 1870–1945*.

29   While wheat and other crops yielded easily to mechanical planting and har-
     vesting, cotton was more complicated. Full mechanization had long been
     slowed by a harvest bottleneck: since mechanical harvesters only worked
     well in the arid flatlands of Texas and California, cotton farmers needed
     hand labor for their harvests; as long as they needed labor for the harvest,
     there was little point in mechanizing the rest of the operation. The process
     did not kick into high gear until after World War II. See Melissa Walker,
     "Shifting Boundaries: Race Relations in the Rural Jim Crow South," in
     African American Life in the Rural South, 1900–1950, 107.

30   Tractors, of course, are not the only measure of mechanization, but they are
     one of the only constants in the agricultural census from 1920 through 1978.
     U.S. Census of Agriculture (Washington: GPO, 1920–1978).

31   Craig Heinicke and Wayne A. Grove, "'Machinery Has Completely Taken
     Over': The Diffusion of the Mechanical Cotton Picker, 1949–1964,"
     Journal of Interdisciplinary History 39:1 (Summer, 2008), 70, 72. See also
     Donald Holley, "Mechanical Cotton Picker," EH.Net Encyclopedia, ed.
     Robert Whaples (16 June 2003), accessed Oct. 16, 2009 at http://eh.net/
     encyclopedia/article/holley.cottonpicker.

32   McWilliams, *Factories in the Field; the Story of Migratory Farm Labor in
     California*, 134; Hahamovitch, *The Fruits of Their Labor: Atlantic Coast
     Farmworkers and the Making of Migrant Poverty, 1870–1945*, 200. For
     more on California farmworkers, see Daniel, *Bitter Harvest, a History of
     California Farmworkers, 1870–1941*; Matt García, *A World of Its Own:
     Race, Labor, and Citrus in the Making of Greater Los Angeles, 1900–
     1970*, Studies in Rural Culture (Chapel Hill: University of North Carolina
     Press, 2001); Don Mitchell, *The Lie of the Land: Migrant Workers and the
     California Landscape* (Minneapolis: University of Minnesota Press, 1996);
     Douglas Cazaux Sackman, *Orange Empire: California and the Fruits of
     Eden* (Berkeley: University of California Press, 2005), 123–153; Steven Stoll,
     *The Fruits of Natural Advantage: Making the Industrial Countryside in
     California* (Berkeley: University of California Press, 1998), 124–154; for a
     counternarrative to worker exploitation, see Vaught, *Cultivating California:
     Growers, Specialty Crops, and Labor, 1875–1920*.

33   John Mebane, "Labor Deficiency Perils Year's Crops," *The Atlanta Journal*
     (June 22, 1947), 10-B. On the BWITLP, see Hahamovitch, *No Man's
     Land*.

34   Louis Kyriakoudes, "'Lookin' for Better All the Time': Rural Migration
     and Urbanization in the South 1900–1950," in *African American Life in
     the Rural South, 1900–1950*, ed. R. Douglas Hurt (Columbia: University
     of Missouri Press, 2011), 26; Joseph H. Baird, "Is Georgia 'Peached Out'?"
     Atlanta Constitution Magazine (June 6, 1971), 36; Steve Oney, "Peaches:
     Picking through Facts and Fantasies about Georgia's Famous Fruit," 10.
     Census statistics reveal a dramatic decrease in the number of tenants in the
     postwar South: from 942,655 white and 506,638 black tenants in 1939 to
     118,153 and 18,235, respectively, in 1969. See Pete Daniel, *Breaking the
     Land: The Transformation of Cotton, Tobacco, and Rice Cultures since 1880*
     (Urbana: University of Illinois Press, 1985), 248.

35 At 70,000 people in 1950, Macon was the largest city in middle Georgia and the fourth largest in the state. Bibb County was 35% black in 1950.

36 Dickey, interview with the author, July 28, 2008.

37 Bateman, interviews with the author, February 22, 2008 and July 29, 2008.

38 R. M. (Jack) Smith, quoted in Hugh Park, "Red-Gold Peaches Big for Picking," *The Atlanta Journal* (July 22, 1965), 1.

39 W. B. Wood, quoted in Park, "Red-Gold Peaches Big for Picking," 23.

40 Bill Wilson, quoted in Baird, "Is Georgia 'Peached Out'?" 34–35.

41 Bateman, interview with the author, July 29, 2008.

42 Rosa Mae Lucas and Anola Jordan, quoted in Rob Levin, "Georgia's Peach Crop Hot Prospect for Pickers," *The Atlanta Constitution* (June 20, 1984), 7A.

43 Henry Luce founded Blue Bird Bus Company in 1932, using peach packing sheds to put together bus bodies. The company started small but grew rapidly. RAFB (originally the Georgia Air Depot) was built in 1942–1943 and has employed around 20,000 most years since then. Woolfolk Chemical manufactured and sold fungicides and pesticides to peach growers in the 1910s and 1920s, but expanded significantly in the post World War II era. See Bernard Palmer, *Wings of Blue Bird* (Fort Valley, GA: Blue Bird Body Company, 1977); William P. Head, "Robins Air Force Base," *New Georgia Encyclopedia*, August 20, 2014, accessed Aug. 9, 2016 at www .georgiaencyclopedia.org/articles/government-politics/robins-air-force-base; E.F. Savage, "History of the Georgia Peach Industry" (Griffin, GA, 1984), 125.

44 Hal Lowman, interview with the author, July 20, 2009, Fort Valley, Georgia.

45 Ibid.

46 Marvin Crafter, quoted in Hollis R. Towns, "The Enduring Peach: Flourishing Fruit Still Packs Punch as a Symbol," *The Atlanta Journal-Constitution* (August 15, 1993), D8.

47 Frank S. Horne, "The Industrial School of the South: A Program for the Future," *Opportunity* (June 1935), 181.

48 Lawrence J. Hanks, *The Struggle for Black Political Empowerment in Three Georgia Counties* (Knoxville: University of Tennessee Press, 1990), 97–99.

49 Citizenship Education Commission, *Information That Black Folk Should Know* I, no. 3 (August 28, 1969), 1–2, copy in possession of author. Thanks to Zachary Young for sharing this document and his interview with his grandfather Marshall Young.

50 Ibid.

51 Marshall Young, interview by Zachary Young, Fort Valley, Georgia, March 12, 2010. Partial transcript in possession of the author. Young's Superfoods was also known as Young's Super Market.

52 Hanks, *The Struggle for Black Political Empowerment in Three Georgia Counties*, 98.

53 Ibid., 100.

288   *Notes to Pages 191–195*

54 Richard J. Morse, *Peachville at Mid-Century: A Descriptive Analysis of the Negro Community* (Fort Valley, GA: The Fort Valley State College, 1969), 40–42.
55 Lois Banks Hollis, "The Political Orientation of Blacks in Three Bi-Racial Predominantly Rural Counties in Georgia: The Cases of Brooks, Burke, and Peach Counties" (PhD diss., Atlanta University: August 1975), 167.
56 CEC, *Information That Black Folk Should Know*, 2.
57 Donnie D. Bellamy, "Whites Sue for Desegregation in Georgia: The Fort Valley State College Case," *The Journal of Negro History* 64, no. 4 (October 1, 1979): 319.
58 Wilbur K. Avera v. W. Lee Burge, et al., Civil Action Number 2732, "Complaint," U.S. District Court, Middle District of Georgia, Macon, 4–5, quoted in Ibid., 320.
59 Bellamy, "Whites Sue for Desegregation in Georgia," 320, 323.
60 Ibid., 335.
61 Ed Dunbar, discussed later in this chapter, is obviously an exception to this generalization.
62 H. G. Riggins to James P. Mitchell, 20 February 1959, Series III: Miscellaneous File, Box 62, John Leonard Pilcher Papers, Richard B. Russell Library for Political Research and Studies, University of Georgia Libraries, Athens.
63 Dickey, interview with the author, July 28, 2008.
64 Bateman, interview with the author, February 22, 2008.
65 John C. Datt, "National Legislation of Interest to Peach Growers," *National Peach Council Proceedings* (February 20–22, 1956, Cairo, IL), 47.
66 Resolutions adopted, *National Peach Council Proceedings* (18–21 February 1968, Charleston, SC), 11.
67 Oscar Jaynes, "Labor and Labor Management," *National Peach Council Proceedings* (February 25–28, 1973, Washington, DC), 104.
68 Gwen Bulman, "Woodrow Cash, Sons and Daughter," *National Peach Council Proceedings* (February 23–26, 1975, Myrtle Beach, SC), 113; and in the same year, "H. T. and L. F. Holmes, Sun Ridge Peaches: A Family-Oriented Peach Factory," 115.
69 Antonio G. Mendez, "How to Discourage Union Organization," *National Peach Council Proceedings* (February 16–19, 1981, Phoenix, AZ), 77.
70 Al Pearson, quoted in Oney, "Peaches," 14.
71 Bateman, interview with the author, July 29, 2008.
72 Dickey, interview with the author, July 28, 2008.
73 "Carolina Migrant Workers Speak out," *The Atlanta Journal-Constitution* (July 9, 1990), B-2; Frank Heflin, "'Sickest of the Sick ... Poorest of the Poor'," *The Atlanta Journal-Constitution* (August 19, 1991), A-3. Diane Alters, "Crack Lures, Holds Workers to S.C. Camp," *The Boston Globe* (August 21, 1989), 1; Peter T. Kilborn, "Days of Fruit Tramp's Painful Harvest Fade," *The New York Times* (July 14, 1990), 1; Ron Chepesiuk, "Peonage for Peach Pickers," *The Progressive* 56, no. 12 (December 1992), 22–24.
74 Other pest problems included: Peach Yellows, which dramatically weakened the Atlantic coast industry in the late nineteenth century; Peach Rosette;

Phony Peach Disease, which left dwarfed trees that produced unmarketable fruit and emerged periodically in the Southeast; oriental fruit moths, peachtree borers, and plant/stink bugs, and ring and root-knot nematodes. See J.E. Adaskaveg et al., "Diseases of Peach Caused by Fungi and Fungal-like Organisms: Biology, Epidemiology and Management"; D.F. Ritchie et al., "Diseases Caused by Prokaryotes – Bacteria and Phytoplasms"; M. Cambra et al., "Viruses and Viroids of Peach Trees"; D.L. Horton et al., "Insects and Mites"; A.P. Nyczepir and D. Esmenjaud, "Nematodes"; all in Desmond R. Layne and Daniele Bassi, *The Peach: Botany, Production and Uses* (Cambridge, MA: CABI, 2008), 352–535.

75 A. B. Groves, "Root Diseases of Deciduous Fruit Trees," *Botanical Review* 24, no. 1 (January 1, 1958): 29–30.

76 Ibid., 26; E. F. Savage, et al., "Clitobyte Root Rot – A Disease of Economic Importance in Georgia Peach Orchards," *American Society for Horticultural Science Proceedings* 64 (1954): 81–86. E. F. Savage had a rather jaundiced opinion of the panic surrounding PTSL in his unpublished "History of the Georgia Peach Industry," 117–119.

77 Groves, "Root Diseases of Deciduous Fruit Trees," 30–31.

78 Ibid., 33, 36; Z. A. Patrick, "The Peach Replant Problem in Ontario: II. Toxic Substances from Microbial Decomposition Products of Peach Root Residues," *Canadian Journal of Botany*, 33(5) (1955): 461–486; and V. E. Prince, et al., "Effect of Soil Treatments in a Greenhouse Study of the Peach Replant Problem," *American Society for Horticultural Science Proceedings*, 65 (1955): 139–148.

79 Karen Kalmar Kelly, "Richard B. Russell, Democrat from Georgia," (Ph.D., University of North Carolina, 1979), 284. For his part, Russell had played a key role in the legislative maneuvering that gave Fort Valley its county seat status, in 1925, when Peach County was created. See the correspondence between Russell and W. H. Harris, Homer J. Avera, and others in the 1920s and 1930s, particularly 1932. Subgroup D: Winder Papers, Box V76, Folder 6, Richard B. Russell, Jr. Papers, Richard B. Russell Library for Political Research and Studies, University of Georgia Libraries, Athens.

80 William J. Wilson to Charles F. Brannan, December 19, 1929; Arthur H. Surprise to Charles F. Brannan, February 15, 1950, Subgroup C, Series VIII: Official, Box 81, Richard B. Russell, Jr. Papers, Richard B. Russell Library for Political Research and Studies, University of Georgia Libraries, Athens.

81 Richard B. Russell, Jr. to William J. Wilson, December 23, 1949, Subgroup C, Series VIII: Official, Box 81, Richard B. Russell, Jr. Papers, Richard B. Russell Library for Political Research and Studies, University of Georgia Libraries, Athens.

82 Georgia Peach Council, "A Proposal to Establish a U.S. Regional Tree Fruit and Nut Crops Laboratory for the Southeast," (January 1962), Series III: Miscellaneous File, Box 62, John Leonard Pilcher Papers, Richard B. Russell Library for Political Research and Studies, University of Georgia Libraries, Athens.

83 Ibid., 3–5.

84 Ibid., 6.
85 *Department of Agriculture and Related Agencies Appropriations for 1963: Hearing Before the Subcommittee of the Committee on Appropriations, United States Senate, Eighty-seventh Congress, Second Session*, March 1, 1962 (statement of Edgar L. Duke, Jr., President, Georgia Peach Council), 1018.
86 Georgia's farm population stood at 165,465 in 1954; by 1964, it was 83,366. The nonwhite tenant farmer population was at 27,429 in 1954; by 1964, it was only 5,062. See the USDA, 1964 Census of Agriculture, vol. 1, part 28, Georgia, Table 3, Farms and Acreage, by Color and Tenure of Operator, 1930–1964, p. 10, accessed Aug. 9, 2016 at http://usda.mannlib.cornell.edu/usda/AgCensusImages/1964/01/28/792/Table-03.pdf.
87 Richard M. Shapiro and Donald S. Safford, interview with Dr. C. L. Ellison, March 7, 1964, box 1, CFLID, USCCR, RG 453, NARA. Quoted in Daniel, *Dispossession: Discrimination against African American Farmers in the Age of Civil Rights*, 38.
88 *Department of Agriculture and Related Agencies Appropriations for 1963: Hearing Before the Subcommittee of the Committee on Appropriations, United States Senate, Eighty-seventh Congress, Second Session*, March 1, 1962 (statement of William J. Wilson), 1022.
89 Richard B. Russell, Jr., to Bennett Rigdon, October 17, 1962, Subgroup C, Series XV: General, Box 244, Richard B. Russell, Jr. Papers, Richard B. Russell Library for Political Research and Studies, University of Georgia Libraries, Athens; The bill authorizing the spending was the appropriations bill for 1963, PL 87–879, accessed Nov. 10, 2015 at www.gpo.gov/fdsys/pkg/STATUTE-76/pdf/STATUTE-76-Pg1203.pdf.
90 Edgar L. Duke, Jr., to Richard B. Russell, Jr., June 13, 1963, Subgroup C, Series XV: General, Box 85, Richard B. Russell, Jr. Papers, Richard B. Russell Library for Political Research and Studies, University of Georgia Libraries, Athens.
91 Some of his supporters acknowledged his "more serious and important work" directly. Editor of the local newspaper and state representative Daniel Grahl telegraphed: "Your interest and work for the farmers is greatly appreciated as well as your stand on Mississippi." Russell replied: "It is a sad day in the history of this country to see the guns of the Federal Government turned on the South, both figuratively and literally, as it seeks to implement the unconstitutional rulings of the Supreme Court." Perhaps recognizing that the winds were shifting, Russell crossed out his note to Grahl. Daniel K. Grahl to Richard B. Russell, Jr., October 15, 1962; Richard B. Russell, Jr. to Daniel K. Grahl, October 16, 1962; both in Subgroup C, Series XV: General, Box 244, Richard B. Russell, Jr. Papers, Richard B. Russell Library for Political Research and Studies, University of Georgia Libraries, Athens.
92 David Steigerwald, *The Sixties and the End of Modern America*, The St. Martin's Series in U.S. History (New York: St. Martin's Press, 1995), 17–18.
93 Gilbert C. Fite, *Richard B. Russell, Jr, Senator from Georgia*, Fred W. Morrison Series in Southern Studies, (Chapel Hill, NC: University of North Carolina Press, 1991), 400–401.

94 Collins, Frederic W. "Senator Russell 'in the Last Ditch': The Powerful Southern Lawmaker, Symbol of Civil-rights Opposition in the Senate, Is Staking All on the Outcome of the Current Battle." *New York Times* (October 20, 1963), sec. 16.

95 H. W. Fogle et al., *Peach Production East of the Rocky Mountains*, Agriculture Handbook 280 (Washington, DC: Agricultural Research Service, U.S. Department of Agriculture, 1965), accessed Aug. 8, 2016 at http://permanent.access.gpo.gov/gpo22282/CAT87208340.pdf. One of the first named rootstocks was Nemaguard, released in 1959 for its resistance to root-knot nematode.

96 D. F. Ritchie and C. N. Clayton, "Peach Tree Short Life: A Complex of Interacting Factors," *Plant Disease* 65, no. 6 (June 1981): 468.

97 Ibid.

98 Southern Regional Project S-97, "Development and Evaluation of Peach Rootstocks." See Ritchie and Clayton, "Peach Tree Short Life: A Complex of Interacting Factors," 468.

99 Ritchie and Clayton, "Peach Tree Short Life: A Complex of Interacting Factors," 468.

100 Ward Sinclair, "The Return of DBCP, a Classic Tale of Pesticide Regulation," *The Washington Post* (February 1, 1983).

101 Ibid.

102 T. G. Beckman et al., "History, Current Status and Future Potential of Guardian(TM) (BY520-9) Peach Rootstock," *Acta Horticulturae* 451 (1997): 251–258; W.R. Okie, interview with the author, September 2016. Tara Weaver, "A Guardian Angel for Peach Trees," *AgResearch* (October 1998), 10–11, accessed on Jan. 29, 2015, at https://www.ars.usda.gov/is/AR/archive/oct98/guard1098.htm.

103 On that longer history, see Tore Olsson, "Agrarian Crossings: The American South, Mexico, and the Twentieth-Century Remaking of the Rural World" (Ph.D. Dissertation, University of Georgia, 2013); and Julie Weise, *Corazón de Dixie: Mexicanos in the U.S. South since 1910* (Chapel Hill: University of North Carolina Press, 2015).

104 Bateman, interview with the author, February 22, 2008. The picking bag request probably reflected experience in Florida groves, where picking bags would have been standard equipment for citrus workers.

105 John D. Studstill and Laura Nieto-Studstill, "Hospitality and Hostility: Latin Immigrants in Southern Georgia," in *Latino Workers in the Contemporary South*, ed. Arthur D. Murphy, Colleen Blanchard, and Jennifer A. Hill (Athens: University of Georgia Press, 2001), 78.

106 Laurie Moses, "Chop Evans: Hot On Hydrocooling," *American Fruit Grower* (June 1992): 4.

107 Johnathan Burns, "Field of Dreams: Migrants No More, Hispanic Farm Workers Make Midstate Home," *The Macon Telegraph* (August 14, 1997), 1B.

108 Studstill and Nieto-Studstill, "Hospitality and Hostility," 79.

109 Ibid.

110 John Brown, quoted in Peter Applebome, "Georgia Harvester Is Fined $1 Million in Alien Smuggling," *The New York Times* (Feb. 8, 1992), 1; Arthur

Brice, "Action against 'Pillars of the Community' Shocks Residents," *The Atlanta Journal-Constitution* (Feb. 8, 1992), B5; Jeffry Scott, "Lane Is One of Georgia's Biggest Packing Companies," *The Atlanta Journal-Constitution* (Feb. 8, 1992), B5.

111 Jorge Durand, Douglas S. Massey, and Emilio A. Parrado, "The New Era of Mexican Migration to the United States," *The Journal of American History* 86 (Sept. 1999): para. 13.

112 Bill McGehee, quoted in David A. Goldberg, "Migrants' Boon, Farmers' Burden: Amnesty Law May Create Farm Labor Crisis," *The Atlanta Journal-Constitution* (July 31, 1989), A-4.

113 Durand et al., "The New Era of Mexican Migration to the United States," para. 19; Robert Carrazco, Jr., interview with the author, July 28, 2008, Musella, GA.

114 Johnathan Burns, "Field of Dreams," 1B.

115 Durand et al., "The New Era of Mexican Migration to the United States," para. 15.

116 Thomas P. Fischer, quoted in Deborah Scroggins, "INS Fines Georgia Firm $1.2 Million," The *Atlanta Journal-Constitution* (February 8, 1992), A1.

117 Ibid.

118 Fischer, quoted in Applebome, "Georgia Harvester Is Fined $1 Million in Alien Smuggling," 1.

119 Charles "Chop" Evans, quoted in Moses, "Chop Evans: Hot on Hydrocooling," 4.

120 Charles "Chop" Evans, quoted in Towns, "The Enduring Peach," D8.

121 Health, Education and Human Services Division, GAO, "H-2A Agricultural Guest Worker Program: Experiences of Individual Vidalia Onion Growers," B-28097, (September 10, 1998), 9.

122 Dickey, interview with the author, July 28, 2008.

123 Ibid.

124 Dickey, interview with the author, February 22, 2008; Statement of Chalmers R. Carr III, President Titan Peach Farms, January 28, 2004, in U.S. House, Committee on Agriculture, Temporary Guest Worker Proposals in the Agriculture Sector Hearing (CIS-NO: 2004-H161-7).

125 Carr Statement, January 28, 2004.

126 Jeffrey H. Cohen, *The Culture of Migration in Southern Mexico*, vol. 1 (Austin: University of Texas Press, 2004), 111, 121; Leon Fink, *The Maya of Morganton: Work and Community in the Nuevo New South* (Chapel Hill: University of North Carolina Press, 2003), 168–169; Griffith, *American Guestworkers*, chs. 3 and 4.

127 Griffith, *American Guestworkers*, 163.

128 *Juan Duque-Tovar et al., v. Georgia Growers Association et al.*, "Memorandum of Law in Support of Plaintiffs' Motion for Conditional Certification and for Court-Authorized Notice," Civil Action No. 1:03-CV-128-2 (WLS), U.S. District Court Middle Division of Georgia, Albany Division, (December 15, 2003), 15.

129 Angelo Surez, quoted in Towns, "The Enduring Peach," D8.

130 Robert Carrazco, interview with the author, July 28, 2008, Musella, GA.

131 Tony Barajas, quoted in Sally Scherer, "Taking root: one family's journey," *The Macon Telegraph* (August 6, 1995), 8E.
132 Bill McGehee, quoted in Jodi White and Sally Scherer, "'Invisible Work Force' Lacking Necessities," *The Macon Telegraph* (August 6, 1995), 9A.
133 Helen Hudson, quoted in Burns, "Field of Dreams," 1B. For more on this welcoming attitude, especially from religious middle Georgians, see Julie Wiese, Julie Meira Weise, *Corazón de Dixie: Mexicanos in the U.S. South since 1910*, especially pp. 120–178.
134 Carr Statement, January 28, 2004.
135 Fort Valley peach growers were also, in this sense, similar to Hancock County's power elite in the 1930s and 1940s. See Schultz, *The Rural Face of White Supremacy: Beyond Jim Crow.*
136 See Agricultural Research Service, *Effects of the March 1955 Freeze on Peach, Pecan, and Tung Trees in the South*, vol. 18, ARS 22 (Washington, DC: U.S. Dept. of Agriculture, 1955), accessed Aug. 9, 2016 at http://archive.org/details/effectsofmarch1918unit.
137 Edward Dunbar, interview with the author, July 15, 2009, Houston County, Georgia.
138 Ibid.
139 Sokol, *There Goes My Everything: White Southerners in the Age of Civil Rights, 1945–1975*, 5.
140 Edward Dunbar, interview with the author.
141 Julie Meira Weise, "Fighting for Their Place: Mexicans and Mexican Americans in the U.S. South, 1910–2008" (Ph.D., Yale University, 2009), 126. Weise has worked extensively with white migrant advocates and Mexican migrants in Fort Valley and develops this argument much more fully. See also her *Corazón de Dixie: Mexicanos in the U.S. South since 1910.*
142 Al Pearson, interview with the author, February 8, 2008.
143 Jenny Coyle, "Nova Scotia, Georgia Allies in Toxic Fight," *The Planet* 5.2 (March 1998) accessed Oct. 16, 2013 at www.sierraclub.org/planet/199803/toxics.html.
144 Region 4: Serving the Southeast US EPA, "Woolfolk Chemical Works, Inc. NPL Site Summary Page," Overview & Factsheets, accessed July 15, 2015, at www.epa.gov/region4/superfund/sites/npl/georgia/wolchemga.html; Environmental Background Information Center, "Analysis of Environmental Justice Issues in Peach County, Georgia" (State College, PA: Environmental Background Information Center, October 31, 2001), 4, accessed Aug. 9, 2016 at www.movementech.org/gis/pdf/fortvalleyrpt.pdf.
145 Vicki Breman, "Hazardous Waste in Georgia," *Southern Changes* 6, no. 4 (September 1984): 7–12; Environmental Background Information Center, "Analysis of Environmental Justice Issues in Peach County, Georgia."
146 US EPA, *Life After Superfund* (Fort Valley, GA), accessed July 9, 2015, at http://epa.gov/superfund/programs/recycle/info/aftersf.html. For more on pesticides, especially in the South, see Pete Daniel, *Toxic Drift: Pesticides*

and Health in the Post-World War II South, The Walter Lynwood Fleming Lectures in Southern History (Baton Rouge: Louisiana State University Press, 2005); and Frederick Rowe Davis, *Banned: A History of Pesticides and the Science of Toxicology* (New Haven, CT: Yale University Press, 2014).

147 US EPA, "Woolfolk Chemical Works, Inc. NPL Site Summary Page"; US EPA, "EPA Superfund Record of Decision: Woolfork Chemical Works, Inc.," Record of Decision (Fort Valley, GA, March 25, 1994), accessed July 9, 2015 at www.epa.gov/superfund/sites/rods/fulltext/r0494171.pdf; Cathy Alden, "All the Pretty Poisons," *Public Health*, Spring 1999, accessed July 9, 2015 at www.whsc.emory.edu/_pubs/ph/phspr99/poison.html.

148 For the Love Canal story, see Elizabeth D. Blum, *Love Canal Revisited: Race, Class, and Gender in Environmental Activism* (Lawrence: University Press of Kansas, 2011); Lois Marie Gibbs, *Love Canal and the Birth of the Environmental Health Movement* (Washington, D.C.: Island Press, 2011); Richard S. Newman, *Love Canal: A Toxic History from Colonial Times to the Present* (New York: Oxford University Press, 2016).

149 Environmental Protection Agency, Proceedings: Superfund Relocation Roundtable Meeting, Pensacola, FL, 2–4 May 1996 (December 1996), 7, 9.

150 Ibid., 9.

151 Coyle, "Nova Scotia, Georgia Allies in Toxic Fight."

152 Christina M. Wright, "BBQ Cookers, Eaters Gather in Fort Valley for ComSouth Hambone Jam," *Macon Telegraph and News*, September 8, 2012, accessed July 9, 2015 at www.macon.com/2012/09/08/2167910/bbq-cookers-eaters-gather-at-fort.html; "World's Largest Peach Cobbler – Georgia Peach Festival," accessed July 15, 2015, at www.gapeachfestival.com/story.cfm; Michael W. Pannell, "Georgia Peach Festival Concludes with Cobbler Gobbling," *Macon Telegraph and News* (June 14, 2014), accessed July 9, 2015 at www.macon.com/2014/06/14/3149590/georgia-peach-festival-concludes.html?sp=/99/100/&ihp=1.

153 US EPA, *Life After Superfund*.

154 Sarah Fay, "Marilynne Robinson, The Art of Fiction No. 198," *Paris Review* (Fall 2008), accessed July 9, 2015 at www.theparisreview.org/interviews/5863/the-art-of-fiction-no-198-marilynne-robinson.

CONCLUSION

1 Hubert Bond Owens, *Georgia's Planting Prelate, Including an Address on Horticulture at Macon, Georgia, in 1851, by the Rt. Rev. Stephen Elliott, Jr.* (Athens: University of Georgia Press, 1945), 51.

2 The acreage figures are from the National Agricultural Statistics Service QuickStats 2.0, "Peaches – Acres Bearing and Non-Bearing," accessed Nov. 17, 2015, at http://quickstats.nass.usda.gov.

3 Mark Lamport-Stokes, "Augusta, Home of the Masters, Admits First Female Members," *Reuters* (Aug. 20, 2012) accessed Aug. 9, 2016 at http://www.reuters.com/article/us-golf-augusta-idUSBRE87J0IE20120820.

4 Jenna Martin, "Augusta-Based Vodka Brand Spreading across State," *Augusta Chronicle* (Apr.1, 2015), accessed Aug. 9, 2016 at http:// m.chronicle.augusta.com/news/business/local-business/2015-04-01/ augusta-based-vodka-brand-spreading-across-state; "Fruitland Augusta, Georgia Peach Vodka & Georgia Peach Tea," accessed Aug. 4, 2014, at www.fruitlandaugusta.com/.

5 Alan Eugene Jackson, "Where I Come From," on *When Somebody Loves You* (Warner/Chappell Music, 2000); Alabam, recording of "Song of the South," by Bob McDill, on *Southern Star* (RCA, 1988); Gladys Knight and the Pips, "Midnight Train to Georgia," by Jim Weatherly, on *Imagination* (Buddah, 1973); Ray Charles, recording of "Georgia On My Mind," by Hoagy Carmichael and Stuart Gorrell, on *The Genius Hits the Road* (ABC-Paramount, 1960).

6 In 2006, the Lane family entered into what they described as a "partnership" with B&H Georgia Orchards, which despite its name is a Florida-based company. Having made their fortune in "Indian River Citrus," the Banacks and Hazels were at this writing apparently part-owners of Lane Packing (the details of the arrangement were not available to the public).

7 Lawton Pearson, interview with the author, July 10, 2009, Lee Pope, GA.

8 David Shields makes a similar point in *Southern Provisions: The Creation and Revival of a Cuisine* (Chicago: University of Chicago Press, 2015), 11–12.

9 Herbert Allen Giles, *A History of Chinese Literature* (New York: D. Appleton, 1901), 128–130.

10 Herbert Allen Giles, *Gems of Chinese Literature* (London: Bernard Quaritch, 1884), 107–108.

11 Ibid.

12 Ibid.

13 Ibid., 108.

14 Aldo Leopold, *A Sand County Almanac, and Sketches Here and There* (New York: Oxford University Press, 1987), 197.

15 Leopold, I think, understood this quite well. But I think we also use this quote to emphasize certain environmental experiences at the expense of others.

16 Tim Ingold, "Hunting, Gathering and Perceiving," in *The Perception of the Environment: Essays on Livelihood, Dwelling and Skill* (London: Routledge, 2011), 57.

17 Tim Ingold, "The Temporality of the Landscape," in *The Perception of the Environment: Essays on Livelihood, Dwelling and Skill* (London: Routledge, 2011), 189.

Index

For EU product safety concerns, contact us at Calle de José Abascal, 56–1°, 28003 Madrid, Spain or eugpsr@cambridge.org.

www.ingramcontent.com/pod-product-compliance
Ingram Content Group UK Ltd.
Pitfield, Milton Keynes, MK11 3LW, UK
UKHW042151130625
459647UK00011B/1291